*Acclaim for*
# The Collected Poems of
# LANGSTON HUGHES

### Poetry

*The Panther and the Lash* (1967)

*Ask Your Mama* (1961)

*Selected Poems of Langston Hughes* (1959)

*Montage of a Dream Deferred* (1951)

*One-Way Ticket* (1949)

*Fields of Wonder* (1947)

*Shakespeare in Harlem* (1942)

*The Dream Keeper* (1932)

*Fine Clothes to the Jew* (1927)

*The Weary Blues* (1926)

### Fiction

*Something in Common and Other Stories* (1963)

*The Sweet Flypaper of Life* (1955)

*Laughing to Keep from Crying* (1952)

*The Ways of White Folks* (1934)

*Not Without Laughter* (1930)

### Drama

*Five Plays by Langston Hughes* (1963)

### Humor

*Simple's Uncle Sam* (1965)

*The Best of Simple* (1961)

*Simple Stakes a Claim* (1957)

*Simple Takes a Wife* (1953)

*Simple Speaks His Mind* (1950)

### For Young People

*First Book of Africa* (1964)

*The First Book of the West Indies* (1956)

*The First Book of Rhythms* (1954)

*The First Book of Jazz* (1954)

*The First Book of the Negroes* (1952)

*Popo and Fifina* (1932)
—with Arna Bontemps

### Biography and Autobiography

*Famous Negro Heroes of America* (1958)

*I Wonder as I Wander* (1956)

*Famous Negro Music Makers* (1955)

*Famous American Negroes* (1964)

*The Big Sea* (1940)

### Anthology

*The Langston Hughes Reader* (1958)

### History

*Black Magic: A Pictorial History of the Negro in American Entertainment* (1967)
—with Milton Meltzer

*Fight for Freedom: The Story of the NAACP* (1962)

*A Pictorial History of the Negro in America* (1956)
—with Milton Meltzer

# The Collected Poems of
# LANGSTON HUGHES

# The Collected Poems of
# LANGSTON HUGHES

**ARNOLD RAMPERSAD**, Editor

**DAVID ROESSEL**, Associate Editor

**VINTAGE CLASSICS**

Vintage Books     A Division of Random House, Inc.     New York

FIRST VINTAGE CLASSICS EDITION, NOVEMBER 1995

Much of the poetry in this collection was originally published,
sometimes in somewhat different form, in the following Alfred A. Knopf,
Inc., titles: *The Weary Blues* (1926), *Fine Clothes to the Jew* (1927), *The
Dream Keeper* (1932), *Shakespeare in Harlem* (1942), *Fields of Wonder*
(1947), *One-Way Ticket* (1949), *Montage of a Dream Deferred* (1951),
*Selected Poems of Langston Hughes* (1959), *Ask Your Mama* (1961),
and *The Panther and the Lash* (1967).

The Library of Congress has cataloged the Knopf edition as follows:
Hughes, Langston, 1902–1967.
[Poems]
The collected poems of Langston Hughes / Arnold Rampersad, editor,
David Roessel, associate editor. — 1st ed.
p.  cm.
Includes index.
ISBN 0-679-42631-0
1. Afro-Americans—Poetry. I. Rampersad, Arnold. II. Roessel, David.
III. Title.
PS3515.U274A17  1994
811'.52—dc20      94-14509
CIP

Vintage ISBN: 0-679-76408-9

Book design by Virginia Tan

Manufactured in the United States of America

30 29 28 27 26 25 24 23 22

*To the memory of*
*George Houston Bass*

# Contents

The Collected Poems of
# LANGSTON HUGHES

# Introduction

> Hang yourself, poet, in your own words.
> Otherwise, you are dead.
>
> LANGSTON HUGHES, 1964

Langston Hughes is one of the more controversial names in the history of American poetry. To many readers of African descent he is their poet laureate, the beloved author of poems steeped in the richness of African American culture, poems that exude Hughes's affection for black Americans across all divisions of region, class, and gender. To many readers who love verse and are also committed to the ideal of social and political justice, he is among the most eloquent American poets to have sung about the wounds caused by injustice. For still other admirers, he is, above all, the author of poems of often touching lyric beauty, beyond issues such as race and justice.

There is, however, another and less flattering aspect to Hughes's reputation. To a substantial number of readers and, especially, scholar-critics, Hughes's approach to poetry was far too simple and unlearned. To them, his verse fails lamentably to satisfy their desire for a modernist literature attuned to the complexities of modern life. Still other readers have found his poetry altogether too radical politically, and a kind of affront to their sense of patriotism.

Langston Hughes never sought to be all things to all people but rather aimed to create a body of work that epitomized the beauty and variety of the African American and the American experiences, as well as the diversity of emotions, thoughts, and dreams that he saw common to all human beings. He started out as a poet with a deep regard for the written word and a strong connection to the American past. He grew up in Lawrence, Kansas, with a grandmother, Mary Langston, whose first husband, Sheridan Leary, had died in 1859 in the celebrated raid on the federal arsenal at Harpers Ferry led by John Brown, who was hanged for his act. John Mercer Langston, one of the most distinguished black Americans of the nineteenth century and the brother of Langston Hughes's maternal grandfather, Charles Langston, published an autobiography; and Langston's mother, Carrie Langston Hughes, wrote verse and yearned for a career on the stage. Lonely as a child, with his mother frequently away and his father, James N. Hughes, a businessman, living in self-imposed exile in Mexico, Langston Hughes for comfort turned to "books, and the wonderful world in books," as he himself remembered. Later he would recall the inspiration of the Bible in his early life, as well as the inspiration of the African American intellectual W. E. B. Du Bois, whose *The Souls of Black Folk*, published the year after Hughes's birth in 1902, defined for many people the essential drama of the lives of people born black in America in the aftermath of the Civil War.

In Hughes's predominantly white but cosmopolitan high school in Cleveland, Ohio, he published his first poems and searched for his authentic voice. Before his graduation in 1920 he had clearly fallen under the spell of the most original of American poets, Walt Whitman, whose *Leaves of Grass* had revolutionized

3

American verse in the nineteenth century. He also learned much from Carl Sandburg, himself one of Whitman's most fervent disciples, whose *Jazz Fantasies* (1919) pointed Hughes in the direction of his own music-inflected verse. Thereafter, Langston Hughes understood that he could have a place in the long tradition of American writing despite the most repressive features of racism. This tradition emphasized the realities of American life and the realities of the American language, as well as the idealism out of which sprang the most radical American democratic beliefs. In 1921, at the age of nineteen, when his poem "The Negro Speaks of Rivers" was printed in Du Bois's *Crisis* magazine, his first appearance in a national publication, Hughes showed that he at last had found his own poetic voice.

That voice would reverberate over the next forty-six years, until his death in 1967. Even as Hughes published works in a wide variety of other forms—novels, plays, short stories, essays, autobiographies, histories, libretti—he saw himself first and foremost as a poet. By 1926, when he published his first volume of verse, *The Weary Blues*, he already had fused into his poetry its key technical commitment: the music of black Americans as the prime source and expression of their cultural truths. In these blues and jazz poems, Hughes wrote a fundamentally new kind of verse—one that told of the joys and sorrows, the trials and triumphs, of ordinary black folk, in the language of their typical speech and composed out of a genuine love of these people.

In the 1930s especially, in response to the Great Depression, certain features of his verse were altered as he began to emphasize the need for radical political action. Hughes then wrote some of the most radical poems ever published by an American, as well as some of the most poignant lamentations of the chasm that often exists between American social ideals and American social reality, as in his 1935 anthem, "Let America Be America Again." Some of his radical poems, especially "Goodbye Christ," would haunt Hughes's career for the rest of his life, with conservative political and religious groups citing them as evidence of his alleged communist beliefs and associations. Under such pressure, Hughes himself eventually repudiated "Goodbye Christ" and in general suppressed the bulk of his radical socialist poetry. "Politics in any country in the world is dangerous," he wrote near the end of his life. "For the poet, politics in any country in the world had better be disguised as poetry. . . . Politics can be the graveyard of the poet. And only poetry can be his resurrection."

Early in the 1940s, closing ranks with his nation in the war effort, he returned as a poet to older themes—or, as he put it ironically, to "Negroes, nature, and love." In the postwar years, and settled now in Harlem, where he would live the rest of his life, Hughes watched the historic evolution of African American culture from its roots in the rural South to its often tangled exfoliation in the cities of the North. His response as a poet was a body of verse, notably from *Montage of a Dream Deferred* (1951) to *Ask Your Mama* (1961), shaped largely by the impact of the transformation of black music, primarily in the complex new dissonant jazz of musicians such as Dizzy Gillespie and Charlie Parker.

Hughes was often called, and sometimes called himself, a folk poet. To some people, this means that his work is almost artless and thus possibly beneath criticism. The truth indeed is that Hughes published many poems that are doggerel. To reach his primary audience—the black masses—he was prepared to write "down" to them. Some of the pieces in this volume were intended for public recitation mainly; some started as song lyrics. Like many democratic poets, such as William Carlos Williams, he believed that the full range of his poetry should reach print as soon as possible; poetry is a form of social action. However, for Hughes, as for all serious poets, the writing of poetry was virtually a sacred commitment. And while he wished to write no verse that was beyond the ability of the masses of people to understand, his poetry, in common with that of other committed writers, is replete with allusions that must be respected and understood if it is to be properly appreciated. To respect Hughes's work, above all one must respect the African American people and their culture, as well as the American people in general and their national culture.

If Hughes kept at the center of his art the hopes and dreams, as well as the actual lived conditions, of African Americans, he almost always saw these factors in the context of the eternally embattled but eternally inspiring American democratic tradition, even as changes in the world order, notably the collapse of colonialism in Africa, redefined the experiences of African peoples around the world. Almost always, too, Hughes attempted to preserve a sense of himself as a poet beyond race and other corrosive social pressures. By his absolute dedication to his art and to his social vision, as well as to his central audience, he fused his unique vision of himself as a poet to his production of art.

"What is poetry?" Langston Hughes asked near his death. He answered, "It is the human soul entire, squeezed like a lemon or a lime, drop by drop, into atomic words." He wanted no definition of the poet that divorced his art from the immediacy of life. "A poet is a human being," he declared. "Each human being must live within his time, with and for his people, and within the boundaries of his country." Hughes constantly called upon himself for the courage and the endurance necessary to write according to these beliefs. "Hang yourself, poet, in your own words," he urged all those who would take up the mantle of the poet and dare to speak to the world. "Otherwise, you are dead."


In preparing *The Collected Poems of Langston Hughes*, we set out to find and include in this volume all the poems by Hughes published in his lifetime. (However, we also include two poems first published *after* Hughes's death, because Hughes submitted these poems for publication before he died.)

In the appendixes, we have gathered poems that Hughes wrote mainly for children, and a group of pieces, including some doggerel, that Hughes wrote for and published through the Associated Negro Press in the 1940s.

We have excluded as juvenilia Hughes's poems in the Central High School (Cleveland) *Monthly Magazine*, the Columbia University *Spectator*, and *The Oracle*, the magazine of Omega Psi Phi fraternity. The poem about Carl Sandburg that appears in Hughes's autobiography *The Big Sea*, among other examples of his high-school verse, has been omitted for the same reason. Only those youthful efforts that Hughes decided to reprint later are included in this volume. Also excluded are poems written by Hughes but never published—most likely because Hughes either never offered them to publishers or because they were rejected by publishers when he offered them. Several hundred unpublished poems may be found in the Langston Hughes papers at the Beinecke Library, Yale University. We also omitted poems that were unpublished during Hughes's lifetime but have since appeared in *Good Morning Revolution: Uncollected Writings of Langston Hughes*, edited by Faith Berry (2nd ed. New York: Citadel Press, 1992), or in biographies.

In general, we have arranged Hughes's poems in chronological order, according to the dates of their first publication. However, we have allowed exceptions to this rule. The books *Montage of a Dream Deferred* and *Ask Your Mama*, which Hughes repeatedly described as peculiarly unified works, are preserved intact. Following standard scholarly practice, the text we offer is of the *last* published version of each poem, so as to include revisions made by the author.

In our notes, we give the basic publication history of each poem: the date and place of publication of our text, plus (where different) the date and place of publication of the first appearance of the poem. We also attempt to document textual changes made by Hughes between the first and last publication. We also provide explanatory notes where they seem useful or necessary, but we make no attempt at literary analysis or criticism.

Our project began following the death of George Houston Bass, to whom we dedicate this volume. Professor Bass, who was the executor-trustee of the Hughes estate at the time of his death, had undertaken to edit the collected poems of Hughes and had signed a contract with Knopf for that purpose. When we took over the project, we inherited from Professor Bass a manuscript of several hundred poems but virtually no notes whatsoever. Therefore, we had to start again from the beginning. In the process, we found many more published poems, which Professor Bass no doubt would also have discovered if he had had time to finish the manuscript.

Scholars perhaps will notice that this volume includes a few dozen more poems than are listed in the standard bibliographic guide to Hughes's work, Donald Dickenson's *A Bio-bibliography of Langston Hughes* (New York: Archon Books, 1967; 2nd ed., revised, 1972). Over the years, this volume has been a useful tool for Hughes scholars. However, it contains numerous errors and omissions—for example, eighteen publications of verse by Hughes in *Messenger* magazine (from 1924 to 1927). In each instance, we have gone directly to the primary source of publication to ascertain the correct text of the poem, as well as the other facts of its publication. We have been careful not to rely simply on clippings or typescripts in the Langston Hughes papers in the Beinecke Library at Yale University, or on notations on the library folders there, notations which are based on *A Bio-bibliography*. These shortcuts have led, in large part, to the many discrepancies between our volume and the work of other editors.

No doubt we too have missed some poems in preparing *The Collected Poems of Langston Hughes* and have made some errors in annotating the texts; however, we hope to correct such omissions and errors in subsequent editions of *The Collected Poems of Langston Hughes*. Our goal has been to set a solid foundation for future scholars and critics interested in the poetry of Langston Hughes.

We would like to record our debt to Judith Jones of Alfred A. Knopf, who served as Hughes's last editor there and has encouraged this effort from the outset, and to her assistant Kathy Zuckerman. We are indebted, too, to A. Walton Litz of Princeton University for his advice on various editorial questions. We would also like to acknowledge the assistance of the staff of Firestone Library at Princeton, especially the interlibrary loan and reference departments; Patricia Canon Willis and the staff at the Beinecke Library at Yale University; the staff at the library of Lincoln University, Pennsylvania, Hughes's alma mater; the Butler Library of Columbia University; the Van Pelt Library of the University of Pennsylvania; the New York Public Library, including the Schomburg Center for Research in Black Culture; the Library of Congress; the San Francisco Public Library; and the Carmel Public Library.

For certain poems published first in South Africa, we thank Stephen Gray. Our thanks also go to our student assistant Sara Jost, as well as to Judith Ferszt of the Program in American Studies at Princeton University. Last but not least, we gratefully acknowledge the help and encouragement of Pamela Beatrice and Marvina White in preparing this volume.

Arnold Rampersad
David Roessel
Princeton University

# A Chronology of the Life of Langston Hughes

1902   Born James Langston Hughes, February 1, Joplin, Missouri, to James Nathaniel Hughes, who was a stenographer with a mining company, and Carrie Mercer Langston Hughes, who wrote verse and acted in amateur theatricals. Following James's departure for Cuba and then Mexico, his mother takes Langston to Lawrence, Kansas, where she had grown up.

Langston and his mother live in a state of poverty at the home of her mother, Mary Langston. Married first to Lewis Sheridan Leary, who was killed in 1859 in John Brown's band at Harpers Ferry, Langston's grandmother had then married Charles Langston, a Virginia-born abolitionist and, after the war, a businessman and Republican politician in Kansas.

1907   When an attempted reconciliation in Mexico fails, Langston and Carrie return to Lawrence. In the frequent absence of his mother, who must look for work, Hughes lives with the aged Mary Langston.

1908   Hughes moves to Topeka, Kansas, to live with his mother. Starts school there.

1909   Returns to Lawrence and his grandmother.

1915   Mary Langston dies. Hughes leaves Lawrence and starts the eighth grade in Lincoln, Illinois, where he lives with his mother and her second husband, Homer Clark, a sometime cook and the father of Hughes's stepbrother, Gwyn "Kit" Clark.

1916   Graduating from the eighth grade, Hughes is named class poet. Enters Central High School in Cleveland, Ohio, where his mother and stepfather, now employed in a steel mill, live.

1918   Begins to publish verse and short stories in the *Central High Monthly Magazine.* Also excels in track and other student activities.

1919   Spends the summer in Toluca, Mexico, where his father is a businessman and landowner. Hughes's verse and fiction in the *Monthly* show the influence of Walt Whitman and Carl Sandburg.

1920   Elected class poet and editor of high-school annual. After graduation in June, lives for one year with his father in Mexico. The two clash frequently over Hughes's desire to be a writer.

1921   In June, publishes "The Negro Speaks of Rivers" in *The Crisis.* Supported unwillingly by his father, he enrolls in September at Columbia University. Meets Jessie Fauset, literary editor of *The Crisis,* and its editor, W. E. B. Du Bois, as well as the young Harlem poet Countee Cullen.

1922   In June, after refusing to return to Mexico to help his father, who has suffered a stroke, Hughes completes his classes and withdraws from Columbia. Works as a delivery boy for a florist, on a vegetable farm on Staten Island, and as a messman on a fleet of ships mothballed up the Hudson River. Continues to publish poems in *The Crisis*.

1923   After visiting a Harlem cabaret, writes "The Weary Blues." In June, sails on the *West Hesseltine*, a steamship trading up and down the west coast of Africa. Visits ports in various regions, including Senegal, the Gold Coast (later Ghana), Nigeria, the Congo, and Portuguese West Africa (later Angola). Returns home in October.

1924   On second voyage to Europe as a seaman, jumps ship and settles in Paris. Works for a few months in the kitchen of Le Grand Duc, a nightclub in Montmartre managed by an American and featuring jazz music. Writes poems influenced by jazz rhythms. Vacations for a month in Italy. Stranded in Genoa after losing his passport, he writes "I, Too," whose first line reads "I, too, sing America."

1925   Spends year with his mother in Washington, D.C. Works in a laundry, as an oysterman in a restaurant, and in the office of the historian Carter G. Woodson, founder of the Association for the Study of Negro Life and History and Negro History Week (later Black History Month).

In April, "The Weary Blues" wins Hughes the first prize in poetry in *Opportunity* magazine's literary contest. Meets Carl Van Vechten, who quickly arranges for a book contract for Hughes with his own publisher, Alfred A. Knopf, as well as for the publication of some poems in *Vanity Fair*. Hughes also meets Alain Locke, editor of *The New Negro* (1925), Arna Bontemps, Zora Neale Hurston, Wallace Thurman, and other stars of the burgeoning Harlem Renaissance. Later, as a busboy at a Washington hotel, he meets Vachel Lindsay and publicizes Lindsay's praise of his verse.

1926   In January, *The Weary Blues* published to good reviews. That month, aided by Amy Spingarn, Hughes enters (at mid-year) Lincoln University, Pennsylvania; for the first time he is a member of a virtually all-black student body. In June, publishes in *The Nation* a landmark essay, "The Negro Artist and the Racial Mountain," asserting the importance of race-feeling as a factor in art by African Americans. Contributes work to the avant-garde Harlem magazine *Fire!!*, which lasts only one issue.

1927   Publishes *Fine Clothes to the Jew* to harsh reviews in the African American press because of its emphasis on allegedly unsavory aspects of the blues culture.

Through Alain Locke, Hughes meets Charlotte Mason, the wealthy, aged widow (known as "Godmother" at her insistence) who becomes his patron for the next three years. In the summer, Hughes visits the South and travels there for some time with Zora Neale Hurston, who is also taken up by Mrs. Mason.

1929   Graduates in June from Lincoln University. Urged on by Mrs. Mason, he completes his first novel.

1930   Funded by Mrs. Mason, he visits Cuba and meets many writers and artists there. His blues poems influence one, Nicolás Guillén, to write *Motivos de Son* (1930), hailed as the first "Negro" poems in Cuba.

Later that year, Godmother breaks with him for reasons not clear to Hughes, although they have clashed previously over his insistence on greater independence as an artist. This conflict leads Zora Neale Hurston to disavow Hughes's co-authorship of their play *Mule Bone* and accuse him of dishonesty. Hughes breaks with Hurston and Alain Locke, who are still supported by Mrs. Mason.

Spends several weeks at Hedgerow Theater, Pennsylvania, working on playwriting with Jasper Deeter. *Not Without Laughter* is published to excellent reviews. Hughes wins the Harmon Foundation Medal and a prize of $400 for his contribution as an African American to literature.

1931    Distraught about his break with Godmother, Hughes spends six weeks in Haiti, near the Citadel at Cap Haïtien. Marking a major ideological turn to the left, he publishes essays and poems critical of capitalism in *New Masses*.

Amy Spingarn's Troutbeck Press, at her home in Amenia, New York, prints a hundred copies of his *Dear Lovely Death*, a small collection of poems about death.

Returning to the U.S., he secures funds from the Rosenwald Foundation, buys a car, and, with a driver, undertakes a yearlong reading tour of the South and the West. In Alabama, he visits the Scottsboro Boys awaiting execution in prison, and sides with the communist International Labor Defense in its fight with the NAACP over the defense of the men.

The Golden Stair Press (started by Hughes and the illustrator Prentiss Taylor) publishes his pamphlet of poems *The Negro Mother*.

1932    Hughes and Taylor publish *Scottsboro Limited* (a brief play and four poems). Later that year, Knopf publishes Hughes's *The Dream Keeper*, a collection of poems intended for young readers. From Macmillan comes *Popo and Fifina: Children of Haiti*, a children's book by Hughes and Arna Bontemps.

Completing his tour, he returns to New York in June to travel to Europe in a band of twenty-two African Americans invited to take part in a film in the Soviet Union about U.S. race relations. Arrives in Moscow in June. The project falters badly and is soon abandoned. Hughes elects to stay in the Soviet Union. Writes and publishes several revolutionary poems, including "Goodbye Christ" and "Good Morning Revolution." Starting in September, he travels extensively in Soviet Asia, including several weeks with Arthur Koestler.

1933    Near the end of January, Hughes returns to Moscow, where he frequents the lively theater scene. In June, crosses the Soviet Union by rail, then visits China, where he dines with Madame Sun Yat-sen, and Japan, from which he is expelled by the police for associating with alleged leftists. In August, Hughes reaches San Francisco.

Supported by the wealthy Noël Sullivan, Hughes begins a year in Carmel, California, living in a cottage owned by Sullivan. Works on a collection of short stories inspired first by certain short stories of D. H. Lawrence, which remind him of his failed relationship with his patron Godmother.

1934    *The Ways of White Folks*, a collection of stories, published by Knopf to critical praise. Labor unrest in California leads to anti-socialist vigilantism in the Carmel area. After rumors circulate about violence planned against Hughes, and he is attacked in a local newspaper, he is forced to leave Carmel for a while. In November, he travels to Mexico following the death of his father there. His father's will does not mention Hughes.

1935   In six months, he translates short stories by various young Mexican writers, and lives for a while with the young French photographer Henri Cartier-Bresson. Hughes returns in June to the U.S. to his mother's home, now in Oberlin, Ohio. Discovers that his play about miscegenation, *Mulatto*, written in 1930, is about to open on Broadway. Travels to New York to find play sensationalized and its producer, Martin Jones, hostile to his protests. *Mulatto* opens to savage reviews, but ingenious publicity keeps it on Broadway. Hughes writes the poem "Let America Be America Again."

1936   Begins a nine-month, $1,500 Guggenheim Foundation fellowship for work on a novel, which never develops. In Cleveland, working with the Karamu Players (founded by Russell and Rowena Jelliffe, whom Hughes had known since 1916), he concentrates on writing plays.

In March, Hughes's farce *Little Ham* produced by the Jelliffes at the Karamu Theater. In November, Karamu stages *Troubled Island*, his historical drama of the Haitian revolution. Neither play promises commercial success. In New York, he meets Ralph Ellison.

1937   Karamu produces *Joy to My Soul*, another comedy by Hughes.

In June, Hughes travels to Europe to cover the Spanish Civil War for the Baltimore *Afro-American* and other black newspapers. In Paris, for the League of American Writers, he addresses the Writers' Congress meeting there in July. Meets Nancy Cunard, Pablo Neruda, W. H. Auden, Berthold Brecht, and other leading writers. In Spain, he travels with Nicolás Guillén, then passes three months in besieged Madrid, where he lives at the local Alianza Para Intellectuales, a center of cultural activity, and meets many writers, including Hemingway. Translates poems by Federico García Lorca.

1938   Early in the year, returns to the U.S. Founds the leftist Harlem Suitcase Theater, whose first production, his *Don't You Want to Be Free?*, runs for thirty-eight performances. The radical International Workers Order publishes *A New Song*, a pamphlet of radical verse with an introduction by Mike Gold.

On June 3, after suffering for some years with breast cancer, his mother Carrie dies in New York.

In July, Langston travels to Paris with Theodore Dreiser as delegates from the League of American Writers to a conference of the leftist International Association of Writers; addresses the gathering. In November, Karamu stages his *Front Porch*, a domestic drama. Desperate for money, including funds to pay for his mother's funeral, Hughes leaves New York for Carmel and Los Angeles.

1939   In Los Angeles, with the actor-singer Clarence Muse, he writes the script of the motion picture *Way Down South*, a vehicle for the boy singer Bobby Breen. To his dismay, progressive critics accuse Hughes of selling out to Hollywood. However, he is able to meet various debts and to work on his autobiography. In June, addressing the Third American Writers' Congress in New York, he emphasizes the plight of blacks in the U.S. In Carmel, settles down at Hollow Hills Farm, where Noël Sullivan now lives.

1940  In the spring and summer, Hughes spends several months in Chicago working on a musical review for the Negro Exposition planned for the summer; he is poorly paid and his scripts are ignored. Hughes and Richard Wright honored at a literary reception given by Jack Conroy and Nelson Algren of *New Anvil* magazine. Hughes's autobiography, *The Big Sea*, published, but overshadowed by the success earlier in the year of Richard Wright's best-seller *Native Son*, which Hughes criticizes as too harsh about black life. Returns to Carmel. In the fall, moves temporarily to Los Angeles to work on a review for the progressive Hollywood Theatre Alliance. On November 15, his appearance at a literary luncheon in Pasadena for *The Big Sea* is picketed by members of an evangelical group attacked in Hughes's 1932 poem "Goodbye Christ." Alarmed, Hughes leaves Los Angeles and the review for Carmel, where he publicly repudiates the poem as an aberration of his youth, and is then attacked by the communist press.

1941  Wins a Rosenwald Fund fellowship to write plays. In November, after two years spent mainly in California, leaves Hollow Hills Farm and returns to the East. In Chicago, he lives at the Good Shepherd Community Center, run by the sociologist Horace Cayton, with an office at the Rosenwald Fund headquarters. Works with the Skyloft Players of Good Shepherd on a new play.

At the urging of Carl Van Vechten, Hughes decides to donate his papers to the James Weldon Johnson Memorial Collection of Negro Arts and Letters, founded by Van Vechten at Yale University.

In December, Hughes relocates to New York, at the one-bedroom apartment of the musician Emerson Harper and his wife, Toy Harper, a seamstress and a long-time friend of Carrie Hughes, at 634 St. Nicholas Avenue, Manhattan.

1942  In February, Knopf publishes his verse collection *Shakespeare in Harlem*, which eschews radicalism and returns to themes and forms of the 1920s, including the blues. In April in Chicago, the Skyloft Players stage his play *The Sun Do Move*.

Starting in August, he spends several weeks at the Yaddo writers' and artists' colony near Saratoga Springs, New York. He meets Carson McCullers, Katherine Anne Porter, and other writers.

On behalf of the war effort, Hughes works on various projects for the Office of Civil Defense and, later, the Writers' War Committee. He devotes much of his time to writing song lyrics but also writes "Stalingrad: 1942," a militant poem inspired by the Soviet defense of the besieged city.

In November, he starts a weekly column, "Here to Yonder," in the Chicago *Defender* newspaper.

1943  A presidential order exempting men over thirty-eight ends Hughes's worries about being drafted into the military service.

On February 13, he introduces Jesse B. Semple, or "Simple," to readers of his column. The exploits of this Harlem everyman, appearing in about one-quarter of the columns, quickly becomes their most popular feature.

His poem or recitation piece "Freedom's Plow" is published by Musette, and a pamphlet of verse about segregation and civil rights, *Jim Crow's Last Stand*, is brought out by the Negro Publishing Society of America. Along with Carl Sandburg, Hughes receives an honorary doctorate at his alma mater, Lincoln University.

On the lecture circuit, Hughes is harassed by conservative forces, notably by supporters of the demagogue Gerald L. K. Smith.

In July, Hughes returns for a residency at Yaddo. On August 1, a major civil disturbance breaks out in Harlem.

1944   Takes part successfully in a debate about segregation on the nationally broadcast radio program "America's Town Meeting of the Air."

The Federal Bureau of Investigation steps up its surveillance of Hughes, begun in 1940, for alleged communist activity. In October, he is attacked by the Special Committee on Un-American Activities of the House of Representatives, then by the influential newspaper columnist George Sokolsky.

For the Common Council of American Unity, Hughes undertakes a success-ful tour of high schools in the New York and New Jersey area. In Holland, the resis-tance publishes a verse collection by Hughes, *Lament for Dark Peoples*.

Hughes begins a lucrative national tour organized by a prominent speakers' agency. The extended tour becomes an annual feature of his schedule and an important source of income.

1945   In July, begins work with Mercer Cook, a professor at Howard University, on *Masters of the Dew*, a translation of *Gouverneurs de la rosée*, a novel by Jacques Roumain of Haiti, whom Hughes had met in Haiti in 1931. Soon after, he also begins work as a lyricist with Kurt Weill and Elmer Rice on a musical adaptation of Rice's play *Street Scene*.

1946   Countee Cullen, Hughes's friend and his major rival as a poet in the Harlem Renaissance, dies in New York.

In May, Hughes receives an award of $1,000 from the American Academy of Arts and Letters for distinguished service as a writer. In December, *Street Scene* tries out in Philadelphia, to hostile reviews.

1947   On January 9, *Street Scene* opens on Broadway in New York at the Adel-phi, where it is hailed as a major event in the American musical theater. The show runs only until May 17, but nets Hughes more than $10,000 in 1947.

On a speaking tour, Hughes visits Kenyon College in Ohio and meets John Crowe Ransom.

In February, Hughes starts a semester of teaching at Atlanta University. *Fields of Wonder*, a book of nonpolitical, lyric verse, appears to unfavorable reviews.

Hughes begins work with the German-born composer Jan Meyerowitz on an opera based on his play *Mulatto*.

In September, he flies to Jamaica for a vacation. He meets Roger Mais, Vic Reid, and other prominent local writers and artists whose work he will include in a proposed anthology of verse with Arna Bontemps. Right-wing attacks on Hughes continue, although he denies ever having been a member of the Communist Party.

1948    Another tour takes him to Springfield, Ohio, where he stays at the home of Vachel Lindsay's sister Olive Lindsay. On April 1, Hughes is denounced as a communist in the U.S. Senate by Albert W. Hawkes of New Jersey. Claude McKay, a major influence on Hughes in his formative years as a writer, dies in Chicago.

In June, Hughes moves into 20 East 127th Street in Harlem, into a townhouse purchased by him with money from *Street Scene*. Moving with him from 634 St. Nicholas Avenue are Emerson and Toy Harper. Mrs. Harper will manage the household, including the regular rental of rooms.

Within a few days in September, Hughes completes most of the poems for a new collection about Harlem, *Montage of a Dream Deferred*.

1949    His anthology with Arna Bontemps, *The Poetry of the Negro 1746–1949* (Doubleday) appears, as well as his latest verse collection *One-Way Ticket* (Knopf), with illustrations by Jacob Lawrence, and his *Cuba Libre: Poems by Nicolás Guillén* (Anderson and Ritchie), translated by Hughes with Ben Frederic Carruthers.

Hughes travels to Chicago to take up a one-semester appointment as a visiting teacher of writing at the Laboratory School (kindergarten through the twelfth grade) of the University of Chicago.

On March 30, *Troubled Island*, Hughes's opera from his play about the Haitian revolution with the African American composer William Grant Still (a collaboration started late in the 1930s) opens at the City Center, New York City. Adverse criticism about the derivative nature of the music dooms the production.

Following an international conference in New York sponsored by the leftist National Council of the Arts, Sciences and Professions, *Life* magazine attacks Hughes and other figures (including Albert Einstein, Paul Robeson, and Leonard Bernstein) as "dupes and fellow travelers" of communism.

1950    To critical praise, Hughes's opera with Jan Meyerowitz, *The Barrier*, plays for ten performances at Columbia University. Later in the year, the opera (with a cast headed by Lawrence Tibbett and Muriel Rahn) will falter in Washington, D.C., and (in November) fail disastrously on Broadway, closing after three performances.

In April, Hughes's first edited collection of Simple sketches, *Simple Speaks His Mind*, appears from Simon and Schuster to brisk sales and excellent reviews. The first scholarly essay on Hughes, John W. Parker's "Tomorrow in the Writings of Langston Hughes," appears in May in *College English*.

Hughes undertakes to write "Battle of Harlem," a biography of the first black patrolman in New York, Thomas Battle; completed at great effort, the manuscript would be rejected by publishers and abandoned. He also begins work on a musical play for Broadway, "Just Around the Corner."

Hughes is attacked in the influential book *Red Channels: The Report of Communist Influence in Radio and Television*.

In October, in Washington, D.C., he visits Ezra Pound at St. Elizabeth's Hospital for the Criminally Insane, where Pound was confined following his conviction for treason. The men had exchanged letters starting in 1931, when Pound was on the board of *Contempo* magazine of Chapel Hill, North Carolina.

1951   *Montage of a Dream Deferred* (Henry Holt) appears to lukewarm reviews. In the fall, a special chapbook number (one thousand copies) of the *Beloit Poetry Journal* is devoted to Hughes's translations (begun in 1937) of Federico García Lorca's *Romancero Gitano,* or *Gypsy Ballads.*

Himself under steady attack from the right, in an October column in the *Defender* Hughes strongly endorses W. E. B. Du Bois, then being tried with other colleagues for alleged communist activity.

1952   In January, Henry Holt publishes Hughes's first collection of short stories since 1934, *Laughing to Keep from Crying.* Hughes begins to devote increasing time to writing books for children and young adults. He publishes an introduction to a centenary edition of Harriet Beecher Stowe's *Uncle Tom's Cabin.* With the composer Elie Siegmeister, he begins work on an opera set in Pennsylvania, "The Wizard of Altoona." Hughes's *The First Book of Negroes* (for children) appears from Franklin Watts.

1953   On March 21, Hughes is served with a subpoena at home to appear before Senator Joseph McCarthy's subcommittee on subversive activities. Before the committee, in Washington, D.C., Hughes concedes past mistakes as a radical but implicates no one else on the left. He is "exonerated" by the committee, but conservative attacks on him continue. In his newspaper column, Hughes defends Walt Whitman against charges of racism.

*Simple Takes a Wife,* his second collection of Simple sketches, appears from Henry Holt. Beset by attacks, Hughes takes a vacation at Noël Sullivan's Hollow Hills Farm in Carmel, California.

1954   In February, *Five Foolish Virgins,* Hughes's oratorio based on a biblical text, with music by Jan Meyerowitz, is presented at Town Hall in Manhattan.

That month, with the national climate of segregation changing, Hughes stays for the first time at a "white" hotel in St. Louis, Missouri.

*Famous American Negroes,* for young readers, is published by Dodd, Mead. The book makes no mention of W. E. B. Du Bois or Paul Robeson, both now closely identified with communism and under strong attack from conservatives.

Hughes agrees to a request from *Drum: Africa's Leading Magazine* (Johannesburg) to help judge its annual short-story competition. This involvement stirs Hughes's interest in the new literature of Africa, and in Africa in general. Begins work on his second volume of autobiography. *The First Book of Rhythms,* another juvenile from Franklin Watts, appears.

1955   On January 7, attends Marian Anderson's long-overdue debut at the Metropolitan Opera in New York in Verdi's *Un Ballo in Maschera.*

*The First Book of Jazz* (Franklin Watts) published. Finishes *Famous Negro Music Makers* (Dodd, Mead), another juvenile. The omission from the latter of Paul Robeson, forced on Hughes by the political climate, draws fire from the left.

In April, his Easter cantata with Jan Meyerowitz, *The Glory Round His Head*, is hailed in its premiere at Carnegie Hall, performed by leading singers with the New York Philharmonic Orchestra. In November, *The Sweet Flypaper of Life* (Simon and Schuster), with a text by Hughes inspired by Harlem photographs taken by Roy De Carava, earns extremely favorable reviews.

1956   Attending the American Jazz Festival in Newport, Rhode Island, Hughes apparently is inspired to break new ground and write a gospel musical play, *Tambourines to Glory*, with music by Jobe Huntley. Hughes then converts the play into a short novel.

In September, *The First Book of the West Indies* (Franklin Watts) appears.

On September 16, Hughes's friend and patron Noël Sullivan of Carmel, California, dies in San Francisco. In October, *I Wonder As I Wander*, Hughes's second volume of autobiography (covering the period 1931 to 1938), is published by Rinehart. His evenhanded treatment of the Soviet Union is applauded in progressive circles, and the book is well received generally.

His *A Pictorial History of the Negro in America* (Crown), edited with Milton Meltzer, who conceived the volume, also appears that month.

1957   In March, he attends the world premiere at the University of Illinois in Champaign-Urbana of his three-act opera with Jan Meyerowitz, *Esther*. In May, addresses the first national assembly of the Authors League of America, parent body of the Authors' Guild and the Dramatists' Guild. *Simple Stakes a Claim* is published as a novel by Rinehart. On May 21, his musical play *Simply Heavenly*, also based on his character Simple, opens at an off-Broadway theater in Manhattan. Farcical aspects of the play draw criticism of Hughes for belittling black life. In August, *Simply Heavenly* opens on Broadway at the 48th Street Playhouse and runs for sixty-two performances.

1958   In February, as part of the poetry-to-jazz trend, Hughes reads his poems at the Village Vanguard nightclub in Greenwich Village to the music of bassist Charles Mingus and the pianist Phineas Newborn. The five-hundred-page *Langston Hughes Reader* (George Braziller) appears, as well as *Selected Poems of Gabriela Mistral* (Indiana University Press), his translation of some of the poems of the Nobel Prize–winning writer Lucila Godoy Alcayaga of Chile. To Hughes's dismay, at least two reviewers question his competence as a translator of Mistral's poems.

*Famous Negro Heroes of America* (Dodd, Mead) appears.

In October, Hughes returns to Lawrence, Kansas, to read at the University of Kansas, then drives to Joplin, Missouri, to his place of birth. His novel *Tambourines to Glory* appears (John Day), as well as *The Book of Negro Folklore*, co-edited with Arna Bontemps for Dodd, Mead.

1959   In March, *Selected Poems* (Knopf) is published to a dismissive review by James Baldwin in *The New York Times Book Review*. At the celebration of African Freedom Day at Carnegie Hall, Hughes meets Tom Mboya, the Kenyan political leader. In May, he records some of his poems for the Library of Congress.

Writes an introduction to a new edition of Mark Twain's *The Tragedy of Pudd'nhead Wilson* (Bantam), and composes liner notes for a recording of spirituals by Harry Belafonte. Visits Trinidad in the West Indies for a series of lectures; there he meets Eric Williams, C. L. R. James, and Derek Walcott. Hughes assists in gathering books for a "Gifts for Ghana" project of the American Society of African Culture.

1960    A reading tour early in the year is marred by bomb threats and other disruptions over Hughes's alleged present and former communist allegiances.

*Shakespeare in Harlem*, by Robert Glenn but based on Hughes's writings, runs for thirty-two performances on Broadway. In March, Hughes gives a poetry reading at Spelman College, Atlanta, in the midst of spirited civil-rights protests by black students nearby. On June 25, in St. Paul, Minnesota, Hughes receives the Spingarn Medal, the highest award of the NAACP.

In July, he takes part in the Newport Jazz Festival, where a riot by fans shut out of the main venue brings the event to a premature end. Before leaving Newport, an excited Hughes begins a long, jazz-driven poem, "Ask Your Mama," based on the "dozens," a ritual of harsh teasing well known in the African American community.

*The First Book of Africa* (Franklin Watts) appears, and *An African Treasury: Articles, Essays, Stories, Poems by Black Africans* (Crown), which is immediately banned in South Africa.

In August, at the Tanglewood Festival in Massachusetts, he attends the world premiere of *Port Town*, his one-act opera with Jan Meyerowitz. Offended by the typical inaudibility of his libretto, and by Meyerowitz's typical (for a composer) refusal to respond to his suggestions, Hughes declares an end to his writing for the operatic stage.

In November, visits Nigeria at the invitation of Nnamdi Azikiwe (a former Lincoln University student) to attend his inauguration as governor general of newly independent Nigeria. Hughes meets and befriends a young policeman, Sunday Osuya, to whom he will eventually leave a significant bequest in his will.

Returns via Rome and Paris, where he visits Richard Wright at his home. In London, a short time later, he learns of Wright's sudden death at a Paris clinic.

1961    In April, inducted into the 250-member National Institute of Arts and Letters; meets Robert Frost. In November, attends luncheon hosted by President Kennedy at the White House for Léopold Sédar Senghor, poet and president of Senegal.

*Ask Your Mama: 12 Moods for Jazz* appears from Knopf, largely to punitive reviews. Hill and Wang publishes *The Best of Simple*, Hughes's fourth collection of Simple sketches.

In time for Christmas, Hughes writes the musical play *Black Nativity*, which is steeped even more deeply than is *Tambourines to Glory* in gospel music; then he quickly finishes a gospel play, *The Prodigal Son*. On December 11, the premiere of *Black Nativity* at a Broadway theater is a huge success.

In December, Hughes visits Lagos, Nigeria, this time with a delegation of performers organized by the American Society of African Culture, or AMSAC. The main concert is panned by local critics, but Hughes acquits himself well.

1962 He agrees to write a weekly column for the (white) New York *Post*. In June, he visits Africa again, to attend a writers' conference at Makerere University College in Kampala, Uganda. Meets Chinua Achebe, Wole Soyinka, and other rising young African writers.

Visits Egypt and then Italy, where *Black Nativity* is playing to rave reviews at Gian Carlo Menotti's Festival of Two Worlds in Spoleto. Returns to Africa, to Accra, Ghana, to speak at the opening of a United States Information Service library.

Hughes's history book, *Fight for Freedom: The Story of the NAACP*, commissioned by the association, appears. In October, during the Cuban missile crisis, Hughes joins other major American poets in the first national poetry festival at the Library of Congress and attends a reception for the writers at the White House.

1963 In speeches and elsewhere, he defends the moderate civil-rights approach of the NAACP and deplores violence. Hill and Wang publishes his collection *Something in Common and Other Stories*, and Indiana University Press publishes *Five Plays by Langston Hughes*, edited by Webster Smalley.

In June, Howard University awards Hughes an honorary doctorate. He finishes a new gospel play, "Jericho-Jim Crow," about the civil-rights struggle. With his secretary, George Bass, Hughes visits Paris, Nice, and Venice, then takes a cruise ship to Dubrovnik, Athens, and Haifa. He returns just after the March on Washington and the news of W. E. B. Du Bois's death in Accra, Ghana.

Indiana University Press publishes Hughes's anthology *Poems from Black Africa, Ethiopia, and Other Countries*. After years of setbacks and delays, the Theatre Guild production of *Tambourines to Glory* opens in November on Broadway to harsh reviews and other criticism, especially as a politically irresponsible representation of black American culture. Within days of the assassination of President Kennedy, the show closes.

1964 Produced on a modest budget at a Greenwich Village theater, and written to strike a more aggressive tone than *Tambourines to Glory*, Hughes's *Jericho-Jim Crow* is lauded by virtually all the critics.

In January, Hughes is honored at the fifty-fourth annual dinner of the Poetry Society of America, then honored again at a testimonial banquet in Detroit on "Langston Hughes Day" there.

His anthology *New Negro Poets: U.S.A.*, with a foreword by Gwendolyn Brooks, is published by Indiana University Press. In June, Hughes receives an honorary degree from Western Reserve University, Cleveland, Ohio.

After the worst riot since 1943 hits Harlem, Hughes defends the community on television and in his *Post* column. He works on an eighteen-part BBC radio series on black America. In September, he participates in the Berlin Folk Festival and reads at the University of Hamburg. In Paris, fêted by various cultural groups, Hughes agrees to edit two volumes, one of his verse, another of black American poetry, for the publisher Pierre Seghers; he also promotes Raymond Quinot's *Langston Hughes, or l'Etoile Noire*, recently published in Brussels.

In December, in New York City, he attends a memorial service for Carl Van Vechten.

**1965** In a column in the *Post*, "That Boy Leroi," Hughes attacks obscenity and profanity in the new militant black writing, even as he privately ridicules the pedantry and high formalism of writers such as the poet Melvin B. Tolson. Defends Martin Luther King, Jr., against attacks by militant blacks.

Hughes hails President Johnson's endorsement of the Civil Rights Act of 1965. With black poets writing and publishing with new freedom, he agrees to revise his 1949 anthology with Arna Bontemps, *The Poetry of the Negro*. Defends himself against charges of communism at a lecture in April at Wichita State University, Kansas. In "America's Casbah," in his column in the New York *Post*, Hughes concedes the spread of vicious crime in the black community but places the ultimate blame on racism and greed in the culture as a whole.

*The Prodigal Son*, a brief play, opens at the Greenwich Mews Theater along with a production of Brecht's *The Exception and the Rule*. For the U.S. State Department, he visits Paris to lecture and read with the young black novelists Paule Marshall and William Melvin Kelley; goes on to Britain and then to Denmark and Germany, all for the U.S. State Department.

Works on the script for "The Strollin' Twenties," a television variety show featuring Sidney Poitier, Harry Belafonte, Duke Ellington, and other major entertainers. Hill and Wang publishes *Simple's Uncle Sam*.

Hughes visits San Francisco for the premiere of his cantata *Let Us Remember*, with music by David Amram, commissioned for the biennial convention of Reformed Judaism.

Hughes arrives in Paris to see a British-based production of his *The Prodigal Son*. However, police are called after the actors refuse to perform and then turn on the producer over nonpayment of wages and other grievances.

**1966** January 8, the Chicago *Defender* announces Hughes's decision to end the Simple saga, and presents Hughes's last Simple column.

Hughes flies to Tunis from Paris on vacation. Back in New York, his *The Book of Negro Humor* appears (Dodd, Mead) to unfavorable reviews. He attends a performance of *Street Scene*, now regarded as a classic of American opera, in a revival at the New York City Opera. At his Harlem home, he receives the young South African "coloured" writer Richard Rive.

Appointed by President Johnson, Hughes travels in March to Dakar, to the First World Festival of Negro Arts, as a leader of the American delegation. President Senghor and festival audiences hail him as a historic figure in black literature. Hughes speaks on "Black Writers in a Troubled World," about racial chauvinism and obscenity in radical contemporary black American writing.

After a month in Senegal, he tours other parts of Africa for the State Department, including Nigeria, Ethiopia (where he is received by Haile Selassie), and Tanzania, before vacationing in Paris. Returns to the U.S. in July, after about four months abroad.

In autumn, works on "Black Magic," a pictorial history of black American entertainers, with Milton Meltzer, and on a collection of his verse emphasizing civil rights.

1967   With his home at 20 East 127th Street undergoing renovations, Hughes moves to the Wellington Hotel in mid-Manhattan. Toy Harper, gravely ill, enters a hospital. In February, Hughes reads at UCLA in Los Angeles and speaks in opposition to the Vietnam War.

In *The Best Short Stories by Negro Writers: An Anthology from 1899 to the Present* (Little, Brown), he includes "To Hell with Dying," the first story published by Alice Walker, then twenty-one years old.

Pays tribute to Marianne Moore at the annual dinner of the Poetry Society of America in Manhattan. *L'Ingénu de Harlem*, a translation of *The Best of Simple*, published in Paris (Editions Robert Laffont).

May 6, enters New York Polyclinic Hospital on West 50th Street in Manhattan, after complaining of illness. May 12, undergoes prostate surgery. Dies May 22 of complications following surgery. After a service at Benta's Funeral Home on St. Nicholas Avenue, his body is cremated.

Posthumously, two volumes appear in 1967: *The Panther and the Lash: Poems of Our Times* (Knopf); and, with Milton Meltzer, *Black Magic: A Pictorial History of the Negro in American Entertainment* (Prentice Hall).

# Poems  **1921–1930**

## The Negro Speaks of Rivers

I've known rivers:
I've known rivers ancient as the world and older than the
     flow of human blood in human veins.

My soul has grown deep like the rivers.

I bathed in the Euphrates when dawns were young.
I built my hut near the Congo and it lulled me to sleep.
I looked upon the Nile and raised the pyramids above it.
I heard the singing of the Mississippi when Abe Lincoln
     went down to New Orleans, and I've seen its muddy
     bosom turn all golden in the sunset.

I've known rivers:
Ancient, dusky rivers.

My soul has grown deep like the rivers.


## Aunt Sue's Stories

Aunt Sue has a head full of stories.
Aunt Sue has a whole heart full of stories.
Summer nights on the front porch
Aunt Sue cuddles a brown-faced child to her bosom
And tells him stories.

Black slaves
Working in the hot sun,
And black slaves
Walking in the dewy night,
And black slaves
Singing sorrow songs on the banks of a mighty river
Mingle themselves softly
In the flow of old Aunt Sue's voice,
Mingle themselves softly
In the dark shadows that cross and recross
Aunt Sue's stories.

And the dark-faced child, listening,
Knows that Aunt Sue's stories are real stories.
He knows that Aunt Sue never got her stories

Out of any book at all,
But that they came
Right out of her own life.

The dark-faced child is quiet
Of a summer night
Listening to Aunt Sue's stories.


## Negro

I am a Negro:
  Black as the night is black,
  Black like the depths of my Africa.

I've been a slave:
  Caesar told me to keep his door-steps clean.
  I brushed the boots of Washington.

I've been a worker:
  Under my hand the pyramids arose.
  I made mortar for the Woolworth Building.

I've been a singer:
  All the way from Africa to Georgia
  I carried my sorrow songs.
  I made ragtime.

I've been a victim:
  The Belgians cut off my hands in the Congo.
  They lynch me still in Mississippi.

I am a Negro:
  Black as the night is black,
  Black like the depths of my Africa.


## Question [1]

When the old junk man Death
Comes to gather up our bodies
And toss them into the sack of oblivion,

I wonder if he will find
The corpse of a white multi-millionaire
Worth more pennies of eternity,
Than the black torso of
A Negro cotton-picker?

## Mexican Market Woman

This ancient hag
Who sits upon the ground
Selling her scanty wares
Day in, day round,
Has known high wind-swept mountains,
And the sun has made
Her skin so brown.

## New Moon

There's a new young moon
Riding the hills tonight.

There's a sprightly young moon
Exploring the clouds.

There's a half-shy young moon
Veiling her face like a virgin
Waiting for a lover.

## My Loves

I love to see the big white moon,
    A-shining in the sky;
I love to see the little stars,
    When the shadow clouds go by.

I love the rain drops falling
    On my roof-top in the night;

I love the soft wind's sighing,
    Before the dawn's gray light.

I love the deepness of the blue,
    In my Lord's heaven above;
But better than all these things I think,
    I love my lady love.

## To a Dead Friend

The moon still sends its mellow light
    Through the purple blackness of the night;
The morning star is palely bright
    Before the dawn.

The sun still shines just as before;
The rose still grows beside my door,
    But you have gone.

The sky is blue and the robin sings;
The butterflies dance on rainbow wings
    Though I am sad.

In all the earth no joy can be;
Happiness comes no more to me,
    For you are dead.

## The South

The lazy, laughing South
With blood on its mouth.
The sunny-faced South,
    Beast-strong,
    Idiot-brained.
The child-minded South
Scratching in the dead fire's ashes
For a Negro's bones.
    Cotton and the moon,
    Warmth, earth, warmth,
    The sky, the sun, the stars,

The magnolia-scented South.
Beautiful, like a woman,
Seductive as a dark-eyed whore,
    Passionate, cruel,
    Honey-lipped, syphilitic—
    That is the South.
And I, who am black, would love her
But she spits in my face.
And I, who am black,
Would give her many rare gifts
But she turns her back upon me.
    So now I seek the North—
    The cold-faced North,
    For she, they say,
    Is a kinder mistress,
And in her house my children
May escape the spell of the South.

## Laughers

Dream-singers,
Story-tellers,
Dancers,
Loud laughers in the hands of Fate—
    My people.
Dish-washers,
Elevator-boys,
Ladies' maids,
Crap-shooters,
Cooks,
Waiters,
Jazzers,
Nurses of babies,
Loaders of ships,
Rounders,
Number writers,
Comedians in vaudeville
And band-men in circuses—
Dream-singers all,—
    My people.
Story-tellers all,—
My people.
    Dancers—

God! What dancers!
   Singers—
God! What singers!
Singers and dancers
Dancers and laughers.
   Laughers?
Yes, laughers . . . laughers . . . laughers—
Loud-mouthed laughers in the hands
   Of Fate.

## Danse Africaine

The low beating of the tom-toms,
The slow beating of the tom-toms,
      Low . . . slow
      Slow . . . low—
      Stirs your blood.
         Dance!
A night-veiled girl
   Whirls softly into a
   Circle of light.
   Whirls softly . . . slowly,
Like a wisp of smoke around the fire—
   And the tom-toms beat,
   And the tom-toms beat,
And the low beating of the tom-toms
   Stirs your blood.

## After Many Springs

Now,
In June,
When the night is a vast softness
Filled with blue stars,
And broken shafts of moon-glimmer
Fall upon the earth,
Am I too old to see the fairies dance?
I cannot find them any more.

## Beggar Boy

What is there within this beggar lad
That I can neither hear nor feel nor see,
That I can neither know nor understand
And still it calls to me?

Is not he but a shadow in the sun —
A bit of clay, brown, ugly, given life?
And yet he plays upon his flute a wild free tune
As if Fate had not bled him with her knife!


## Song for a Banjo Dance

Shake your brown feet, honey,
Shake your brown feet, chile,
Shake your brown feet, honey,
Shake 'em swift and wil' —
   Get way back, honey,
   Do that rockin' step.
   Slide on over, darling,
     Now! Come out
     With your left.
Shake your brown feet, honey,
Shake 'em, honey chile.

Sun's going down this evening —
Might never rise no mo'.
The sun's going down this very night —
Might never rise no mo' —
So dance with swift feet, honey,
   (The banjo's sobbing low)
Dance with swift feet, honey —
   Might never dance no mo'.

Shake your brown feet, Liza,
Shake 'em, Liza, chile,
Shake your brown feet, Liza,
   (The music's soft and wil')
Shake your brown feet, Liza,
   (The banjo's sobbing low)
The sun's going down this very night —
Might never rise no mo'.

## Mother to Son

Well, son, I'll tell you:
Life for me ain't been no crystal stair.
It's had tacks in it,
And splinters,
And boards torn up,
And places with no carpet on the floor—
Bare.
But all the time
I'se been a-climbin' on,
And reachin' landin's,
And turnin' corners,
And sometimes goin' in the dark
Where there ain't been no light.
So boy, don't you turn back.
Don't you set down on the steps
'Cause you finds it's kinder hard.
Don't you fall now—
For I'se still goin', honey,
I'se still climbin',
And life for me ain't been no crystal stair.

## When Sue Wears Red

When Susanna Jones wears red
Her face is like an ancient cameo
Turned brown by the ages.

Come with a blast of trumpets,
    Jesus!

When Susanna Jones wears red
A queen from some time-dead Egyptian night
Walks once again.

Blow trumpets, Jesus!

And the beauty of Susanna Jones in red
Burns in my heart a love-fire sharp like pain.

Sweet silver trumpets,
    Jesus!

## A Black Pierrot

I am a black Pierrot:
      She did not love me,
      So I crept away into the night
      And the night was black, too.

I am a black Pierrot:
      She did not love me,
      So I wept until the dawn
      Dripped blood over the eastern hills
      And my heart was bleeding, too.

I am a black Pierrot:
      She did not love me,
      So with my once gay-colored soul
      Shrunken like a balloon without air,
      I went forth in the morning
      To seek a new brown love.

## Justice

That Justice is a blind goddess
Is a thing to which we black are wise.
Her bandage hides two festering sores
That once perhaps were eyes.

## Monotony

Today like yesterday
Tomorrow like today;
The drip, drip, drip,
      Of monotony
Is wearing my life away;
Today like yesterday,
Tomorrow like today.

## Dreams

Hold fast to dreams
For if dreams die
Life is a broken-winged bird
That cannot fly.

Hold fast to dreams
For when dreams go
Life is a barren field
Frozen with snow.

## Poem [1]

For the portrait of an African boy after the manner of Gauguin

All the tom-toms of the jungles beat in my blood,
And all the wild hot moons of the jungles shine in my
      soul.
I am afraid of this civilization—
    So hard,
        So strong,
            So cold.

## Our Land

Poem for a Decorative Panel

We should have a land of sun,
Of gorgeous sun,
And a land of fragrant water
Where the twilight
Is a soft bandanna handkerchief
Of rose and gold,
And not this land where life is cold.

We should have a land of trees,
Of tall thick trees
Bowed down with chattering parrots

Brilliant as the day,
And not this land where birds are grey.

Ah, we should have a land of joy,
Of love and joy and wine and song,
And not this land where joy is wrong.

Oh, sweet away!
Ah, my beloved one, away!

## The Last Feast of Belshazzar

The jeweled entrails of pomegranates
     bled on the marble floor.
The jewel-heart of a virgin broke at the
     golden door.
The laughter of a drunken lord hid the sob
     of a silken whore.

*Mene,*
Wrote a strange hand,
*Mene Tekel Upharsin,* —
And Death stood at the door.

## Young Prostitute

Her dark brown face
Is like a withered flower
On a broken stem.
Those kind come cheap in Harlem
So they say.

# Jazzonia

Oh, silver tree!
Oh, shining rivers of the soul!

In a Harlem cabaret
Six long-headed jazzers play.
A dancing girl whose eyes are bold
Lifts high a dress of silken gold.

Oh, singing tree!
Oh, shining rivers of the soul!

Were Eve's eyes
In the first garden
Just a bit too bold?
Was Cleopatra gorgeous
In a gown of gold?

Oh, shining tree!
Oh, silver rivers of the soul!

In a whirling cabaret
Six long-headed jazzers play.


# Shadows

We run,
We run,
We cannot stand these shadows!
Give us the sun.

We were not made
For shade,
For heavy shade,
And narrow space of stifling air
That these white things have made.
We run,
Oh, God,
We run!
We must break through these shadows,
We must find the sun.

## Cabaret

Does a jazz-band ever sob?
They say a jazz-band's gay.
Yet as the vulgar dancers whirled
And the wan night wore away,
One said she heard the jazz-band sob
When the little dawn was grey.

## Winter Moon

How thin and sharp is the moon tonight!
How thin and sharp and ghostly white
Is the slim curved crook of the moon tonight!

## Young Singer

One who sings "chansons vulgaires"
In a Harlem cellar
Where the jazz-band plays
From dark to dawn
Would not understand
Should you tell her
That she is like a nymph
For some wild faun.

## Prayer Meeting

Glory! Hallelujah!
The dawn's a-comin'!
Glory! Hallelujah!
The dawn's a-comin'!
A black old woman croons
In the amen-corner of the
Ebecaneezer Baptist Church.
A black old woman croons—
The dawn's a-comin'!

## My People

The night is beautiful,
So the faces of my people.

The stars are beautiful,
So the eyes of my people.

Beautiful, also, is the sun.
Beautiful, also, are the souls of my people.

## Migration

A little Southern colored child
Comes to a Northern school
And is afraid to play
With the white children.

At first they are nice to him,
But finally they taunt him
And call him "nigger."

The colored children
Hate him, too,
After awhile.

He is a little dark boy
With a round black face
And a white embroidered collar.

Concerning this
Little frightened child
One might make a story
Charting tomorrow.

## My Beloved

Shall I make a record of your beauty?
Shall I write words about you?
Shall I make a poem that will live a thousand
    years and paint you in the poem?

## The White Ones

I do not hate you,
For your faces are beautiful, too.
I do not hate you,
Your faces are whirling lights of loveliness and splendor, too.
Yet why do you torture me,
O, white strong ones,
Why do you torture me?


## Gods

The ivory gods,
And the ebony gods,
And the gods of diamond and jade,
Sit silently on their temple shelves
While the people
Are afraid.
Yet the ivory gods,
And the ebony gods,
And the gods of diamond-jade,
Are only silly puppet gods
That the people themselves
Have made.


## Grant Park

The haunting face of poverty,
The hands of pain,
The rough, gargantuan feet of fate,
The nails of conscience in a soul
That didn't want to do wrong—
You can see what they've done
To brothers of mine
In one back-yard of Fifth Avenue.
You can see what they've done
To brothers of mine—
Sleepers on iron benches
Behind the Library in Grant Park.

## Fire-Caught

The gold moth did not love him
So, gorgeous, she flew away.
But the gray moth circled the flame
    Until the break of day.
And then, with wings like a dead desire,
She fell, fire-caught, into the flame.


## Exits

The sea is deep,
A knife is sharp,
And a poison acid burns—
But they all bring rest,
They all bring peace
For which the tired
Soul yearns.
They all bring rest
In a nothingness
From where
No soul returns.


## Prayer for a Winter Night

O, Great God of Cold and Winter,
Wrap the earth in an icy blanket
And freeze the poor in their beds.
All those who haven't enough cover
To keep them warm,
Nor food enough to keep them strong—
Freeze, dear God.
Let their limbs grow stiff
And their hearts cease to beat,
Then tomorrow
They'll wake up in some rich kingdom of nowhere
Where nothingness is everything and
Everything is nothingness.

## Lament for Dark Peoples

I was a red man one time,
But the white men came.
I was a black man, too,
But the white men came.

They drove me out of the forest.
They took me away from the jungles.
I lost my trees.
I lost my silver moons.

Now they've caged me
In the circus of civilization.
Now I herd with the many—
Caged in the circus of civilization.


## Fascination

Her teeth are as white as the meat of an apple,
Her lips are like dark ripe plums.
I love her.
Her hair is a midnight mass, a dusky aurora.
I love her.
And because her skin is the brown of an oak leaf in autumn, but a softer color,
I want to kiss her.


## Youth

We have tomorrow
Bright before us
Like a flame.

Yesterday
A night-gone thing,
A sun-down name.

And dawn-today
Broad arch above the road we came.

We march!

## Mammy

I'm waiting for ma mammy,—
    She is Death.

Say it very softly.
Say it very slowly if you choose.

I'm waiting for ma mammy,—
    Death.

## Dream Variations

To fling my arms wide
In some place of the sun,
To whirl and to dance
Till the white day is done.
Then rest at cool evening
Beneath a tall tree
While night comes on gently,
    Dark like me—
That is my dream!

To fling my arms wide
In the face of the sun,
Dance! Whirl! Whirl!
Till the quick day is done.
Rest at pale evening . . .
A tall, slim tree . . .
Night coming tenderly
    Black like me.

## Subway Face

That I have been looking
For you all my life
Does not matter to you.
You do not know.

You never knew.
Nor did I.
Now you take the Harlem train uptown;
I take a local down.

# Afraid

> We cry among the skyscrapers
> As our ancestors
> Cried among the palms in Africa
> Because we are alone,
> It is night,
> And we're afraid.

# A Song to a Negro Wash-woman

> Oh, wash-woman,
>     Arms elbow-deep in white suds,
>     Soul washed clean,
>     Clothes washed clean,—
>     I have many songs to sing you
>     Could I but find the words.
>
> Was it four o'clock or six o'clock on a winter afternoon,
>     I saw you wringing out the last shirt in Miss White
>     Lady's kitchen? Was it four o'clock or six o'clock?
>     I don't remember.
>
> But I know, at seven one spring morning you were on
>     Vermont Street with a bundle in your arms going to
>     wash clothes.
> And I know I've seen you in a New York subway train in
>     the late afternoon coming home from washing clothes.
>
> Yes, I know you, wash-woman.
> I know how you send your children to school, and high-
>     school, and even college.
> I know how you work and help your man when times are
>     hard.
> I know how you build your house up from the wash-tub
>     and call it home.
> And how you raise your churches from white suds for the
>     service of the Holy God.
>
> And I've seen you singing, wash-woman. Out in the back-
>     yard garden under the apple trees, singing, hanging
>     white clothes on long lines in the sun-shine.
> And I've seen you in church a Sunday morning singing,
>     praising your Jesus, because some day you're going to
>     sit on the right hand of the Son of God and forget

you ever were a wash-woman. And the aching back
and the bundles of clothes will be unremembered
then.
Yes, I've seen you singing.

And for you,
O singing wash-woman,
For you, singing little brown woman,
Singing strong black woman,
Singing tall yellow woman,
Arms deep in white suds,
Soul clean,
Clothes clean,—
For you I have many songs to make
Could I but find the words.

## Poppy Flower

A wild poppy-flower
Withered and died.

The day-people laughed—
But the night-people cried.

A wild poppy-flower
Withered and died.

## Troubled Woman

She stands
In the quiet darkness,
This troubled woman
Bowed by
Weariness and pain
Like an
Autumn flower
In the frozen rain,
Like a
Wind-blown autumn flower
That never lifts its head
Again.

## Johannesburg Mines

In the Johannesburg mines
There are 240,000
Native Africans working.
What kind of poem
Would you
Make out of that?
240,000 natives
Working in the
Johannesburg mines.

## To Certain Intellectuals

You are no friend of mine
For I am poor,
Black,
Ignorant and slow,—
Not your kind.
You yourself
Have told me so,—
No friend of mine.

## Steel Mills

The mills
That grind and grind,
That grind out new steel
And grind away the lives
Of men,—
In the sunset
Their stacks
Are great black silhouettes
Against the sky.
In the dawn
They belch red fire.
The mills,—
Grinding out new steel,
Old men.

## Negro Dancers

"Me an' ma baby's
Got two mo' ways,
Two mo' ways to do de Charleston!
   Da, da,
    Da, da, da!
Two mo' ways to do de Charleston!"

Soft light on the tables,
Music gay,
Brown-skin steppers
In a cabaret.

White folks, laugh!
White folks, pray!

"Me an' ma baby's
   Got two mo' ways,
Two mo' ways to do de Charleston!"

## Liars

It is we who are liars:
The Pretenders-to-be who are not
And the Pretenders-not-to-be who are.
It is we who use words
As screens for thoughts
And weave dark garments
To cover the naked body
Of the too white Truth.
It is we with the civilized souls
   Who are liars.

## Sea Charm

Sea charm
The sea's own children
Do not understand.
They know
But that the sea is strong
Like God's hand.
They know

But that sea wind is sweet
Like God's breath,
And that the sea holds
A wide, deep death.

## The Dream Keeper

Bring me all of your dreams,
You dreamers,
Bring me all of your
Heart melodies
That I may wrap them
In a blue cloud-cloth
Away from the too-rough fingers
Of the world.

## Song

Lovely, dark, and lonely one,
Bare your bosom to the sun.
Do not be afraid of light,
You who are a child of night.

Open wide your arms to life,
Whirl in the wind of pain and strife,
Face the wall with the dark closed gate,
Beat with bare, brown fists—
And wait.

## Walkers with the Dawn

Being walkers with the dawn and morning,
Walkers with the sun and morning,
We are not afraid of night,
Nor days of gloom,
Nor darkness—
Being walkers with the sun and morning.

## Earth Song

It's an earth song—
And I've been waiting long
For an earth song.
It's a spring song!
I've been waiting long
For a spring song:
    Strong as the bursting of young buds,
    Strong as the shoots of a new plant,
    Strong as the coming of the first child
    From its mother's womb—
An earth song!
A body song!
A spring song!
And I've been waiting long
For an earth song.

## I, Too

I, too, sing America.

I am the darker brother.
They send me to eat in the kitchen
When company comes,
But I laugh,
And eat well,
And grow strong.

Tomorrow,
I'll be at the table
When company comes.
Nobody'll dare
Say to me,
"Eat in the kitchen,"
Then.

Besides,
They'll see how beautiful I am
And be ashamed—

I, too, am America.

# Drama for Winter Night (Fifth Avenue)

You can't sleep here,
My good man,
You can't sleep here.
This is the house of God.

The usher opens the church door and he goes out.

You can't sleep in this car, old top,
Not here.
If Jones found you
He'd give you to the cops.
Get-the-hell out now,
This ain't home.
You can't stay here.

The chauffeur opens the door and he gets out.

Lord! You can't let a man lie
In the streets like this.
Find an officer quick.
Send for an ambulance.
Maybe he is sick but
He can't die on this corner,
Not here!
He can't die here.

Death opens a door.

Oh, God,
Lemme git by St. Peter.
Lemme sit down on the steps of your throne.
Lemme rest somewhere.
What did yuh say, God?
What did yuh say?
You can't sleep here. . . .
Bums can't stay. . . .

The man's raving.
Get him to the hospital quick.
He's attracting a crowd.
He can't die on this corner.
No, no, not here.

## God to Hungry Child

Hungry child,
I didn't make this world for you.
You didn't buy any stock in my railroad.
You didn't invest in my corporation.
Where are your shares in standard oil?
I made the world for the rich
And the will-be-rich
And the have-always-been-rich.
Not for you,
Hungry child.

## Rising Waters

To you
Who are the
Foam on the sea
And not the sea—
What of the jagged rocks,
And the waves themselves,
And the force of the mounting waters?
You are
But foam on the sea,
You rich ones—
Not the sea.

## Poem to a Dead Soldier

"Death is a whore who consorts with all men."

Ice-cold passion
And a bitter breath
Adorned the bed
Of Youth and Death—
Youth, the young soldier
Who went to the wars
And embraced white Death,
the vilest of whores.

Now we spread roses
Over your tomb—

We who sent you
To your doom.
Now we make soft speeches
And sob soft cries
And throw soft flowers
And utter soft lies.

We would mould you in metal
And carve you in stone,
Not daring to make statue
Of your dead flesh and bone,
Not daring to mention
The bitter breath
Nor the ice-cold passion
Of your love-night with Death.

We make soft speeches.
We sob soft cries
We throw soft flowers,
And utter soft lies.
And you who were young
When you went to the wars
Have lost your youth now
With the vilest of whores.

## Park Benching

I've sat on the park benches in Paris
Hungry.
I've sat on the park benches in New York
Hungry.
And I've said:
I want a job.
I want work.
And I've been told:
There are no jobs.
There is no work.
So I've sat on the park benches
Hungry.
Mid-winter,
Hungry days,
No jobs,
No work.

# The Weary Blues

Droning a drowsy syncopated tune,
Rocking back and forth to a mellow croon,
    I heard a Negro play.
Down on Lenox Avenue the other night
By the pale dull pallor of an old gas light
    He did a lazy sway. . . .
    He did a lazy sway. . . .
To the tune o' those Weary Blues.
With his ebony hands on each ivory key
He made that poor piano moan with melody.
    O Blues!
Swaying to and fro on his rickety stool
He played that sad raggy tune like a musical fool.
    Sweet Blues!
Coming from a black man's soul.
    O Blues!
In a deep song voice with a melancholy tone
I heard that Negro sing, that old piano moan—
    "Ain't got nobody in all this world,
        Ain't got nobody but ma self.
        I's gwine to quit ma frownin'
        And put ma troubles on the shelf."

Thump, thump, thump, went his foot on the floor.
He played a few chords then he sang some more—
    "I got the Weary Blues
        And I can't be satisfied.
        Got the Weary Blues
        And can't be satisfied—
        I ain't happy no mo'
        And I wish that I had died."
And far into the night he crooned that tune.
The stars went out and so did the moon.
The singer stopped playing and went to bed
While the Weary Blues echoed through his head.
He slept like a rock or a man that's dead.

## Empty House

It was in the empty house
That I came to dwell
And in the empty house
I found an empty hell.

Why is it that an empty house,
Untouched by human strife,
Can hold more woe
Than the wide world holds,
More pain than a cutting knife?

## Prayer [1]

I ask you this:
Which way to go?
I ask you this:
Which sin to bear?
Which crown to put
Upon my hair?
I do not know,
Lord God,
I do not know.

## Ways

A slash of the wrist,
A swallow of scalding acid,
The crash of a bullet through the brain—
And Death comes like a mother
To hold you in her arms.

## Poem [2]  (To F.S.)

I loved my friend.
He went away from me.
There's nothing more to say.
The poem ends,
Soft as it began,—
I loved my friend.

## America

Little dark baby,
Little Jew baby,
Little outcast,
America is seeking the stars,
America is seeking tomorrow.
You are America.
I am America
America—the dream,
America—the vision.
America—the star-seeking I.
Out of yesterday
The chains of slavery;
Out of yesterday,
The ghettos of Europe;
Out of yesterday,
The poverty and pain of the old, old world,
The building and struggle of this new one,
We come
You and I,
Seeking the stars.
You and I,
You of the blue eyes
And the blond hair,
I of the dark eyes
And the crinkly hair.
You and I
Offering hands
Being brothers,
Being one,
Being America.
You and I.
And I?
Who am I?
You know me:

I am Crispus Attucks at the Boston Tea Party;
Jimmy Jones in the ranks of the last black troops
    marching for democracy.
I am Sojourner Truth preaching and praying
    for the goodness of this wide, wide land;
Today's black mother bearing tomorrow's America.
Who am I?
You know me,
Dream of my dreams,
I am America.
I am America seeking the stars.
America—
Hoping, praying
Fighting, dreaming.
Knowing
There are stains
On the beauty of my democracy,
I want to be clean.
I want to grovel
No longer in the mire.
I want to reach always
After stars.
Who am I?
I am the ghetto child,
I am the dark baby,
I am you
And the blond tomorrow
And yet
I am my one sole self,
America seeking the stars.

## Better

Better in the quiet night
To sit and cry alone
Than rest my head on another's shoulder
After you have gone.

Better, in the brilliant day,
Filled with sun and noise,
To listen to no song at all
Than hear another voice.

## Change

The moon is fat and old tonight,
Yellow and gross with pain.
The moon is fat and old tonight,
But she'll be young again.
Whereas my love, who's fair and sweet,
My love, who's sweet and fair,
Will wither like the autumn rose
In winter air.


## Poem [3]   (When Young Spring Comes)

When young spring comes,
With silver rain
One almost
Could be good again.

But then comes summer,
Whir of bees . . .
Crimson poppies . . . anemones,
The old, old god of Love
To please.


## Love Song for Antonia

If I should sing
All of my songs for you
And you would not listen to them,
If I should build
All of my dream houses for you
And you would never live in them,
If I should give
All of my hopes to you
And you would laugh and say: I do not care,
Still I would give you my love
Which is more than my songs,
More than any houses of dreams,
Or dreams of houses—
I would still give you my love
Though you never looked at me.

# A Wooing

I will bring you big things:
Colors of dawn-morning,
Beauty of rose leaves,
And a flaming love.

But you say
Those are not big things,
That only money counts.

Well,
Then I will bring you money.
But do not ask me
For the beauty of rose leaves,
Nor the colors of dawn-morning,
Nor a flaming love.

# To Certain "Brothers"

You sicken me with lies,
With truthful lies.
And with your pious faces.
And your wide, out-stretched,
    mock-welcome, Christian hands.
While underneath
Is dirt and ugliness,
And rottening hearts,
And wild hyenas howling
In your soul's waste lands.

# Suicide's Note

The calm,
Cool face of the river
Asked me for a kiss.

## Fantasy in Purple

Beat the drums of tragedy for me.
Beat the drums of tragedy and death.
And let the choir sing a stormy song
To drown the rattle of my dying breath.

Beat the drums of tragedy for me,
And let the white violins whir thin and slow,
But blow one blaring trumpet note of sun
To go with me
              to the darkness
                       where I go.


## Young Bride

They say she died,—
Although I do not know,
They say she died of grief
And in the earth-dark arms of Death
Sought calm relief,
And rest from pain of love
In loveless sleep.


## The Jester

In one hand
I hold tragedy
And in the other
Comedy,—
Masks for the soul.
Laugh with me.
You would laugh!
Weep with me.
You would weep!
Tears are my laughter.
Laughter is my pain.
Cry at my grinning mouth,
If you will.
Laugh at my sorrow's reign.

I am the Black Jester,
The dumb clown of the world,
The booted, booted fool of silly men.
Once I was wise.
Shall I be wise again?


## Soledad    A Cuban Portrait

The shadows
Of too many nights of love
Have fallen beneath your eyes.
Your eyes,
So full of pain and passion,
So full of lies.
So full of pain and passion,
Soledad,
So deeply scarred,
So still with silent cries.


## To Midnight Nan at Leroy's

Strut and wiggle,
Shameless gal.
Wouldn't no good fellow
Be your pal.

*Hear dat music. . . .*
*Jungle night.*
*Hear dat music. . . .*
*And the moon was white.*

Sing your Blues song,
Pretty baby.
You want lovin'
And you don't mean maybe.

*Jungle lover. . . .*
*Night black boy. . . .*

*Two against the moon*
*And the moon was joy.*

Strut and wiggle,
Shameless Nan.
Wouldn't no good fellow
Be your man.


**Poem [4]**   To the Black Beloved

Ah,
My black one,
Thou art not beautiful
Yet thou hast
A loveliness
Surpassing beauty.

Oh,
My black one,
Thou art not good
Yet thou hast
A purity
Surpassing goodness.

Ah,
My black one,
Thou art not luminous
Yet an altar of jewels,
An altar of shimmering jewels,
Would pale in the light
Of thy darkness,
Pale in the light
Of thy nightness.


**Cross**

My old man's a white old man
And my old mother's black.
If ever I cursed my white old man
I take my curses back.

If ever I cursèd my black old mother
And wished she were in hell,
I'm sorry for that evil wish
And now I wish her well.

My old man died in a fine big house.
My ma died in a shack.
I wonder where I'm gonna die,
Being neither white nor black?

## Summer Night

The sounds
Of the Harlem night
Drop one by one into stillness.
The last player-piano is closed.
The last victrola ceases with the
"Jazz Boy Blues."
The last crying baby sleeps
And the night becomes
Still as a whispering heartbeat.
I toss
Without rest in the darkness,
Weary as the tired night,
My soul
Empty as the silence,
Empty with a vague,
Aching emptiness,
Desiring,
Needing someone,
Something.

I toss without rest
In the darkness
Until the new dawn,
Wan and pale,
Descends like a white mist
Into the court-yard.

## Disillusion

I would be simple again,
Simple and clean
Like the earth,
Like the rain,
Nor ever know,
Dark Harlem,
The wild laughter
Of your mirth
Nor the salt tears
Of your pain.
Be kind to me,
Oh, great dark city.
Let me forget.
I will not come
To you again.

## Jazz Band in a Parisian Cabaret

Play that thing,
Jazz band!
Play it for the lords and ladies,
For the dukes and counts,
For the whores and gigolos,
For the American millionaires,
And the school teachers
Out for a spree.
Play it,
Jazz band!
You know that tune
That laughs and cries at the same time.
You know it.

    May I?
    Mais oui.
    Mein Gott!
    Parece una rumba.
Play it, jazz band!
You've got seven languages to speak in
And then some,
Even if you do come from Georgia.
    Can I go home wid yuh, sweetie?
    Sure.

## Minstrel Man

Because my mouth
Is wide with laughter
And my throat
Is deep with song,
You do not think
I suffer after
I have held my pain
So long?

Because my mouth
Is wide with laughter,
You do not hear
My inner cry?
Because my feet
Are gay with dancing,
You do not know
I die?

## Nude Young Dancer

What jungle tree have you slept under,
Midnight dancer of the jazzy hour?
What great forest has hung its perfume
Like a sweet veil about your bower?

What jungle tree have you slept under,
Night-dark girl of the swaying hips?
What star-white moon has been your mother?
To what clean boy have you offered your lips?

## Songs to the Dark Virgin

I

Would
That I were a jewel,
A shattered jewel,
That all my shining brilliants
Might fall at thy feet,
Thou dark one.

II

Would
That I were a garment,
A shimmering, silken garment,
That all my folds
Might wrap about thy body,
Absorb thy body,
Hold and hide thy body,
Thou dark one.

III

Would
That I were a flame,
But one sharp, leaping flame
To annihilate thy body,
Thou dark one.

## Young Sailor

He carries
His own strength
And his own laughter,
His own today
And his own hereafter—
This strong young sailor
Of the wide seas.

What is money for?
To spend, he says.
And wine?
To drink.
And women?
To love.
And today?
For joy.
And the green sea
For strength,
And the brown land
For laughter.

And nothing hereafter.

## Joy

I went to look for Joy,
Slim, dancing Joy,
Gay, laughing Joy,
Bright-eyed Joy—
And I found her
Driving the butcher's cart
In the arms of the butcher boy!
Such company, such company,
As keeps this young nymph, Joy!

## Fog

Singing black boatmen
An August morning
In the thick white fog at Sekondi
Coming out to take cargo
From anchored alien ships,
You do not know the fog
We strange so-civilized ones
Sail in always.

## Strange Hurt

In times of stormy weather
She felt queer pain
That said,
"You'll find rain better
Than shelter from the rain."

Days filled with fiery sunshine
Strange hurt she knew
That made
Her seek the burning sunlight
Rather than the shade.

In months of snowy winter
When cozy houses hold,
She'd break down doors
To wander naked
In the cold.

# Star Seeker

I have been a seeker
Seeking a flaming star,
And the flame white star
Has burned my hands
Even from afar.

Walking in a dream-dead world
Circled by iron bars,
I sought a singing star's
Wild beauty.
Now behold my scars.

# Lullaby   (For a Black Mother)

My little dark baby,
My little earth-thing,
My little love-one,
What shall I sing
For your lullaby?

Stars,
Stars,
A necklace of stars
Winding the night.

My little black baby,
My dark body's baby,
What shall I sing
For your lullaby?

Moon,
Moon,
Great diamond moon,
Kissing the night.

Oh, little dark baby,
Night black baby,

Stars, stars,
Moon,
Night stars,
Moon,

For your sleep-song lullaby.

# The Ring

Love is the master of the ring
And life a circus tent.
What is this silly song you sing?
Love is the master of the ring.

I am afraid!
Afraid of Love
And of Love's bitter whip!
Afraid,
Afraid of Love
And Love's sharp, stinging whip.

What is this silly song you sing?
Love is the master of the ring.

# Midwinter Blues

In the middle of the winter,
Snow all over the ground.
In the middle of the winter,
Snow all over the ground—
'Twas the night befo' Christmas
My good man turned me down.

Don't know's I'd mind his goin'
But he left me when the coal was low.
Don't know's I'd mind his goin'
But he left when the coal was low.
Now, if a man loves a woman
That ain't no time to go.

He told me that he loved me
But he must a been tellin' a lie.
He told me that he loved me.
He must a been tellin' a lie.
But he's the only man I'll
Love till the day I die.

I'm gonna buy me a rose bud
An' plant it at my back door,
Buy me a rose bud,
Plant it at my back door,
So when I'm dead they won't need
No flowers from the store.

# Gypsy Man

Ma man's a gypsy
Cause he never does come home.
Ma man's a gypsy,—
He never does come home.
I'm gonna be a gypsy woman
Fer I can't stay here alone.

Once I was in Memphis,
I mean Tennessee.
Once I was in Memphis,
Said Tennessee.
But I had to leave cause
Nobody there was good to me.

I met a yellow papa,
He took ma last thin dime.
Met a yellow papa,
He took ma last thin dime.
I give it to him cause I loved him
But I'll have mo' sense next time.

Love, Oh, love is
Such a strange disease.
Love, Oh, love is
Such a strange disease.
When it hurts yo' heart you
Sho can't find no ease.

# Ma Man

When ma man looks at me
He knocks me off ma feet.
When ma man looks at me
He knocks me off ma feet.
He's got those 'lectric-shockin' eyes an'
De way he shocks me sho is sweet.

He kin play a banjo.
Lordy, he kin plunk, plunk, plunk.
He kin play a banjo.
I mean plunk, plunk . . . plunk, plunk.
He plays good when he's sober
An' better, better, better when he's drunk.

Eagle-rockin',
Daddy, eagle-rock with me.
Eagle rockin',
Come an' eagle-rock with me.
Honey baby,
Eagle-rockish as I kin be!

## Teacher

Ideals are like the stars,
    Always above our reach.
Humbly I tried to learn,
    More humbly did I teach.

On all honest virtues
    I sought to keep firm hold.
I wanted to be a good man
    Though I pinched my soul.

But now I lie beneath cool loam
    Forgetting every dream;
And in this narrow bed of earth
    No lights gleam.

In this narrow bed of earth
    Star-dust never scatters,
And I tremble lest the darkness teach
    Me that nothing matters.

## Love Song for Lucinda

Love
Is a ripe plum
Growing on a purple tree.
Taste it once
And the spell of its enchantment
Will never let you be.

Love
Is a bright star
Glowing in far Southern skies.
Look too hard
And its burning flame
Will always hurt your eyes.

Love
Is a high mountain
Stark in a windy sky.
If you
Would never lose your breath.
Do not climb too high.


## Minnie Sings Her Blues

Cabaret, cabaret!
That's where ma man an' me go.
Cabaret, cabaret!
That's where we go, —
Leaves de snow outside
An' our troubles at de door.

Jazz band, jazz band!
Ma man an' me dance.
When I cuddles up to him
No other gal's got a chance.

Baby, O, Baby,
I'm midnight mad.
If ma daddy didn't love me
It sho would be sad.
If he didn't love me
I'd go away
An' dig me a grave this very day.

Blues . . . blues!
Blue, blue, blues!
I'd sho have them blues.


## Listen Here Blues

Sweet girls, sweet girls,
Listen here to me.
All you sweet girls,
Listen here to me:
Gin an' whiskey
Kin make you lose yo' 'ginity.

I used to be a good chile,
Lawd, in Sunday School.
Used to be a good chile,—
Always in Sunday School,
Till these licker-headed rounders
Made me everybody's fool.

Good girls, good girls,
Listen here to me.
Oh, you good girls,
Better listen to me:
Don't you fool wid no men cause
They'll bring you misery.


## Lament over Love

I hope my child'll
Never love a man.
I say I hope my child'll
Never love a man.
Love can hurt you
Mo'n anything else can.

I'm goin' down to the river
An' I ain't goin' there to swim;

Down to the river,
Ain't goin' there to swim.
My true love's left me
And I'm goin' there to think about him.

Love is like whiskey,
Love is like red, red wine.
Love is like whiskey,
Like sweet red wine.
If you want to be happy
You got to love all the time.

I'm goin' up in a tower
Tall as a tree is tall,
Up in a tower
Tall as a tree is tall.
Gonna think about my man—
And let my fool-self fall.

## Fortune Teller Blues

I went to de gypsy,
De gypsy took hold o' my hand.
Went to de gypsy,
Gypsy took hold o' my hand.
She looked at me and tole me
Chile, you gonna lose yo' man.

These fortune tellers
Never tell me nothin' kind.
I say fortune tellers
Never tell me nothin' kind.
I'd give a hundred dollars
To de one that would ease my mind.

Cause I'll holler an' scream an'
Fall down on de flo'.
Say I'll holler an' scream an'
Fall down on de flo'.
If my man leaves me
I won't live no mo'.

## Judgment Day

They put ma body in the ground,
Ma soul went flyin' o' the town,

Went flyin' to the stars an' moon
A-shoutin', God, I's comin' soon.

O Jesus!

Lord in heaven,
Crown on His head,
Says don't be 'fraid
Cause you ain't dead.

Kind Jesus!

An' now I'm settin' clean an' bright
In the sweet o' ma Lord's sight—
    Clean an' bright,
        Clean an' bright.


## Wide River

Ma baby lives across de river
An' I ain't got no boat.
She lives across de river.
I ain't got no boat.
I ain't a good swimmer
An' I don't know how to float.

Wide, wide river
'Twixt ma love an' me.
Wide, wide river
'Twixt ma love an' me.
I never knowed how
Wide a river can be.

Got to cross that river
An' git to ma baby somehow.
Cross that river,
Git to ma baby somehow—
Cause if I don't see ma baby
I'll lay down an' die right now.

## Homesick Blues

De railroad bridge's
A sad song in de air.
De railroad bridge's
A sad song in de air.
Ever time de trains pass
I wants to go somewhere.

I went down to de station.
Ma heart was in ma mouth.
Went down to de station.
Heart was in ma mouth.
Lookin' for a box car
To roll me to de South.

Homesick blues, Lawd,
'S a terrible thing to have.
Homesick blues is
A terrible thing to have.
To keep from cryin'
I opens ma mouth an' laughs.


## Pale Lady

Pale, delightful lady,
How I love you!
I would spread cool violets
At your feet
And bring you lovely jewels
For your hair,
And put a tiny golden ring
Upon your finger
And leave it there
As a sign and symbol of my love,
My bright, bright love for you.
Oh, pale, delightful lady,
How I love you!

## Ruby Brown

She was young and beautiful
And golden like the sunshine
That warmed her body.
And because she was colored
Mayville had no place to offer her,
Nor fuel for the clean flame of joy
That tried to burn within her soul.

One day,
Sitting on old Mrs. Latham's back porch
Polishing the silver,
She asked herself two questions
And they ran something like this:
What can a colored girl do
On the money from a white woman's kitchen?
And ain't there any joy in this town?

Now the streets down by the river
Know more about this pretty Ruby Brown,
And the sinister shuttered houses of the bottoms
Hold a yellow girl
Seeking an answer to her questions.
The good church folk do not mention
Her name any more.

But the white men,
Habitués of the high shuttered houses,
Pay more money to her now
Than they ever did before,
When she worked in their kitchens.

## New Year

The years
Fall like dry leaves
From the top-less tree
Of eternity.
Does it matter
That another leaf has fallen?

## Epitaph [1]

Within this grave lie,
Yes, I.
Why laugh, good people,
Or why cry?
Within this grave
Lies nothing more
Than I.

## Autumn Note

The little flowers of yesterday
Have all forgotten May.
The last gold leaf
Has turned to brown.
The last bright day is grey.
The cold of winter comes apace
And you have gone away.

## Formula

Poetry should treat
        Of lofty things
Soaring thoughts
        And birds with wings.

The Muse of Poetry
        Should not know
That roses
        In manure grow.

The Muse of Poetry
        Should not care
That earthly pain
        Is everywhere.

Poetry!
        Treats of lofty things:
Soaring thoughts
        And birds with wings.

## For Dead Mimes

O white-faced mimes,
May rose leaves
Cover you
Like crimson
Snow.

And may Pierrette,
The faithful,
Rest forever
With Pierrot.

## To Beauty

To worship
At the altar of Beauty,
To feel her loveliness and pain,
To thrill
At the wonder of her gorgeous moon
Or the sharp, swift, silver swords
Of falling rain.

To walk in a golden garden
When an autumn sun
Has almost set,
When near-night's purple splendor
Shimmers to a star-shine net.
To worship
At the altar of Beauty
Is a pleasure divine,
Not given to the many many
But to fools
Who drink Beauty's wine.
Not given to the many many
But to fools
Who seek no other goddess
Nor grapes
Plucked from another's
Vine.

## Bound No'th Blues

Goin' down the road, Lawd,
Goin' down the road.
Down the road, Lawd,
Way, way down the road.
Got to find somebody
To help me carry this load.

Road's in front o' me,
Nothin' to do but walk.
Road's in front o' me,
Walk . . . an' walk . . . an' walk.
I'd like to meet a good friend
To come along an' talk.

Hates to be lonely,
Lawd, I hates to be sad.
Says I hates to be lonely,
Hates to be lonely an' sad,
But ever friend you finds seems
Like they try to do you bad.

Road, road, road, O!
Road, road . . . road . . . road, road!
Road, road, road, O!
On the no'thern road.
These Mississippi towns ain't
Fit fer a hoppin' toad.

## Lonesome Place

I got to leave this town.
It's a lonesome place.
Got to leave this town cause
It's a lonesome place.
A po', po' boy can't
Find a friendly face.

Goin' down to de river
Flowin' deep an' slow.
Goin' down to de river
Deep an' slow,—
Cause there ain't no worries
Where de waters go.

I'm weary, weary,
Weary as I can be.
Weary, weary,
Weary as can be.
This life's so weary,
'S 'bout to overcome me.

## Misery

Play the blues for me.
Play the blues for me.
No other music
'Ll ease my misery.

Sing a soothin' song.
Said a soothin' song,
Cause the man I love's done
Done me wrong.

Can't you understand,
O, understand
A good woman's cryin'
For a no-good man?

Black gal like me,
Black gal like me
'S got to hear a blues
For her misery.

## Bad Luck Card

Cause you don't love me
Is awful, awful hard.
Gypsy done showed me
My bad luck card.

There ain't no good left
In this world for me.
Gypsy done tole me—
Unlucky as can be.

I don't know what
Po' weary me can do.
Gypsy says I'd kill my self
If I was you.

## Feet o' Jesus

At the feet o' Jesus,
Sorrow like a sea.
Lordy, let yo' mercy
Come driftin' down on me.

At the feet o' Jesus
At yo' feet I stand.
O, ma little Jesus,
Please reach out yo' hand.

## Down and Out

Baby, if you love me
Help me when I'm down and out.
If you love me, baby,
Help me when I'm down and out,
I'm a po' gal
Nobody gives a damn about.

The credit man's done took ma clothes
And rent time's nearly here.
I'd like to buy a straightenin' comb,
An' I need a dime fo' beer.

I need a dime fo' beer.


## Pictures to the Wall

Shall I tell you of my old, old dreams
Lost at the earth's strange turnings,
Some in the sea when the waves foamed high,
Some in a garret candle's burnings?

Shall I tell you of bitter, forgotten dreams—
You who are still so young, so young?
You with your wide brown singing eyes
And laughter at the tip of your tongue.

Shall I tell you of weary, weary dreams,—
You who have lost no dreams at all,
Or shall I keep quiet and let turn
My ugly pictures to the wall?


## Walls

Four walls can hold
So much pain,
Four walls that shield
From the wind and rain.

Four walls can shelter
So much sorrow
Garnered from yesterday
And held for tomorrow.

## Beale Street Love

Love
Is a brown man's fist
With hard knuckles
Crushing the lips,
Blackening the eyes,—
Hit me again,
Says Clorinda.

## Dressed Up

I had ma clothes cleaned
Just like new.
I put 'em on but
I still feels blue.

I bought a new hat,
Sho is fine,
But I wish I had back that
Old gal o' mine.

I got new shoes,—
They don't hurt ma feet,
But I ain't got nobody
For to call me sweet.

## A House in Taos

*Rain*

Thunder of the Rain God:
   And we three
   Smitten by beauty.

Thunder of the Rain God:
   And we three
   Weary, weary.

Thunder of the Rain God:
   And you, she, and I
   Waiting for nothingness.

Do you understand the stillness
  Of this house
   In Taos
Under the thunder of the Rain God?

## Sun

That there should be a barren garden
About this house in Taos
Is not so strange,
But that there should be three barren hearts
In this one house in Taos—
Who carries ugly things to show the sun?

## Moon

Did you ask for the beaten brass of the moon?
We can buy lovely things with money,
You, she, and I,
Yet you seek,
As though you could keep,
This unbought loveliness of moon.

## Wind

Touch our bodies, wind.
Our bodies are separate, individual things.
Touch our bodies, wind,
But blow quickly
Through the red, white, yellow skins
Of our bodies
To the terrible snarl,
Not mine,
Not yours,
Not hers,
But all one snarl of souls.
Blow quickly, wind,
Before we run back
Into the windlessness—
With our bodies—
Into the windlessness
Of our house in Taos.

## Suicide

Ma sweet good man has
Packed his trunk and left.
Ma sweet good man has
Packed his trunk and left.
Nobody to love me:
I'm gonna kill ma self.

I'm gonna buy me a knife with
A blade ten inches long.
Gonna buy a knife with
A blade ten inches long.
Shall I carve ma self or
That man that done me wrong?

'Lieve I'll jump in de river
Eighty-nine feet deep.
'Lieve I'll jump in de river
Eighty-nine feet deep.
Cause de river's quiet
An' a po', po' gal can sleep.


## Hard Luck

When hard luck overtakes you
Nothin' for you to do.
When hard luck overtakes you
Nothin' for you to do.
Gather up yo' fine clothes
An' sell 'em to de Jew.

Jew takes yo' fine clothes,
Gives you a dollar an' a half.
Jew takes yo' fine clothes,
Gives you a dollar an' a half.
Go to de bootleg's,
Git some gin to make you laugh.

If I was a mule I'd
Git me a waggon to haul.
If I was a mule I'd
Git a waggon to haul.
I'm so low-down I
Ain't even got a stall.

## Po' Boy Blues

When I was home de
Sunshine seemed like gold.
When I was home de
Sunshine seemed like gold.
Since I come up North de
Whole damn world's turned cold.

I was a good boy,
Never done no wrong.
Yes, I was a good boy,
Never done no wrong,
But this world is weary
An' de road is hard an' long.

I fell in love with
A gal I thought was kind.
Fell in love with
A gal I thought was kind.
She made me lose ma money
An' almost lose ma mind.

Weary, weary,
Weary early in de morn.
Weary, weary,
Early, early in de morn.
I's so weary
I wish I'd never been born.

## Red Roses

I'm waitin' for de springtime
When de tulips grow—
Sweet, sweet springtime
When de tulips grow;
Cause if I'd die in de winter
They'd bury me under snow.

Un'neath de snow, Lawd,
Oh, what would I do?
Un'neath de snow,

I say what would I do?
It's bad enough to die but
I don't want freezin' too.

I'm waitin' for de springtime
An' de roses red,
Waitin' for de springtime
When de roses red
'Ll make a nice coverin'
Fer a gal that's dead.

## Railroad Avenue

Dusk dark
On Railroad Avenue.
Lights in the fish joints,
Lights in the pool rooms.
A box-car some train
Has forgotten
In the middle of the
Block.
A player piano,
A victrola.
942
Was the number.
A boy
Lounging on a corner.
A passing girl
With purple powdered skin.
Laughter
Suddenly
Like a taut drum.
Laughter
Suddenly
Neither truth nor lie.
Laughter
Hardening the dusk dark evening.
Laughter
Shaking the lights in the fish joints,
Rolling white balls in the pool rooms,
And leaving untouched the box-car
Some train has forgotten.

## Elevator Boy

I got a job now
Runnin' an elevator
In the Dennison Hotel in Jersey.
Job ain't no good though.
No money around.
    Jobs are just chances
    Like everything else.
    Maybe a little luck now,
    Maybe not.
    Maybe a good job sometimes:
    Step out o' the barrel, boy.
Two new suits an'
A woman to sleep with.
    Maybe no luck for a long time.
    Only the elevators
    Goin' up an' down,
    Up an' down,
    Or somebody else's shoes
    To shine,
    Or greasy pots in a dirty kitchen.
I been runnin' this
Elevator too long.
Guess I'll quit now.

## Stars

O, sweep of stars over Harlem streets,
O, little breath of oblivion that is night.
    A city building
    To a mother's song.
    A city dreaming
    To a lullaby.
Reach up your hand, dark boy, and take a star.
Out of the little breath of oblivion
    That is night,
    Take just
    One star.

## Brass Spittoons

Clean the spittoons, boy.
  Detroit,
  Chicago,
  Atlantic City,
  Palm Beach.
Clean the spittoons.
The steam in hotel kitchens,
And the smoke in hotel lobbies,
And the slime in hotel spittoons:
Part of my life.
  Hey, boy!
  A nickel,
  A dime,
  A dollar,
Two dollars a day.
  Hey, boy!
  A nickel,
  A dime,
  A dollar,
  Two dollars
Buys shoes for the baby.
House rent to pay.
Gin on Saturday,
Church on Sunday.
  My God!
Babies and gin and church
and women and Sunday
all mixed up with dimes and
dollars and clean spittoons
and house rent to pay.
  Hey, boy!
A bright bowl of brass is beautiful to the Lord.
Bright polished brass like the cymbals
Of King David's dancers,
Like the wine cups of Solomon.
  Hey, boy!
A clean spittoon on the altar of the Lord.
A clean bright spittoon all newly polished,—
At least I can offer that.
  Come 'ere, boy!

## The New Cabaret Girl

That little yaller gal
Wid blue-green eyes:
If her daddy ain't white
Would be a surprise.

She don't drink gin
An' she don't like corn.
I asked her one night
Where she was born.

An' she say, Honey,
I don't know
Where I come from
Or where I go.

That crazy little yaller gal
Wid blue-green eyes:
If her daddy ain't fay
Would be a surprise.

An' she set there a cryin'
In de cabaret
A lookin' all sad
When she ought to play.

My God, I says,
You can't live that way!
Babe you can't
Live that way!

## Argument [1]

Now lookahere, gal,
Don't you talk 'bout me.
I got mo' hair 'n you evah did see,
An' if I ain't high yaller
I ain't coal black,
So what you said 'bout me
You bettah take it back.

Now, listen, Corrine,
I don't talk 'bout you.

I's got much mo'
Important things to do.

All right, gal,
But I'm speakin' ma mind:
You bettah keep yo' freight train
Off ma line.

## Saturday Night

Play it once.
O, play some more.
Charlie is a gambler
An' Sadie is a whore.
  A glass o' whiskey
  An' a glass o' gin:
  Strut, Mr. Charlie,
  Till de dawn comes in.
Pawn yo' gold watch
An' diamond ring.
Git a quart o' licker,
Let's shake dat thing!
  Skee-de-dad! De-dad!
  Doo-doo-doo!
  Won't be nothin' left
  When de worms git through
  An' you's a long time
  Dead
  When you is
  Dead, too.
So beat dat drum, boy!
Shout dat song:
Shake 'em up an' shake 'em up
All night long.
  Hey! Hey!
  Ho . . . Hum!
  Do it, Mr. Charlie,
  Till de red dawn come.

## The Cat and the Saxophone (2 a.m.)

EVERYBODY
Half-pint,—
Gin?
No, make it
LOVES MY BABY
corn. You like
liquor,
don't you, honey?
BUT MY BABY
Sure. Kiss me,
DON'T LOVE NOBODY
daddy.
BUT ME.
Say!
EVERYBODY
Yes?
WANTS MY BABY
I'm your
BUT MY BABY
sweetie, ain't I?
DON'T WANT NOBODY
Sure.
BUT
Then let's
ME,
do it!
SWEET ME.
Charleston,
mamma!
!

## To a Little Lover-Lass, Dead

She
Who searched for lovers
In the night
Has gone the quiet way

Into the still,
Dark land of death
Beyond the rim of day.

Now like a little lonely waif
She walks
An endless street
And gives her kiss to nothingness.
Would God his lips were sweet!


## Harlem Night Club

Sleek black boys in a cabaret.
Jazz-band, jazz-band,—
Play, plAY, PLAY!
Tomorrow. . . . who knows?
Dance today!

White girls' eyes
Call gay black boys.
Black boys' lips
Grin jungle joys.

Dark brown girls
In blond men's arms.
Jazz-band, jazz-band,—
Sing Eve's charms!

White ones, brown ones,
What do you know
About tomorrow
Where all paths go?

Jazz-boys, jazz-boys,—
Play, plAY, PLAY!
Tomorrow. . . . is darkness.
Joy today!

## Midnight Dancer

(To a Black Dancer in "The Little Savoy")

Wine-maiden
Of the jazz-tuned night,
Lips
Sweet as purple dew,
Breasts
Like the pillows of all sweet dreams,
Who crushed
The grapes of joy
And dripped their juice
On you?

## Blues Fantasy

Hey! Hey!
That's what the
Blues singers say.
Singing minor melodies
They laugh,
Hey! Hey!

My man's done left me,
Chile, he's gone away.
My good man's left me,
Babe, he's gone away.
Now the cryin' blues
Haunts me night and day.

Hey! . . . Hey!

Weary,
Weary,
Trouble, pain.
Sun's gonna shine
Somewhere
Again.

I got a railroad ticket,
Pack my trunk and ride.

Sing 'em, sister!

Got a railroad ticket,
Pack my trunk and ride.

And when I get on the train
I'll cast my blues aside.

Laughing,
Hey! . . . Hey!
Laugh a loud,
Hey! Hey!

## Lenox Avenue: Midnight

The rhythm of life
Is a jazz rhythm,
Honey.
The gods are laughing at us.

The broken heart of love,
The weary, weary heart of pain, —
        Overtones,
        Undertones,
To the rumble of street cars,
To the swish of rain.

Lenox Avenue,
Honey.
Midnight,
And the gods are laughing at us.

## Poème d'Automne

The autumn leaves
Are too heavy with color.
The slender trees
On the Vulcan Road
Are dressed in scarlet and gold
Like young courtesans
Waiting for their lovers.
But soon

The winter winds
Will strip their bodies bare
And then
The sharp, sleet-stung
Caresses of the cold
Will be their only
Love.

## March Moon

The moon is naked.
The wind has undressed the moon.
The wind has blown all the cloud-garments
Off the body of the moon
And now she's naked,
Stark naked.

But why don't you blush,
O shameless moon?
Don't you know
It isn't nice to be naked?

## As I Grew Older

It was a long time ago.
I have almost forgotten my dream.
But it was there then,
In front of me,
Bright like a sun—
My dream.

And then the wall rose,
Rose slowly,
Slowly,
Between me and my dream.
Rose slowly, slowly,
Dimming,

Hiding,
The light of my dream.
Rose until it touched the sky—
The wall.

Shadow.
I am black.

I lie down in the shadow.
No longer the light of my dream before me,
Above me.
Only the thick wall.
Only the shadow.

My hands!
My dark hands!
Break through the wall!
Find my dream!
Help me to shatter this darkness,
To smash this night,
To break this shadow
Into a thousand lights of sun,
Into a thousand whirling dreams
Of sun!

## Harlem Night Song

Come,
Let us roam the night together
Singing.

I love you.

Across
The Harlem roof-tops
Moon is shining.
Night sky is blue.
Stars are great drops
Of golden dew.

Down the street
A band is playing.

I love you.

Come,
Let us roam the night together
Singing.

## Ardella

I would liken you
To a night without stars
Were it not for your eyes.
I would liken you
To a sleep without dreams
Were it not for your songs.

## Pierrot

I work all day,
Said Simple John,
Myself a house to buy.
I work all day,
Said Simple John,
But Pierrot wondered why.

For Pierrot loved the long white road,
And Pierrot loved the moon,
And Pierrot loved a star-filled sky,
And the breath of a rose in June.

I have one wife,
Said Simple John,
And, faith, I love her yet.
I have one wife,
Said Simple John,
But Pierrot left Pierrette.

For Pierrot saw a world of girls,
And Pierrot loved each one,

And Pierrot thought all maidens fair
As flowers in the sun.

Oh, I am good,
Said Simple John,
The Lord will take me in.
Yes, I am good,
Said Simple John,
But Pierrot's steeped in sin.

For Pierrot played on a slim guitar,
And Pierrot loved the moon,
And Pierrot ran down the long white road
With the burgher's wife one June.

## Water-Front Streets

The spring is not so beautiful there—
    But dream ships sail away
To where the spring is wondrous rare
    And life is gay.

The spring is not so beautiful there—
    But lads put out to sea
Who carry beauties in their hearts
    And dreams, like me.

## A Farewell

With gypsies and sailors,
Wanderers of the hills and seas,
I go to seek my fortune.
With pious folk and fair
I must have a parting.
But you will not miss me,—
You who live between the hills
And have never seen the seas.

# Long Trip

The sea is a wilderness of waves,
A desert of water.
We dip and dive,
Rise and roll,
Hide and are hidden
On the sea.
    Day, night,
    Night, day,
The sea is a desert of waves,
A wilderness of water.

# Port Town

Hello, sailor boy,
In from the sea!
Hello, sailor,
Come with me!

Come on drink cognac.
Rather have wine?
Come here, I love you.
Come and be mine.

Lights, sailor boy,
Warm, white lights.
Solid land, kid.
Wild, white nights.

Come on, sailor,
Out o' the sea.
Let's go, sweetie!
Come with me.

# Sea Calm

How still,
How strangely still
The water is today.
It is not good
For water
To be so still that way.

## Caribbean Sunset

God having a hemorrhage,
Blood coughed across the sky,
Staining the dark sea red,
That is sunset in the Caribbean.

## Seascape

Off the coast of Ireland
　　As our ship passed by
We saw a line of fishing ships
　　Etched against the sky.

Off the coast of England
　　As we rode the foam
We saw an Indian merchantman
　　Coming home.

## Natcha

Natcha, offering love,
For ten shillings offering love.
Offering: A night with me, honey.
A long, sweet night with me.
　　Come, drink palm wine.
　　Come, drink kisses.
A long, dream night with me.

# Death of an Old Seaman

We buried him high on a windy hill,
But his soul went out to sea.
I know, for I heard, when all was still,
His sea-soul say to me:

Put no tombstone at my head,
For here I do not make my bed.
Strew no flowers on my grave,
I've gone back to the wind and wave.
Do not, do not weep for me,
For I am happy with my sea.


# Sick Room

How quiet
It is in this sick room
Where on the bed
A silent woman lies between two lovers—
Life and Death,
And all three covered with a sheet of pain.


# To the Dark Mercedes of "El Palacio de Amor"

Mercedes is a jungle-lily in a death house.
Mercedes is a doomed star.
Mercedes is a charnel rose.
Go where gold
Will fall at the feet of your beauty,
Mercedes.
Go where they will pay you well
For your loveliness.

# Mulatto

*I am your son, white man!*

Georgia dusk
And the turpentine woods.
One of the pillars of the temple fell.

> *You are my son!*
> *Like hell!*

The moon over the turpentine woods.
The Southern night
Full of stars,
Great big yellow stars.
   What's a body but a toy?
      Juicy bodies
      Of nigger wenches
      Blue black
      Against black fences.
      O, you little bastard boy,
      What's a body but a toy?
The scent of pine wood stings the soft night air.
      *What's the body of your mother?*
Silver moonlight everywhere.
      *What's the body of your mother?*
Sharp pine scent in the evening air.
      A nigger night,
      A nigger joy,
      A little yellow
      Bastard boy.

> *Naw, you ain't my brother.*
> *Niggers ain't my brother.*
> *Not ever.*
> *Niggers ain't my brother.*

The Southern night is full of stars,
Great big yellow stars.
      O, sweet as earth,
      Dusk dark bodies
      Give sweet birth
To little yellow bastard boys.

> *Git on back there in the night,*
> *You ain't white.*

The bright stars scatter everywhere.
Pine wood scent in the evening air.
    A nigger night,
    A nigger joy.

*I am your son, white man!*

    A little yellow
    Bastard boy.


## A Letter to Anne

Since I left you, Anne,
I have seen nothing but you.
Every day
Has been your face,
And every night your hand
And every road
Your voice calling me.
And every rock and every flower and tree
Has been a touch of you.
Nowhere
Have I seen anything else but you,
Anne.


## In the Mist of the Moon

In the mist of the moon I saw you,
O, Nanette,
And you were lovelier than the moon.
    You were darkness,
    And the body of darkness.
    And light,
    And the body of light.
In the mist of the moon I saw you,
Dark Nanette.

## Spirituals

Rocks and the firm roots of trees.
The rising shafts of mountains.
Something strong to put my hands on.

Sing, O Lord Jesus!
Song is a strong thing.
I heard my mother singing
When life hurt her:

*Gonna ride in my chariot some day!*

The branches rise
From the firm roots of trees.
The mountains rise
From the solid lap of earth.
The waves rise
From the dead weight of sea.

Sing, O black mother!
Song is a strong thing.


## For an Indian Screen

Clutching at trees and clawing rocks
And panting and climbing
Until he reached the top
A tiger in India
Surmounted a cliff one day
When the hunters were behind him
And his lair was far away.
A black and golden tiger
Climbed a red cliff's side
And men in black and golden gowns
Sought the tiger's hide.

O, splendid, supple animal:
Against the cliff's red face:
A picture for an Indian screen
Woven in silks of subtle sheen
And broidered in yellow lace,
A picture for an Indian screen
As a prince's gift to some ebony queen
In a far-off land like a fairy scene.

# Day

Where most surely comes a day
When all the sweets you've gorged
Will turn your stomach sick
And all the friends you've loved
Will go away
And every gold swift hour
Will be an hour of pain
And every sun-filled cloud
A cloud of rain
And even the withered flowers
Will lose their long-held faint perfume
And you alone will be with you
In that last room,—
Only your single selves together
Facing a single doom.

# Passing Love

Because you are to me a song
I must not sing you over-long.

Because you are to me a prayer
I cannot say you everywhere.

Because you are to me a rose—
You will not stay when summer goes.

# Lincoln Monument: Washington

Let's go see old Abe
Sitting in the marble and the moonlight,
Sitting lonely in the marble and the moonlight,
Quiet for ten thousand centuries, old Abe.
Quiet for a million, million years.

Quiet—

And yet a voice forever
Against the
Timeless walls
Of time—
Old Abe.

## Song for a Dark Girl

Way Down South in Dixie
    (Break the heart of me)
They hung my black young lover
    To a cross roads tree.

Way Down South in Dixie
    (Bruised body high in air)
I asked the white Lord Jesus
    What was the use of prayer.

Way Down South in Dixie
    (Break the heart of me)
Love is a naked shadow
    On a gnarled and naked tree.

## Gal's Cry for a Dying Lover

Heard de owl a hootin',
Knowed somebody's 'bout to die.
Heard de owl a hootin',
Knowed somebody's 'bout to die.
Put ma head un'neath de kiver,
Started in to moan an' cry.

Hound dawg's barkin'
Means he's gonna leave this world.
Hound dawg's barkin'
Means he's gonna leave this world.
O, Lawd have mercy
On a po' black girl.

Black an' ugly
But he sho do treat me kind.
I'm black an' ugly
But he sho do treat me kind.
High-in-heaben Jesus,
Please don't take this man o' mine.

# Desire

Desire to us
Was like a double death,
Swift dying
Of our mingled breath,
Evaporation
Of an unknown strange perfume
Between us quickly
In a naked
Room.

# Poem for Youth

Raindrops
On the crumbling walls
Of tradition,
Sunlight
Across mouldy pits
Of yesterday.

Oh,
Wise old men,
What do you say
About the fiddles
And the jazz
And the loud Hey! Hey!
About the dancing girls,
And the laughing boys,
And the brilliant lights,
And the blaring joys,
The firecracker days
And the nights,—
Love-toys?

Staid old men,
What do you say
About sun-filled rain
Drowning yesterday?

## The Naughty Child

The naughty child
Who ventured to go cut flowers,
Fell into the mill-pond
And was drowned.
But the good children all
Are living yet,
Nice folks now
In a very nice town.

## Girl

She lived in sinful happiness
And died in pain.
She danced in sunshine
And laughed in rain.

She went one summer morning
When flowers spread the plain,
But she told everybody
She was coming back again.

Folks made a coffin
And hid her deep in earth.
Seems like she said:
*My body*
*Brings new birth.*

For sure there grew flowers
And tall young trees
And sturdy weeds and grasses
To sway in the breeze.

And sure she lived
In growing things
With no pain
To laugh in sunshine
And dance in rain.

## Wise Men

Let me become dead eyed
Like a fish,—
I'm sure then I'd be wise
For all the wise men I've seen
Have had dead eyes.

Let me learn to fit all things
Into law and rule:
I'd be the proper person then
To teach a school.

## Ma Lord

Ma Lord ain't no stuck-up man.
Ma Lord, he ain't proud.
When he goes a-walkin'
He gives me his hand.
"You ma friend," he 'lowed.

Ma Lord knowed what it was to work.
He knowed how to pray.
Ma Lord's life was trouble, too,
Trouble ever day.

Ma Lord ain't no stuck-up man.
He's a friend o' mine.
When He went to heaben,
His soul on fire,
He tole me I was gwine.
He said, "Sho you'll come wid Me
An' be ma friend through eternity."

## Tapestry

Men who ride strange wild horses
Down dangerous glens and glades,
Men who draw keen sharp swords,
Toledo or Damascus blades,
Men who swear and laugh and love
And live and sing like troubadours,—
Wrinkled old beldams somewhere
Are dreaming of old amours.

## Success

Here I sit with my belly full
And he who might have been my brother
Walks hungry in the rain.

Here I sit with my belly full
And she I might have loved
Seeks someone in the shadows
To whom she may sell her body.

Here I sit with my belly full,
No longer in the rain,
No longer the shadows for the
Woman I love,
No longer hunger.

Success is a great big beefsteak
With onions on it,
And I eat.

## Nocturne for the Drums

Gay little devils
That hide in gin
And tickle black boys
Under the chin
And make them laugh,
Gay little devils
That lurk in kisses,
And shine in the eyes
Of ebony misses,
Shine in their eyes:
Whee-e-e!!
O-o-o-o . . . Boom!
Jazz band in a cabaret!
The quick red hour
Before the day.

## For Salome

There
Is no sweetness
In the kiss
Of a mouth
Unwarm and dead,
And even passion's
Flaming bliss
Turns ashen
In a charnel bed.
Salome
Of the wine-red lips,
What would you with death's head?


## Being Old

It's because you are so young,—
You do not understand.
        But we are old
        As the jungle trees
        That bloomed forever,
        Old as the forgotten rivers
        That flowed into the earth.
Surely we know what you do not know;
        Joy of living,
        Uselessness of things.
You are too young to understand yet.
        Build another skyscraper
        Touching the stars.
We sit with our backs against a tree
And watch skyscrapers tumble
And stars forget.
        Solomon built a temple
        And it must have fallen down.
        It isn't here now.
We know some things, being old,
You do not understand.

## Freedom Seeker

I see a woman with wings
Trying to escape from a cage
And the cage door
Has fallen on her wings.
They are long wings
Which drag on the ground
When she stands up,
But she hasn't enough strength
To pull them away
From the weight of the cage door,
She is caught and held by her wings.

## Parisian Beggar Woman

Once you were young.
Now, hunched in the cold,
Nobody cares
That you are old.

Once you were beautiful.
Now, in the street,
No one remembers
Your lips were sweet.

Oh, withered old woman
Of rue Fontaine,
Nobody but death
Will kiss you again.

## I Thought It Was Tangiers I Wanted

I know now
That Notre Dame is in Paris.
And the Seine is more to me now
Than a wriggling line on a map
Or a name in travel stories.

I know now
There is a Crystal Palace in Antwerp
Where a hundred women sell their naked bodies,

And the night-lovers of sailors
Wait for men on docks in Genoa.

I know now
That a great golden moon
Like a picture-book moon
Really rises behind palm groves
In Africa,
And tom-toms do beat
In village squares under the mango trees.

I know now
That Venice is a church dome
And a net-work of canals,
Tangiers a whiteness under sun.
I thought
It was Tangiers I wanted,
Or the gargoyles of Notre Dame,
Or the Crystal Palace in Antwerp,
Or the golden palm-grove moon in Africa,
Or a church dome and a net-work of canals.

Happiness lies nowhere,
Some old fool said,
If not within oneself.

It's a sure thing
Notre Dame is in Paris, —
But I thought it was Tangiers I wanted.


## Dreamer

I take my dreams
And make of them a bronze vase,
And a wide round fountain
With a beautiful statue in its center,
And a song with a broken heart,
And I ask you:
Do you understand my dreams?
Sometimes you say you do
And sometimes you say you don't.
Either way
It doesn't matter.
I continue to dream.

## Hey!

Sun's a settin',
This is what I'm gonna sing.
Sun's a settin',
This is what I'm gonna sing:
I feels de blues a comin',
Wonder what de blues'll bring?

## Hey! Hey!

Sun's a risin',
This is gonna be ma song.
Sun's a risin',
This is gonna be ma song.
I could be blue but
I been blue all night long.

## Bad Man

I'm a bad, bad man
Cause everybody tells me so.
I'm a bad, bad man.
Everybody tells me so.
I takes ma meanness and ma licker
Everwhere I go.

I beats ma wife an'
I beats ma side gal too.
Beats ma wife an'
Beats ma side gal too.
Don't know why I do it but
It keeps me from feelin' blue.

I'm so bad I
Don't even want to be good.
So bad, bad, bad I
Don't even want to be good.
I'm goin' to de devil an'
I wouldn't go to heaben if I could.

## Closing Time

Starter!

    Her face is pale
    In the doorway light.
    Her lips blood red
    And her skin blue white.

Taxi!

    I'm tired.

Deep . . . River. . . .

    O, God, please!

The river and the moon hold memories.

    Cornets play.
    Dancers whirl.
    Death, be kind.

What was the cover charge, kid?

    To a little drowned girl.


## Prize Fighter

Only dumb guys fight.
    If I wasn't dumb
    I wouldn't be fightin'.
    I could make six dollars a day
    On the docks
    And I'd save more than I do now.
Only dumb guys fight.

## Crap Game

Lemme roll 'em, boy.
I got ma tail curled!
If a seven don't come
'Leven ain't far away.
An' if I craps,
Dark baby,
Trouble
Don't last all de time.
Hit 'em, bones!

## Ballad of Gin Mary

Carried me to de court,
Judge was settin' there.
Looked all around me,
Didn't have a friend nowhere.

Judge Pierce he says, Mary.
Old Judge says, Mary Jane,
Ever time I mounts this bench
I sees yo' face again.

O, Lawd! O, Lawd!
O, Lawd . . . Lawdee!
Seems like bad licker,
Judge, won't let me be.

Old Judge says you's a drunkard.
Fact is you worries me.
Gwine give you eighteen months
So licker'll let you be.

Eighteen months in jail!
O, eighteen months locked in!
Won't be so bad in jail
But I'll miss ma gin.

O, please sir, Judge, have mercy!
Have mercy, please, on me!
Old hard-faced Judge says eighteen months
Till licker'll let you be.

# Death of Do Dirty: A Rounder's Song

O, you can't find a buddy
Any old time
'Ll help you out
When you ain't got a dime.

He was a friend o' mine.

They called him Do Dirty
Cause he was black
An' had cut his gal
An' shot a man in de back.

Ma friend o' mine.

But when I was hungry,
Had nothin' to eat,
He bought me corn bread
An' a stew o' meat.

Good friend o' mine.

An' when de cops got me
An' put me in jail
If Dirty had de money
He'd go ma bail.

O, friend o' mine.

That night he got kilt
I was standin' in de street.
Somebody comes by
An' says yo' boy is gettin' beat.

Ma friend o' mine.

But when I got there
An' seen de ambulance
A guy was sayin'
He ain't got a chance.

Best friend o' mine.

An' de ones that kilt him,—
Damn their souls,—
I'm gonna fill 'em up full o'
Bullet holes.

Ma friend o' mine.

## Porter

I must say
Yes, sir,
To you all the time.
Yes, sir!
Yes, sir!
All my days
Climbing up a great big mountain
Of yes, sirs!

Rich old white man
Owns the world.
Gimme yo' shoes
To shine.

Yes, sir!

## Sport

Life
For him
Must be
The shivering of
A great drum
Beaten with swift sticks
Then at the closing hour
The lights go out
And there is no music at all
And death becomes
An empty cabaret
And eternity an unblown saxophone
And yesterday
A glass of gin
Drunk long
Ago.

## Shout

Listen to yo' prophets,
Little Jesus!
Listen to yo' saints!

## Fire

Fire,
Fire, Lord!
Fire gonna burn ma soul!

I ain't been good,
I ain't been clean—
I been stinkin', low-down, mean.

Fire,
Fire, Lord!
Fire gonna burn ma soul!

Tell me, brother,
Do you believe
If you wanta go to heaben
Got to moan an' grieve?

Fire,
Fire, Lord!
Fire gonna burn ma soul!

I been stealin',
Been tellin' lies,
Had more women
Than Pharaoh had wives.

Fire,
Fire, Lord!
Fire gonna burn ma soul!
I means Fire, Lord!
Fire gonna burn ma soul!

## Moan

I'm deep in trouble,
Nobody to understand,
    Lord, Lord!

Deep in trouble,
Nobody to understand,
    O, Lord!

Gonna pray to ma Jesus,
Ask him to gimme His hand.
    Ma Lord!

I'm moanin', moanin',
Nobody cares just why.
    No, Lord!

Moanin', moanin',
Feels like I could die.
    O, Lord!

Sho, there must be peace,
    Ma Jesus,
Somewhere in yo' sky.
    Yes, Lord!

## Angels Wings

The angels wings is white as snow,
    O, white as snow,
        White
            as
                snow.
The angels wings is white as snow,
    But I drug ma wings
    In the dirty mire.
    O, I drug ma wings
    All through the fire.
But the angels wings is white as snow,
        White
            as
                snow.

## Sinner

Have mercy, Lord!

Po' an' black
An' humble an' lonesome
An' a sinner in yo' sight.

Have mercy, Lord!

## Cora

I broke my heart this mornin',
Ain't got no heart no more.
Next time a man comes near me
Gonna shut an' lock my door
Cause they treat me mean—
The ones I love.
They always treat me mean.

## Workin' Man

I works all day
Wid a pick an' a shovel.
Comes home at night,—
It ain't nothin' but a hovel.

I calls for ma woman
When I opens de door.
She's out in de street,—
Ain't nothin' but a 'hore.

I does her good
An' I treats her fine,
But she don't gimme lovin'
Cause she ain't de right kind.

I'm a hard workin' man
An' I sho pays double
Cause I tries to be good
An' gits nothin' but trouble.

## Baby

Albert!
Hey, Albert!
Don't you play in dat road.
    You see dem trucks
    A-goin' by.
    One run ovah you
    An' you die.
Albert, don't you play in dat road.

## Evil Woman

I ain't gonna mistreat ma
Good gal any more.
I'm just gonna kill her
Next time she makes me sore.

I treats her kind but
She don't do me right.
She fights an' quarrels most
Ever night.

I can't have no woman's
Got such low-down ways,
Cause a blue-gummed woman
Ain't de style now days.

I brought her from de South
An' she's goin' on back
Else I'll use her head
For a carpet tack.

## A Ruined Gal

Standin' by de lonesome riverside
After de boat's done gone,
    Po' weary me
    Won't be nobody's bride
    Cause I is long gone wrong.

Standin' by de weary riverside
When de boat comes in,
Po' lonesome me
Won't meet nobody
Cause I ain't got no friend.

By de edge o' de weary riverside
Night-time's comin' down.
Ain't nothin' for a ruined gal
But jump overboard an' drown.

O, de lonesome riverside,
O, de wicked water.
Damn ma black old mammy's soul
For ever havin' a daughter.


## Black Gal

I's always been a workin' girl.
I treated Albert fine.
Ain't cut him wid no razor,
Ain't never been unkind.

Yet it seems like always
Men takes all they can from me
Then they goes an' finds a yaller gal
An' lets me be.

I dressed up Albert Johnson.
I bought him suits o' clothes,
An' soon as he got out de barrel
Then out ma door he goes.

Yet I ain't never been no bad one.
Can't help it cause I'm black.
I hates them rinney yaller gals
An' I wants ma Albert back.
Ma little, short, sweet, brownskin boy,—
Oh, God, I wants him back!

## Sun Song

Sun and softness,
Sun and the beaten hardness of the earth,
Sun and the song of all the sun-stars
Gathered together—
Dark ones of Africa,
I bring you my songs
To sing on the Georgia roads.

## Magnolia Flowers

The quiet fading out of life
In a corner full of ugliness.

I went lookin' for magnolia flowers
But I didn't find 'em.
I went lookin' for magnolia flowers in the dusk
And there was only this corner
Full of ugliness.

*'Scuse me,*
*I didn't mean to stump ma toe on you, lady.*

There ought to be magnolias
Somewhere in this dusk.

*'Scuse me,*
*I didn't mean to stump ma toe on you.*

## Red Silk Stockings

Put on yo' red silk stockings,
Black gal.
Go out an' let de white boys
Look at yo' legs.

Ain't nothin' to do for you, nohow,
Round this town,—

You's too pretty.
Put on yo' red silk stockings, gal,
An' tomorrow's chile'll
Be a high yaller.

Go out an' let de white boys
Look at yo' legs.

## Young Gal's Blues

I'm gonna walk to the graveyard
'Hind ma friend Miss Cora Lee.
Gonna walk to the graveyard
'Hind ma dear friend Cora Lee
Cause when I'm dead some
Body'll have to walk behind me.

I'm goin' to the po' house
To see ma old Aunt Clew.
Goin' to the po' house
To see ma old Aunt Clew.
When I'm old an' ugly
I'll want to see somebody, too.

The po' house is lonely
An' the grave is cold.
O, the po' house is lonely,
The graveyard grave is cold.
But I'd rather be dead than
To be ugly an' old.

When love is gone what
Can a young gal do?
When love is gone, O,
What can a young gal do?
Keep on a-lovin' me, daddy,
Cause I don't want to be blue.

## Hard Daddy

I went to ma daddy,
Says Daddy I have got the blues.
Went to ma daddy,
Says Daddy I have got the blues.
Ma daddy says, Honey,
Can't you bring no better news?

I cried on his shoulder but
He turned his back on me.
Cried on his shoulder but
He turned his back on me.
He said a woman's cryin's
Never gonna bother me.

I wish I had wings to
Fly like the eagle flies.
Wish I had wings to
Fly like the eagle flies.
I'd fly on ma man an'
I'd scratch out both his eyes.

## Sunset—Coney Island

The sun,
Like the red yolk of a rotten egg,
Falls behind the roller-coaster
And the horizon sticks
With a putrid odor of colors.
Down on the beach
A little Jewish tailor from the Bronx,
With a bad stomach,
Throws up the hot-dog sandwiches
He ate in the afternoon
While life to him
Is like a sick tomato
In a garbage can.

## Lover's Return

My old time daddy
Came back home last night.
His face was pale and
His eyes didn't look just right.

He says, "Mary, I'm
Comin' home to you—
So sick and lonesome
I don't know what to do."

    *Oh, men treats women*
    *Just like a pair o' shoes—*
    *You kicks 'em round and*
    *Does 'em like you choose.*

I looked at my daddy—
Lawd! and I wanted to cry.
He looked so thin—
Lawd! that I wanted to cry.
But the devil told me:
    *Damn a lover*
    *Come home to die!*

## Nonette

You wound my soul with a thousand spears,
You bathe my wounds in a flood of tears,
Nonette.

You give me a rose whose breath is sweet,
Whose petals are poison and death to eat,
Nonette.

And when I am dead you do not cry,
But your poor heart breaks, too, and you, too, die.

## Alabama Earth

(At Booker Washington's grave)

Deep in Alabama earth
His buried body lies—
But higher than the singing pines
And taller than the skies
And out of Alabama earth
To all the world there goes
The truth a simple heart has held
And the strength a strong hand knows,
While over Alabama earth
These words are gently spoken:
Serve—and hate will die unborn.
Love—and chains are broken.

## Mazie Dies Alone in the City Hospital

I hate to die this way with the quiet
Over everything like a shroud.
I'd rather die where the band's a-playin'
Noisy and loud.

I'd rather die in the way I lived,—
Drunk and rowdy and gay!
God! why did you ever curse me
Makin' me die this way?

## Hurt

Who cares
About the hurt in your heart?

Make a song like this
      for a jazz band to play:

      Nobody cares.
      Nobody cares.

Make a song like that
From your lips.

      Nobody cares.

126

## Lady in Cabaret

She knows
The end of the evening will come,—
It has come before.
And if it should never come again.
Well,—
Just that much more
A bore.

## Dear Lovely Death

Dear lovely Death
That taketh all things under wing—
Never to kill—
Only to change
Into some other thing
This suffering flesh,
To make it either more or less,
But not again the same—
Dear lovely Death,
Change is thy other name.

## Flight

Plant your toes in the cool swamp mud.
Step and leave no track.
Hurry, sweating runner!
The hounds are at your back.

*No I didn't touch her*
*White flesh ain't for me.*

Hurry! Black boy, hurry!
They'll swing you to a tree.

## Aesthete in Harlem

Strange,
That in this nigger place,
I should meet Life face to face
When for years, I had been seeking
Life in places gentler speaking
Until I came to this near street
And found Life—stepping on my feet!

## Anne Spencer's Table

On Anne Spencer's table
There lies an unsharpened pencil—
As though she has left unwritten
Many things she knows to write.

## Spring for Lovers

Desire weaves its fantasy of dreams,
And all the world becomes a garden close
In which we wander, you and I together,
Believing in the symbol of the rose,
Believing only in the heart's bright flower—
Forgetting—flowers wither in an hour.

## Tower

Death is a tower
To which the soul ascends
To spend a meditative hour—
That never ends.

# The English

In ships all over the world
The English comb their hair for dinner,
Stand watch on the bridge,
Guide by strange stars,
Take on passengers,
Slip up hot rivers,
Nose across lagoons,
Bargain for trade,
Buy, sell or rob,
Load oil, load fruit,
Load cocoa beans, load gold
In ships all over the world,
Comb their hair for dinner.


# Afro-American Fragment

So long,
So far away
Is Africa.
Not even memories alive
Save those that history books create,
Save those that songs
Beat back into the blood—
Beat out of blood with words sad-sung
In strange un-Negro tongue—
So long,
So far away
Is Africa.

Subdued and time-lost
Are the drums—and yet
Through some vast mist of race
There comes this song
I do not understand
This song of atavistic land,
Of bitter yearnings lost
Without a place—
So long,
So far away
Is Africa's
Dark face.

## Rent-Party Shout: For a Lady Dancer

Whip it to a jelly!
Too bad Jim!
Mamie's got ma man—
An' I can't find him.
Shake that thing! O!
Shake it slow!
That man I love is
Mean an' low.
Pistol an' razor!
Razor an' gun!
If I sees ma man he'd
Better run—
For I'll shoot him in de shoulder,
Else I'll cut him down,
Cause I knows I can find him
When he's in de ground—
Then can't no other women
Have him layin' round.
So play it, Mr. Nappy!
Yo' music's fine!
I'm gonna kill that
Man o' mine!

## Black Seed

World-wide dusk
Of dear dark faces
Driven before an alien wind,
Scattered like seed
From far-off places
Growing in soil
That's strange and thin,
Hybrid plants
In another's garden,
Flowers
In a land
That's not your own,
Cut by the shears
Of the white-faced gardeners—

Tell them to leave you alone!

# Militant

Let all who will
Eat quietly the bread of shame.
I cannot,
Without complaining loud and long,
Tasting its bitterness in my throat,
And feeling to my very soul
It's wrong.
For honest work
You proffer me poor pay,
For honest dreams
Your spit is in my face,
And so my fist is clenched
Today—
To strike your face.

# Negro Servant

All day subdued, polite,
Kind, thoughtful to the faces that are white.
    O, tribal dance!
    O, drums!
    O, veldt at night!
Forgotten watch-fires on a hill somewhere!
    O, songs that do not care!
At six o'clock, or seven, or eight,
    You're through.
    You've worked all day.
    Dark Harlem waits for you.
    The bus, the sub—
    Pay-nights a taxi
    Through the park.
O, drums of life in Harlem after dark!
    O, dreams!
    O, songs!
    O, saxophones at night!
O, sweet relief from faces that are white!

# Merry Christmas

Merry Christmas, China,
From the gun-boats in the river,
Ten-inch shells for Christmas gifts,
And peace on earth forever.

Merry Christmas, India,
To Gandhi in his cell,
From righteous Christian England,
Ring out, bright Christmas bell!

Ring Merry Christmas, Africa,
From Cairo to the Cape!
Ring Hallehuiah! Praise the Lord!
(For murder and for rape.)

Ring Merry Christmas, Haiti!
(And drown the voodoo drums—
We'll rob you to the Christian hymns
Until the next Christ comes.)

Ring Merry Christmas, Cuba!
(While Yankee domination
Keeps a nice fat president
In a little half-starved nation.)

And to you down-and-outers,
("Due to economic laws")
Oh, eat, drink, and be merry
With a bread-line Santa Claus—

While all the world hails Christmas,
While all the church bells sway!
While, better still, the Christian guns
Proclaim this joyous day!

While holy steel that makes us strong
Spits forth a mighty Yuletide song:
SHOOT Merry Christmas everywhere!
Let Merry Christmas GAS the air!

# Poems 1931—1940

# Tired

I am so tired of waiting,
Aren't you,
For the world to become good
And beautiful and kind?
Let us take a knife
And cut the world in two—
And see what worms are eating
At the rind.

# Call to Creation

Listen!
All you beauty-makers,
Give up beauty for a moment.
Look at harshness, look at pain,
Look at life again.
Look at hungry babies crying,
Listen to the rich men lying,
Look at starving China dying.
Hear the rumble in the East:
"In spite of all,
Life must not cease."
In India with folded arms,
In China with the guns,
In Africa with bitter smile—
See where the murmur runs:
"Life must not cease,
Because the fat and greedy ones
Proclaim their thieving peace."
Their peace far worse than war and death—
For this is better than living breath:
Free! To be Free!

Listen!
Futile beauty-makers—
Work for awhile with the pattern-breakers!
Come for a march with the new-world-makers:
Let beauty be!

## To Certain Negro Leaders

Voices crying in the wilderness
At so much per word
From the white folks:
"Be meek and humble,
All you niggers,
And do not cry
Too loud."

## A Christian Country

God slumbers in a back alley
With a gin bottle in His hand.
Come on, God, get up and fight
Like a man.

## To the Little Fort of San Lazaro
## on the Ocean Front, Havana

Watch tower once for pirates
That sailed the sun-bright seas—
Red pirates, great romantics.

DRAKE
DE PLAN,
EL GRILLO

Against such as these
Years and years ago
You served quite well—
When time and ships were slow.
But now,
Against a pirate called
THE NATIONAL CITY BANK
What can you do alone?
Would it not be
Just as well you tumbled down,
Stone by helpless stone?

# Drum

Bear in mind
That death is a drum
Beating forever
Till the last worms come
To answer its call,
Till the last stars fall,
Until the last atom
Is no atom at all,
Until time is lost
And there is no air
And space itself
Is nothing nowhere,
Death is a drum,
A signal drum,
Calling life
To come!
Come!
Come!

# Snake

He glides so swiftly
Back into the grass—
Gives me the courtesy of road
To let me pass,
That I am half ashamed
To seek a stone
To kill him.

# Negro Ghetto

I looked at their black faces
And this is what I saw:
The wind imprisoned in the flesh,
The sun bound down by law.
I watched them moving, moving,
Like water down the street,
And this is what moved in my heart:
Their far-too-humble feet.

## House in the World

I'm looking for a house
In the world
Where the white shadows
Will not fall.

*There is no such house,*
*Dark brothers,*
*No such house*
*At all.*

## Union

Not me alone—
I know now—
But all the whole oppressed
Poor world,
White and black,
Must put their hands with mine
To shake the pillars of those temples
Wherein the false gods dwell
And worn-out altars stand
Too well defended,
And the rule of greed's upheld—
That must be ended.

## Prayer [2]

Gather up
In the arms of your pity
The sick, the depraved,
The desperate, the tired,
All the scum
Of our weary city

Gather up
In the arms of your pity.
Gather up
In the arms of your love—
Those who expect
No love from above.

## Dying Beast

Sensing death,
The buzzards gather—
Noting the last struggle
Of flesh under weather,
Noting the last glance
Of agonized eye
At passing wind
And boundless sky.
Sensing death,
The buzzards overhead
Await that still moment
When life—

Is dead.

## Sailor

He sat upon the rolling deck
Half a world away from home,
And smoked a Capstan cigarette
And watched the blue waves tipped with foam.

He had a mermaid on his arm,
An anchor on his breast,
And tattooed on his back he had
A blue bird in a nest.

# God

I am God—
Without one friend,
Alone in my purity
World without end.

Below me young lovers
Tread the sweet ground—
But I am God—
I cannot come down.

Spring!
Life is love!
Love is life only!
Better to be human
Than God—and lonely.

# Sylvester's Dying Bed

I woke up this mornin'
'Bout half-past three.
All the womens in town
Was gathered round me.

Sweet gals was a-moanin',
"Sylvester's gonna die!"
And a hundred pretty mamas
Bowed their heads to cry.

I woke up little later
'Bout half-past fo',
The doctor 'n' undertaker's
Both at ma do'.

Black gals was a-beggin',
"You can't leave us here!"
Brown-skins cryin', "Daddy!
Honey! Baby! Don't go, dear!"

But I felt ma time's a-comin',
And I know'd I's dyin' fast

I seed the River Jerden
A-creepin' muddy past—
But I's still Sweet Papa 'Vester,
Yes, sir! Long as life do last!

So I hollers, "Com'ere, babies,
Fo' to love yo' daddy right!"
And I reaches up to hug 'em—
When the Lawd put out the light.

Then everything was darkness
In a great . . . big . . . night.

## October 16: The Raid

Perhaps
You will remember
John Brown.

John Brown
Who took his gun,
Took twenty-one companions
White and black,
Went to shoot your way to freedom
Where two rivers meet
And the hills of the
North
And the hills of the
South
Look slow at one another—
And died
For your sake.

Now that you are
Many years free,
And the echo of the Civil War
Has passed away,
And Brown himself
Has long been tried at law,
Hanged by the neck,

And buried in the ground—
Since Harpers Ferry
Is alive with ghosts today,
Immortal raiders
Come again to town—

Perhaps
You will recall
John Brown.


## Scottsboro

8 BLACK BOYS IN A SOUTHERN JAIL.
    WORLD, TURN PALE!

8 black boys and one white lie.
Is it much to die?

Is it much to die when immortal feet
March with you down Time's street,
When beyond steel bars sound the deathless drums
Like a mighty heart-beat as They come?

Who comes?

Christ,
Who fought alone.

John Brown.

That mad mob
That tore the Bastille down
Stone by stone.

Moses.

Jeanne d'Arc.

Dessalines.

Nat Turner.

Fighters for the free.

Lenin with the flag blood red.

(Not dead! Not dead!
None of those is dead.)

Gandhi.

Sandino.

Evangelista, too,
To walk with you—

8 BLACK BOYS IN A SOUTHERN JAIL.
WORLD, TURN PALE!

## Christ in Alabama

Christ is a nigger,
Beaten and black:
Oh, bare your back!

Mary is His mother:
Mammy of the South,
Silence your mouth.

God is His father:
White Master above
Grant Him your love.

Most holy bastard
Of the bleeding mouth,
Nigger Christ
On the cross
Of the South.

## Advertisement for the Waldorf-Astoria

*Fine living . . . à la carte??*
*Come to the Waldorf-Astoria!*

LISTEN, HUNGRY ONES!
Look! See what *Vanity Fair* says about the
new Waldorf-Astoria:

"All the luxuries of private home. . . ."
Now, won't that be charming when the last flop-house
    has turned you down this winter?
    Furthermore:
"It is far beyond anything hitherto attempted in the hotel
    world. . . ." It cost twenty-eight million dollars. The fa-
    mous Oscar Tschirky is in charge of banqueting.
    Alexandre Gastaud is chef. It will be a distinguished
    background for society.
So when you've got no place else to go, homeless and hungry
    ones, choose the Waldorf as a background for your rags—
(Or do you still consider the subway after midnight good
    enough?)


                          ROOMERS
Take a room at the new Waldorf, you down-and-outers—
    sleepers in charity's flop-houses where God pulls a
    long face, and you have to pray to get a bed.
They serve swell board at the Waldorf-Astoria. Look at this menu, will you:


            GUMBO CREOLE
            CRABMEAT IN CASSOLETTE
            BOILED BRISKET OF BEEF
            SMALL ONIONS IN CREAM
            WATERCRESS SALAD
            PEACH MELBA


Have luncheon there this afternoon, all you jobless.
    Why not?
Dine with some of the men and women who got rich off of
    your labor, who clip coupons with clean white fingers
    because your hands dug coal, drilled stone, sewed gar-
    ments, poured steel to let other people draw dividends
    and live easy.
(Or haven't you had enough yet of the soup-lines and the bit-
    ter bread of charity?)
Walk through Peacock Alley tonight before dinner, and get
    warm, anyway. You've got nothing else to do.


                    EVICTED FAMILIES
All you families put out in the street:
    Apartments in the Towers are only $10,000 a year.
        (Three rooms and two baths.) Move in there until
        times get good, and you can do better. $10,000 and $1.00
        are about the same to you, aren't they?
Who cares about money with a wife and kids homeless, and

nobody in the family working? Wouldn't a duplex
high above the street be grand, with a view of the rich-
est city in the world at your nose?
"A lease, if you prefer, or an arrangement terminable at will."

## NEGROES

Oh, Lawd, I done forgot Harlem!
Say, you colored folks, hungry a long time in 135th Street—
    they got swell music at the Waldorf-Astoria. It sure is a
    mighty nice place to shake hips in, too. There's dancing
    after supper in a big warm room. It's cold as hell
    on Lenox Avenue. All you've had all day is a cup of
    coffee. Your pawnshop overcoat's a ragged banner on
    your hungry frame. You know, downtown folks are just
    crazy about Paul Robeson! Maybe they'll like you, too,
    black mob from Harlem. Drop in at the Waldorf this
    afternoon for tea. Stay to dinner. Give Park Avenue a
    lot of darkie color—free for nothing! Ask the Junior
    Leaguers to sing a spiritual for you. They probably
    know 'em better than you do—and their lips won't be
    so chapped with cold after they step out of their closed
    cars in the undercover driveways.
        *Hallelujah! Undercover driveways!*
        *Ma soul's a witness for de Waldorf-Astoria!*
(A thousand nigger section-hands keep the roadbeds smooth,
    so investments in railroads pay ladies with diamond
    necklaces staring at Sert murals.)
        *Thank God A-mighty!*
(And a million niggers bend their backs on rubber planta-
    tions, for rich behinds to ride on thick tires to the
    Theatre Guild tonight.)
        *Ma soul's a witness!*
(And here we stand, shivering in the cold, in Harlem.)
        *Glory be to God—*
        *De Waldorf-Astoria's open!*

## EVERYBODY

So get proud and rare back; everybody! The new Waldorf-Astoria's
    open!
(Special siding for private cars from the railroad yards.)
    You ain't been there yet?
(A thousand miles of carpet and a million bathrooms.)
        What's the matter?
 You haven't seen the ads in the papers? Didn't you get a card?
        Don't you know they specialize in American cooking?
        Ankle on down to 49th Street at Park Avenue. Get up

off that subway bench tonight with the evening POST
for cover! Come on out o' that flop-house! Stop shivering
your guts out all day on street corners under the El.
Jesus, ain't you tired yet?

### CHRISTMAS CARD

Hail Mary, Mother of God!
the new Christ child of the Revolution's about to be
born.
(Kick hard, red baby, in the bitter womb of the mob.)
Somebody, put an ad in *Vanity Fair* quick!
Call Oscar of the Waldorf—for Christ's sake!!
It's almost Christmas, and that little girl—turned whore
because her belly was too hungry to stand it anymore—
wants a nice clean bed for the Immaculate Conception.
Listen, Mary, Mother of God, wrap your new born babe in
the red flag of Revolution: the Waldorf-Astoria's the
best manger we've got. For reservations: Telephone EL.
5-3000.

## Helen Keller

She,
In the dark,
Found light
Brighter than many ever see.
She,
Within herself,
Found loveliness,
Through the soul's own mastery.
And now the world receives
From her dower:
The message of the strength
Of inner power.

# The Colored Soldier

A dramatic recitation to be done in the half-dark by a young brown fellow who has a vision of his brother killed in France while fighting for the United States of America. Martial music on a piano, or by an orchestra, may accompany the recitation—echoing softly, "Over There," "There's a Rose That Grows in No-Man's Land," "Joan of Arc," and various other war-time melodies.

| THE MOOD | THE POEM |
|---|---|
| *Calmly* | My brother died in France—but I came back. |
| *telling* | We were just two colored boys, brown and black, |
| *the story.* | Who joined up to fight for the U.S.A. |
| *Proudly* | When the Nation called us that mighty day. |
| *and* | We were sent to training camp, then overseas— |
| *expectantly* | And me and my brother were happy as you please |
| *with* | Thinking we were fighting for Democracy's true reign |
| *head up,* | And that our dark blood would wipe away the stain |
| *shoulders* | Of prejudice, and hate, and the false color line— |
| *back,* | And give us the rights that are yours and mine. |
| *and eyes* | They told us America would know no black or white: |
| *shining.* | So we marched to the front, happy to fight. |
| *Quietly* | |
| *recalling* | Last night in a dream my brother came to me |
| *the vision.* | Out of his grave from over the sea, |
| *The dead* | Back from the acres of crosses in France, |
| *man speaks* | And said to me, "Brother, you've got your chance, |
| *with his* | And I hope you're making good, and doing fine— |
| *face* | 'Cause when I was living, I didn't have mine. |
| *full of* | Black boys couldn't work then anywhere like they can |
| *light* | today, |
| *and faith,* | Could hardly find a job that offered decent pay. |
| *confident* | The unions barred us; the factories, too, |
| *that a* | But now I know we've got plenty to do. |
| *new world* | We couldn't eat in restaurants; had Jim Crow cars; |
| *has been* | Didn't have any schools; and there were all sorts of |
| *made.* | bars |
| *Proud* | To a colored boy's rising in wealth or station— |
| *and* | But now I know well that's not our situation: |
| *smiling.* | The world's been made safe for Democracy |
| *But* | And no longer do we know the dark misery |
| *the* | Of being held back, of having no chance— |
| *living,* | Since the colored soldiers came home from France. |
| *remembering* | Didn't our government tell us things would be fine |
| *with a* | When we got through fighting, Over There, and dying? |
| *half-sob* | So now I know we blacks are just like any other— |
| *and* | 'Cause that's what I died for—isn't it, Brother?" |
| *bowing* | And I saw him standing there, straight and tall, |
| *his head* | In his soldier's uniform, and all. |
| | Then his dark face smiled at me in the night— |

147

*in shame,*
*becomes*
*suddenly*
*fierce*
*and*
*angry.*

But the dream was cruel—and bitter—and somehow
    not right.
It was awful—facing that boy who went out to die,
For what could I answer him, except, "It's a lie!"

It's a lie! It's a lie! Every word they said.
And it's better a thousand times you're in France dead.
For here in the South there's no votes and no right.
And I'm still just a "nigger" in America tonight.

*Then*
*he sadly*
*recalls*
*the rows*
*of white*
*crosses*
*in France.*

Then I woke up, and the dream was ended—
But broken was the soldier's dream, too bad to be
    mended.
And it's a good thing all the black boys lying dead
    Over There
Can't see! And don't know! And won't ever care!


## Broke

A complaint to be given by a dejected looking fellow shuffling along in an old suit and
a battered hat, to the tune of a slow-drag stomp or a weary blues.


Uh! I sho am tired.
Been walkin' since five this mornin'.
Up and down, and they just *ain't* no jobs in this man's town.
Answerin' them want-ads not nary bit o' fun,
'Cause 'fore you gets there, ten thousand and one
Done beat you to de place, standin' outside de do'
Talkin' 'bout "we'll work for 50¢ a day, if we can't get no mo'."
And one old funny boy said, "I'll work at any price
Just only providin' de boss man is nice!"
You all out there laughin', but that ain't no joke—
When you're broke.

Last job I had, went to work at five in de mornin', or little mo'
And de man come tellin' me I better get there at fo'.
I mean four—before daylight—s'pose to've done hit yo' first stroke—
Folks sho is gettin' hard on you—just 'cause you broke.
So I say, "Mister, I ain't no sweepin' machine."
So de man say, "I'll get somebody else, then, to clean,"—
So here I is, broke.

Landlady 'lowed to me last week, "Sam, ain't you got no money?"
I say, "Now, baby, you know I ain't got none, honey."
And don't you know that old woman swelled up like a speckled toad
And told me I'd *better* pay her for my room rent and board!
After all them dollars I gived her these last two years,
And she been holdin' 'em so tight till de eagle's in tears—
I wouldn't pay her a penny now if I was to croak—
Come bawlin' me out, 'cause I'm broke.
(I don't care nothin' 'bout her myself!)

Um-mm! Sign here says they wants somebody to shovel coal.
Well, ain't never done it, but for to keep body and soul
Together, reckon I'll try . . . Sho, I wants de job! Yes, sir!
Has I did it befo'? Certainly!
What I don't know 'bout shovelin' coal, ain't no mo' to know!
Willing worker? Un-uh! Yes! What's that you say?
De time is fourteen hours a day?
Well, er—er . . . how much does you pay?
Six dollars a week? Whee-ooo! You sho pays well!
You can take that job and go to——I hope you choke,
Even if I is broke.

But I sho been lookin' round hard lately for ways and means
O' gettin' a new winter coat, or havin' that old one cleaned.
Tried to find one o' them little elevator and switchboard jobs they used
        to have,
But they givin' 'em to school boys now and payin' just about half.
So I went down town to a hotel where I used to work at night,
And de man come tellin' me they ain't hirin' no mo' colored—just white.
I can't even get de money for to buy myself a smoke,
I tell you it's awful, when you're broke.

And I sho had a pretty gal, too, up yonder on Sugar Hill.
She bought a new hat last week and come sendin' me the bill.
I said, "Baby, you know I loves you, and all like that
But right long through here now, I can't 'ford to buy you no hat."
So when I got ready to go, I said, "I'll be seein' you soon, Marie."
And she come tellin' me, she ain't got no mo' evenings free!
I thought love was a dream, but I sho have awoke—
Since I'm broke.

'Course, you hears plenty 'bout this-here unemployment relief—
But you don't see no presidents dyin' o' grief—
All this talkin' ain't nothin' but tinklin' symbols and soundin' brass:

149

Lawd, folkses, how much longer is this gonna last?
It's done got me so crazy, feel like I been takin' coke,
But I can't even buy a paper—I'm so broke.

Aw-oo! Yonder comes a woman I used to know way down South.
(Ain't seen her in six years! Used to go with her, too!)
She would be alright if she wasn't so bow-legged, and cross-eyed,
And didn't have such a big mouth.
Howdy-do, daughter! Caledonia, how are you?
Yes, indeedy, I sho have missed *you*, too!
All these years you say you been *workin'* here?
You got a good job? Yes! Well, I sho am glad to see *you*, dear!
Is I married? No, all these-here girls up North is too light.
Does I wanta? Well, can't say but what I might—
If a pretty gal like you was willin', I'd bite.
You still bakes biscuits? Fried chicken every night? Is that true?
Certainly, chile, I always was crazy 'bout you!
Let's get married right now! Yes! What do you say?
(Is you lookin' at me, baby, or some other way?)
'Cause I'm just dyin' to take on that there marriage yoke.
Yes, um-hum! You sho is sweet! Can you pay fo' de license, dear?
'Cause I'm broke.

## The Black Clown

A dramatic monologue to be spoken by a pure-blooded Negro in the white
suit and hat of a clown, to the music of a piano, or an orchestra.

| THE MOOD | THE POEM |
|---|---|
| *A gay and*<br>*low-down blues.*<br>*Comic entrance*<br>*like the clowns*<br>*in the circus.*<br>*Humorous*<br>*defiance.*<br>*Melancholy*<br>*jazz. Then*<br>*defiance again*<br>*followed by*<br>*loud joy.* | You laugh<br>Because I'm poor and black and funny—<br>Not the same as you—<br>Because my mind is dull<br>And dice instead of books will do<br>For me to play with<br>When the day is through.<br><br>I am the fool of the whole world.<br>Laugh and push me down.<br>Only in song and laughter<br>I rise again—a black clown. |

*A burst of*
*music. Strutting*
*and dancing.*
*Then sudden*
*sadness again.*
*Back bent as*
*in the fields.*
*The slow step.*
*The bowed head.*
*"Nobody knows*
*de trouble I've*
*had."*
*Flinching*
*under the whip.*
*The spiritual*
*syncopated.*
*Determined to*
*laugh.*
*A bugle call.*
*Gay, martial*
*music. Walking*
*proudly, almost*
*prancing.*
*But gradually*
*subdued to a*
*slow, heavy*
*pace. "Some-*
*times I feel*
*like a mother-*
*less chile."*
*Turning futilely*
*from one side*
*to the other.*
*But now a harsh*
*and bitter note*
*creeps into*
*the music.*
*Over-burdened.*
*Backing away*
*angrily.*
*Frantic*
*with*
*humiliation*

Strike up the music.
Let it be gay.
Only in joy
Can a clown have his day.

Three hundred years
In the cotton and the cane,
Plowing and reaping
With no gain—
Empty handed as I began.

A slave—under the whip,
Beaten and sore.
God! Give me laughter
That I can stand more.

God! Give me the spotted
Garments of a clown
So that the pain and the shame
Will not pull me down.

Freedom!
Abe Lincoln done set me free—
One little moment
To dance with glee.

Then sadness again—
No land, no house, no job,
No place to go.
Black—in a white world
Where cold winds blow.
The long struggle for life:
No schools, no work—
Not wanted here; not needed there—
Black—you can die.
Nobody will care—

Yet clinging to the ladder,
Round by round,
Trying to climb up,
Forever pushed down.

Day after day
White spit in my face—

*and helpless-*
*ness.*
*The music*
*is like*
*a mourn-*
*ful tom-tom*
*in the dark!*
*But out of*
*sadness*
*it rises to*
*defiance*
*and determina-*
*tion. A hymn*
*of faith*
*echoes the*
*fighting*
*"Marseillaise."*
*Tearing off*
*his clown's*
*suit, throwing*
*down the hat*
*of a fool,*
*and standing*
*forth,*
*straight*
*and strong,*
*in the clothes*
*of a modern*
*man, he proclaims*
*himself.*

Worker and clown am I
For the "civilized" race.

Nigger! Nigger! Nigger!
Scorn crushing me down.
Laugh at me! Laugh at me!
Just a black clown!

Laugh at me then,
All the world round—
From Africa to Georgia
I'm only a clown!

But no! Not forever
Like this will I be:
Here are my hands
That can really make me free!

Suffer and struggle.
Work, pray, and fight.
Smash my way through
To Manhood's true right.

Say to all foemen:
You can't keep me down!
Tear off the garments
That make me a clown!

Rise from the bottom,
Out of the slime!
Look at the stars yonder
Calling through time!

Cry to the world
That all might understand:
I was once a black clown
But now—
I'm a man!

# The Big-Timer

A moral poem to be rendered by a man in a straw hat with a bright band, a diamond ring, cigarette holder, and a cane, to the music of piano or orchestra.

| THE MOOD | THE POEM |
|---|---|
| *Syncopated music.* | Who am I? |
| | It ain't so deep: |
| *Telling his story* | I'm the guy the home folks call— |
| *in a hard,* | The Black Sheep. |
| *brazen,* | |
| *cynical* | I ran away. |
| *fashion.* | Went to the city. |
| *Careless,* | Look at me now and |
| *and half-* | Laugh—or take pity. |
| *defiant* | |
| *echoes* | I'm the bad egg, see! |
| *of the* | Didn't turn out right. |
| *"St. James* | My people disowned me— |
| *Infirmary"* | So I'm hustlin' in the night. |
| *as the music* | |
| *takes* | Drinkin' and gamblin' now, |
| | And livin' on gals. |
| *on a* | Red-hot—that's me, |
| *blues* | With a lot o' sporty pals. |
| *strain,* | |
| *gradually* | Spendin' money like water. |
| *returning to* | Drinkin' life like wine. |
| *a sort of* | Not livin' like I oughter, |
| *barrel-house* | But—ain't my life mine? |
| *jazz.* | |
| *Showing-off.* | I got a high-yaller. |
| *Strutting* | Got a diamond ring. |
| *about* | I got a furnished-up flat, |
| *proudly,* | And all that kind o' thing. |
| *bragging* | |
| *and* | I got a big car |
| *boasting,* | And I steps on the gas, |
| *like a* | And whoever don't like it |
| *cheap* | Just gimme some sass, |
| *bully. But* | |
| *suddenly* | 'Cause I carries a switch-blade |
| *looking ahead:* | And I swing it a-hummin', |
| *shrugging his* | And if I don't get you goin', |
| | I'll cut you down comin'. |
| | |
| | You say I'll meet a bad endin', heh? |
| | Well, maybe I will. |

*shoulders*
*at fate.*
*Accepting*
*his position —*
*but inside*
*himself un-*
*happy and blue.*
*Hiding his*
*discontent*
*as thoughts*
*of a*
*better life*
*overcome him.*
*Assuming*
*a false*
*and bragging*
*self-assurance,*
*and a*
*pretended*
*strength he*
*doesn't*
*really feel.*
*Gay,*
*loud,*
*unhappy*
*jazz.*
*Baring*
*his inner*
*heartaches*
*and loneliness*
*to the*
*ironic*
*gaiety of*
*the music.*
*Then*
*pulling*

But while I'm livin' — I'm livin'!
And when I'm dead — I'll keep still.

I'm a first class hustler,
Rounder and sport.
Sometimes I'm settin' pretty,
And again money's short.

But if I wanted to go straight
I'd starve and — oh, well —
I'm just a good-timer
On my road to hell.

Lots of old schoolmates are married now;
Home, kids, and everything fine.
But I ain't got nothin' real
That I can call mine.

But don't let it matter to you,
'Cause I'm all right.
I'm eatin' and lovin',
And holdin' things tight.

So don't worry 'bout me,
Folks, down yonder at home.
I guess I can stand the racket
And fight it out alone.

I guess I know what I'm up against.
I don't cry over troubles.
Look 'em in the face and
Bust 'em like bubbles.

I turn on the radio,
Mix up a drink,
Make lots o' noise,
Then I don't have to think.

Call in a gang o' women
And let 'em have my money,
And forget that they lyin'
When they callin' me honey.

So what's the use o' worryin'
Or thinkin' at all?

| | |
|---|---|
| *himself together,* | We only got one life |
| *boasting* | And I guess that one's all— |
| *loudly again,* | |
| *but realizing* | So I'm takin' it easy |
| *within* | And I don't give a damn— |
| *the tragic* | I'm just a big-timer, |
| *emptiness* | That's all I am! |
| *of his* | |
| *life.* | That's . . . all . . . I . . . am. |

## The Negro Mother

Children, I come back today
To tell you a story of the long dark way
That I had to climb, that I had to know
In order that the race might live and grow.
Look at my face—dark as the night—
Yet shining like the sun with love's true light.
I am the child they stole from the sand
Three hundred years ago in Africa's land.
I am the dark girl who crossed the wide sea
Carrying in my body the seed of the free.
I am the woman who worked in the field
Bringing the cotton and the corn to yield.
I am the one who labored as a slave,
Beaten and mistreated for the work that I gave—
Children sold away from me, husband sold, too.
No safety, no love, no respect was I due.
Three hundred years in the deepest South:
But God put a song and a prayer in my mouth.
God put a dream like steel in my soul.
Now, through my children, I'm reaching the goal.
Now, through my children, young and free,
I realize the blessings denied to me.
I couldn't read then. I couldn't write.
I had nothing, back there in the night.
Sometimes, the valley was filled with tears,
But I kept trudging on through the lonely years.
Sometimes, the road was hot with sun,
But I had to keep on till my work was done:
I *had* to keep on! No stopping for me—

I was the seed of the coming Free.
I nourished the dream that nothing could smother
Deep in my breast—the Negro mother.
I had only hope then, but now through you,
Dark ones of today, my dreams must come true:
All you dark children in the world out there,
Remember my sweat, my pain, my despair.
Remember my years, heavy with sorrow—
And make of those years a torch for tomorrow.
Make of my past a road to the light
Out of the darkness, the ignorance, the night.
Lift high my banner out of the dust.
Stand like free men supporting my trust.
Believe in the right, let none push you back.
Remember the whip and the slaver's track.
Remember how the strong in struggle and strife
Still bar you the way, and deny you life—
But march ever forward, breaking down bars.
Look ever upward at the sun and the stars.
Oh, my dark children, may my dreams and my prayers
Impel you forever up the great stairs—
For I will be with you till no white brother
Dares keep down the children of the Negro mother.

## Dark Youth of the U.S.A.

A recitation to be delivered by a Negro boy, bright, clean, and neatly dressed,
carrying his books to school.

Sturdy I stand, books in my hand—
Today's dark child, tomorrow's strong man:
    The hope of my race
    To mould a place
In America's magic land.

American am I, none can deny:
He who oppresses me, him I defy!
    I am Dark Youth
    Seeking the truth
Of a free life beneath our great sky.

Long a part of the Union's heart—
Years ago at the nation's start
    Attucks died
    That right might abide
And strength to our land impart.

To be wise and strong, then, studying long,
Seeking the knowledge that rights all wrong—
    That is my mission.
Lifting my race to its rightful place
Till beauty and pride fills each dark face
    Is my ambition.

So I climb toward tomorrow, out of past sorrow,
    Treading the modern way
With the White and the Black whom nothing holds back—
    The American Youth of today.


## The Consumptive

All day in the sun
That he loved so
He sat,
Feeling life go.

All night in bed
Waiting for sleep
He lay,
Feeling death creep—
Creeping like fire

Creeping like fire from a slow spark
Choking his breath
And burning the dark.

## Two Things

Two things possess the power,
Two things deserve the name,
Two things can reawaken
Perpetually the flame.
Two things are full of wonder,
Two things cast off all shame.

One is known by the name of Death.
And the other has no name
Except the name each gives it—
In no single mouth the same.

## Demand

Listen!
Dear dream of utter aliveness—
Touching my body of utter death—
Tell me, O quickly! dream of aliveness,
The flaming source of your bright breath.
Tell me, O dream of utter aliveness—
Knowing so well the wind and the sun—
Where is this light
Your eyes see forever?
And what is this wind
You touch when you run?

## Florida Road Workers

Hey, Buddy!
Look at me!

I'm makin' a road
For the cars to fly by on,
Makin' a road
Through the palmetto thicket
For light and civilization
To travel on.

I'm makin' a road
For the rich to sweep over

In their big cars
And leave me standin' here.

Sure,
A road helps everybody.
Rich folks ride —
And I get to see 'em ride.
I ain't never seen nobody
Ride so fine before.

Hey, Buddy, look!
*I'm makin' a road!*

## Garden

Strange
Distorted blades of grass,
Strange
Distorted trees,
Strange
Distorted tulips
On their knees.

## Pennsylvania Station

The Pennsylvania Station in New York
Is like some vast basilica of old
That towers above the terror of the dark
As bulwark and protection to the soul.
Now people who are hurrying alone
And those who come in crowds from far away
Pass through this great concourse of steel and stone
To trains, or else from trains out into day.
And as in great basilicas of old
The search was ever for a dream of God,
So here the search is still within each soul
Some seed to find to root in earthly sod,
Some seed to find that sprouts a holy tree
To glorify the earth — and you — and me.

# Open Letter to the South

White workers of the South
    Miners,
    Farmers,
    Mechanics,
    Mill hands,
    Shop girls,
    Railway men,
    Servants,
    Tobacco workers,
    Sharecroppers,
    GREETINGS!

I am the black worker,
    Listen:
That the land might be ours,
And the mines and the factories and the office towers
At Harlan, Richmond, Gastonia, Atlanta, New Orleans;
That the plants and the roads and the tools of power
Be ours:

Let us forget what Booker T. said,
"Separate as the fingers."

Let us become instead, you and I,
One single hand
That can united rise
To smash the old dead dogmas of the past—
To kill the lies of color
That keep the rich enthroned
And drive us to the time-clock and the plow
Helpless, stupid, scattered, and alone—as now—
Race against race,
Because one is black,
Another white of face.

Let us new lessons learn,
All workers,
New life-ways make,
One union form:
Until the future burns out
Every past mistake
Let us together, say:
"You are my brother, black or white,
You my sister—now—today!"
For me, no more, the great migration to the North.

Instead: migration into force and power—
Tuskegee with a new flag on the tower!
On every lynching tree, a poster crying FREE
Because, O poor white workers,
You have linked your hands with me.

We did not know that we were brothers.
Now we know!
Out of that brotherhood
Let power grow!
We did not know
That we were strong.
Now we see
In union lies our strength.
Let union be
The force that breaks the time-clock,
Smashes misery,
Takes land,
Takes factories,
Takes office towers,
Takes tools and banks and mines.
Railroads, ships and dams,
Until the forces of the world
Are ours!

White worker,
Here is my hand.

Today,
We're Man to Man.


## Ph.D.

He never was a silly little boy
Who whispered in the class or threw spit balls,
Or pulled the hair of silly little girls,
Or disobeyed in any way the laws
That made the school a place of decent order
Where books were read and sums were proven true
And paper maps that showed the land and water
Were held up as the real wide world to you.
Always, he kept his eyes upon his books:

And now he has grown to be a man
He is surprised that everywhere he looks
Life rolls in waves he cannot understand,
And all the human world is vast and strange—
And quite beyond his Ph.D.'s small range.


## Good Morning Revolution


Good-morning, Revolution:
    You're the very best friend
    I ever had.
We gonna pal around together from now on.
Say, listen, Revolution:
You know, the boss where I used to work,
The guy that gimme the air to cut down expenses,
He wrote a long letter to the papers about you:
Said you was a trouble maker, a alien-enemy,
In other words a son-of-a-bitch.
He called up the police
And told 'em to watch out for a guy
Named Revolution.

You see,
The boss knows you're my friend.
He sees us hangin' out together.
He knows we're hungry, and ragged,
And ain't got a damn thing in this world—
And are gonna do something about it.

The boss's got all he needs, certainly,
    Eats swell,
    Owns a lotta houses,
    Goes vacationin',
    Breaks strikes,
    Runs politics, bribes police,
    Pays off congress,
    And struts all over the earth—

But me, I ain't never had enough to eat.
Me, I ain't never been warm in winter.
Me, I ain't never known security—

All my life, been livin' hand to mouth,
    Hand to mouth.

Listen, Revolution,
    We're buddies, see—
    Together,
    We can take everything:
    Factories, arsenals, houses, ships,
    Railroads, forests, fields, orchards,
    Bus lines, telegraphs, radios,
    (Jesus! Raise hell with radios!)
    Steel mills, coal mines, oil wells, gas,
    All the tools of production,
    (Great day in the morning!)
    Everything—
    And turn 'em over to the people who work.
    Rule and run 'em for us people who work.

Boy! Them radios—
Broadcasting that very first morning to USSR:
*Another member the International Soviet's done come*
*Greetings to the Socialist Soviet Republics*
*Hey you rising workers everywhere greetings—*
    And we'll sign it: *Germany*
    Sign it: *China*
    Sign it: *Africa*
    Sign it: *Poland*
    Sign it: *Italy*
    Sign it: *America*
    Sign it with my one name: *Worker*
On that day when no one will be hungry, cold, oppressed,
Anywhere in the world again.

    That's our job!

    I been starvin' too long,
    Ain't you?

    Let's go, Revolution!

# Chant for Tom Mooney

Tom Mooney!
Tom Mooney!
Tom Mooney!
A man with the title of governor has spoken:
   And you do not go free.
A man with the title of governor has spoken:
And the steel bars surround you,
And the prison walls wrap you about,
   And you do not go free.
But the man with the title of governor
   Does not know
That all over the earth today
The workers speak the name:
      Tom Mooney!
      Tom Mooney!
      Tom Mooney!
And the sound vibrates in waves
   From Africa to China,
   India to Germany,
   Russia to the Argentine,
   Shaking the bars,
   Shaking the walls,
   Shaking the earth
Until the whole world falls into the hands of
      The workers.
Of course, the man with the title of governor
Will be forgotten then
On the scrap heap of time—
He won't matter at all.
But remembered forever will be the name:
   TOM MOONEY.
   Schools will be named:
   TOM MOONEY.
   Farms will be named:
   TOM MOONEY.
   Dams will be named:
   TOM MOONEY.
   Ships will be named:
   TOM MOONEY.
   Factories will be named:
   TOM MOONEY.
   And all over the world—
Banner of force and labor, strength and union,
Life forever through the workers' power—
   Will be the name:
   TOM MOONEY.

## Always the Same

It is the same everywhere for me:
On the docks at Sierra Leone,
In the cotton fields of Alabama,
In the diamond mines of Kimberley,
On the coffee hills of Haiti,
The banana lands of Central America,
The streets of Harlem,
And the cities of Morocco and Tripoli.

Black:
Exploited, beaten and robbed,
Shot and killed.
Blood running into

    Dollars
    Pounds
    Francs
    Pesetas
    Lire

For the wealth of the exploiters—
Blood that never comes back to me again.
Better that my blood
Runs into the deep channels of Revolution,
Runs into the strong hands of Revolution,
Stains all flags red,
Drives me away from

    Sierra Leone
    Kimberley
    Alabama
    Haiti
    Central America
    Harlem
    Morocco
    Tripoli

And all the black lands everywhere.
The force that kills,
The power that robs,
And the greed that does not care.

Better that my blood makes one with the blood
Of all the struggling workers in the world—
Till every land is free of

Dollar robbers
Pound robbers
Franc robbers
Peseta robbers
Lire robbers
Life robbers —

Until the Red Armies of the International Proletariat
Their faces, black, white, olive, yellow, brown,
Unite to raise the blood-red flag that
Never will come down!

## Goodbye Christ

Listen, Christ,
You did alright in your day, I reckon —
But that day's gone now.
They ghosted you up a swell story, too,
Called it Bible —
But it's dead now,
The popes and the preachers've
Made too much money from it.
They've sold you to too many

Kings, generals, robbers, and killers —
Even to the Tzar and the Cossacks,
Even to Rockefeller's Church,
Even to THE SATURDAY EVENING POST.
You ain't no good no more.
They've pawned you
Till you've done wore out.

Goodbye,
Christ Jesus Lord God Jehova,
Beat it on away from here now.
Make way for a new guy with no religion at all —
A real guy named
Marx Communist Lenin Peasant Stalin Worker ME —

I said, ME!

Go ahead on now,
You're getting in the way of things, Lord.
And please take Saint Ghandi with you when you go,
And Saint Pope Pius,
And Saint Aimee McPherson,
And big black Saint Becton
Of the Consecrated Dime.
And step on the gas, Christ!
Move!

Don't be so slow about movin'!
The world is mine from now on—
And nobody's gonna sell ME
To a king, or a general,
Or a millionaire.

## Irish Wake

In the dark they fell a-crying
For the dead who'd gone away,
And you could hear the drowsy wailing
Of those compelled to stay—
But when the sun rose making
All the dooryard bright and clear
The mourners got up smiling,
Happy they were here.

## Reasons Why

Just because I loves you—
That's de reason why
Ma soul is full of color
Like de wings of a butterfly.

Just because I loves you
That's de reason why
Ma heart's a fluttering aspen leaf
When you pass by.

# The Town of Scottsboro

Scottsboro's just a little place:
No shame is writ across its face —
Its court, too weak to stand against a mob,
Its people's heart, too small to hold a sob.

# Columbia

Columbia,
My dear girl,
You really haven't been a virgin for so long
It's ludicrous to keep up the pretext.
You're terribly involved in world assignations
And everybody knows it.
You've slept with all the big powers
In military uniforms,
And you've taken the sweet life
Of all the little brown fellows
In loin cloths and cotton trousers.
When they've resisted,
You've yelled, "Rape,"
At the top of your voice
And called for the middies
To beat them up for not being gentlemen
And liking your crooked painted mouth.
(You must think the moons of Hawaii
Disguise your ugliness.)
Really,
You're getting a little too old,
Columbia,
To be so naive, and so coy.
Being one of the world's big vampires,
Why don't you come on out and say so
Like Japan, and England, and France,
And all the other nymphomaniacs of power
Who've long since dropped their
Smoke-screens of innocence
To sit frankly on a bed of bombs?

O, *sweet mouth of India,*
*And Africa,*
*Manchuria, and Haiti.*

Columbia,
You darling,
Don't shoot!
I'll kiss you!

## Letter to the Academy

The gentlemen who have got to be classics and are now old with beards (or
    dead and in their graves) will kindly come forward and speak upon the
    subject

Of the Revolution. I mean the gentlemen who wrote lovely books about the
    defeat of the flesh and the triumph of the spirit that sold in the hundreds
    of thousands and are studied in the high schools and read by the best
    people will kindly come forward and

Speak about the Revolution—where the flesh triumphs (as well as the spirit)
    and the hungry belly eats, and there are no best people, and the poor are
    mighty and no longer poor, and the young by the hundreds of thousands
    are free from hunger to grow and study and love and propagate, bodies
    and souls unchained without My Lord saying a commoner shall never
    marry my daughter or the Rabbi crying cursed be the mating of Jews and
    Gentiles or Kipling writing never the twain shall meet—

For the twain have met. But please—all you gentlemen with beards who are
    so wise and old and who write better than we do and whose souls have
    triumphed (in spite of hungers and wars and the evils about you) and
    whose books have soared in calmness and beauty aloof from the struggle
    to the library shelves and the desks of students and who are now clas-
    sics—come forward and speak upon

The subject of the Revolution.

We want to know what in the hell you'd say?

# Song of the Revolution

Sing me a song of the Revolution
Marching like fire over the world,
Weaving from the earth its bright red banner
For the hands of the masses to unfurl.

Sing me a song of the Revolution
Drowning the past with a thunderous shout:
Filled with the strength of youth and laughter,
And never the echo of a doubt.

O mighty roll of the Revolution,
Ending the centuries of bloody strife,
Ending the tricks of kings and liars,
Big with the laughter of a new life.

Breaking the bonds of the darker races,
Breaking the chains that have held for years,
Breaking the barriers dividing the people,
Smashing the gods of terror and tears,

Cutting, O flame of the Revolution,
Fear from the world like a surgeon's knife,
So that the children of all creation
Waken, at last, to the joy of life.

# A New Song

I speak in the name of the black millions
Awakening to action.
Let all others keep silent a moment.
I have this word to bring,
This thing to say,
This song to sing:

Bitter was the day
When I bowed my back
Beneath the slaver's whip.

That day is past.

Bitter was the day
When I saw my children unschooled,
My young men without a voice in the world,

My women taken as the body-toys
Of a thieving people.

That day is past.

Bitter was the day, I say,
When the lyncher's rope
Hung about my neck,
And the fire scorched my feet,
And the oppressors had no pity,
And only in the sorrow songs
Relief was found.

That day is past.

I know full well now
Only my own hands,
Dark as the earth,
Can make my earth-dark body free.
O, thieves, exploiters, killers,
No longer shall you say
With arrogant eyes and scornful lips:
"You are my servant,
Black man—
I, the free!"

That day is past—

For now,
In many mouths—
Dark mouths where red tongues burn
And white teeth gleam—
New words are formed,
Bitter
With the past
But sweet
With the dream.
Tense,
Unyielding,
Strong and sure,
They sweep the earth—

Revolt! Arise!

The Black
And White World

Shall be one!
The Worker's World!

The past is done!

A new dream flames
Against the
Sun!

## Black Workers

The bees work.
Their work is taken from them.
We are like the bees—
But it won't last
Forever.

## Black Dancers

We
Who have nothing to lose
Must sing and dance
Before the riches
Of the world
Overcome
Us.

We
Who have nothing to lose
Must laugh and dance
Lest our laughter
Goes from
Us.

# Havana Dreams

The dream is a cocktail at Sloppy Joe's—
(Maybe—nobody knows.)

The dream is the road to Batabano.
(But nobody knows if that is so.)

Perhaps the dream is only her face—
Perhaps it's a fan of silver lace—
Or maybe the dream's a Vedado rose—
(*Quien sabe?* Who really knows?)

# Dream

Last night I dreamt
This most strange dream,
And everywhere I saw
What did not seem could ever be:

*You were not there with me!*

Awake,
I turned
And touched you
Asleep,
Face to the wall.

I said,
How dreams
Can lie!

*But you were not there at all!*

# Personal

In an envelope marked:
    *Personal*
God addressed me a letter.
In an envelope marked:
    *Personal*
I have given my answer.

# Wait

PICKERS
CHAPEI
FORD
STRIKERS
ALABAMA
NEGROES
CUBA
UNEMPLOYED
MILLIONS
MEERUT
CHILD
LABOR
SCOTTSBORO
GERMAN
COMMUNISTS
POOR
FARMERS
BLACK
AFRICA
GRAPE
PICKERS
JAPANESE
CONSCRIPTS
JOHANNESBURG
MINERS

I am the Silent One,
Saying nothing,
Knowing no words to write,
Feeling only the bullets
And the hunger
And the stench of gas
Dying.
And nobody knows my name
But someday,
I shall raise my hand
And break the heads of you
Who starve me.
I shall raise my hand
And smash the spines of you
Who shoot me.

I shall take your guns
And turn them on you.

Starting with the bankers and
 the bosses
Traders and missionaries
Who pay the militarists
Who pay the soldiers
Who back the police
Who kill me—
And break my strikes
And break my rising—
I, silently,
And without a single learned word
Shall begin the slaughter
That will end my hunger
And your bullets
And the gas of capitalism
And make the world
My own.
When that is done,
I shall find words to speak

Wait!

MEERUT
HAITI
KOREA
CHILD
LABOR
SUGAR
HAITI
BONUS
KOREA
MEERUT
CHILD
LABOR
BONUS
HAITI
KOREA
SUGAR
CHILD
LABOR
HAITI
BONUS
KOREA
BLACK
HAITI
SUGAR
MEERUT

HAITI UNEMPLOYED MILLIONS CALIFORNIA CHERRY PICKERS STRIKING MINERS ALABAMA SUGAR BEET WORKERS INDIAN MASSES SCOTTSBORO SHANGHAI COOLIES PATTERSON SUGAR BEET WORKERS COLONIAL ASIA FRICK'S MINERS CUBA POOR FARMERS JAPANESE CONSCRIPTS WORKERS JOHANNESBURG MINERS CHAPEI ALABAMA NEGROES OXNARD SUGAR BEET WORKERS INDIAN MASSES BONUS MARCHERS FORD STRIKERS HAITI

## Revolution

Great mob that knows no fear—
Come here!
And raise your hand
Against this man
Of iron and steel and gold
Who's bought and sold
You—
Each one—
For the last thousand years,
Come here,
Great mob that has no fear,
And tear him limb from limb,
Split his golden throat
Ear to ear,
And end his time forever,
Now—
This year—
Great mob that knows no fear.

## Cubes

In the days of the broken cubes of Picasso
And in the days of the broken songs of the young men
A little too drunk to sing
And the young women
A little too unsure of love to love—
I met on the boulevards of Paris
An African from Senegal.

God
Knows why the French
Amuse themselves bringing to Paris
Negroes from Senegal.

It's the old game of the boss and the bossed,
    boss and the bossed,
       amused
         and
       amusing,
   worked and working,
Behind the cubes of black and white,
       black and white,
   black and white

But since it is the old game,
For fun
They give him the three old prostitutes of
  France—
Liberty, Equality, Fraternity—
And all three of 'em sick
In spite of the tax to the government
And the legal houses
And the doctors
And the *Marseillaise.*

Of course, the young African from Senegal
Carries back from Paris
A little more disease
To spread among the black girls in the palm huts.
He brings them as a gift
  disease—
From light to darkness
   disease—
From the boss to the bossed
    disease—
From the game of black and white
  disease
From the city of the broken cubes of Picasso
  d
   i
  s
 e
  a
   s
  e

# One More "S" in the U.S.A.

Put one more s in the U.S.A.
To make it Soviet.
One more s in the U.S.A.
Oh, we'll live to see it yet.
When the land belongs to the farmers
And the factories to the working men—
The U.S.A. when we take control
Will be the U.S.S.A. then.

Now across the water in Russia
They have a big U.S.S.R.
The fatherland of the Soviets—
But that is mighty far
From New York, or Texas, or California, too.
So listen, fellow workers,
This is what we have to do.

    Put one more S in the U.S.A.
       [Repeat chorus]

But we can't win by just talking.
So let us take things in our hand.
Then down and away with the bosses' sway—
Hail Communistic land.
So stand up in battle and wave our flag on
    high,
And shout out fellow workers
Our new slogan in the sky:

    Put one more S in the U.S.A.

But we can't join hands together
So long as whites are lynching black,
So black and white in one union fight
And get on the right track.
By Texas, or Georgia, or Alabama led
Come together, fellow workers
Black and white can all be red:

    Put one more S in the U.S.A.

Oh, the bankers they all are planning
For another great big war.
To make them rich from the worker's dead,
That's all the war is for.
So if you don't want to see bullets holding sway
Then come on, all you workers,
And join our fight today:

    Put one more S in the U.S.A.
    To make it Soviet.
    One more S in the U.S.A.
    Oh, we'll live to see it yet.
    When the land belongs to the farmers
    And the factories to the working men—
    The U.S.A. when we take control
    Will be the U.S.S.A. then.

## Moonlight Night: Carmel

Tonight the waves march
In long ranks
Cutting the darkness
With their silver shanks,
Cutting the darkness
And kissing the moon
And beating the land's
Edge into a swoon.

## Ballad of Roosevelt

The pot was empty,
The cupboard was bare.
I said, Papa,
What's the matter here?
I'm waitin' on Roosevelt, son,
Roosevelt, Roosevelt,
Waitin' on Roosevelt, son.

The rent was due
And the lights was out.
I said, Tell me, Mama,
What's it all about?
We're waitin' on Roosevelt, son,
Roosevelt, Roosevelt,
Just waitin' on Roosevelt.

Sister got sick
And the doctor wouldn't come
Cause we couldn't pay him
The proper sum—
A-waitin' on Roosevelt,
Roosevelt, Roosevelt,
A-waitin' on Roosevelt.

Then one day
They put us out o' the house.
Ma and Pa was
Meek as a mouse
Still waitin' on Roosevelt,
Roosevelt, Roosevelt.

But when they felt those
Cold winds blow

And didn't have no
Place to go
Pa said, I'm tired
O' waitin' on Roosevelt,
Roosevelt, Roosevelt.
Damn tired o' waitin' on Roosevelt.

I can't git a job
And I can't git no grub.
Backbone and navel's
Doin' the belly-rub—
A-waitin' on Roosevelt,
Roosevelt, Roosevelt.

And a lot o' other folks
What's hungry and cold
Done stopped believin'
What they been told
By Roosevelt,
Roosevelt, Roosevelt—

Cause the pot's still empty,
And the cupboard's still bare,
And you can't build a bungalow
Out o' air—
Mr. Roosevelt, listen!
What's the matter here?

## History

The past has been a mint
Of blood and sorrow.
That must not be
True of tomorrow.

## Death in Harlem

Arabella Johnson and the Texas Kid
Went bustin into Dixie's bout one a.m.
The night was young—

179

But for a wise night-bird
The pickin's weren't bad on a 133rd.
The pickin's weren't bad—
His roll wasn't slim—
And Arabella Johnson had her
Hands on him.

At a big piano a little dark girl
Was playin jazz for a midnight world.
    Whip it, Miss Lucy!
    Aw, pick that rag!
    The Texas Kid's on a
    High-steppin jag.
A dumb little jigaboo from
Somewhere South.
A row of gold in his upper mouth.
A roll of bills in his left-hand pocket.
    Do it, Arabella!
    Honey baby, sock it!

Dancin close, and dancin sweet,
Down in a cellar back from the street,
In Dixie's place on 133rd
When the night is young—
For an old night-bird.
    Aw, pick it, Miss Lucy!
    Jazz it slow!
    It's good like that when you
    Bass so low!

Folks at the tables drink and grin.
(Dixie makes his money on two-bit gin.)
Couples on the floor rock and shake.
(Dixie rents rooms at a buck a break.)
Loungers at the bar laugh out loud.
Everybody's happy. It's a spendin crowd—
Big time sports and girls who know
Dixie's ain't no place for a gang that's slow.
    Rock it, Arabella,
    Babe, you sho can go!
She says to the waiter,
Gin rickeys for two.
Says to Texas,
How'd a dance strike you?
Says to Lucy,
Play a long time, gal!
Says to the world,

Here's my sugar-daddy pal.
Whispers to Texas,
Boy, you're sweet!
She gurgles to Texas,
What you like to eat?
Spaghetti and gin, music and smoke,
And a woman cross the table when a man ain't broke—
When a man's won a fight in a big man's town—
    Aw, plunk it, Miss Lucy,
    Cause we dancin down!
A party of whites from Fifth Avenue
Came tippin into Dixie's to get a view.
Came tippin into Dixie's with smiles on their faces,
Knowin they can buy a dozen colored places.
Dixie grinned. Dixie bowed.
Dixie rubbed his hands and laughed out loud—
While a tall white woman
In an ermine cape
Looked at the blacks and
Thought of rape,
Looked at the blacks and
Thought of a rope,
Looked at the blacks and
Thought of flame,
And thought of something
Without a name.
    Aw, play it, Miss Lucy!
    Lawd!
    Ain't you shame?
Lucy was a-bassin it, boom, boom, boom,
When Arabella went to the LADIES' ROOM.
She left the Texas Kid settin by himself
All unsuspectin of the chippie on his left—
Her name was Bessie. She was brown and bold.
And she sat on her chair like a sweet jelly roll.
She cast her eyes on Texas, hollered,
Listen, boy,
While the music's playin let's
Spread some joy!

Now, Texas was a lover.
Bessie was, too.
They loved one another till
The music got through.
While Miss Lucy played it, boom, boom, boom,
And Arabella was busy in the LADIES' ROOM.
When she come out

She looked across the place—
And there was Bessie
Settin in her place!
(It was just as if somebody
Kicked her in the face.)

Arabella drew her pistol.
She uttered a cry.
Everybody dodged as
A ball passed by.
    A shot rang out.
Bessie pulled a knife,
But Arabella had her gun.
Stand back folkses, let us
Have our fun.
    And a shot rang out.
Some began to tremble and
Some began to scream.
Bessie stared at Bella
Like a woman in a dream
    As the shots rang out.
A white lady fainted.
A black woman cried.
But Bessie took a bullet to her
Heart and died
    As the shots rang out.
A whole slew of people
Went rushin for the door
And left poor Bessie bleedin
In that cellar on the floor
    When the shots rang out.
Then the place was empty,
No music didn't play,
And whoever loved Bessie was
Far away.
    Take me,
    Jesus, take me
    Home today!

Oh, they nabbed Arabella
And drove her off to jail
Just as the sky in the
East turned pale
And night like a reefer-man
Slipped away
And the sun came up and

It was day—
But the Texas Kid,
With lovin in his head,
Picked up another woman and
Went to bed.

## Park Bench

I live on a park bench.
You, Park Avenue.
Hell of a distance
Between us two.

I beg a dime for dinner—
You got a butler and maid.
But I'm wakin' up!
Say, ain't you afraid

That I might, just maybe,
In a year or two,
Move on over
To Park Avenue?

## Ballads of Lenin

Comrade Lenin of Russia,
High in a marble tomb,
Move over, Comrade Lenin,
And give me room.

I am Ivan, the peasant,
Boots all muddy with soil.
I fought with you, Comrade Lenin.
Now I have finished my toil.

Comrade Lenin of Russia,
Alive in a marble tomb,
Move over, Comrade Lenin,
And make me room.

I am Chico, the Negro,
Cutting cane in the sun.

I lived for you, Comrade Lenin.
Now my work is done.

Comrade Lenin of Russia,
Honored in a marble tomb,
Move over, Comrade Lenin,
And leave me room.

I am Chang from the foundries
On strike in the streets of Shanghai.
For the sake of the Revolution
I fight, I starve, I die.

Comrade Lenin of Russia
Speaks from the marble tomb:
*On guard with the workers forever—*
*The world is our room!*


## Call of Ethiopia

Ethiopia
Lift your night-dark face,
Abyssinian
Son of Sheba's race!
Your palm trees tall
And your mountains high
Are shade and shelter
To men who die
For freedom's sake—
But in the wake of your sacrifice
May all Africa arise
With blazing eyes and night-dark face
In answer to the call of Sheba's race:

Ethiopias free!
Be like me,
All of Africa,
Arise and be free!
All you black peoples,
Be free! Be free!

## Share-Croppers

                    Just a herd of Negroes
                    Driven to the field,
                    Plowing, planting, hoeing,
                    To make the cotton yield.

                    When the cotton's picked
                    And the work is done
                    Boss man takes the money
                    And we get none,

                    Leaves us hungry, ragged
                    As we were before.
                    Year by year goes by
                    And we are nothing more

                    Than a herd of Negroes
                    Driven to the field—
                    Plowing life away
                    To make the cotton yield.


## Air Raid over Harlem    Scenario for a Little Black Movie

                    Who you gonna put in it?
                    *Me.*
                    Who the hell are you?
                    *Harlem.*
                    Alright, then.

                    AIR RAID OVER HARLEM

                    You're not talkin' 'bout Harlem, are you?
                    That's where my home is,
                    My bed is, my woman is, my kids is!
                    Harlem, that's where I live!
                    Look at my streets
                    Full of black and brown and
                    Yellow and high-yellow
                    Jokers like me.
                    Lenox, Seventh, Edgecombe, 145th.
                    Listen,
                    Hear 'em talkin' and laughin'?
                    Bombs over Harlem'd kill
                    People like me—

Kill ME!
Sure, I know
The Ethiopian war broke out last night:
BOMBS OVER HARLEM
Cops on every corner
Most of 'em white
COPS IN HARLEM
Guns and billy-clubs
Double duty in Harlem
Walking in pairs
Under every light
Their faces
WHITE
In Harlem
And mixed in with 'em
A black cop or two
For the sake of the vote in Harlem
GUGSA A TRAITOR TOO
No, sir,
I ain't talkin' 'bout you,
Mister Policeman!
No, indeed!
I know we got to keep
ORDER OVER HARLEM
Where the black millions sleep
Shepherds over Harlem
Their armed watch keep
Lest Harlem stirs in its sleep
And maybe remembers
And remembering forgets
To be peaceful and quiet
And has sudden fits
Of raising a black fist
Out of the dark
And that black fist
Becomes a red spark
PLANES OVER HARLEM
Bombs over Harlem
*You're just making up*
*A fake funny picture, ain't you?*
*Not real, not real?*
Did you ever taste blood
From an iron heel
Planted in your mouth
In the slavery-time South
Where to whip a nigger's

Easy as hell—
And not even a *living* nigger
Has a tale to tell
Lest the kick of a boot
Baring more blood to his mouth
In the slavery-time South
And a long billy-club
Split his head wide
And a white hand draw
A gun from its side
And send bullets splaying
Through the streets of Harlem
Where the dead're laying
Lest you stir in your sleep
And remember something
You'd best better keep
In the dark, in the dark
Where the ugly things hide
Under the white lights
With guns by their side
In Harlem?

*Say, what are yuh tryin' to do?*
*Start a riot?*
*You keep quiet!*
*You niggers keep quiet!*

BLACK WORLD
Never wake up
Lest you knock over the cup
Of gold that the men who
Keep order guard so well
And then—well, then
There'd be hell
To pay
And bombs over Harlem

AIR RAID OVER HARLEM

Bullets through Harlem
And someday
A sleeping giant waking
To snatch bombs from the sky
And push the sun up with a loud cry
Of to hell with the cops on the corners at night
Armed to the teeth under the light

Lest Harlem see red
And suddenly sit on the edge of its bed
And shake the whole world with a new dream
As the squad cars come and the sirens scream
And a big black giant snatches bombs from the sky
And picks up a cop and lets him fly
Into the dust of the Jimcrow past
And laughs and Hollers
Kiss my
!x!&!

Hey!
Scenario for a Little Black Movie,
You say?
A RED MOVIE TO MR. HEARST
Black and white workers united as one
In a city where
There'll never be
Air raids over Harlem
FOR THE WORKERS ARE FREE

What workers are free?
THE BLACK AND WHITE WORKERS —
You and me!
Looky here, everybody!
Look at me!

I'M HARLEM!


## Ballad of Ozie Powell

Red is the Alabama road,
    Ozie, Ozie Powell,
Redder now where your blood has flowed,
    Ozie, Ozie Powell.

Strong are the bars and steel the gate,
    Ozie, Ozie Powell,
The High Sheriff's eyes are filled with hate,
    Ozie, Ozie Powell.

The High Sheriff shoots and he shoots to kill
    Black young Ozie Powell.

The Law's a Klansman with an evil will,
    Ozie, Ozie Powell.

Nine old men in Washington,
    Ozie, Ozie Powell,
Never saw the High Sheriff's gun
    Aimed at Ozie Powell.

Nine old men so rich and wise,
    Ozie, Ozie Powell,
They never saw the High Sheriff's eyes
    Stare at Ozie Powell.

But nine black boys know full well,
    Don't they, Ozie Powell?
What it is to live in hell,
    Ozie, Ozie Powell.

The devil's a Kleagle with an evil will,
    Ozie, Ozie Powell,
A white High Sheriff who shoots to kill
    Black young Ozie Powell.

And red is that Alabama road,
    Ozie, Ozie Powell,
But redder now where your life's blood flowed,
    Ozie! Ozie Powell!

## Let America Be America Again

Let America be America again.
Let it be the dream it used to be.
Let it be the pioneer on the plain
Seeking a home where he himself is free.

(America never was America to me.)

Let America be the dream the dreamers dreamed—
Let it be that great strong land of love
Where never kings connive nor tyrants scheme
That any man be crushed by one above.

(It never was America to me.)

O, let my land be a land where Liberty
Is crowned with no false patriotic wreath,
But opportunity is real, and life is free,
Equality is in the air we breathe.

(There's never been equality for me,
Nor freedom in this "homeland of the free.")

*Say, who are you that mumbles in the dark?*
*And who are you that draws your veil across the stars?*

I am the poor white, fooled and pushed apart,
I am the Negro bearing slavery's scars.
I am the red man driven from the land,
I am the immigrant clutching the hope I seek—
And finding only the same old stupid plan
Of dog eat dog, of mighty crush the weak.

I am the young man, full of strength and hope,
Tangled in that ancient endless chain
Of profit, power, gain, of grab the land!
Of grab the gold! Of grab the ways of satisfying need!
Of work the men! Of take the pay!
Of owning everything for one's own greed!

I am the farmer, bondsman to the soil.
I am the worker sold to the machine.
I am the Negro, servant to you all.
I am the people, humble, hungry, mean—
Hungry yet today despite the dream.
Beaten yet today—O, Pioneers!
I am the man who never got ahead,
The poorest worker bartered through the years.

Yet I'm the one who dreamt our basic dream
In that Old World while still a serf of kings,
Who dreamt a dream so strong, so brave, so true,
That even yet its mighty daring sings
In every brick and stone, in every furrow turned
That's made America the land it has become.
O, I'm the man who sailed those early seas
In search of what I meant to be my home—
For I'm the one who left dark Ireland's shore,
And Poland's plain, and England's grassy lea,

And torn from Black Africa's strand I came
To build a "homeland of the free."

The free?

Who said the free? Not me?
Surely not me? The millions on relief today?
The millions shot down when we strike?
The millions who have nothing for our pay?
For all the dreams we've dreamed
And all the songs we've sung
And all the hopes we've held
And all the flags we've hung,
The millions who have nothing for our pay—
Except the dream that's almost dead today.

O, let America be America again—
The land that never has been yet—
And yet must be—the land where *every* man is free.
The land that's mine—the poor man's, Indian's, Negro's, ME—
Who made America,
Whose sweat and blood, whose faith and pain,
Whose hand at the foundry, whose plow in the rain,
Must bring back our mighty dream again.

Sure, call me any ugly name you choose—
The steel of freedom does not stain.
From those who live like leeches on the people's lives,
We must take back our land again,
America!

O, yes,
I say it plain,
America never was America to me,
And yet I swear this oath—
America will be!

Out of the rack and ruin of our gangster death,
The rape and rot of graft, and stealth, and lies,
We, the people, must redeem
The land, the mines, the plants, the rivers.
The mountains and the endless plain—
All, all the stretch of these great green states—
And make America again!

# Broadcast on Ethiopia

The little fox is still.
   The dogs of war have made their kill.

   Addis Ababa
   Across the headlines all year long.
   Ethiopia—
   Tragi-song for the news reels.
   Haile
   With his slaves, his dusky wiles,
   His second-hand planes like a child's,
   But he has no gas—so he cannot last.
   Poor little joker with no poison gas!
   Thus his people now may learn
   How Il Duce makes butter from an empty churn
   To butter the bread
   (If bread there be)
   Of civilization's misery.

### MISTER CHRISTOPHER COLUMBUS

DJIBOUTI, French Somaliland, May 4 (AP)—Emperor Haile Selassie
and imperial family, in flight from his crumbling empire, reached the
sanctuary of French soil and a British destroyer today. . . .

### HE USED RHYTHM FOR HIS COMPASS

   Hunter, hunter, running, too—
   Look what's after you:

PARIS, May 4 (UP)—COMMUNISTS TOP FRANCE'S SWEEP LEFT.
Minister of Colonies Defeated. Rise From 10 to 85 Seats.

   France ain't Italy!

   No, but Italy's cheated
   When *any* Minister anywhere's
   Defeated by Communists.
   Goddamn! I swear!
   Hitler,
   Tear your hair!
   Mussolini,
   Grit your teeth!
   Civilization's gone to hell!
   Major Bowes, ring your bell!

      (Gong!)

Station XYZW broadcasting:
MISTER CHRISTOPHER COLOMBO
Just made a splendid kill.
The British Legation stands solid on its hill
The natives run wild in the streets.
The fox is still.

Addis Ababa
In headlines all year long.
Ethiopia—tragi-song.


## Dusk

Wandering in the dusk,
Sometimes
You get lost in the dusk—
And sometimes not.

Beating your fists
Against the wall,
You break your bones
Against the wall—
But sometimes not.

Walls have been known
To fall,
Dusk turn to dawn,
And chains be gone!


## Elderly Leaders

The old, the cautious, the over-wise—
Wisdom reduced to the personal equation:
Life is a system of half-truths and lies,
 Opportunistic, convenient evasion.
      Elderly,
      Famous,

Very well paid,
They clutch at the egg
Their master's
Goose laid:
$$$$$
$$$$
$$$
$$
$
•

## White Man

Sure I know you!
You're a White Man.
I'm a Negro.
You take all the best jobs
And leave us the garbage cans to empty
    and
The halls to clean.
You have a good time in a big house at
    Palm Beach
And rent us the back alleys
And the dirty slums.
You enjoy Rome—
And *take* Ethiopia.
White Man! White Man!
Let Louis Armstrong play it—
And you copyright it
And make the money.
You're the smart guy, White Man!
You got everything!
But now,
I hear your name ain't really White
    Man.
I hear it's something
Marx wrote down
Fifty years ago—
That rich people don't like to read.
Is that true, White Man?

Is your name in a book
Called the *Communist Manifesto?*
   Is your name spelled
   C-A-P-I-T-A-L-I-S-T?
   Are you always a White Man?
   Huh?

# Song of Spain

Come now, all you who are singers,
And sing me the song of Spain.
Sing it very simply that I might understand.

   What is the song of Spain?

*Flamenco* is the song of Spain:
Gypsies, guitars, dancing
Death and love and heartbreak
To a heel tap and a swirl of fingers
On three strings.
*Flamenco* is the song of Spain.

   I do not understand.

*Toros* are the song of Spain:
The bellowing bull, the red cape,
A sword thrust, a horn tip,
The torn suit of satin and gold,
Blood on the sand
Is the song of Spain.

   I do not understand.

*Pintura* is the song of Spain:
Goya, Velasquez, Murillo,
Splash of color on canvass,
Whirl of cherub-faces.
La Maja Desnuda's
The song of Spain.

   What's that?

*Don Quixote! España!*
*Aquel rincon de la Mancha de*
*Cuyo nombre no quiero acordarme. . . .*
That's the song of Spain.
You wouldn't kid me, would you?
A bombing plane's
The song of Spain.
Bullets like rain's
The song of Spain.
Poison gas is Spain.
A knife in the back
And its terror and pain is Spain.

*Toros, flamenco*, paintings, books—
    Not Spain.
The people are Spain:
The people beneath that bombing plane
With its wings of gold for which I pay—
I, a worker, letting my labor pile
Up millions for bombs to kill a child—
I bought those bombs for Spain!
Workers made those bombs for a Fascist Spain!
Will I make them again, and yet again?
    Storm clouds move fast,
    Our sky is gray.
    The white devils of the terror
    Await their day
When bombs'll fall not only on Spain—
    But on me and you!
    Workers, make no bombs again!
    Workers, mine no gold again!
    Workers, lift no hand again
    To build up profits for the rape of Spain!
    Workers, see yourselves as Spain!
    Workers, know that we too can cry.
    Lift arms in vain, run, hide, die:
        Too late!
        The bombing plane!
    Workers, make no bombs again
    Except that they be made for us
        To hold and guard
    Lest some Franco steal into our backyard
Under the guise of a patriot
Waving a flag and mouthing rot

And dropping bombs from a Christian steeple
    On the people.

I made those bombs for Spain.
I must not do it again.
I made those bombing planes.
I must not do it again.

I made rich the grandees and lords
Who hire Franco to lead his gang-hordes
Against Spain.

I must never do that again.

I must drive the bombers out of Spain!
I must drive the bombers out of the world!
I must take the world for my own again —

    A workers' world
    Is the song of Spain.


## Sister Johnson Marches


Here am I with my head held high!
*What's de matter, honey?*
I just want to cry:
It's de first of May!

Here I go with my banner in my hand!
*What's de matter, chile?*
Why we owns de land!
It's de first of May!

*Who are all them people*
*Marching in a mass?*
Lawd! Don't you know?
That's de working class!

It's de first of May!

## Genius Child

This is a song for the genius child.
Sing it softly, for the song is wild.
Sing it softly as ever you can—
Lest the song get out of hand.

*Nobody loves a genius child.*

Can you love an eagle,
Tame or wild?

Wild or tame,
Can you love a monster
Of frightening name?

*Nobody loves a genius child.*

*Kill him*—and let his soul run wild!

## Roar China!

Roar, China!
Roar, old lion of the East!
Snort fire, yellow dragon of the Orient,
Tired at last of being bothered.
Since when did you ever steal anything
From anybody,
Sleepy wise old beast
Known as the porcelain-maker,
Known as the poem-maker,
Known as maker of firecrackers?
A long time since you cared
About taking other people's lands
Away from them.
THEY must've thought you didn't care
About your own land either—
So THEY came with gunboats,
Set up Concessions,
Zones of influence,
International Settlements,
Missionary houses,
Banks,
And Jim Crow Y.M.C.A.'s.
THEY beat you with malacca canes

And dared you to raise your head—
Except to cut it off.
Even the yellow men came
To take what the white men
Hadn't already taken.
The yellow men dropped bombs on Chapei.
The yellow men called you the same names
The white men did:
> *Dog! Dog! Dog!*
> *Coolie dog!*
> *Red! . . . Lousy red!*
> *Red coolie dog!*
And in the end you had no place
To make your porcelain,
Write your poems,
Or shoot your firecrackers on holidays.
In the end you had no peace
Or calm left at all.
PRESIDENT, KING, MIKADO
Thought you really were a dog.
THEY kicked you daily
Via radiophone, via cablegram,
Via gunboats in her harbor,
Via malacca canes.
THEY thought you were a tame lion.
A sleepy, easy, tame old lion!
> Ha! Ha!
> Haaa-aa-a! . . . Ha!
Laugh, little coolie boy on the docks of Shanghai, laugh!
> You're no tame lion.
Laugh, red generals in the hills of Sian-kiang, laugh!
> You're no tame lion.
Laugh, child slaves in the factories of the foreigners!
> You're no tame lion.
Laugh—and roar, China! Time to spit fire!
Open your mouth, old dragon of the East.
To swallow up the gunboats in the Yangtse!
Swallow up the foreign planes in your sky!
Eat bullets, old maker of firecrackers—
And spit out freedom in the face of your enemies!
Break the chains of the East,
> Little coolie boy!
Break the chains of the East,
> Red generals!
Break the chains of the East,
> Child slaves in the factories!

Smash the iron gates of the Concessions!
Smash the pious doors of the missionary houses!
Smash the revolving doors of the Jim Crow Y.M.C.A.'s.
Crush the enemies of land and bread and freedom!
    Stand up and roar, China!
    You know what you want!
    The only way to get it is
    To take it!
    Roar, China!

## Note in Music

Life is for the living.
Death is for the dead.
Let life be like music.
And death a note unsaid.

## Search

All life is but the climbing of a hill
To seek the sun that ranges far beyond
Confused with stars and lesser lights anon,
And planets where the darkness reigneth still.

All life is but the seeking for that sun
That never lets one living atom die —
That flames beyond the circles of the eye
Where Never and Forever are as one.

And seeking always through this human span
That spreads its drift of years beneath the sky
Confused with living, goeth simple man
Unknowing and unknown into the Why —
The Why that flings itself beyond the Sun
And back in space to where Time was begun.

# Today

This is earthquake
Weather!
Honor and Hunger
Walk lean
Together.


# Letter from Spain

Addressed to Alabama

Lincoln Battalion,
International Brigades,
November Something, 1937.

Dear Brother at home:

We captured a wounded Moor today.
He was just as dark as me.
I said, Boy, what you been doin' here
Fightin' against the free?

He answered something in a language
I couldn't understand.
But somebody told me he was sayin'
They nabbed him in his land

And made him join the fascist army
And come across to Spain.
And he said he had a feelin'
He'd never get back home again.

He said he had a feelin'
This whole thing wasn't right.
He said he didn't know
The folks he had to fight.

And as he lay there dying
In a village we had taken,
I looked across to Africa
And seed foundations shakin'.

Cause if a free Spain wins this war,

The colonies, too, are free—
Then something wonderful'll happen
To them Moors as dark as me.

I said, I guess that's why old England
And I reckon Italy, too,
Is afraid to let a workers' Spain
Be too good to me and you—

Cause they got slaves in Africa—
And they don't want 'em to be free.
Listen, Moorish prisoner, hell!
Here, shake hands with me!

I knelt down there beside him,
And I took his hand—
But the wounded Moor was dyin'
And he didn't understand.

                    Salud,
                        Johnny


# Postcard from Spain

Addressed to Alabama


                    Lincoln-Washington Battalion,
                    April, 1938


Dear Folks at home:

I went out this mornin'
Old shells was a-fallin'
Whistlin' and a-fallin'
When I went out this mornin'.

I'm way over here
A long ways from home,
Over here in Spanish country
But I don't feel alone.

Folks over here don't treat me
Like white folks used to do.

When I was home they treated me
Just like they treatin' you.

I don't think things'll ever
Be like that again:
I done met up with folks
Who'll fight for me now
Like I'm fightin' now for Spain.

> Salud,
> Johnny

## Convent

Tell me,
Is there peace
Behind your high stone walls—
Peace
Where no worldly duty calls—
Or does some strange
Insistence beckon
With a challenge
That appalls?

## In Time of Silver Rain

In time of silver rain
The earth
Puts forth new life again,
Green grasses grow
And flowers lift their heads,
And over all the plain
The wonder spreads
    Of life,
    Of life,
    Of life!

In time of silver rain
The butterflies
Lift silken wings

To catch a rainbow cry,
And trees put forth
New leaves to sing
In joy beneath the sky
As down the roadway
Passing boys and girls
Go singing, too,
In time of silver rain
    When spring
    And life
    Are new.


## August 19th . . .      A Poem for Clarence Norris


What flag will fly for me
When I die?
What flag of red and white and
    blue,
Half-mast, against the sky?
I'm not the President,
Nor the Honorable So-and-So.
But only one of the
Scottsboro Boys
Doomed "by law" to go.
**August 19th is the date.**
Put it in your book.
The date that I must keep with
    death.
Would you like to come and look?
You will see a black boy die.
Would you like to come and cry?
Maybe tears politely shed
Help the dead.
Or better still, they may help you—
For if you let the "law" kill me,
Are you free?
**August 19th is the date.**
Clarence Norris is my name.
The sentence, against me,
Against you, the same.
**August 19th is the date.**
Thunder in the sky.

In Alabama
A young black boy will die.
**August 19th is the date.**
Judges in high places
Still preserve their dignity
And dispose of cases.
**August 19th is the date.**
Rich people sit and fan
And sip cool drinks and do no work—
Yet they rule the land.
**August 19th is the date.**
The electric chair.
Swimmers on cool beaches
With their bodies bare.
**August 19th is the date.**
European tours.
Summer camps for the kids.
If they are yours.
Me, I never had no kids.
I never had no wife.
**August 19th is the date.**
To take my life.
**August 19th is the date.**
Will your church bells ring?
**August 19th is the date.**
Will the choir sing?
**August 19th is the date.**
Will the ball games stop?
**August 19th is the date.**
Will the jazz bands play?
**August 19th is the date.**
When I go away.
**August 19th is the date.**
Thunder in the sky.
**August 19th is the date.**
Scottsboro Boy must die.
**August 19th is the date.**
Judges in high places—
**August 19th is the date—**
Still dispose of cases.
**August 19th is the date.**
Rich people sit and fan.
**August 19th is the date.**
Who shall rule our land?
**August 19th is the date.**
Swimmers on cool beaches.

**August 19th is the date.**
World!
stop *all the leeches*
*That suck your life away and mine.*
World!
stop *all the leeches*
*That use their power to strangle*
*hope,*
*That make of the law a lyncher's*
*rope,*
*That drop their bombs on China*
*and Spain,*
*That have no pity for hunger or*
*pain,*
*That always, forever, close the door*
*Against the likes of me, the poor,*
AUGUST 19th IS THE DATE.
*What flag will fly for me?*
AUGUST 19th IS THE DATE.
*So deep my grave will be.*
AUGUST 19th IS THE DATE.
*I'm not the honorable So-and-So.*
AUGUST 19th IS THE DATE.
*Just a poor boy doomed to go.*
AUGUST 19th IS THE DATE.

AUGUST 19th IS THE DATE.
*Can you make death wait?*
AUGUST 19th IS THE DATE.
*Will you let me die?*
AUGUST 19th IS THE DATE.
*Can we make death wait?*
AUGUST 19th IS THE DATE.
*Will you let me die?*
AUGUST 19th IS THE DATE.
AUGUST 19th IS THE DATE.
AUGUST 19th . . . AUGUST 19th . . .
AUGUST 19th . . . AUGUST 19th . . .
AUGUST 19th . . .

# Beauty

They give to beauty here—
The same as everywhere—
Adulation, but no care.

# Song for Ourselves

Czechoslovakia lynched on a swastika cross!
    Blow, bitter winds, blow!
    Blow, bitter winds, blow!
Nails in her hands and nails in her feet,
    Left to die slow!
    Left to die slow!
Czechoslovakia! Ethiopia! Spain!
    One after another!
    One after another!
Where will the long snake of greed strike
    again?
    Will it be here, brother?

# Air Raid: Barcelona

Black smoke of sound
Curls against the midnight sky.

Deeper than a whistle,
Louder than a cry,
Worse than a scream
Tangled in the wail
Of a nightmare dream,
    The siren
Of the air raid sounds.

Flames and bombs and
Death in the ear!
The siren announces
Planes drawing near.
Down from bedrooms
Stumble women in gowns.
Men, half-dressed,
Carrying children rush down.

Up in the sky-lanes
Against the stars
A flock of death birds
Whose wings are steel bars
Fill the sky with a low dull roar
Of a plane,
      two planes,
            three planes,
                  five planes,
                       or more.
The anti-aircraft guns bark into space.
The searchlights make wounds
On the night's dark face.
The siren's wild cry
Like a hollow scream
Echoes out of hell in a nightmare dream.
      Then the BOMBS fall!
All other noises are nothing at all
    When the first BOMBS fall.
All other noises are suddenly still
    When the BOMBS fall.
All other noises are deathly still
As blood spatters the wall
And the whirling sound
Of the iron star of death
Comes hurtling down.
No other noises can be heard
As a child's life goes up
In the night like a bird.
Swift pursuit planes
Dart over the town,
Steel bullets fly
Slitting the starry silk
    Of the sky:
A bomber's brought down
In flames orange and blue,
And the night's all red
Like blood, too.
    The last BOMB falls.

The death birds wheel East
To their lairs again
Leaving iron eggs
In the streets of Spain.
With wings like black cubes
Against the far dawn,

The stench of their passage
Remains when they're gone.
In what was a courtyard
A child weeps alone.

Men uncover bodies
From ruins of stone.


## Chant for May Day

To be read by a Workman with, for background, the rhythmic waves of rising and
re-rising Mass Voices, multiplying like the roar of the sea.

|              |                                           |
|-------------:|-------------------------------------------|
| WORKER:      | The first of May:                         |
|              | When the flowers break through the earth, |
|              | When the sap rises in the trees.          |
|              | When the birds come back from the South.  |
|              | Workers:                                  |
|              | Be like the flowers,                      |
| 10 VOICES:   | Bloom in the strength of your unknown     |
|              | power,                                    |
| 20 VOICES:   | Grow out of the passive earth,            |
| 40 VOICES:   | Grow strong with Union,                   |
|              | All hands together —                      |
|              | To beautify this hour, this spring,       |
|              | And all the springs to come              |
| 50 VOICES:   | Forever for the workers!                  |
| WORKER:      | Workers:                                  |
| 10 VOICES:   | Be like the sap rising in the trees,      |
| 20 VOICES:   | Strengthening each branch,                |
| 40 VOICES:   | No part neglected —                       |
| 50 VOICES:   | Reaching all the world.                   |
| WORKER:      | All workers:                              |
| 10 VOICES:   | White workers,                            |
| 10 OTHERS:   | Black workers,                            |
| 10 OTHERS:   | Yellow workers,                           |
| 10 OTHERS:   | Workers in the islands of the sea —       |
| 50 VOICES:   | Life is everywhere for you,               |
| WORKER:      | When the sap of your own strength rises   |
| 50 VOICES:   | Life is everywhere.                       |
| 10 VOICES:   | May Day!                                   |
| 20 VOICES:   | May Day!                                   |
| 40 VOICES:   | May Day!                                   |
| 50 VOICES:   | When the earth is new,                    |

| WORKER: | Proletarians of all the world: |
| 20 VOICES: | Arise, |
| 40 VOICES: | Grow strong, |
| 60 VOICES: | Take Power, |
| 80 VOICES: | Till the forces of the earth are yours |
| 100 VOICES: | From this hour. |

## Kids Who Die

This is for the kids who die,
Black and white,
For kids will die certainly.
The old and rich will live on awhile,
As always,
Eating blood and gold,
Letting kids die.

Kids will die in the swamps of Mississippi
Organizing sharecroppers.
Kids will die in the streets of Chicago
Organizing workers.
Kids will die in the orange groves of California
Telling others to get together.
Whites and Filipinos,
Negroes and Mexicans,
All kinds of kids will die
Who don't believe in lies, and bribes, and contentment,
And a lousy peace.

Of course, the wise and the learned
Who pen editorials in the papers,
And the gentlemen with Dr. in front of their names,
White and black,
Who make surveys and write books,
Will live on weaving words to smother the kids who die,
And the sleazy courts,
And the bribe-reaching police,
And the blood-loving generals,
And the money-loving preachers
Will all raise their hands against the kids who die,
Beating them with laws and clubs and bayonets and bullets
To frighten the people—
For the kids who die are like iron in the blood of the people—

And the old and rich don't want the people
To taste the iron of the kids who die,
Don't want the people to get wise to their own power,
To believe an Angelo Herndon, or ever get together.

Listen, kids who die—
Maybe, now, there will be no monument for you
Except in our hearts.
Maybe your bodies'll be lost in a swamp,
Or a prison grave, or the potter's field,
Or the rivers where you're drowned like Liebknecht,
But the day will come—
You are sure yourselves that it is coming—
When the marching feet of the masses
Will raise for you a living monument of love,
And joy, and laughter,
And black hands and white hands clasped as one,
And a song that reaches the sky—
The song of the new life triumphant
Through the kids who die.

## Six-Bits Blues

Gimme six-bits' worth o' ticket
On a train that runs somewhere.
I say six-bits' worth o' ticket
On a train that runs somewhere.
I don't care where it's goin'
Just so it goes away from here.

Baby, gimme a little lovin',
But don't make it too long.
A little lovin', babe, but
Don't make it too long.
Make it short and sweet, your lovin',
So I can roll along.

*I got to roll along!*

## Poet to Patron

What right has anyone to say
That I
Must throw out pieces of my heart
For pay?

For bread that helps to make
My heart beat true,
I must sell myself
To you?

A factory shift's better,
A week's meagre pay,
Than a perfumed note asking:
*What poems today?*

## Red Clay Blues

(by Langston Hughes and Richard Wright)

I miss that red clay, Lawd, I
Need to feel it in my shoes.
Says miss that red clay, Lawd, I
Need to feel it in my shoes.
I want to get to Georgia cause I
Got them red clay blues.

Pavement's hard on my feet, I'm
Tired o' this concrete street.
Pavement's hard on my feet, I'm
Tired o' this city street.
Goin' back to Georgia where
That red clay can't be beat.

I want to tramp in the red mud, Lawd, and
Feel the red clay round my toes.
I want to wade in that red mud,
Feel that red clay suckin' at my toes.
I want my little farm back and I
Don't care where that landlord goes.

I want to be in Georgia, when the
Big storm starts to blow.

Yes, I want to be in Georgia when that
Big storm starts to blow.
I want to see the landlords runnin' cause I
Wonder where they gonna go!

I got them red clay blues.


# Hey-Hey Blues

I can HEY on water
Same as I can HEY-HEY on beer.
HEY on water
Same as I can HEY-HEY on beer.
But if you gimme good corn whisky
I can HEY-HEY-HEY—and cheer!

If you can whip de blues, boy,
Then whip 'em all night long.
Boy, if you can whip de blues,
Then whip 'em all night long.
Just play 'em, perfesser,
Till you don't know right from wrong.

While you play 'em,
I will sing 'em, too.
And while you play 'em,
I'll sing 'em, too.
I don't care how you play 'em
I'll keep right up with you.

Cause I can HEY on water,
I said HEY-HEY on beer—
HEY on water
And HEY-HEY on beer—
But gimme good corn whisky
And I'll HEY-HEY-HEY—and cheer!

*Yee-ee-e-who-ooo-oo-o!*

# Lynching Song

Pull at the rope!
O, pull it high!
Let the white folks live
And the black boy die.

Pull it, boys,
With a bloody cry.
Let the black boy spin
While the white folks die.

*The white folks die?*
*What do you mean—*
*The white folks die?*

That black boy's
Still body
Says:
NOT I.


# How Thin a Blanket

There is so much misery in the world,
So much poverty and pain,
So many who have no food
Nor shelter from the rain,
So many wandering friendless,
So many facing cold,
So many gnawing bitter bread
And growing old!

What can I do?
And you?
What can we do alone?
How short a way
The few spare crumbs
We have will go!
How short a reach
The hand stretched out
To those who know
No handshake anywhere.

How little help our love
When they themselves
No longer care.
How thin a blanket ours
For the withered body
Of despair!

## Visitors to the Black Belt

You can talk about
*Across* the railroad tracks—
To me it's *here*
On this side of the tracks.

You can talk about
*Up* in Harlem—
To me it's *here*
In Harlem.

You can say
Jazz on the South Side—
To me it's hell
On the South Side:

Kitchenettes
With no heat
And garbage
In the halls.

Who're you, outsider?

Ask me who am I.

## Note on Commercial Theatre

You've taken my blues and gone—
You sing 'em on Broadway
And you sing 'em in Hollywood Bowl,
And you mixed 'em up with symphonies

And you fixed 'em
So they don't sound like me.
Yep, you done taken my blues and gone.

You also took my spirituals and gone.
You put me in *Macbeth* and *Carmen Jones*
And all kinds of *Swing Mikados*
And in everything but what's about me—
But someday somebody'll
Stand up and talk about me,
And write about me—
Black and beautiful—
And sing about me,
And put on plays about me!
I reckon it'll be
Me myself!

Yes, it'll be me.


## Love Again Blues

My life ain't nothin'
But a lot o' Gawd-knows-what.
I say my life ain't nothin'
But a lot o' Gawd-knows-what.
Just one thing after 'nother
Added to de trouble that I got.

When I got you I
Thought I had an angel-chile.
When I got you
Thought I had an angel-chile.
You turned out to be a devil
That mighty nigh drove me wild!

Tell me, tell me,
What makes love such an ache and pain?
Tell me what makes
Love such an ache and pain?
It takes you and it breaks you—
But you got to love again.

# Out of Work

I walked de streets till
De shoes wore off my feet.
I done walked de streets till
De shoes wore off my feet.
Been lookin' for a job
So's that I could eat.

I couldn't find no job
So I went to de WPA.
Couldn't find no job
So I went to de WPA.
WPA man told me:
You got to live here a year and a day.

A year and a day, Lawd,
In this great big lonesome town!
A year and a day in this
Great big lonesome town!
I might starve for a year but
That extra day would get me down.

Did you ever try livin'
On two-bits minus two?
I say did you ever try livin'
On two-bits minus two?
Why don't you try it, folks,
And see what it would do to you?

# Seven Moments of Love

An un-sonnet sequence in Blues

### 1. Twilight Reverie

Here I set with a bitter old thought,
Something in my mind better I forgot.
Setting here thinking feeling sad.
Keep feeling like this I'm gonna start acting bad.
Gonna go get my pistol, I said forty-four—
Make you walk like a ghost if you bother me any more.
Gonna go get my pistol, I mean thirty-two,
And shoot all kinds o' shells into you.
Yal, here I set thinking—a bitter old thought
About two kinds o' pistols that I ain't got.

If I just had a Owl Head, old Owl Head would do,
Cause I'd take that Owl Head and fire on you.
But I ain't got no Owl Head and you done left town
And here I set thinking with a bitter old frown.
It's dark on this stoop, Lawd! The sun's gone down!

## 2. Supper Time

I look in the kettle, the kettle is dry.
Look in the bread box, nothing but a fly.
Turn on the light and look real good!
I would make a fire but there ain't no wood.
Look at that water dripping in the sink.
Listen at my heartbeats trying to think.
Listen at my footprints walking on the floor.
That place where your trunk was, ain't no trunk no more.
Place where your clothes hung's empty and bare.
Stay away if you want to, and see if I care!
If I had a fire I'd make me some tea
And set down and drink it, myself and me.
Lawd! I got to find me a woman for the WPA—
Cause if I don't they'll cut down my pay.

## 3. Bed Time

If this radio was good I'd get KDQ
And see what Count Basie's playing new.
If I had some money I'd stroll down the street
And jive some old broad I might meet.
Or if I wasn't so drowsy I'd look up Joe
And start a skin game with some chumps I know.
Or if it wasn't so late I might take a walk
And find somebody to kid and talk.
But since I got to get up at day,
I might as well put it on in the hay.
I can sleep *so* good with you away!
House is *so* quiet! . . . Listen at them mice.
Do I see a couple? Or did I count twice?
Dog-gone little mouses! I wish I was you!
A human gets lonesome if there ain't two.

## 4. Daybreak

Big Ben, I'm gonna bust you bang up side the wall!
Gonna hit you in the face and let you fall!
Alarm clock here ringing so damn loud

You must think you got to wake up a crowd!
You ain't got to wake up *no* body but me.
I'm the only one's got to pile out in the cold,
Make this early morning time to keep body and soul
Together in my big old down-home frame.
Say! You know I believe I'll change my name,
Change my color, change my ways,
And be a white man the rest of my days!
I wonder if white folks ever feel bad,
Getting up in the morning lonesome and sad?

5. Sunday

All day Sunday didn't even dress up.
Here by myself, I do as I please.
Don't have to go to church.
Don't have to go nowhere.
I wish I could tell you how much I don't care
How far you go, nor how long you stay—
Cause I'm sure enjoying myself today!
Set on the front porch as long as I please.
I wouldn't take you back if you come on your knees.
But this house is mighty quiet!
They ought to be some noise. . . .
I'm gonna get up a poker game and invite the boys.
But the boys is all married! Pshaw!
Ain't that too bad?
They ought to be like me setting here—feeling glad!

6. Pay day

This whole pay check's just for me.
Don't have to share it a-tall.
Don't have to hear nobody say,
"This week I need it all."
I'm gonna get it cashed,
Buy me a few things.
Ain't gonna pay a cent on that radio
Nor them two diamond rings
We bought for the wedding that's
Turned out so bad.
I'm gonna tell the furniture man to come
And take back all them things we had
That's been keeping my nose to the grindstone.
I never did like the installment plan

And I won't need no furniture living alone—
Cause I'm going back to rooming and be a free man.
I'm gonna rent me a cubby-hole with a single bed.
Ain't even gonna dream 'bout the womens I had.
Women's abominations! Just like a curse!
You was the best—but you *the worst.*

### 7. Letter

Dear Cassie: Yes, I got your letter.
It come last night.
What do you mean, why I didn't write?
What do you mean, just a little spat?
How did I know where you done gone at?
And even if I did, I was mad—
Left me by myself in a double bed.
Sure, I missed your trunk—but I didn't miss you.
Yal, come on back—I know you want to.
I might not forget and I might not forgive,
But you just as well be here where you due to live.
And if you think I been too mean before,
 I'll try not to be that mean no more.
I can't get along with you, I can't get along without—
So let's just forget what this fuss was about.
Come on home and bake some corn bread,
And crochet a quilt for our double bed,
And wake me up gentle when the dawn appears
Cause that old alarm clock sho hurts my ears.
Here's five dollars, Cassie. Buy a ticket back.
I'll meet you at the bus station.
        Your baby,
        Jack.

## Daybreak in Alabama

When I get to be a composer
I'm gonna write me some music about
Daybreak in Alabama
And I'm gonna put the purtiest songs in it
Rising out of the ground like a swamp mist
And falling out of heaven like soft dew.
I'm gonna put some tall tall trees in it
And the scent of pine needles

And the smell of red clay after rain
And long red necks
And poppy colored faces
And big brown arms
And the field daisy eyes
Of black and white black white black people
And I'm gonna put white hands
And black hands and brown and yellow hands
And red clay earth hands in it
Touching everybody with kind fingers
And touching each other natural as dew
In that dawn of music when I
Get to be a composer
And write about daybreak
In Alabama.

## Comment on War

Let us kill off youth
For the sake of *truth*.

We who are old know what truth is—
*Truth* is a bundle of vicious lies
Tied together and sterilized—
A war-makers' bait for unwise youth
To kill off each other
For the sake of
*Truth*.

## Ballad of the Miser

He took all his money
And put it in a sock
Till that sock got full
Then he got another sock.
He put all the sox
In a safe place

Behind the bricks
In the fireplace.
He worked and schemed
To stash all he could
And went around in rags
Like a beggar would.
When he died he didn't
Will a thing to anyone—
To a miser saving money's
Too much fun.

## Ballad of Little Sallie

Little Sallie, Little Sallie,
I've tried every way I know
To make you like me, Little Sallie,
Now I guess I'll go.

Listen, Jimmy, listen!
You mean you're gone for good?

Little Sallie, I mean always.
I've stood all a good man could.

Then wait a minute, Jimmy.
I want you to stay.
If you went off and left me
You'd take my heart away.

Little Sallie, Little Sallie,
Then I'll marry you.
We'll put one and one together—
To make three instead of two.

That's what we'll do!

# Poems **1941–1950**

# Evenin' Air Blues

Folks, I come up North
Cause they told me de North was fine.
I come up North
Cause they told me de North was fine.
Been up here six months—
I'm about to lose my mind.

This mornin' for breakfast
I chawed de mornin' air.
This mornin' for breakfast
Chawed de mornin' air.
But this evenin' for supper,
I got evenin' air to spare.

Believe I'll do a little dancin'
Just to drive my blues away—
A little dancin'
To drive my blues away,
Cause when I'm dancin'
De blues forgets to stay.

But if you was to ask me
How de blues they come to be,
Says if you was to ask me
How de blues they come to be—
You wouldn't need to ask me:
Just look at me and see!

# Aspiration

I wonder how it feels
To do cart wheels?
I sure would like
To know.

To walk a high wire
Is another desire,
In this world before
I go.

## Little Lyric (*Of Great Importance*)

> I wish the rent
> Was heaven sent.

## Curious

> I can see your house, babe,
> But I can't see you.
> I can see your house,
> But I can't see you.
> When you're in your house, baby
> Tell me, what do you do?

## *If*-ing

> If I had some small change
> I'd buy me a mule,
> Get on that mule and
> Ride like a fool.
>
> If I had some greenbacks
> I'd buy me a Packard,
> Fill it up with gas and
> Drive that baby backward.
>
> If I had a million
> I'd get me a plane
> And everybody in America'd
> Think I was insane.
>
> But I ain't got a million,
> Fact is, ain't got a dime—
> So just by *if*-ing
> I have a good time!

# Evil

Looks like what drives me crazy
Don't have no effect on you—
But I'm gonna keep on at it
Till it drives you crazy, too.

# Southern Mammy Sings

Miss Gardner's in her garden.
Miss Yardman's in her yard.
Miss Michaelmas is at de mass
And I am gettin' tired!
    Lawd!
I am gettin' tired!

The nations they is fightin'
And the nations they done fit.
Sometimes I think that white folks
Ain't worth a little bit.
    No, m'am!
Ain't worth a little bit.

Last week they lynched a colored boy.
They hung him to a tree.
That colored boy ain't said a thing
But we all should be free.
    Yes, m'am!
We all should be free.

Not meanin' to be sassy
And not meanin' to be smart—
But sometimes I think that white folks
Just ain't got no heart.
    No, m'am!
Just ain't got no heart.

# Black Maria

Must be the Black Maria
That I see,
The Black Maria that I see—

But I hope it
Ain't comin' for me.

Hear that music playin' upstairs?
Aw, my heart is
Full of cares—
But that music playin' upstairs
*Is* for me.

Babe, did you ever
See the sun
Rise at dawnin' full of fun?
Says, did you ever see the sun rise
Full of fun, full of fun?
Then you know a new day's
Done begun.

Black Maria passin' by
Leaves the sunrise in the sky—
And a new day,
Yes, a new day's
Done begun!


## Dustbowl


The land
Wants me to come back
To a handful of dust in autumn,
To a raindrop
In the palm of my hand
In spring.

The land
Wants me to come back
To a broken song in October,
To a snowbird on the wing.

The land
Wants me
To come back.

## Addition [1]

$7 \times 7 + \text{love} =$
An amount
Infinitely above:
$7 \times 7 - \text{love}.$

## Kid Sleepy

Listen, Kid Sleepy,
Don't you want to run around
To the other side of the house
Where the shade is?
It's sunny here
And your skin'll turn
A reddish-purple in the sun.

    Kid Sleepy said,
    *I don't care.*

Listen, Kid Sleepy,
Don't you want to get up
And go to work down-
Town somewhere
To earn enough
For lunches and car fare?

    Kid Sleepy said,
    *I don't care.*

Or would you rather,
Kid Sleepy, just
Stay here?

    *Rather just*
    *Stay here.*

## Stony Lonesome

They done took Cordelia
Out to stony lonesome ground.
Done took Cordelia
To stony lonesome,
Laid her down.
They done put Cordelia
Underneath that
Grassless mound.
  Ay-Lord!
   Ay-Lord!
    Ay-Lord!
She done left po' Buddy
To struggle by his self.
Po' Buddy Jones,
Yes, he's done been left.
She's out in stony lonesome,
Lordy! Sleepin' by herself.
  Cordelia's
   In stony
    Lonesome
     Ground!

## NAACP

I see by the papers
Where the NAACP
Is meeting down in Houston
And I'd like to be there to see
What they intend to do
In these trying times today
Cause we need to take some solid steps
To drive Jim Crow away.
We need a delegation to
Go see the President
And tell him from the shoulder
Just why we are sent:
Tell him we've heard his speeches
About Democracy—
But to enjoy what he's talking about
*What* color must you be?
I'm cook or dishwasher in the Navy.

In the Marines I can't be either.
The Army still segregates me—
And we ain't run by Hitler neither!
The Jim Crow car's still dirty.
The color line's still drawn.
Yet up there in Washington
They're blowing freedom's horn!
The NAACP meets in Houston.
Folks, turn out in force!
We got to take some drastic steps
To break old Jim Crow's course.

## Early Evening Quarrel

Where is that sugar, Hammond,
I sent you this morning to buy?
I say, where is that sugar
I sent you this morning to buy?
Coffee without sugar
Makes a good woman cry.

*I ain't got no sugar, Hattie,*
*I gambled your dime away.*
*Ain't got no sugar, I*
*Done gambled that dime away.*
*If you's a wise woman, Hattie,*
*You ain't gonna have nothin to say.*

I ain't no wise woman, Hammond.
I am evil and mad.
Ain't no sense in a good woman
Bein treated so bad.

*I don't treat you bad, Hattie,*
*Neither does I treat you good.*
*But I reckon I could treat you*
*Worser if I would.*

Lawd, these things we women
Have to stand!
I wonder is there nowhere a
Do-right man?

## Watch Out, Papa

When you thrill with joy
At the songs of yesteryear
And declare the ditties
Of today quite drear—
Watch out! You're getting old!

When you extoll the solid
Virtues of *your* youth
And pronounce the young folks
Of *this* age uncouth—
Uh-huh! You're getting old!

Watch Out!
Else you won't know what it's
All about.
Watch Out!

## Snob

If your reputation
In the community is good
Don't snub the other fellow—
It might be misunderstood—
Because a good reputation
Can commit suicide
By holding its head
Too far to one side.

## Heaven

Heaven is
The place where
Happiness is
Everywhere.

Animals
And birds sing—
As does
Everything.

To each stone,
"How-do-you-do?"
Stone answers back,
"Well! And you?"

## Enemy

It would be nice
In any case,
To someday meet you
Face to face
Walking down
The road to hell . . .
As I come up
Feeling swell.

## Snail

Little snail,
Dreaming you go.
Weather and rose
Is all you know.

Weather and rose
Is all you see,
Drinking
The dewdrop's
Mystery.

## One

Lonely
As the wind
On the Lincoln
Prairies.

Lonely
As a bottle of licker
On a table
All by itself.

## Young Negro Girl

You are like a warm dark dusk
In the middle of June-time
When the first violets
Have almost forgotten their names
And the deep red roses bloom.

You are like a warm dark dusk
In the middle of June-time
Before the hot nights of summer
Burn white with stars.

## Silence

I catch the pattern
Of your silence
Before you speak.

I do not need
To hear a word.

In your silence
Every tone I seek
Is heard.

# Big Sur

Great lonely hills.
Great mountains.
Mighty touchstones of song.

# Gypsy Melodies

Songs that break
And scatter
Out of the moon:
Rockets of joy
Dimmed too soon.

# Refugee

Loneliness terrific beats on my heart,
Bending the bitter broken boughs of pain.
Stunned by the onslaught that tears the sky apart
I stand with unprotected head against the rain.

Loneliness terrific turns to panic and to fear.
I hear my footsteps on the stairs of yesteryear,
Where are you? Oh, where are you?
Once so dear.

# It Gives Me Pause

I would like to be a sinner
Sinning just for fun
But I always suffer so
When I get my sinning done.

## Some Day

Once more
The guns roar.
Once more
The call goes forth for men.
Again
The war begins,
Again
False slogans become a bore.
Yet no one cries:
ENOUGH! NO MORE!
Like angry dogs the human race
Loves the snarl upon its face
It loves to kill.
The pessimist says
It always will.

That I do not believe.

Some day
The savage in us will wear away.
Some day quite clearly
Men will see
How clean and happy life can be
And how,
Like flowers planted in the sun,
We, too, can give forth blossoms,
Shared by everyone.

## Death in Africa

To die
And never know what killed you
When death comes swift
Like a mountain
In the path of a speeding plane
Is O.K. But to die
When death comes slow
Like the tax collector
Year after year
Or the white boss in Africa
Who never goes away,
That's another story.

The drums and the witch doctors, helpless.
The missionaries, helpless.
Damballa,
Helpless, too?


## Sunset in Dixie

The sun
Is gonna go down
In Dixie
Some of these days
With such a splash
That everybody who ever knew
What yesterday was
Is gonna forget—
When that sun
Goes down in Dixie.


## Gangsters

The gangsters of the world
Are riding high.
It's not the underworld
Of which I speak.
They leave that loot to smaller fry.
Why should they great Capone's
Fallen headpiece seek
When stolen crowns
Sit easier on the head—
Or Ethiopia's band of gold
For higher prices
On the market can be sold—
Or Iraq oil—
Than any vice or bootleg crown of old?
The gangsters of the world ride high—
But not small fry.

## Southern Negro Speaks

I reckon they must have
Forgotten about me
When I hear them say they gonna
Save Democracy.
Funny thing about white folks
Wanting to go and fight
Way over in Europe
For freedom and light
When right here in Alabama—
Lord have mercy on me!—
They declare I'm a Fifth Columnist
If I say the word, *Free*.
Jim Crow all around me.
Don't have the right to vote.
Let's leave our neighbor's eye alone
And look after our own mote—
Cause I sure don't understand
What the meaning can be
When folks talk about freedom—
And Jim Crow me?

## This Puzzles Me

They think we're simple children:
Watermelon in the sun,
Shooting dice and shouting,
Always having fun.
They think we're simple children,
Grown up never be—
But other simple children
Seem simpler than we.
Other simple children
Play with bombs for toys,
Kill and slaughter every day,
Make a frightful noise,
Strew the world with misery,
Stain the earth with blood,
Slay and maim each other
And evidently think it good—
For when we dark-skinned children
Try to search for right and light

These other simple children
Think it isn't right—
Unless it's white.
Talmadge down in Georgia,
Dies in Washington
Seem to feel that all we need
Is melon in the sun.
They think we're simple children—
*Simpler* than they—
But why they think it, is a puzzle
When you see the world today.


## Vagabonds

We are the desperate
Who do not care,
The hungry
Who have nowhere
To eat,
No place to sleep,
The tearless
Who cannot
Weep.


## Me and the Mule

My old mule,
He's got a grin on his face.
He's been a mule so long
He's forgot about his race.

I'm like that old mule—
Black—and don't give a damn!
You got to take me
Like I am.

## Big Buddy

Big Buddy, Big Buddy,
Ain't you gonna stand by me?
Big Buddy, Big Buddy,
Ain't you gonna stand by me?
If I got to fight,
I'll fight like a man.
But say, Big Buddy,
Won't you lend a hand?
Ain't you gonna stand by me?

Big Buddy, Big Buddy,
Don't you hear this hammer ring?
Hey, Big Buddy,
Don't you hear this hammer ring?
I'm gonna split this rock
And split it wide!
When I split this rock,
Stand by my side.
Say, Big Buddy,
Don't you hear this hammer ring?

## Merry-Go-Round    Colored child at carnival

Where is the Jim Crow section
On this merry-go-round,
Mister, cause I want to ride?
Down South where I come from
White and colored
Can't sit side by side.
Down South on the train
There's a Jim Crow car.
On the bus we're put in the back—
But there ain't no back
To a merry-go-round!
Where's the horse
For a kid that's black?

## 403 Blues

You lucky to be a spider
Cause it's bad luck to kill you.
Lucky to be a spider.
It's bad luck to kill you.
But if you wasn't a spider
Your day would sure be through.

Evil as I feel this morning
I could whip my weight in lime.
Evil's I feel this morning,
Could whip my weight in lime.
Don't cross my path no mo', spider,
Cause this ain't crossin' time.

Why do you s'pose she left me
Just when I got my 403?
Why do you s'pose my baby left me
When I got my 403?
I reckon, all the time she
Must not of cared for me.


## Sunday Morning Prophecy

An old Negro minister concludes his sermon in his loudest voice,
having previously pointed out the sins of this world:


. . . and now
When the rumble of death
Rushes down the drain
Pipe of eternity,
And hell breaks out
Into a thousand smiles,
And the devil licks his chops
Preparing to feast on life,
And all the little devils
Get out their bibs
To devour the corrupt bones
Of this world—
Oh-ooo-oo-o!
Then my friends!
Oh, then! Oh, then!
What will you do?

You will turn back
And look toward the mountains.

You will turn back
And grasp for a straw.
You will holler,
*Lord-d-d-d-d-ah!*
*Save me, Lord!*
*Save me!*
And the Lord will say,
*In the days of your greatness*
*I did not hear your voice!*
The Lord will say,
*In the days of your richness*
*I did not see your face!*
The Lord will say,
*No-oooo-ooo-oo-o!*
*I will not save you now!*

And your soul
Will be lost!

Come into the church this morning,
Brothers and Sisters,
And be saved—
And give freely
In the collection basket
That I who am thy shepherd
Might live.

Amen!

## The Bitter River

(Dedicated to the memory of Charlie Lang and Ernest Green, each
fourteen years old when lynched together beneath the Shubuta Bridge
over the Chicasawhay River in Mississippi, October 12th, 1942.)

There is a bitter river
Flowing through the South.
Too long has the taste of its water
Been in my mouth.
There is a bitter river
Dark with filth and mud.

Too long has its evil poison
Poisoned my blood.

I've drunk of the bitter river
And its gall coats the red of my tongue,
Mixed with the blood of the lynched boys
From its iron bridge hung,
Mixed with the hopes that are drowned there
In the snake-like hiss of its stream
Where I drank of the bitter river
That strangled my dream:
The book studied—but useless,
Tool handled—but unused,
Knowledge acquired but thrown away,
Ambition battered and bruised.
Oh, water of the bitter river
With your taste of blood and clay,
You reflect no stars by night,
No sun by day.

The bitter river reflects no stars—
It gives back only the glint of steel bars
And dark bitter faces behind steel bars:
The Scottsboro boys behind steel bars,
Lewis Jones behind steel bars,
The voteless share-cropper behind steel bars,
The labor leader behind steel bars,
The soldier thrown from a Jim Crow bus behind steel bars,
The 15¢ mugger behind steel bars,
The girl who sells her body behind steel bars,
And my grandfather's back with its ladder of scars,
Long ago, long ago—the whip and steel bars—
The bitter river reflects no stars.

"Wait, be patient," you say.
"Your folks will have a better day."
But the swirl of the bitter river
Takes your words away.
"Work, education, patience
Will bring a better day."
The swirl of the bitter river
Carries your "patience" away.
"Disrupter! Agitator!
Trouble maker!" you say.

The swirl of the bitter river
Sweeps your lies away.
I did not ask for this river
Nor the taste of its bitter brew.
I was given its water
As a gift from you.
Yours has been the power
To force my back to the wall
And make me drink of the bitter cup
Mixed with blood and gall.

You have lynched my comrades
Where the iron bridge crosses the stream,
Underpaid me for my labor,
And spit in the face of my dream.
You forced me to the bitter river
With the hiss of its snake-like song—
Now your words no longer have meaning—
I have drunk at the river too long:
Dreamer of dreams to be broken,
Builder of hopes to be smashed,
Loser from an empty pocket
Of my meagre cash,
Bitter bearer of burdens
And singer of weary song,
I've drunk at the bitter river
With its filth and its mud too long.
Tired now of the bitter river,
Tired now of the pat on the back,
Tired now of the steel bars
Because my face is black,
I'm tired of segregation,
Tired of filth and mud,
I've drunk of the bitter river
And it's turned to steel in my blood.

Oh, tragic bitter river
Where the lynched boys hung,
The gall of your bitter water
Coats my tongue.
The blood of your bitter water
For me gives back no stars.
I'm tired of the bitter river!
Tired of the bars!

# Hope [1]

Sometimes when I'm lonely,
Don't know why,
Keep thinkin' I won't be lonely
By and by.

# Harlem Sweeties

Have you dug the spill
Of Sugar Hill?
Cast your gims
On this sepia thrill:
Brown sugar lassie,
Caramel treat,
Honey-gold baby
Sweet enough to eat.
Peach-skinned girlie,
Coffee and cream,
Chocolate darling
Out of a dream.
Walnut tinted
Or cocoa brown,
Pomegranate lipped
Pride of the town.
Rich cream colored
To plum-tinted black,
Feminine sweetness
In Harlem's no lack.
Glow of the quince
To blush of the rose.
Persimmon bronze
To cinnamon toes.
Blackberry cordial,
Virginia Dare wine—
All those sweet colors
Flavor Harlem of mine!
Walnut or cocoa,
Let me repeat:
Caramel, brown sugar,
A chocolate treat.
Molasses taffy,
Coffee and cream,
Licorice, clove, cinnamon

To a honey-brown dream.
Ginger, wine-gold,
Persimmon, blackberry,
All through the spectrum
Harlem girls vary—
So if you want to know beauty's
Rainbow-sweet thrill,
Stroll down luscious,
Delicious, *fine* Sugar Hill.

## Declaration

If I was a sea-lion
Swimming in the sea,
I would swim to China
And you never would see me.
    No!
    You never would
    See me.

If I was a rich boy
I'd buy myself a car,
Fill it up with gas
And drive so far, so far.
    Yes!
    I would drive
    So far.

Hard-hearted and unloving!
Hard-hearted and untrue!
If I was a bird I'd
Fly away from you.
    Yes, way
    Away
    From
    You.

## Statement

Down on '33rd Street
They cut you
Every way they is.

## Present

De lady I work for
Told her husband
She wanted a
Robe o' love—
But de damn fool
Give her
A fur coat!

Yes,
He did!

## Free Man

You can catch the wind,
You can catch the sea,
But you can't, pretty mama,
Ever catch me.

You can tame a rabbit,
Even tame a bear,
But you'll never, pretty mama,
Keep me caged up here.

## Brief Encounter

I was lookin' for a sandwich, Judge,
Any old thing to eat.
I was walkin' down de street, Judge,
Lookin' for any old thing to eat—

When I come across that woman
That I didn't want to meet.

Judge, she is de woman
That put de mix on me.
She is de woman, Judge,
That put de mix on me.
If there's anybody on this earth, Judge,
I didn't want to see!

Fact that I hurt her, Judge,
De fact that she is dead,
Fact that I hurt her,
Fact that she is dead—
She was de wrongest thing, Judge,
That I ever had!

## Morning After

I was so sick last night I
Didn't hardly know my mind.
So sick last night I
Didn't know my mind.
I drunk some bad licker that
Almost made me blind.

Had a dream last night I
Thought I was in hell.
I drempt last night I
Thought I was in hell.
Woke up and looked around me—
Babe, your mouth was open like a well.

I said, Baby! Baby!
Please don't snore so loud.
Baby! Please!
Please don't snore so loud.
You jest a little bit o' woman but you
Sound like a great big crowd.

## Mississippi Levee

Been workin' on de levee,
Workin' like a tuck-tail dog.
Workin' on de levee
Like a tuck-tail dog.
When this flood is over,
Gonna sleep like a water-log.

Don't know why I build this levee
And de levee don't do no good.
Don't know why I build this levee
When de levee don't do no good.
I pack a million bags o' sand
But de water still makes a flood.

Levee, levee,
How high have you got to be?
Levee, levee,
How high have you got to be
To keep them cold muddy waters
From washin' over me?

## In a Troubled Key

Do not sell me out, baby,
Please do not sell me out.
Do not sell me out, baby.
Do not sell me out.
I used to believe in you, baby,
Now I begins to doubt.

Still I can't help lovin' you,
Even though you do me wrong.
Says I can't help lovin' you
Though you do me wrong—
But my love might turn into a knife
Instead of to a song.

# Only Woman Blues

I want to tell you 'bout that woman,
My used-to-be—
She was de meanest woman
I ever did see.
But she's de only
Woman that could mistreat me!

She could make me holler like a sissie,
Bark like a dog.
She could chase me up a tree
And then cut down de log—
Cause she's de only
Woman that could mistreat me.

She had long black hair,
Big black eyes,
Glory! Hallelujah!
Forgive them lies!
She's de only
Woman's gonna mistreat me.

I got her in Mississippi.
Took her to Alabam'.
When she left
I said, Go, hot damn!
You de last and only
Woman's gonna mistreat me.

# Wake

Tell all my mourners
To mourn in red—
Cause there ain't no sense
In my bein' dead.

## Cabaret Girl Dies on Welfare Island

I hate to die this way with the quiet
Over everything like a shroud.
I'd rather die where the band's a-playin'
Noisy and loud.

Rather die the way I lived—
Drunk and rowdy and gay!
God! Why did you ever curse me
Makin' me die this way?

## Crossing

It was that lonely day, folks,
When I walked all by myself.
My friends was all around me
But it was as if they'd left.
I went up on a mountain
In a high cold wind
And the coat that I was wearing
Was mosquito-netting thin.
I went down in the valley
And I crossed an icy stream
And the water I was crossing
Was no water in a dream
And the shoes I was wearing
No protection for that stream.
Then I stood out on a prairie
And as far as I could see
Wasn't nobody on that prairie
Looked like me.
It was that lonely day, folks,
I walked all by myself:
My friends was right there with me
But was just as if they'd left.

## West Texas

Down in West Texas where the sun
Shines like the evil one
I had a woman
And her name
Was Joe.

Pickin' cotton in the field
Joe said I wonder how it would feel
For us to pack up
Our things
And go?

So we cranked up our old Ford
And we started down the road
Where we was goin'
We didn't know—
Nor which way.

But West Texas where the sun
Shines like the evil one
Ain't no place
For a colored
Man to stay!

## Ku Klux

They took me out
To some lonesome place.
They said, "Do you believe
In the great white race?"

I said, "Mister,
To tell you the truth,
I'd believe in anything
If you'd just turn me loose."

The white man said, "Boy,
Can it be
You're a-standin' there
A-sassin' me?"

They hit me in the head
And knocked me down.
And then they kicked me
On the ground.

A klansman said, "Nigger,
Look me in the face—
And tell me you believe in
The great white race."

## Ballad of the Sinner

I went down the road,
Dressed to kill—
Straight down the road
That leads to hell.

Mother warned me,
Warned me true.
Father warned me,
And Sister, too.

But I was bold,
Headstrong and wild.
I did not act like
My mother's child.

She begged me, please,
Stay on the right track.
But I was drinking licker,
Jitterbugging back,

Going down that road,
All dressed to kill—
The road that leads
Right straight to hell.

*Pray for me, Mama!*

# Ballad of the Killer Boy

Bernice said she wanted
A diamond or two.
I said, Baby,
I'll get 'em for you.

Bernice said she wanted
A Packard car.
I said, Sugar,
Here you are.

Bernice said she needed
A bank full of cash.
I said, Honey,
That's nothing but trash.

I pulled that job
In the broad daylight.
The cashier trembled
And turned dead white.

He tried to guard
Other people's gold.
I said to hell
With your stingy soul!

There ain't no reason
To let you live!
I filled him full of holes
Like a sieve.

Now they've locked me
In the death house.
I'm gonna die!

Ask that woman—
*She knows why.*

# Ballad of the Fortune Teller

Madam could look in your hand—
Never seen you before—
And tell you more than
You'd want to know.

She could tell you about love,
And money, and such.
And she wouldn't
Charge you much.

A fellow came one day.
Madam took him in.
She treated him like
He was her kin.

Gave him money to gamble.
She gave him bread,
And let him sleep in her
Walnut bed.

Friends tried to tell her
Dave meant her no good.
Looks like she could've knowed it
If she only would.

He mistreated her terrible,
Beat her up bad.
Then went off and left her.
Stole all she had.

She tried to find out
What road he took.
There wasn't a trace
No way she looked.

That woman who could foresee
What *your* future meant,
Couldn't tell, to save her,
Where Dave went.

## Ballad of the Girl Whose Name Is Mud

A girl with all that raising,
It's hard to understand
How she could get in trouble
With a no-good man.

The guy she gave her all to
Dropped her with a thud.
Now amongst decent people,
Dorothy's name is mud.

But nobody's seen her shed a tear,
Nor seen her hang her head.
Ain't even heard her murmur,
*Lord, I wish I was dead!*

No! The hussy's telling everybody—
Just as though it was no sin—
That if she had a chance
*She'd do it agin'!*


## Ballad of the Gypsy

I went to the Gypsy's.
Gypsy settin' all alone.
I said, Tell me, Gypsy,
When will my gal be home?

Gypsy said, Silver,
Put some silver in my hand
And I'll look into the future
And tell you all I can.

I crossed her palm with silver,
Then she started in to lie.
She said, Now, listen, Mister,
She'll be here by and by.

    *Aw, what a lie!*

I been waitin' and a-waitin'
And she ain't come home yet.
Something musta happened
To make my gal forget.

Uh! I hates a lyin' Gypsy
Will take good money from you,
Tell you pretty stories
And take your money from you—

But if I was a Gypsy
I would take your money, too.


## Ballad of the Pawnbroker

This gold watch and chain
That belonged to my father?
Two bucks on it?
Never mind! Don't bother.

How about this necklace?
Pure jade.
Chinese? . . . Hell, no!
It's union-made.

Can I get Ten on this suit
I bought two weeks ago?
I don't know why it looks
Worn so.

Feel the weight, Mr. Levy,
Of this silver bowl.
Stop hunting for the price tag!
It ain't stole.

O.K. You don't want it?
Then I'll go.
But a man's got to live,
You know.

Say! On the last thing I own,
Pawnbroker, old friend—
  Me!
  My self!
  Life!
What'll you lend?

# Ballad of the Man Who's Gone

No money to bury him.
The relief gave Forty-Four.
The undertaker told 'em,
You'll need Sixty more

For a first-class funeral,
A hearse and two cars—
And maybe your friends'll
Send some flowers.

His wife took a paper
And went around.
Everybody that gave something
She put 'em down.

She raked up a Hundred
For her man that was dead.
His buddies brought flowers.
A funeral was had.

A minister preached—
And charged Five
To bless him dead
And praise him alive.

Now that he's buried—
God rest his soul—
Reckon there's no charge
For graveyard mold.

*I wonder what makes*
*A funeral so high?*
*A poor man ain't got*
*No business to die!*


# Midnight Chippie's Lament

I looked down 31st Street,
Not a soul but Lonesome Blue.
Down on 31st Street,
Nobody but Lonesome Blue.
I said come here, Lonesome,
And I will love you, too.

Feelin' so sad, Lawd,
Feelin' so sad and lone.
So sad, Lawd!
So sad and lone!
I said, please, Mr. Lonesome,
Don't leave me here alone.

Lonesome said, listen!
Said, listen! Hey!
Lonesome said, listen!
Woman, listen! Say!
Buy you two for a quarter
On State Street any day.

I said, Mr. Lonesome,
Don't ig me like you do.
Cripple Mr. Lonesome,
Please don't ig me like you do.
Lonesome said when a two-bit woman
Gives love away she's through.

Girls, don't stand on no corner
Cryin' to no Lonesome Blue!
I say don't stand on no corner
Cryin' to no Lonesome Blue!
Cry by yourself, girls,
So nobody can't low-rate you.

## Widow Woman

Oh, that last long ride is a
Ride everybody must take.
Yes, that last long ride's a
Ride everybody must take.
And that final stop is a
Stop everybody must make.

When they put you in the ground and
They throw dirt in your face,
I say put you in the ground and
Throw dirt in your face,
That's one time, pretty papa,
You'll sure stay in your place.

You was a mighty lover and you
Ruled me many years.
A mighty lover, baby, cause you
Ruled me many years—
If I live to be a thousand
I'll never dry these tears.

I don't want nobody else and
Don't nobody else want me.
I say don't want nobody else
And don't nobody else want me—

*Yet you never can tell when a*
*Woman like me is free!*


## Shakespeare in Harlem

Hey ninny neigh!
And a hey nonny noe!
Where, oh, where
Did my sweet mama go?

Hey ninny neigh
With a tra-la-la-la!
They say your sweet mama
Went home to her ma.


## Fired

Awake all night with loving
The bright day caught me
Unawares—asleep.

"Late to work again,"
The boss man said.
"You're fired!"

So I went on back to bed—
And dreamed the sweetest dream
With Caledonia's arm
Beneath my head.


## Announcement

I had a gal,
She was driving alone,
Doing eighty
In a twenty-mile zone.

Had to pay her ticket.
It took all I had.
What makes a woman
Treat a man so bad?

Come to find out
(If I'd a-only knew it)
She had another joker
In my Buick!

So from now on,
I want the world to know,
That gal don't drive my
Car no more.


## 50–50

I'm all alone in this world, she said,
Ain't got nobody to share my bed,
Ain't got nobody to hold my hand—
The truth of the matter's
I ain't got no man.

Big Boy opened his mouth and said,
Trouble with you is

You ain't got no head!
If you had a head and used your mind
You could have *me* with you
All the time.

She answered, Babe, what must I do?

He said, Share your bed—
*And your money, too.*


## Evil Morning

It must have been yesterday,
(I know it ain't today)
Must have been yesterday
I started feeling this a-way.

I feel so mean I could
Bite a nail in two.
But before I'd bite a nail
I'd pulverize you.

You're the cause
O' my feeling like a dog
With my feet in the mire
And my heart in a bog.

Uh! It sure is awful to
Feel bad two days straight.
Get out o' my sight be-
Fore it is too late!


## Reverie on the Harlem River

Did you ever go down to the river—
Two a.m. midnight by your self?
Sit down by the river
And wonder what you got left?

Did you ever think about your mother?
God bless her, dead and gone!
Did you ever think about your sweetheart
And wish she'd never been born?

Down on the Harlem River:
    Two a.m.
    Midnight!
    By your self!
Lawd, I wish I could die—
But who would miss me if I left?

## Love

Love is a wild wonder
And stars that sing,
Rocks that burst asunder
And mountains that take wing.

John Henry with his hammer
Makes a little spark.
That little spark is love
Dying in the dark.

## Freedom's Plow

When a man starts out with nothing,
When a man starts out with his hands
Empty, but clean,
When a man starts out to build a world,
He starts first with himself
And the faith that is in his heart—
The strength there,
The will there to build.

First in the heart is the dream.
Then the mind starts seeking a way.
His eyes look out on the world,

On the great wooded world,
On the rich soil of the world,
On the rivers of the world.

The eyes see there materials for building,
See the difficulties, too, and the obstacles.
The hand seeks tools to cut the wood,
To till the soil, and harness the power of the waters.
Then the hand seeks other hands to help,
A community of hands to help—
Thus the dream becomes not one man's dream alone,
But a community dream.
Not my dream alone, but *our* dream.
Not my world alone,
But *your world and my world,*
Belonging to all the hands who build.

A long time ago, but not too long ago,
Ships came from across the sea
Bringing Pilgrims and prayer-makers,
Adventurers and booty seekers,
Free men and indentured servants,
Slave men and slave masters, all new—
To a new world, America!

With billowing sails the galleons came
Bringing men and dreams, women and dreams.
In little bands together,
Heart reaching out to heart,
Hand reaching out to hand,
They began to build our land.
Some were free hands
Seeking a greater freedom,
Some were indentured hands
Hoping to find their freedom,
Some were slave hands
Guarding in their hearts the seed of freedom.
But the word was there always:
    FREEDOM.

Down into the earth went the plow
In the free hands and the slave hands,
In indentured hands and adventurous hands,

Turning the rich soil went the plow in many hands
That planted and harvested the food that fed
And the cotton that clothed America.
Clang against the trees went the ax in many hands
That hewed and shaped the rooftops of America.
Splash into the rivers and the seas went the boat-hulls
That moved and transported America.
Crack went the whips that drove the horses
Across the plains of America.
Free hands and slave hands,
Indentured hands, adventurous hands,
White hands and black hands
Held the plow handles,
Ax handles, hammer handles,
Launched the boats and whipped the horses
That fed and housed and moved America.
Thus together through labor,
All these hands made America.
Labor! Out of labor came the villages
And the towns that grew to cities.
Labor! Out of labor came the rowboats
And the sailboats and the steamboats,
Came the wagons, stage coaches,
Out of labor came the factories,
Came the foundries, came the railroads,
Came the marts and markets, shops and stores,
Came the mighty products moulded, manufactured,
Sold in shops, piled in warehouses,
Shipped the wide world over:
Out of labor—white hands and black hands—
Came the dream, the strength, the will,
And the way to build America.
Now it is Me here, and You there.
Now it's Manhattan, Chicago,
Seattle, New Orleans,
Boston and El Paso—
Now it is the U.S.A.

A long time ago, but not too long ago, a man said:

    ALL MEN ARE CREATED EQUAL . . .
    ENDOWED BY THEIR CREATOR
    WITH CERTAIN INALIENABLE
       RIGHTS . . .

> AMONG THESE, LIFE, LIBERTY
> AND THE PURSUIT OF HAPPINESS.

His name was Jefferson. There were slaves then,
But in their hearts the slaves believed him, too,
And silently took for granted
That what he said was also meant for them.
It was a long time ago,
But not so long ago at that, Lincoln said:

> NO MAN IS GOOD ENOUGH
> TO GOVERN ANOTHER MAN
> WITHOUT THAT OTHER'S CONSENT.

There were slaves then, too,
But in their hearts the slaves knew
What he said must be meant for every human being—
Else it had no meaning for anyone.
Then a man said:

> BETTER TO DIE FREE,
> THAN TO LIVE SLAVES.

He was a colored man who had been a slave
But had run away to freedom.
And the slaves knew
What Frederick Douglass said was true.
With John Brown at Harpers Ferry, Negroes died.
John Brown was hung.
Before the Civil War, days were dark,
And nobody knew for sure
When freedom would triumph.
"Or if it would," thought some.
But others knew it had to triumph.
In those dark days of slavery,
Guarding in their hearts the seed of freedom,
The slaves made up a song:

> KEEP YOUR HAND ON THE PLOW!
> HOLD ON!

That song meant just what it said: *Hold on!*
Freedom will come!

> KEEP YOUR HAND ON THE PLOW!
> HOLD ON!

Out of war, it came, bloody and terrible!
But it came!
Some there were, as always,
Who doubted that the war would end right,
That the slaves would be free,
Or that the union would stand.
But now we know how it all came out.
Out of the darkest days for a people and a nation,
We know now how it came out.
There was light when the battle clouds rolled away.
There was a great wooded land,
And men united as a nation.

America is a dream.
The poet says it was promises.
The people say it *is* promises—that will come true.
The people do not always say things out loud,
Nor write them down on paper.
The people often hold
Great thoughts in their deepest hearts
And sometimes only blunderingly express them,
Haltingly and stumbling say them,
And faultily put them into practice.
The people do not always understand each other.
But there is, somewhere there,
Always the *trying* to understand,
And the *trying* to say,
"You are a man. Together we are building our land."

America!
Land created in common,
Dream nourished in common,
Keep your hand on the plow! Hold on!
If the house is not yet finished,
Don't be discouraged, builder!
If the fight is not yet won,
Don't be weary, soldier!
The plan and the pattern is here,
Woven from the beginning
Into the warp and woof of America:

ALL MEN ARE CREATED EQUAL.

NO MAN IS GOOD ENOUGH
TO GOVERN ANOTHER MAN WITHOUT
THAT OTHER'S CONSENT.

BETTER DIE FREE,
THAN LIVE SLAVES.

Who said those things? Americans!
Who owns those words? America!
Who is America? You, me!
We are America!
To the enemy who would conquer us from without,
We say, NO!
To the enemy who would divide
and conquer us from within,
We say, NO!

FREEDOM!
BROTHERHOOD!
DEMOCRACY!

To all the enemies of these great words:
We say, NO!

A long time ago,
An enslaved people heading toward freedom
Made up a song:
    *Keep Your Hand On The Plow! Hold On!*
That plow plowed a new furrow
Across the field of history.
Into that furrow the freedom seed was dropped.
From that seed a tree grew, is growing, will ever grow.
That tree is for everybody,
For all America, for all the world.
May its branches spread and its shelter grow
Until all races and all peoples know its shade.

KEEP YOUR HAND ON THE PLOW!
HOLD ON!

## Wisdom

I stand most humbly
Before man's wisdom,
Knowing we are not
Really wise:

If we were
We'd open up the kingdom
And make earth happy
As the dreamed of skies.

## Words Like Freedom

There are words like *Freedom*
Sweet and wonderful to say.
On my heartstrings freedom sings
All day everyday.

There are words like *Liberty*
That almost make me cry.
If you had known what I know
You would know why.

## Madam and the Number Writer

Number runner
Come to my door.
I had swore
I wouldn't play no more.

He said, Madam,
6-0-2
Looks like a likely
Hit for you.

I said, Last night,
I dreamed 7-0-3.
He said, That might
Be a hit for me.

He played a dime,
I played, too,

Then we boxed 'em.
Wouldn't you?

But the number that day
Was 3-2-6—
And we both was in
The *same* old fix.

I said, I swear I
Ain't gonna play no more
Till I get over
To the other shore—

Then I can play
On them golden streets
Where the number not only
Comes out—but repeats!

The runner said, Madam,
That's all very well—
But suppose
You goes to hell?


## Dimout in Harlem

Down the street young Harlem
In the dusk is walking
In the dusky dimout
Down the street is walking

Shadows veil his darkness
Shadows veiling shadows
Soft as dusk the darkness
Veiling shadows

Laughter
Then a silence
Silence
Then laughter

Shadows veiling silence
Silence veiling shadows

Silence and the shadows
Veiling Harlem's laughter

Silence
No one talking
Down the street young Harlem
In the dark

## Little Old Letter

It was yesterday morning
I looked in my box for mail.
The letter that I found there
Made me turn right pale.

Just a little old letter,
Wasn't even one page long—
But it made me wish
I was in my grave and gone.

I turned it over,
Not a word writ on the back.
I never felt so lonesome
Since I was born black.

Just a pencil and paper,
You don't need no gun nor knife—
A little old letter
Can take a person's life.

## Dear Mr. President

President Roosevelt, you
Are our Commander in Chief.
As such, I appeal
To you for relief.

Respectfully, sir,
I await your reply

As I train here to fight,
Perhaps to die.

I am a soldier
Down in Alabam
Wearing the uniform
Of Uncle Sam.

But when I get on the bus
I have to ride in the back.
Rear seats only
For a man who's black.

When I get on the train,
It's the Jim Crow car—
That don't seem to jibe
With what we're fighting for.

Mr. President, sir,
I don't understand
Democracy that
Forgets the black man.

Respectfully, therefore,
I call your attention
To these Jim Crow laws
Your speeches don't mention.

I ask why YOUR soldiers
Must ride in the back,
Segregated—
Because we are black?

I train to fight,
Perhaps to die.
Urgently, sir,
I await your reply.

## Broadcast to the West Indies

Radio Station: Harlem
Wave Length: The Human Heart

                    Hello, Jamaica!
                    Hello, Haiti!
                    Hello, Cuba!
                    Hello, Panama!
                    Hello, St. Kitts!
                    Hello, Bahamas!
          All you islands and all you lands
          That rim the sun-warmed Carribean!
          Hello! Hello! Hello! Hello!
                    I, Harlem,
                    Speak to you!

                    I, Harlem,
                    Island, too.
          In the great sea of this day's turmoil.
                    I, Harlem,
                    Little land, too,
          Bordered by the sea that washes
                    and mingles
          With all the other waters of the
                    world.

                    I, Harlem,
          Island within an island, but not
                    alone.

                    I, Harlem,
          Dark-faced, great, enormous
                    Negro city
          On Manhattan Island, New York,
                    U.S.A.

                    I, Harlem, say:
                    HELLO, WEST INDIES!
          You are dark like me,
          Colored with many bloods like me,
          Verging from the sunrise to the
                    dusk like me,
          From day to night, from black to
                    white like me.
                    HELLO! HELLO!
                    HELLO, WEST INDIES!

          They say—the Axis—
          That the U.S.A. is bad:

It lynches Negroes,
Starves them, pushes them aside.
In some states the vote is dead.
Those things are partly true.
They say—the enemy—
Via short wave every day,
That there is now no way
For you to put any faith at all
In what the Yankees say—
They have no love for you
Or any colored people anywhere.
That's also partly true.
There are people here
Who still place greed and power
Above the needs of this most
    crucial hour—
Just as with you there are those
    who place
Imperial will above the needs of
    men.
But here, as there, *their day will
    end.*
Listen, West Indies, they
Are not the U.S.A.

Certain things we know in common:
    Suffering,
    Domination,
    Segregation—
    Locally called
    Jim Crow.

In common certain things we know:
    We are tired!
    *Those things
    Must go!*

It's a long ways
From where you live to where I
    live—
But there's a direct line
From your heart to mine—
West Indies—Harlem!
Harlem—West Indies!
I like your people, your fruit,
Your sunrise and your song,

Your strength, your sense
Of right and wrong.
We care for each other—

You for me and I for you—
Because we share so much in common,
And because we are aware
Of vast explosions in the air:
        FREEDOM!
        FOR FREEDOM!
        WE PREPARE!
        Hello, West Indies!
        Hello, Jamaica!
        Hello, Haiti!
        Hello, Cuba!
        Hello, Panama!
        Hello, St. Kitts!
        Hello, Bahamas!
        Hello! Hello!
        Hello, West Indies!


## Madam and the Rent Man

The rent man knocked.
He said, Howdy-do?
I said, What
Can I do for you?
He said, You know
Your rent is due.

I said, Listen,
Before I'd pay
I'd go to Hades
And rot away!

The sink is broke,
The water don't run,
And you ain't done a thing
You promised to've done.

Back window's cracked,
Kitchen floor squeaks,

There's rats in the cellar,
And the attic leaks.

He said, Madam,
It's not up to me.
I'm just the agent,
Don't you see?

I said, Naturally,
You pass the buck.
If it's money you want
You're out of luck.

He said, Madam,
I ain't pleased!
I said, Neither am I.

So we agrees!


## Madam and the Charity Child

Once I adopted
A little girl child.
She grew up and got ruint,
Nearly drove me wild.

Then I adopted
A little boy.
He used a switch-blade
For a toy.

What makes these charity
Children so bad?
Ain't had no luck
With none I had.

Poor little things,
Born behind the 8-rock,

With parents that don't even
Stop to take stock.

The county won't pay me
But a few bucks a week.
Can't raise no child on that,
So to speak.

And the lady from the
Juvenile Court
Always coming around
Wanting a report.

Last time I told her,
Report, my eye!
Things is bad—
*You* figure out why!


## Blind


I am blind.
I cannot see.
Color is no bar to me.
I know neither
Black nor white.
I walk in night.
Yet it seems I see mankind
More tortured than the blind.
Can it be that those who know
Sight are often doomed to woe?
Or is it that, seeing,
They never see
With the infinite eyes
Of one like me?

## Shall the Good Go Down?

All over the world
Shall the good go down?

Lidice?
Were they good there?
Or did some devil come
To scourge their evil bare?

Shall the good go down?

Who makes fine speeches
Far from the ravaged town?

Spain?
Were folks good there?
Or did some god
Mete punishment
Who did not care?

Who makes fine speeches
Far from the beaten town?

Shall the good go down?

Are we good?
Did we care?
Or did we weary when they said,
Your theme wears bare?
PROPAGANDA—
Boring anywhere.

Shall the good go down?

Who are the good?
Where is their
Town?


## Crowing Hen Blues

I was setting on the hen-house steps
When the hen begin to crow.
Setting on the hen-house steps

When the hen begin to crow.
I ain't gonna set on
Them hen-house steps no mo'!

I had a cat, I called him
Battling Tom McCann.
Had a big black cat, I called him
Battling Tom McCann.
Last night that cat riz up and
Started talking like a man.

I said to Baby,
Baby, what do you hear?
I said, Baby,
What on earth do you hear?
Baby said, I don't hear nothin'
But your drunken snorin', dear.

Ummmm-mmm-m-huh! I wish that
Domineck hen wouldn't crow!
Oh-ooo-oo-o, Lawd! Nor that
Black cat talk no mo'!
But, woman, if you don't like it,
Find someplace else to sleep and snore—
Cause I'm gonna drink my licker
Till they burn the licker store.


## The Underground

(To the Anti-Fascists of the Occupied Countries of Europe and Asia.)

Still you bring us with our hands bound,
Our teeth knocked out, our heads broken,
Still you bring us shouting curses,
Or crying, or silent as tomorrow,
Still you bring us to the guillotine,
The shooting wall, the headsman's block.
Or the mass grave in the long trench.

But you can't kill all of us!
You can't silence all of us!
You can't stop all of us!
From Norway to Slovakia, Manchuria to Greece,

We are like those rivers
That fill with the melted snow in spring
And flood the land in all directions.

Our spring will come.

The pent up snows of all the brutal years
Are melting beneath the rising sun of freedom.
The rivers of the world
Will be flooded with strength
And you will be washed away—
You murderers of the people—
You Nazis, Fascists, headsmen,
Appeasers, liars, Quislings,
You will be washed away,
And the land will be fresh and clean again,
Denuded of the past—
For time will give us
Our spring
At last.


## Too Blue


I got those sad old weary blues.
I don't know where to turn.
I don't know where to go.
Nobody cares about you
When you sink so low.

What shall I do?
What shall I say?
Shall I take a gun
And put myself away?

I wonder if
One bullet would do?
As hard as my head is,
It would probably take two.

But I ain't got
Neither bullet nor gun—
And I'm too blue
To look for one.

# Beaumont to Detroit: 1943

Looky here, America
What you done done—
Let things drift
Until the riots come.

Now your policemen
Let your mobs run free.
I reckon you don't care
Nothing about me.

You tell me that hitler
Is a mighty bad man.
I guess he took lessons
From the ku klux klan.

You tell me mussolini's
Got an evil heart.
Well, it mus-a been in Beaumont
That he had his start—

Cause everything that hitler
And mussolini do,
Negroes get the same
Treatment from you.

You jim crowed me
Before hitler rose to power—
And you're STILL jim crowing me
Right now, this very hour.

Yet you say we're fighting
For democracy.
Then why don't democracy
Include me?

I ask you this question
Cause I want to know
How long I got to fight
BOTH HITLER—AND JIM CROW.

# The Ballad of Margie Polite

If Margie Polite
Had of been white
She might not've cussed
Out the cop that night.

In the lobby
Of the Braddock Hotel
She might not've felt
The urge to raise hell.

A soldier took her part.
He got shot in the back
By a white cop—
The soldier were black.

*They killed a colored soldier!*
Folks started to cry it—
The cry spread over Harlem
And turned into riot.

They taken Margie to jail
And kept her there.
DISORDERLY CONDUCT
The charges swear.

Margie warn't nobody
Important before—
But she ain't just *nobody*
Now no more.

She started the riots!
Harlemites say
August 1st is
MARGIE'S DAY.

Mark August 1st
As decreed by fate
For Margie and History
To have a date.

Mayor La Guardia
Riding up and down.
Somebody yelled,

*What about*
*Stuyvesant Town?*

Colored leaders
In sound trucks.
Somebody yelled,
*Go home, you hucks!*

*They didn't kill the soldier,*
A race leader cried.
Somebody hollered,
*Naw! But they tried!*

Margie Polite!
Margie Polite!
Kept the Mayor—
And Walter White—
And everybody
Up all night!

When the PD car
Taken Margie away—
It wasn't Mother's
Nor Father's—
It were
MARGIE'S DAY!

## Madam and the Army

They put my boy-friend
In 1-A.
But I can't figure out
How he got that way.

He wouldn't work,
Said he wasn't able.
Just drug himself
To the dinner table.

Couldn't get on relief,
Neither WPA.

He wouldn't even try
Cause he slept all day.

I nagged at him
Till I thought he was deaf—
But I never could get him
Above 4-F.

But Uncle Sam
Put him in 1-A
And now has taken
That man away.

If Uncle Sam
Makes him lift a hand,
Uncle's really
A powerful man!

## Madam and the Movies

I go to the movies
Once-twice a week.
I love romance.
That's where I'm weak.

But I never could
Understand
Why real life ain't got
No romance-man.

I pay my quarter
And for two hours
Romance reigns
And true love flowers.

Then I come home
And unlock the door—
And there ain't no
Romance any more.

## Madam and Her Madam

I worked for a woman,
She wasn't mean—
But she had a twelve-room
House to clean.

Had to get breakfast,
Dinner, and supper, too—
Then take care of her children
When I got through.

Wash, iron, and scrub,
Walk the dog around—
It was too much,
Nearly broke me down.

I said, Madam,
Can it be
You trying to make a
Pack-horse out of me?

She opened her mouth.
She cried, Oh, no!
You know, Alberta,
I love you so!

I said, Madam,
That may be true—
But I'll be dogged
If I love you!


## Stalingrad: 1942

There are the inactive ones who,
By their inaction,
Aid in the breaking of your dreams.
There are the ones
Who burn to help you,
But do not know how—
Can only fling words in the air,

Petition: Second Front,
Give money,
Beg, curse, pray,
Bitterly care.

I know—
Those who wreck your dream
Wreck my dream, too,
Reduce my heart to ashes
As they reduce you.

Stalingrad—
Never Paradise—
Just a city on the Volga
Trying peacefully to grow,
A city where some few small dreams
Men dreamt come true.
A simple city
Where all worked, all ate,
All children went to school.
No beggars,
No sick without attention,
No prostitutes,
For women had jobs
And men had wives.
People respected
Each other's lives.
Communal brotherhood,
A city growing toward the good.
Stalingrad—not Paradise—
Yet not bad.

Then out of the West the wreckers came—
Luftwaffe! Panzers! Storm Troopers!
Men with guns and an evil name: Nazis!
Invaders! Bombers! Throwers of flame!
Thieves of the common grain!

>     Did we go to help?
>         No.
>     Did the Second Front open?
>         No.
>     Did the RAF arrive?
>         No.

Did the AEF get there?
     No.
Did Stalingrad fall?
Did Stalingrad fall?
Did it fall?

Out of the rubble from a dead hand lifted —
Out of the rubble from a lost voice calling —
I gather instead another world is falling:
Lies and blunders and fear and greed
Are meagre feed for the people —
As quick as steel or *ersatz* swill, they kill.

     But no one can kill
     The dream of men
     To be men again.

Beyond the Volga —
Or some more distant stream —
Beyond the desert
Still will live the dream.
In deep hearts
Where now dismayed it lies,
Tomorrow it will rise!

This Hitler understands —
He tries so hard to kill it
Quickly in all lands —
But Stalingrad will rise again,
Rebuilt by hands around the world
That care — as we care — by hands
That grope now in the dark
And don't know why,
Or how to help — but cry
At headlines in the news that say:
STALINGRAD GIVES WAY.

Ethiopia — let it go!
(Retrieved at bloody cost.)
Czechoslovakia — let it go!
     (Lost.)
Spain — let the dogs have it!
India — freedom? The Japs?
They're puzzled at the choice.

(They wait. Too little and too late.)
The same old story—yet today?
The same old patterns—still in power
Even at this hour—as Stalingrad gives way?

Gives way? Oh, no!
Though the last walls fall,
And the last man dies,
And the last bullets go,
Stalingrad does not give way!
Fight on, brave city!
Deathless in song and story,
Yours is the final triumph!

VICTORY—your glory!

## The Black Man Speaks

I swear to the Lord
I still can't see
Why Democracy means
Everybody but me.

I swear to my soul
I can't understand
Why Freedom don't apply
To the black man.

I swear, by gum,
I really don't know
Why in the name of Liberty
You treat me so.

Down South you make me ride
In a Jim Crow car.
From Los Angeles to London
You spread your color bar.

Jim Crow Army,
And Navy, too—

Is Jim Crow Freedom the best
I can expect from you?

I simply raise these questions
Cause I want you to state
What kind of a world
We're fighting to create.

If we're fighting to create
A free world tomorrow,
Why not end *right now*
Old Jim Crow's sorrow?

## Freedom [1]

Freedom will not come
Today, this year
    Nor ever
Through compromise and fear.

I have as much right
As the other fellow has
    To stand
On my two feet
And own land.

I tire so of hearing people say,
*Let things take their course.*
*Tomorrow is another day.*
I do not need freedom when I'm dead.
I cannot live on tomorrow's bread.
    Freedom
    Is a strong seed
    Planted
    In a great need.
    I live here, too.
    I want freedom
    Just as you.

## Color

Wear it
Like a banner
For the proud—
Not like a shroud.
Wear it
Like a song
Soaring high—
Not moan or cry.

## Freedom [2]

Some folks think
By burning books
They burn Freedom.

Some folks think
By imprisoning Nehru
They imprison Freedom.

Some folks think
By lynching a Negro
They lynch Freedom.

But Freedom
Stands up and laughs
In their faces
And says,

*You'll never kill me!*

## Red Cross

The Angel of Mercy's
Got her wings in the mud,
And all because of
Negro blood.

## Note to All Nazis Fascists and Klansmen

You delight,
So it would seem,
At making mince-meat
Of my dream.

If you keep on,
Before you're through,
I'll make mince-meat
Out of you.


## How About It, Dixie

The President's Four Freedoms
Appeal to me.
I would like to see those Freedoms
Come to be.

If you believe
In the Four Freedoms, too,
Then share 'em with me—
Don't keep 'em all for you.

Show me that you mean
Democracy, please—
Cause from Bombay to Georgia
I'm beat to my knees.

You can't lock up Gandhi,
Club Roland Hayes,
Then make fine speeches
About Freedom's ways.

Looks like by now
Folks ought to know
It's hard to beat Hitler
Protecting Jim Crow.

Freedom's not just
To be won Over There.
It means Freedom at home, too—
Now—*right here!*

## Blue Bayou

I went walkin'
By the blue bayou
And I saw the sun go down.
I thought about old Greeley
And I thought about Lou
And I saw the sun go down.

White man
Makes me work all day
And I work too hard
For too little pay—
Then a white man
Takes my woman away.

I'll kill old Greeley.

The blue bayou
Turns red as fire.
*Put the black man*
*On a rope*
*And pull him higher!*

I saw the sun go down.

*Put him on a rope*
*And pull him higher!*

The blue bayou's
A pool of fire.
And I saw the sun go down,
Down,
    Down,
Lawd I saw the sun go down!


## Motherland

Dream of yesterday
And far-off long tomorrow:
Africa imprisoned
In her bitter sorrow.

# To Captain Mulzac
(Negro Skipper of the Booker T. Washington Sailing with a Mixed Crew)

Dangerous
Are the western waters now,
And all the waters of the world.
Somehow,
Again mankind has lost its course,
Been driven off its way,
Down paths of death and darkness
Gone astray—
But there are those who still hold out
A chart and compass
For a better way—
And there are those who fight
To guard the harbor entrance
To a brighter day.

There are those, too, who for so long
Could not call their house, *their* house.
Nor their land, *their* land—
Formerly the beaten and the poor
Who did not own
The things they made, nor their own lives—
But stood, individual and alone,
Without power—
They have found their hour.
The clock is moving forward here—
But backward in the lands where Fascist fear
Has taken hold,
And tyranny again is bold.

Yes, dangerous are the wide world's waters still,
Menaced by the will
Of those who would keep, or once more make
Slaves of men.
We Negroes have been slaves before.
We will *not* be again.
Alone, I know, no one is free.
But we have joined hands—
Black workers with white workers—
I, with you! You, with me!
Together we have launched a ship
That sails these dangerous seas—
But more than ship,
Our symbol of new liberties.
We've put a captain on that ship's bridge there,
A man, spare, swarthy, strong, foursquare—

But more than these,
He, too, a symbol of new liberties.

There is a crew of many races, too,
Many bloods—yet all of one blood still:
The blood of brotherhood,
Of courage, of good-will,
And deep determination geared to kill
The evil forces that would destroy
Our charts, our compass and bell-buoy
That guide us toward the harbor of the new world
We will to make—
The world where every ugly past mistake
Of hate and greed and race
Will have no place.

In union, you, White Man,
And I, Black Man,
Can be free.
More than ship then,
Captain Mulzac,
Is the BOOKER T.,
And more than captain
You who guide it on its way.
Your ship is mankind's deepest dream
Daring the sea—
Your ship is flagship
Of a newer day.

Let the winds rise then!
Let the great waves beat!
Your ship is Victory,
And not defeat.
Let the great waves rise
And the winds blow free!
        Your ship is
        Freedom,
        Brotherhood,
        Democracy!

# Still Here

I've been scared and battered.
My hopes the wind done scattered.
Snow has friz me, sun has baked me.
    Looks like between 'em
    They done tried to make me
Stop laughin', stop lovin', stop livin'—
    But I don't care!
    I'm still here!

# Ballad of Sam Solomon

Sam Solomon said,
You may call out the Klan
But you must've forgot
That a Negro is a MAN.
It was down in Miami
A few years ago.
Negroes never voted but
Sam said, It's time to go
To the polls election day
And make your choice known
Cause the vote is not restricted
To white folks alone.
The fact we never voted
In the past
Is something that surely
Ain't due to last.
Sam Solomon called on
Every colored man
To qualify and register
And take a stand
And be up and out and ready
On election day
To vote at the polls,
Come what may.
The crackers said, Sam,
If you carry this through,
Ain't no telling what
We'll do to you.
Sam Solomon answered,
I don't pay you no mind.
The crackers said, Boy,

Are you deaf, dumb, and blind?
Sam Solomon said, I'm
Neither one nor the other—
But we intend to vote
On election day, brother.
The crackers said, Sam,
Are you a fool or a dunce?
Sam Solomon said, A MAN
Can't die but once.
They called out the Klan.
They had a parade.
But Sam Solomon
Was not afraid.
On election day
He led his colored delegation
To take their rightful part
In the voting of a nation.
The crackers thought
The Ku Klux was tough—
But the Negroes in Miami
Called their bluff.
Sam Solomon said,
Go *get* out your Klan—
But you must've forgotten
A Negro is a MAN.


## Me and My Song


Black
As the gentle night
Black
As the kind and quiet night
Black
As the deep productive earth
Body
Out of Africa
Strong and black
As iron
First smelted in
Africa
Song
Out of Africa
Deep and mellow song

Rich
As the black earth
Strong
As black iron
Kind
As the black night
My song
From the dark lips
Of Africa
Deep
As the rich earth
Beautiful
As the black night
Strong
As the first iron
Black
Out of Africa
Me and my
Song

## Good Morning, Stalingrad

Goodmorning, Stalingrad!
Lots of folks who don't like you
Had give you up for dead.
But you ain't dead!

Goodmorning, Stalingrad!
Where I live down in Dixie
Things is bad—
But they're not so bad
I still can't say,
Goodmorning, Stalingrad!
And I'm not so dumb
I still don't know
That as long as your red star
Lights the sky,
We won't die.

Goodmorning, Stalingrad!
You're half a world away or more
But when your guns roar,
They roar for me—

And for everybody
Who want to be free.

Goodmorning, Stalingrad!
Some folks try to tell me down this way
That you're our ally just for today.
That may be so—for those who want it so.
But as for me—you're my ally
Until we *all* are free.

Goodmorning, Stalingrad!
When crooks and klansmen
Lift their heads and things is bad,
I can look way across the sea
And see where simple working folks like me
Lift their heads, too, with gun in hand
To drive the fascists from the land.
You've stood between us well,
Stalingrad!
The folks who hate you'd
Done give you up for dead—
They were glad.

*But you ain't dead!*

And you won't be
As long as I am you
And you are me—
For you have allies everywhere,
All over the world, who care.
And they
Are with you more
Than just today.

Listen! I don't own no radio—
Can't send no messages through the air.
But I reckon you can hear me,
Anyhow, away off there.
And I know you know
I mean it when I say,
(Maybe in a whisper
To keep the Klan away)
Goodmorning, Stalingrad!
  I'm glad
  You ain't dead!

GOODMORNING, STALINGRAD!

# Jim Crow's Last Stand

There was an old Crow by the name of Jim.
The Crackers were in love with him.
They liked him so well they couldn't stand
To see Jim Crow get out of hand.
But something happened, Jim's feathers fell.
Now that Crow's begun to look like hell.

DECEMBER 7, 1941:

Pearl Harbor put Jim Crow on the run.
That Crow can't fight for Democracy
And be the same old Crow he used to be —
Although right now, even yet today,
He still tries to act in the same old way.
But India and China and Harlem, too,
Have made up their minds Jim Crow is through.
Nehru said, before he went to jail,
Catch that Jim Crow bird, pull the feathers out his tail!
Marian Anderson said to the DAR,
I'll sing for you — but drop that color bar.
Paul Robeson said, out in Kansas City,
To Jim Crow my people is a pity.
Mrs. Bethune told Martin Dies,
You ain't telling nothing but your Jim Crow lies —
If you want to get old Hitler's goat,
Abolish poll tax so folks can vote.
Joe Louis said, We gonna win this war
Cause the good Lord knows what *we're* fighting for!

DECEMBER 7, 1941:

When Dorie Miller took gun in hand —
Jim Crow started his last stand.
Our battle yet is far from won
But when it is, Jim Crow'll be done.
We gonna bury that son-of-a-gun!

# Salute to Soviet Armies

Mighty Soviet armies marching on the West,
Red star on your visor, courage on your breast!
Mighty Soviet armies, warriors brave and strong,

Freedom is your watchword as you forge along!
The eyes of all the people, poor upon the earth,
Follow your great battle for mankind's rebirth.
Mighty Soviet armies, allies, comrades, friends,
We will march beside you until fascism ends.

Mighty Soviet armies, guard your fatherland!
The earth of your union warms the hope of man.
Fascist foes surround you with their ring of steel,
But your warriors crush them with a workman's heel.
Never will the people let them rise again.
Death to the fascist tyrants! Death to the Nazi's reign!
Mighty Soviet armies, allies of the free,
We will fight beside you until victory!
Mighty Soviet armies, now as one we stand,
Allies all together for the cause of man!
Salute to the Soviet armies—from our land!

## Poem for an Intellectual on the Way Up to Submit to His Lady

Do not call me Dr.
If I get a Ph.D.
Just keep on calling me *Sweetie*
Cause that is good to me.

Do not call me Rev.
If I go into the church.
Address me, *Loving Daddy*,
And my heart will give a lurch.

Don't dare call me Hon.
If I get to be a judge.
Simply call me *Honey Bunch*,
I'll call you *Sugar Fudge*.

I don't believe in titles
When it comes to love,
So, please, do not call me Dr.—
Just call me *Turtle Dove*.

## Madam's Past History

My name is Johnson—
Madam Alberta K.
The Madam stands for business.
I'm smart that way.

I had a
HAIR-DRESSING PARLOR
Before
The depression put
The prices lower.

Then I had a
BARBECUE STAND
Till I got mixed up
With a no-good man.

Cause I had a insurance
The WPA
Said, We can't use you
Wealthy that way.

I said,
DON'T WORRY 'BOUT ME!
Just like the song,
You WPA folks take care of yourself—
And I'll get along.

I do cooking,
Day's work, too!
Alberta K. Johnson—
*Madam* to you.

## Madam's Calling Cards

I had some cards printed
The other day.
They cost me more
Than I wanted to pay.

I told the man
I wasn't no mint,

But I hankered to see
My name in print.

MADAM JOHNSON,
ALBERTA K.
He said, Your name looks good
Madam'd that way.

Shall I use Old English
Or a Roman letter?
I said, Use American.
American's better.

There's nothing foreign
To my pedigree:
Alberta K. Johnson—
*American* that's me.


## Uncle Tom  [1]


Uncle Tom is a legend and a dream.
Uncle Tom is a groan and a scream.
Uncle Tom is a lash on the back.
Uncle Tom is a man who's black.
     But Uncle Tom
     Was long ago.
     Gone is the lash
     And the slaver's blow.
     Ours is the freedom
     Tom did not know—
So tend your freedom that the lash and the pain
And his head bowed down be not in vain.
Tend your freedom that tomorrow may see
Uncle Tom's children wholly free!

# Will V-Day Be Me-Day Too?

(A Negro Fighting Man's Letter to America)

                                        Over There,
                                        World War II.

Dear Fellow Americans,
I write this letter
Hoping times will be better
When this war
Is through.
I'm a Tan-skinned Yank
Driving a tank.
I ask, WILL V-DAY
BE ME-DAY, TOO?

I wear a U.S. uniform.
I've done the enemy much harm,
I've driven back
The Germans and the Japs,
From Burma to the Rhine.
On every battle line,
I've dropped defeat
Into the Fascists' laps.

I am a Negro American
Out to defend my land
Army, Navy, Air Corps—
I am there.
I take munitions through,
I fight—or stevedore, too.
I face death the same as you do
Everywhere.

I've seen my buddy lying
Where he fell.
I've watched him dying
I promised him that I would try
To make our land a land
Where his son could be a man—
And there'd be no Jim Crow birds
Left in our sky.

So this is what I want to know:
When we see Victory's glow,
Will you still let old Jim Crow
Hold me back?
When all those foreign folks who've waited—

Italians, Chinese, Danes—are liberated.
Will I still be ill-fated
Because I'm black?

Here in my own, my native land,
Will the Jim Crow laws still stand?
Will Dixie lynch me still
When I return?
Or will you comrades in arms
From the factories and the farms,
Have learned what this war
Was fought for us to learn?

When I take off my uniform,
Will I be safe from harm—
Or will you do me
As the Germans did the Jews?
When I've helped this world to save,
Shall I still be color's slave?
Or will Victory change
Your antiquated views?

You can't say I didn't fight
To smash the Fascists' might.
You can't say I wasn't with you
In each battle.
As a soldier, and a friend.
When this war comes to an end,
Will you herd me in a Jim Crow car
Like cattle?

Or will you stand up like a man
At home and take your stand
For Democracy?
That's all I ask of you.
When we lay the guns away
To celebrate
Our Victory Day
WILL V-DAY BE ME-DAY, TOO?
That's what I want to know.

                        Sincerely,
                           GI Joe.

## Ennui

It's such a
Bore
Being always
Poor.

## Breath of a Rose

Love is like dew
On lilacs at dawn:
Comes the swift sun
And the dew is gone.

Love is like star-light
In the sky at morn:
Star-light that dies
When day is born.

Love is like perfume
In the heart of a rose:
The flower withers,
The perfume goes —

Love is no more
Than the breath of a rose,
No more
Than the breath of a rose.

## Silhouette

Southern gentle lady,
Do not swoon.
They've just hung a black man
In the dark of the moon.

They've hung a black man
To a roadside tree
In the dark of the moon

For the world to see
How Dixie protects
Its white womanhood.

Southern gentle lady,
 Be good!
 Be good!

## Moonlight in Valencia: Civil War

Moonlight in Valencia:
The moon meant planes.
The planes meant death.
And not heroic death.
Like death on a poster:
An officer in a pretty uniform
Or a nurse in a clean white dress—
But death with steel in your brain,
Powder burns on your face,
Blood spilling from your entrails,
And you didn't laugh
Because there was no laughter in it.
You didn't cry PROPAGANDA either.
The propaganda was too much
For everybody concerned.
It hurt you to your guts.
It was real
As anything you ever saw
In the movies:
Moonlight. . . .
*Me caigo en la ostia!*
Bombers over
Valencia.

# Madam and the Minister

Reverend Butler came by
My house last week.
He said, Have you got
A little time to speak?

He said, I am interested
In your soul.
Has it been saved,
Or is your heart stone-cold?

I said, Reverend,
I'll have you know
I was baptized
Long ago.

He said, What have you
Done since then?
I said, None of your
Business, friend.

He said, Sister
Have you back-slid?
I said, It felt good—
If I did!

He said, Sister,
Come time to die,
The Lord will surely
Ask you why!
I'm gonna pray
For you!
Goodbye!

I felt kinder sorry
I talked that way
After Rev. Butler
Went away—
So I ain't in no mood
For sin today.

## Madam and the Wrong Visitor

A man knocked three times.
I never seen him before.
He said, Are you Madam?
I said, What's the score?

He said, I reckon
You don't know my name,
But I've come to call
On you just the same.

I stepped back
Like he had a charm.
He said, I really
Don't mean no harm.

I'm just Old Death
And I thought I might
Pay you a visit
Before night.

He said, You're Johnson—
Madam Alberta K.?
I said, Yes—but *Alberta*
Ain't goin' with you today!

No sooner had I told him
Than I awoke.
The doctor said, Madam,
Your fever's broke—

Nurse, put her on a diet,
And buy her some chicken.
I said, Better buy *two*—
Cause I'm still here kickin'!

## Madam and the Newsboy

Newsboy knocks,
I buy the DEFENDER.
These colored papers
Is a solid sender.

I read all about
The murdering news,

And who killed who
With the love sick blues.

Then I read
The lynchings and such,
Come to the conclusion
White folks ain't much.

Then I turn over
And read the scandal
In the gossip column,
Initials for a handle.

Then the pictures:
Marva looks well—
But if Joe was my husband,
I'd also look swell.

It's just a matter
Of Who is Who—
If I was Marva I'd be
In the papers, too.
Wouldn't you?

## Madam and Her Might-Have-Been

I had two husbands.
I could of had three—
But my Might-Have-Been
Was too good for me.

When you grow up the hard way
Sometimes you don't know
What's too good to be true,
Just might be so.

He worked all the time,
Spent his money on me—
First time in my life
I had anything free.

I said, Do you love me?
Or am I mistaken?

You're always giving
And never taking.

He said, Madam, I swear
All I want is you.
Right then and there
I knowed we was through!

I told him, Jackson,
You better leave —
You got some'n else
Up your sleeve:

When you think you got bread
It's always a stone —
Nobody loves nobody
For yourself alone.

He said, In me
You've got no trust.
I said, I don't want
My heart to bust.

## Madam and the Insurance Man

Insurance man,
I heard his knock.
But he couldn't get in
Cause my door was locked.

Week ago Tuesday
He came back agin.
This time, I thought,
I'll let him in.

Insurance man said,
It's paying time.
Madam, you are
Six weeks behind.

I said, Mister,
Just let it slumber.
I'll pay in full
When I hit the number.

Insurance man said,
Suppose you die—
Who would bury you?
I said, WHY?

## I Dream a World

I dream a world where man
No other man will scorn,
Where love will bless the earth
And peace its paths adorn.
I dream a world where all
Will know sweet freedom's way,
Where greed no longer saps the soul
Nor avarice blights our day.
A world I dream where black or white,
Whatever race you be,
Will share the bounties of the earth
And every man is free,
Where wretchedness will hang its head
And joy, like a pearl,
Attends the needs of all mankind—
Of such I dream, my world!

## The Heart of Harlem

The buildings in Harlem are brick and stone
And the streets are long and wide,
But Harlem's much more than these alone,
Harlem is what's inside—
It's a song with a minor refrain,

It's a dream you keep dreaming again.
It's a tear you turn into a smile.
It's the sunrise you know is coming after a while.
It's the shoes that you get half-soled twice.
It's the kid you hope will grow up nice.
It's the hand that's working all day long.
It's a prayer that keeps you going along—
     That's the Heart of Harlem!

It's Joe Louis and Dr. W. E. B.,
A stevedore, a porter, Marian Anderson, and me.
It's Father Divine and the music of Earl Hines,
Adam Powell in Congress, our drivers on bus lines.
It's Dorothy Maynor and it's Billie Holiday,
The lectures at the Schomburg and the Apollo down
     the way.
It's Father Shelton Bishop and shouting Mother Horne.
It's the Rennie and the Savoy where new dances are
     born.
It's Canada Lee's penthouse at Five-Fifty-Five.
It's Small's Paradise and Jimmy's little dive.
It's 409 Edgecombe or a cold-water walk-up flat—
But it's where I live and it's where my love is at
     Deep in the Heart of Harlem!

It's the pride all Americans know.
It's the faith God gave us long ago.
It's the strength to make our dreams come true.
It's a feeling warm and friendly given to you.
It's that girl with the rhythmical walk.
It's my boy with the jive in his talk.
It's the man with the muscles of steel.
It's the right to be free a people never will yield.
A dream . . . a song . . . half-soled shoes . . . dancing shoes
A tear . . . a smile . . . the blues . . . sometimes the
     blues
Mixed with the memory . . . and forgiveness . . . of our
     wrong.
But more than that, it's freedom—
Guarded for the kids who came along—
     Folks, that's the Heart of Harlem!

## Little Green Tree

It looks like to me
My good-time days done past.
Nothin' in this world
Is due to last.

I used to play
And I played so dog-gone hard.
Now old age has
Dealt my bad-luck card.

I look down the road
And I see a little tree.
A little piece down the road.
I see a little tree.

Them cool green leaves
Is waitin' to shelter me.

O, *little tree!*


## Give Us Our Peace

Give us a peace equal to the war
Or else our souls will be unsatisfied,
And we will wonder what we have fought for
And why the many died.

Give us a peace accepting every challenge—
The challenge of the poor, the black, of all denied,
The challenge of the vast colonial world
That long has had so little justice by its side.

Give us a peace that dares us to be wise.
Give us a peace that dares us to be strong.
Give us a peace that dares us still uphold
Throughout the peace our battle against wrong.

Give us a peace that is not cheaply used,
A peace that is no clever scheme,
A people's peace for which men can enthuse,
A peace that brings reality to our dream.

Give us a peace that will produce great schools—
As the war produced great armament,

A peace that will wipe out our slums—
As war wiped out our foes on evil bent.

Give us a peace that will enlist
A mighty army serving human kind,
Not just an army geared to kill,
But trained to help the living mind.

An army trained to shape our common good
And bring about a world of brotherhood.


## Lonesome Corner

I went down to the corner.
I stood there feelin' blue—
I used to go *round* the corner,
Babe, and call on you.

Old lonesome corner!
People pass by me—
But none of them peoples
Is who I want to see.


## Harlem Night

Harlem
Knows a song
Without a tune—
The rhythm's there:
But the melody's
Bare.

Harlem
Knows a night
Without a moon.
The stars
Are where?

# Graduation

Cinnamon and rayon,
Jet and coconut eyes,
Mary Lulu Jackson
Smooths the skirt
At her thighs.

Mama, portly oven,
Brings remainders from the kitchen
Where the people all are icebergs
Wrapped in checks and wealthy.

𝕯𝖎𝖕𝖑𝖔𝖒𝖆 in its new frame:
Mary Lulu Jackson,
Eating chicken,
Tells her mama she's a typist
And the clicking of the keys
Will spell the name
Of a job in a fine office
Far removed from basic oven,
Cookstoves,
And iceberg's kitchen.

Mama says, *Praise Jesus!*
*Until then*
*I'll bring home chicken!*

The 𝕯𝖎𝖕𝖑𝖔𝖒𝖆 bursts its frame
To scatter star-dust in their eyes.

Mama says, *Praise Jesus!*
*The colored race will rise!*

Mama says,
*Praise Jesus!*

Then,
Because she's tired,
She sighs.

# Peace Conference in an American Town

At the back fence calling,
    Mrs. Jones!
At the back fence calling,
    Mrs. Greene!
At the back fence calling,
    Mrs. Brown!
    My blueberry pie's
    the best in town.

At the back fence calling,
    Johnny Jones!
At the back fence calling,
    Kenny Greene!
At the back fence calling,
    Buddy Brown!
    Come on, let's
    bat a ball around.

At the back fence calling,
    Neighbor! Neighbor!
At the back fence calling,
    Neighbor! Friend!
At the back fence calling,
    Neighbor! When
    is all this trouble
    gonna end?

At the back fence calling
    Colored, White.
At the back fence calling
    Gentile, Jew.
At the back fence calling
    Neighbor!

At the back fence calling
    You!

# Labor Storm

Now it is time
For the strike-breakers to come out:
The boys with the shifting eyes,
The morons,
The discriminated ones
Too bitter to understand,
The goons,
The gangsters of defeat and death,
The strong-armed mercenaries
With the alley breath.

Now it is time for the worms
To come out of their holes,
And the little snakes
Who wrap themselves around
The big snakes,
Time for the white bellied things
To bare their atavistic fangs
For dollars and gray shame.

Man knows well
The use of man against men,
The greedy few
Against the needy many,
The decayed against the healthy,
The snakes
Against the runners in the sun.

Too often in the past
The snakes have won.

Time now that men awake
To their old past mistake
Of trust in snakes
Who wear a tailored skin—
But when in trouble
Call less stylish vipers in,
Moccasins that strike
The unprotected heel of hunger
Without shame—
Since no great respected firm
Bears that anonymous name:

STRIKEBREAKER—
At least, not on the door.

The storm
That calls up varmints
From the earth
Is coming.

Workers beware!
It's almost
Here!

## Lenin

Lenin walks around the world.
Frontiers cannot bar him.
Neither barracks nor barricades impede.
Nor does barbed wire scar him.

Lenin walks around the world.
Black, brown, and white receive him.
Language is no barrier.
The strangest tongues believe him.

Lenin walks around the world.
The sun sets like a scar.
Between the darkness and the dawn
There rises a red star.

## First of May

I believe it to be true,
You see,
Tomorrow
Now belongs to me—
And so
Let not too many tears

Water these unhappy years.
Being poor and black today,
I await
My first of May.


## Conservatory Student Struggles with Higher Instrumentation

The saxophone
Has a vulgar tone.
I wish it would
Let me alone.

The saxophone
Is ordinary.
More than that,
It's mercenary!

The saxophone's
An instrument
By which I wish
I'd never been
Sent!


## Comment

Spiral Death
The snake must be—
Yet he's never
Murdered me.

Fanged death
The tiger, too—
But has he ever
Murdered you?

More dangerous death
Man indeed

Who often kills
When there's no need.

For man will kill
Animal—or you—
For strife, for sport,
Or just a stew.


## Summer Evening (Calumet Avenue)


Mothers pass,
Sweet watermelon in a baby carriage,
Black seed for eyes
And a rose pink mouth.
Pimps in gray go by,
Boots polished like a Murray head,
Or in reverse
Madam Walker
On their shoe tips.
I. W. Harper
Stops to listen to gospel songs
From a tent at the corner
Where the carnival is Christian.
Jitneys go by
Full of chine bones in dark glasses,
And a blind man plays an accordion
Gurgling *Jericho.*

Theresa Belle Aletha
Throws a toothpick from her window,
And the four bells she's awaiting
Do not ring, not even murmur.
But maybe before midnight
The tamale man will come by,
And if Uncle Mac brings beer
Night will pull its slack taut
And wrap a string around its finger
So as not to forget
That tomorrow is Monday.

*A dime on those two bottles.*
*Yes, they are yours,*
*Too!*

And in another week
It will again
Be Sunday.

## Yesterday and Today

O, I wish that yesterday,
Yesterday was today!
Yesterday you was here.
Today you gone away.

I miss you, Lulu,
I miss you so bad—
There ain't no way for me
To get you out of my head.

Yesterday I was happy.
I thought you was happy, too.
I don't know how you feel today—
But, baby, I feel blue.

## Blues on a Box

Play your guitar, boy,
Till yesterday's
Black cat
Runs out tomorrow's
Back door
And evil old
Hard luck
Ain't no more!

# Who but the Lord?

I looked and I saw
That man they call the Law.
He was coming
Down the street at me!
I had visions in my head
Of being laid out cold and dead,
Or else murdered
By the third degree.

I said, O, *Lord, if you can,*
*Save me from that man!*
*Don't let him make a pulp out of me!*
But the Lord he was not quick.
The Law raised up his stick
And beat the living hell
Out of me!

Now I do not understand
Why God don't protect a man
From police brutality.
Being poor and black,
I've no weapon to strike back
So who but the Lord
Can protect me?

*We'll see.*


# Seashore Through Dark Glasses (Atlantic City)

Beige sailors with large noses
Binocular the Atlantic.

At Club Harlem it's eleven
And seven cats go frantic.
Two parties from Philadelphia
Dignify the place
And murmur:

*Such Negroes*
*disgrace the race!*

On Artic Avenue
Sea food joints
Scent salty-colored
Compass points.


## Birth

Oh, fields of wonder
Out of which
Stars are born,
And moon and sun
And me as well,
Like stroke
Of lightning
In the night
Some mark
To make
Some word
To tell.


## Freedom Train

I read in the papers about the
     Freedom Train.
I heard on the radio about the
     Freedom Train.
I seen folks talkin' about the
     Freedom Train.
Lord, I been a-waitin' for the
     Freedom Train!

Down South in Dixie only train I see's
Got a Jim Crow car set aside for me.
I hope there ain't no Jim Crow on the Freedom Train,
No back door entrance to the Freedom Train,

No signs FOR COLORED on the Freedom Train,
No WHITE FOLKS ONLY on the Freedom Train.

    I'm gonna check up on this
        Freedom Train.

Who's the engineer on the Freedom Train?
Can a coal black man drive the Freedom Train?
Or am I still a porter on the Freedom Train?
Is there ballot boxes on the Freedom Train?
When it stops in Mississippi will it be made plain
Everybody's got a right to board the Freedom Train?

    Somebody tell me about this
        Freedom Train!

The Birmingham station's marked COLORED and WHITE.
The white folks go left, the colored go right—
They even got a segregated lane.
Is that the way to get aboard the Freedom Train?

    I got to know about this
        Freedom Train!

If my children ask me, *Daddy, please explain*
*Why there's Jim Crow stations for the Freedom Train?*
What shall I tell my children? . . . *You* tell me—
'Cause freedom ain't freedom when a man ain't free.

    But maybe they explains it on the
        Freedom Train.

When my grandmother in Atlanta, 83 and black,
Gets in line to see the Freedom,
Will some white man yell, *Get back!*
*A Negro's got no business on the Freedom Track!*

    Mister, I thought it were the
        Freedom Train!

Her grandson's name was Jimmy. He died at Anzio.
He died for real. It warn't no show.
The freedom that they carryin' on this Freedom Train,
Is it for real—or just a show again?

Jimmy wants to know about the
    Freedom Train.

Will *his* Freedom Train come zoomin' down the track
Gleamin' in the sunlight for white and black?
Not stoppin' at no stations marked COLORED nor WHITE,
Just stoppin' in the fields in the broad daylight,
Stoppin' in the country in the wide-open air
Where there never was no Jim Crow signs nowhere,
No Welcomin' Committees, nor politicians of note,
No Mayors and such for which colored can't vote,
And nary a sign of a color line—
For the Freedom Train will be yours and mine!

Then maybe from their graves in Anzio
The G.I.'s who fought will say, *We wanted it so!*
Black men and white will say, *Ain't it fine?*
*At home they got a train that's yours and mine!*

    Then I'll shout, *Glory for the*
        *Freedom Train!*
    I'll holler, *Blow your whistle,*
        *Freedom Train!*
    *Thank God-A-Mighty! Here's the*
        *Freedom Train!*
    *Get on board our Freedom Train!*

## Border Line

I used to wonder
About living and dying—
I think the difference lies
Between tears and crying.

I used to wonder
About here and there—
I think the distance
Is nowhere.

## Night: Four Songs

Night of the two moons
And the seventeen stars,
Night of the day before yesterday
And the day after tomorrow,
Night of the four songs unsung:
    Sorrow! Sorrow!
    Sorrow! Sorrow!

## Burden

It is not weariness
That bows me down,
But sudden nearness
To song without sound.

## Beale Street

The dream is vague
And all confused
With dice and women
And jazz and booze.

The dream is vague,
Without a name,
Yet warm and wavering
And sharp as flame.

The loss
Of the dream
Leaves nothing
The same.

# Circles

The circles spin round
And the circles spin round
And meet their own tail.

Seasons come, seasons go,
The years build their bars
Till we're in jail.

Like a squirrel in a cage—
For the jail is round—
We sometimes find
Ourselves upside down.

# Grave Yard

Here is that sleeping place,
Long resting place,
No stretching place,
That never-get-up-no-more
        Place
        Is here.

# Montmartre

Pigalle:
A neon rose
In a champagne bottle.
At dawn
The petals
Fall.

## Fragments

Whispers
Of springtime.

Death in the night.

A song
With too many
Tunes.

## Desert

Anybody
Better than
Nobody.

In the barren dusk
Even the snake
That spirals
Terror on the sand—

Better than nobody
In this lonely
Land.

## End

There are
No clocks on the wall,
And no time,
No shadows that move
From dawn to dusk
Across the floor.

There is neither light
Nor dark
Outside the door.

*There is no door!*

# Heart

Pierrot
Took his heart
And hung it
On a wayside wall.

He said,
"Look, Passers-by,
Here is my heart!"

But no one was curious.
No one cared at all
That there hung
Pierrot's heart
On the public wall.

So Pierrot
Took his heart
And hid it
Far away.

Now people wonder
Where his heart is
Today.

# Remembrance

To wander through this living world
And leave uncut the roses
Is to remember fragrance where
The flower no scent encloses.

## Fulfillment

The earth-meaning
Like the sky-meaning
Was fulfilled.

We got up
And went to the river,
Touched silver water,
Laughed and bathed
In the sunshine.

Day
Became a bright ball of light
For us to play with,
Sunset
A yellow curtain,
Night
A velvet screen.

The moon,
Like an old grandmother,
Blessed us with a kiss
And sleep
Took us both in
Laughing.

## Night Song

In the dark
Before the tall
Moon came,
Little short
Dusk
Was walking
Along.

In the dark
Before the tall
Moon came,
Little short
Dusk

Was singing
A song.

In the dark
Before the tall
Moon came,
A lady named
Day
Fainted away
In the
Dark.

## Carolina Cabin

There's hanging moss
And holly
And tall straight pine
About this little cabin
In the wood.

Inside
A crackling fire,
Warm red wine,
And youth and life
And laughter
That is good.

Outside
The world is gloomy,
The winds of winter cold,
As down the road
A wandering poet
Must roam.

But here there's peace
And laughter
And love's old story told—
Where two people
Make a home.

## Songs

I sat there singing her
Songs in the dark.

She said,
*I do not understand*
*The words.*

I said,
*There are*
*No words.*

## Sleep

When the lips
And the body
Are done
She seeks your hand,
Touches it,
And sleep comes,
Without wonder
And without dreams,
When the lips
And the body
Are done.

## Juliet

Wonder
And pain
And terror,
And sick silly songs
Of sorrow,
And the marrow
Of the bone
Of life
Are smeared across
Her mouth.

The road
From Verona
To Mantova
Is dusty
With the drought.

## Man

I was a boy then.
I did not understand—
I thought that friendship lay
In the grip of hand to hand.
I thought that love must be
Her body close to mine.
I thought that drunkenness
Was real—
In wine.

But I was a boy then,
I didn't understand
The things a young lad
Learns so soon
When he's
A man.

## Luck

Sometimes a crumb falls
From the tables of joy,
Sometimes a bone
Is flung.

To some people
Love is given,
To others
Only heaven.

## Chippy

Rose of neon darkness,
Rose of the sharp-thorned stem
And the rouge-bright petals,
Rose of nothing but yesterdays
Too bitter to remember—
Little dollar rose
Of the bar stools
Facing a two-bit
December.

## Dancers

Stealing from the night
A few
Desperate hours
Of pleasure.

Stealing from death
A few
Desperate days
Of life.

## Grief

Eyes
That are frozen
From not crying.

Heart
That knows
No way of dying.

## Old Sailor

He has been
Many places
In ships
That cross the sea,
Has studied varied faces,
Has tasted mystery,
In Oriental cities
Has breasted
Monstrous pities
And to all
Fleshly pleasures
Known the key.
Now,
Paralyzed,
He suns himself
In charity's poor chair—
And dreams
That women he has left
Lament him
Everywhere.

## Faithful One

Though I go drunken
To her door,
I'm ever so sure
She'll let me in.

Though I wander and stray
And wound her sore,
She'll open the latch
When I come again.

No matter what
I do or say,
She waits for me
At the end of day.

## Dream Dust

Gather out of star-dust,
    Earth-dust,
    Cloud-dust,
    Storm-dust,
And splinters of hail,
One handful of dream-dust
    Not for sale.


## Little Song

Lonely people
In the lonely night
Grab a lonely dream
And hold it tight.

Lonely people
In the lonely day
Work to salt
Their dream away.


## Jaime

He sits on a hill
And beats a drum
For the great earth spirits
That never come.

He sits on a hill
Looking out to sea
Toward a mirage-land
That will never be.

## Sailing Date

Twisted and strange
Their lives
With bitter range
From salt sea water
To a whiskey shore.

On sailing date,
Old seamen
Who've weathered
A thousand storms,
Two wars
And submarines
From here to there,
Go up the gangplank
To the Nevermore—
Perhaps—
Or just another
Trip.

Why care?
It's sailing date.
Their captain's
There.

## There

Where death
Stretches its wide horizons
And the sun gallops no more
Across the sky,
There where nothing
Is all,
I,
Who am nobody,
Will become Infinity,
Even perhaps
Divinity.

# Trumpet Player

The Negro
With the trumpet at his lips
Has dark moons of weariness
Beneath his eyes
Where the smoldering memory
Of slave ships
Blazed to the crack of whips
About his thighs.

The Negro
With the trumpet at his lips
Has a head of vibrant hair
Tamed down,
Patent-leathered now
Until it gleams
Like jet—
Were jet a crown.

The music
From the trumpet at his lips
Is honey
Mixed with liquid fire.
The rhythm
From the trumpet at his lips
Is ecstasy
Distilled from old desire—

Desire
That is longing for the moon
Where the moonlight's but a spotlight
In his eyes,
Desire
That is longing for the sea
Where the sea's a bar-glass
Sucker size.

The Negro
With the trumpet at his lips
Whose jacket
Has a *fine* one-button roll,
Does not know
Upon what riff the music slips

Its hypodermic needle
To his soul—

But softly
As the tune comes from his throat
Trouble
Mellows to a golden note.


## Harlem Dance Hall

It had no dignity before.
But when the band began to play,
Suddenly the earth was there,
        And flowers,
        Trees,
        And air,
And like a wave the floor—
That had no dignity before!


## Communion

I was trying to figure out
What it was all about
But I could not figure out
What it was all about
So I gave up and went
To take the sacrament
And when I took it
It felt good to shout!

# When the Armies Passed

Mama, I found this soldier's cap
Lying in the snow.
It has a red star on it.
Whose is it, do you know?
>*I do not know*
>*Whose cap it is, son,*
>*All stained*
>*With wet and mud.*

But it has a red star on it!
>*Are you sure*
>*It is not blood?*

I thought I saw red stars, mother,
Scattered all over the snow.
But if they were blood, mother—
Whose?
>*Son, I do not know.*
>*It might have been*
>*Your father's blood,*
>*Perhaps blood*
>*Of your brother.*

See! When you wipe the mud away,
It *is* a red star, mother!


# Oppression

Now dreams
Are not available
To the dreamers,
Nor songs
To the singers.

In some lands
Dark night
And cold steel
Prevail—
But the dream
Will come back,
And the song
Break
Its jail.

# Peace

We passed their graves:
The dead men there,
Winners or losers,
Did not care.

In the dark
They could not see
Who had gained
The victory.

# To Dorothy Maynor

As though her lips
Are touched
With cooling water
The calmness of her song
Is blessed
With peace.

# Barefoot Blues

Papa, don't you see my shoes?
Papa, don't you see my shoes?
    What you want
    Yo' little boy to do,
    Keep on goin' round
    Feelin' blue?
Walkin' with them barefoot blues.

Papa, don't you see my feet?
Looky, don't you see my feet?
    How you want
    Yo' sugar-lump to walk,
    Pattin' leather
    On the street?

Papa, is yo' money gone?
Tell me, is yo' money gone?
    I'm as cold
    As cold can be!
    What you gonna do
    'Bout these shoes and me?
Papa, is your money gone?

## Wealth

From Christ to Ghandi
Appears this truth—
St. Francis of Assisi
Proves it, too:
Goodness becomes grandeur
Surpassing might of kings.
Halos of kindness
Brighter shine
Than crowns of gold,
And brighter
Than rich diamonds
Sparkles
The simple dew
Of love.

## Wisdom and War

We do not care—
That much is clear.
Not enough
Of us care
Anywhere.

We are not wise—
For that reason,
Mankind dies.

To think
Is much against
The will.

Better—
And easier—
To kill.


## From Selma

In places like
Selma, Alabama,
Kids say,
> In places like
> Chicago and New York. . . .

In places like
Chicago and New York
Kids say,
> In places like
> London and Paris. . . .

In places like
London and Paris
Kids say,
> In places like
> Chicago and New York. . . .


## Ballad of the Seven Songs    A Poem for Emancipation Day

Seven letters,
Seven songs.
The seven letters
F-R-E-E-D-O-M
Spell *Freedom*.
The seven songs

Capture segments of its history
In terms of black America.

Seven songs,
Seven names:
      Cudjoe
      Sojourner Truth
      Harriet Tubman
      Frederick Douglass
      Booker T. Washington
      Dr. Carver
      Jackie
Seven men and women
From unrecorded slavery to recorded free:

For Emancipation Day
Seven songs,
Seven men,
Seven letters
That spell *Freedom*.

It was an easy name to give a slave
So they called him Cudjoe.
There were four million Cudjoes
Before Emancipation came.

What did it mean to be a slave?
That you could not choose your own son's name,
Nor your own son's father or mother,
Nor your own son's home, or work, or way of life,
(Nor indeed could you choose your own)
Nor choose to have or not have a son.
No part of life or self
Belonged to Cudjoe—slave.

To Cudjoe—slave—
Only a dream belonged.
Seven letters spelled the dream:
*F-R-E-E-D-O-M*
Freedom!
But in the cane fields, in the rice fields,
In the bondage of the cotton,
In the deep dark of the captive heart
Sometimes Freedom seemed so far away,
Farther away than the farthermost star,

So far, so far—
That only over Jordan was there a dream
Called Freedom.
Cudjoe's song was:

> *Deep river,*
> *My home is over Jordan.*
> *Deep river, Lord,*
> *I want to cross over into camp ground.*
> *O, don't you want to go to that gospel feast,*
> *That promised land where all is peace? . . .*
> *Deep river, Lord,*
> *I want to cross over into camp ground.*

Death was a deep river,
And only over Jordan, Freedom.
Oh, night! Oh, moon! Oh, stars!
Oh, stars that guide lone sailing boats
Across the great dark sea,
Star, guide thou me!

Star! Star! Star!
North Star! North.
I cannot catch my breath
For fear of that one star
And that one word:
Star—Free—Freedom—North Star!
Where is the road that leads me to that star?
Ah, ha! The road?
Dogs guard that road,
Patrollers guard that road,
Bloodhounds with dripping muzzles
Guard that road!
Gun, lash, and noose
Guard that road!

Freedom was not a word:
Freedom was the dark swamp crossed,
And death defied,
Fear laid aside,
And a song that whispered, crooned,
And while it whispered cried:

> *Oh, Freedom!*
> *Freedom over me!*
> *Before I'd be a slave,*

*I'd be buried in my grave*
*And go home to my Lord*
*And be free!*

Harriet Tubman—slave.
She wanted to be free.
She'd heard of that word with seven letters.
She could not read the word,
Nor spell the word,
But she smelled the word,
Tasted the word,
On the North wind heard the word.
And she saw it in a star.

*Before I'd be a slave,*
*I'd be buried in my grave*
*And go home to my Lord*
*And be free!*

Sojourner Truth—slave.
She wanted to be free.
Her sons and daughters sold away,
Still she wanted to be free.
She said:
    I look up at de stars,
    My chillun look up at de stars.
    They don't know where I be
    And I don't know where they be.
    God said, Sojourner, go free!
Go free! Free! Freedom! Free!

*Before I'd be a slave*
*I'd be buried in my grave. . . .*

Before Emancipation thousands of slaves
Made their way to freedom—
Through swamp and brier, over field and hill,
By dark of night, prayer-guided, star-guided,
Guided by that human will that makes men love
A word called Freedom—

And the deep river was not Jordan, but the Ohio,
Home was not heaven, but the North.
North! North Star! North!

Frederick Douglass called his paper
"The North Star."

Douglass had made his way to freedom.
Sojourner Truth made her way to freedom.
Harriet Tubman made her way to freedom;
Then she went back into slavery land,
And back again, and back again, and again, again,
Each time bringing a band of slave
(Who once were slaves, now slaves no more)
To freedom!
Before the Civil War,
Long before '61,
Before Emancipation,
Freedom had begun!

> *Go down, Moses,*
> *Way down in Egypt land*
> *Tell old Pharaoh*
> *To let my people go!*

Linking arms for freedom
With the one-time slaves,
With Douglass, Harriet, Sojourner,
Were Whittier, Garrison, Lovejoy, Lowell—
Great Americans who believed in all men being free.
And thousands more—white, too, but not so famous—
Dared arrest and scorn and persecution
That black men might be free:
The stations of the underground railroad to freedom
Became many—
And the North Star found a million friends.
And of that time a book was born, "Uncle Tom's Cabin."
And a spirit was born, John Brown.
And a song was born:

*Mine eyes have seen the glory of the coming of the Lord:*
*He is trampling out the vintage where the grapes of wrath are stored;*
*He hath loosed the fateful lightning of his terrible swift sword. . . .*

And a war was born:

*John Brown's body lies*
*A-mouldering in the grave—*
*But his soul goes marching on!*

And a voice to set the nation right:

*With malice toward none,*
*With charity for all. . . .*

Lincoln . . .

*In the beauty of the lilies Christ was born across the sea,*

Abraham . . .

*With a glory in His bosom that transfigures you and me;*

Lincoln . . .

*As he died to make men holy, let us die to make men free,*

Abraham . . .

*While God is marching on.*

Lincoln . . .

*In giving freedom to the slave*
*we assure freedom to the free. . . .*

Abraham . . .

*No man is good enough to govern another*
*man without that other's consent.*

Lincoln . . .

*I do ordain . . . thenceforward and forever free.*

But the fields still needed planting,
The cane still needed cutting,
The cotton still needed picking,
The old mule still needed a hand to guide the plow:

> De cotton needs pickin'
> So bad, so bad, so bad!
> De cotton needs pickin' so bad!
> Gonna glean all over this field!

And on the river boats the song:

> Roll dat bale, boy!
> Roll dat bale! . . .

Up the river to Memphis, Cairo, St. Louis,
Work and song, work and song—stevedores, foundry men,
Brick layers, builders, makers, section hands, railroad shakers:

> There ain't no hammer
> In this mountain
> Rings like mine, boys,
> Rings like mine!

Freedom is a mighty word,
But not an easy word.
You have to hold hard to freedom.
And as somebody said,
Maybe you have to win it all over again every generation.
There are no color lines in freedom.
But not all the "free" are free.
Still it's a long step from Cudjoe—slave,
From Harriet Tubman—slave,
Sojourner Truth—slave
Frederick Douglass—slave
Who had to run away to freedom—
It's a long step to Booker T. Washington
Building Tuskegee,
To Dr. W. E. B. Du Bois building a culture for America.
It's a long step from Cudjoe—slave
Hoeing cotton—
To George Washington Carver—once slave—

349

Giving his discoveries in agricultural chemistry to the world.
It's a long song from:

> *Before I'd be a slave*
> *I'd be buried in my grave. . . .*

To Dorothy Maynor singing, *"Depuis le jour."*
It's a long step from Cudjoe—slave—
To Jackie Robinson hitting a homer.

Yet to some Freedom is still
Only a part of a word:
Some of the letters are missing.
Yet it's enough of a word
To lay hands on and hope,
It's enough of a word
To be a universal star—
Not just a North Star anymore:

*Thenceforward and forever—free!*

> *Oh, Freedom!*
> *Freedom over me!*
> *Before I'd be a slave*
> *I'd be buried in my grave*
> *And go home to my Lord*
> *And be free!*


## Dare


          Let darkness
          Gather up its roses
          Cupping softness
          In the hand—
          Till the hard fist
          Of sunshine
          Dares the dark
          To stand.

# Slave Song

I can see down there
That star that brings no peace—
I can see in the East
It does shine.

I can see in the West
The star that does not care—
But the star in the North
    Is mine!

        Guiding star!
        Wishing star!
        North star!

        How far?

# Second Generation: New York

Mama
Remembers the four-leaf clover
And the bright blue Irish sky.

I
Remember the East River Parkway
And the tug boats passing by.

I
Remember Third Avenue
And the el trains overhead,
And our one window sill geranium
Blooming red.

Mama
Remembers Ireland.
All I remember is here—
And it's dear!

Papa
Remembers Poland,
Sleighs in the wintertime,
Tall snow-covered fir trees,
And faces frosty with rime.

Papa
Remembers pogroms
And the ghetto's ugly days.
I remember Vocational High,
Park concerts,
Theatre Guild plays.

Papa
Remembers Poland.
All I remember is here—
　　This house,
　　This street,
　　This city—
And they're dear!

## Homecoming

I went back in the alley
And I opened up my door.
All her clothes was gone:
She wasn't home no more.

I pulled back the covers,
I made down the bed.
A *whole* lot of room
Was the only thing I had.

## From Spain to Alabama

Where have the people gone
That they do not sing
Their *flamencos?*

　　*The people*
　　*Have gone nowhere:*
　　*They still sing*
　　*Their flamencos.*

Where have the people gone
That they do not sing
Their blues?

*The people*
*Have gone nowhere:*
*They still sing*
*Their blues.*


## Madam and the Phone Bill

You say I O.K.ed
LONG DISTANCE?
O.K.ed it when?
My goodness, Central,
That was *then!*

I'm mad and disgusted
With that Negro now.
I don't pay no REVERSED
CHARGES nohow.

You say, I will pay it—
Else you'll take out my phone?
You better let
My phone alone.

I didn't ask him
To telephone me.
Roscoe knows darn well
LONG DISTANCE
Ain't free.

If I ever catch him,
Lawd, have pity!
Calling me up
From Kansas City

Just to say he loves me!
I knowed that was so.

Why didn't he tell me some'n
I don't know?

For instance, what can
Them other girls do
That Alberta K. Johnson
Can't do—*and more, too?*

What's that, Central?
You say you don't care
Nothing about my
Private affair?

Well, even less about your
PHONE BILL does I care!

Un-humm-m! . . . Yes!
You say I gave my O.K.?
Well, that O.K. you may keep—

But I *sure* ain't gonna pay!


## Madam and the Fortune Teller

Fortune teller looked in my hand.
Fortune teller said,
Madam, It's just good luck
You ain't dead.

Fortune teller squeeze my hand.
She squinted up her eyes.
Fortune teller said,
Madam, you ain't wise.

I said, Please explain to me
What you mean by that?
She said, You must recognize
Where your fortune's at.

I said, Madam, tell me—
For she was *Madam*, too—

Where *is* my fortune at?
I'll pay some mind to you.

She said, Your fortune, honey,
Lies right in yourself.
You ain't gonna find it
On nobody else's shelf.

I said, What *man* you're talking 'bout?
She said, Madam! Be calm—
For one more dollar and a half,
I'll read your other palm.


## Madam and the Census Man

The census man,
The day he came round,
Wanted my name
To put it down.

I said, JOHNSON,
ALBERTA K.
But he hated to write
The K that way.

He said, What
Does K stand for?
I said, K—
And nothing more.

He said, I'm gonna put it
K—A—Y.
I said, If you do,
You lie.

My mother christened me
ALBERTA K.
You leave my name
Just that way!

He said, Mrs.,
(With a snort)

Just a K
Makes your name too short.

I said, I don't
Give a damn!
Leave me and my name
Just like I am!

Furthermore, rub out
That MRS., too—
I'll have you know
I'm *Madam* to you!

## Mama and Daughter

*Mama, please brush off my coat.*
*I'm going down the street.*

Where're you going, daughter?

*To see my sugar-sweet.*

Who is your sugar, honey?
Turn around—I'll brush behind.

*He is that young man, mama,*
*I can't get off my mind.*

Daughter, once upon a time—
Let me brush the hem—
Your father, yes, he was the one!
I felt like that about him.

But it was a long time ago
He up and went his way.
I hope that wild young son-of-a-gun
Rots in hell today!

*Mama, dad couldn't be still young.*

He *was* young yesterday.
He *was* young when he—
Turn around!
So I can brush your back, I say!


## S-sss-ss-sh!

Her great adventure ended
As great adventures should
In life being created
Anew—and good.

> *Except the neighbors*
> *And her mother*
> *Did not think it good!*

Nature has a way
Of not caring much
About marriage
Licenses and such.

> *But the neighbors*
> *And her mother*
> *Cared very much!*

The baby came one morning,
Almost with the sun.

> *The neighbors—*
> *And its grandma—*
> *Were outdone!*

But mother and child
Thought it fun.

## Life Is Fine

I went down to the river,
I set down on the bank.
I tried to think but couldn't,
So I jumped in and sank.

I came up once and hollered!
I came up twice and cried!
If that water hadn't a-been so cold
I might've sunk and died.

    *But it was*
    *Cold in that water!*
    *It was cold!*

I took the elevator
Sixteen floors above the ground.
I thought about my baby
And thought I would jump down.

I stood there and I hollered!
I stood there and I cried!
If it hadn't a-been so high
I might've jumped and died.

    *But it was*
    *High up there!*
    *It was high!*

So since I'm still here livin',
I guess I will live on.
I could've died for love —
But for livin' I was born.

Though you may hear me holler,
And you may see me cry —
I'll be dogged, sweet baby,
If you gonna see me die.

    *Life is fine!*
    *Fine as wine!*
    *Life is fine!*

## Honey Babe

Honey babe,
You braid your hair too tight—
But the good Lord knows
Your heart is right.

I asked you for a dollar.
You gimme two.
That, honey babe,
Is what I like about you.

I knock on your door
About two-three a.m.
You jump out of bed,
Says, *I know it's him!*

There's many another woman
In this wide wide world—
But nary a one
Like my little girl.

## Stranger in Town

I walked all over the zoo and the park.
I set down on a stone.
I kept wishing I had a girl-friend
Who would be my very own—
   But I didn't have nary one,
   Not nary one a-tall.

I asked my landlady did I have privileges.
My landlady, she said, No!
I said, It don't make no difference nohow,
Cause I ain't nobody's beau.
   Nobody a-tall—
   I ain't nobody's beau.

Of course, I'm just a stranger
In this strange old town—
But after I been here awhile
I'll know my way around.
   Yes, I'll know
   My way around.

## Lincoln Theatre

The head of Lincoln looks down from the wall
While movies echo dramas on the screen.
The head of Lincoln is serenely tall
Above a crowd of black folk, humble, mean.
The movies end. The lights flash gaily on.
The band down in the pit bursts into jazz.
The crowd applauds a plump brown-skin bleached
    blonde
Who sings the troubles every woman has.
She snaps her fingers, slowly shakes her hips,
And cries, all careless-like from reddened lips!
    *De man I loves has*
    *Gone and done me wrong . . .*
While girls who wash rich white folks clothes by day
And sleek-haired boys who deal in love for pay
Press hands together, laughing at her song.


## Song for Billie Holiday

What can purge my heart
        Of the song
        And the sadness?
What can purge my heart
        But the song
        Of the sadness?
What can purge my heart
        Of the sadness
        Of the song?

Do not speak of sorrow
With dust in her hair,
Or bits of dust in eyes
A chance wind blows there.
The sorrow that I speak of
Is dusted with despair.

Voice of muted trumpet,
Cold brass in warm air.
Bitter television blurred
By sound that shimmers—
        Where?

# One-Way Ticket

I pick up my life
And take it with me
And I put it down in
Chicago, Detroit,
Buffalo, Scranton,
Any place that is
North and East—
And not Dixie.

I pick up my life
And take it on the train
To Los Angeles, Bakersfield,
Seattle, Oakland, Salt Lake,
Any place that is
North and West—
And not South.

I am fed up
With Jim Crow laws,
People who are cruel
And afraid,
Who lynch and run,
Who are scared of me
And me of them.

I pick up my life
And take it away
On a one-way ticket—
Gone up North,
Gone out West,
Gone!

# Restrictive Covenants

When I move
Into a neighborhood
Folks fly.

Even every foreigner
That can move, moves.

Why?

*The moon doesn't run.*
*Neither does the sun.*

In Chicago
They've got covenants
Restricting me —
Hemmed in
On the South Side,
Can't breathe free.

*But the wind blows there.*
*I reckon the wind*
*Must care.*


## Juice Joint: Northern City


There is a gin mill on the avenue
Where singing black boys dance and play each night
Until the stars pale and the sky turns blue
And dawn comes down the street all wanly white.
They sell beer foaming there in mug-like cups,
Gin is sold in glasses finger-tall.
Women of the streets stop by for sups
Of whiskey as they start out for a ball.
Sometimes a black boy plays a song
That once was sung beneath the sun
In lazy far-off drowsy Southern days
Before this long hegira had begun
   That brought dark faces
   And gay dancing feet
   Into this gin mill
   On this city street.

Play your guitars, grinning night-dark boys,
And let your songs drift through the swinging doors.
Let your songs hold all the sunny joys
That goad black feet to dancing on bare floors.
Let those women with their lips too red
Turn from the bar and join you in your song,
And switch their skirts and lift their straightened heads
To sing about the men who've done them wrong —

While blues as mellow as the Southern air
And weary as a drowsy Southern rain
Echo the age-less, age-long old despair
That fills a woman's age-less, age-long pain—
　　As every swaying
　　Guitar-playing boy
　　Forgets he ever sang
　　A song of joy.

O, in this tavern on the city street
Where black men come to drink and play and sing,
And women, too, whom anyone may meet
And handle easy like a purchased thing,
Where two old brown men stand behind the bar—
Still after hours pouring drinks the law forbids—
Dark dancers dance and dreamers seek a star
And some forget to laugh who still are kids.
But suddenly a guitar-playing lad
Whose languid lean brings back the sunny South
Strikes up a tune all gay and bright and glad
To keep the gall from biting in his mouth,
　　Then drowsy as the rain
　　Soft sad black feet
　　Dance in this juice joint
　　On the city street.

## Harlem [1]

　　Here on the edge of hell
　　Stands Harlem—
　　Remembering the old lies,
　　The old kicks in the back,
　　The old "Be patient"
　　They told us before.

　　Sure, we remember.
　　Now when the man at the corner store
　　Says sugar's gone up another two cents,
　　And bread one,
　　And there's a new tax on cigarettes—
　　We remember the job we never had,

Never could get,
And can't have now
Because we're colored.

So we stand here
On the edge of hell
In Harlem
And look out on the world
And wonder
What we're gonna do
In the face of what
We remember.

## Man into Men

A nigger comes home from work:
  Jostle of fur coats
  Jostle of dirty coats
  Jostle of women who shop
  Jostle of women who work
  Jostle of men with good jobs
  Jostle of men in the ditches.

A Negro comes home from work:
  Wondering about fur coats
  Dirty coats
  White skins
  Black skins
  Good jobs
  Ditches

A man comes home from work:
  Knowing all things
  Belong
  To the man
  Who becomes
  Men.

# Warning

Negroes,
Sweet and docile,
Meek, humble, and kind:
Beware the day
They change their mind!

Wind
In the cotton fields,
Gentle breeze:
Beware the hour
It uproots trees!

# Late Last Night

Late last night I
Set on my steps and cried.
Wasn't nobody gone,
Neither had nobody died.

I was cryin'
Cause you broke my heart in two.
You looked at me cross-eyed
And broke my heart in two—

So I was cryin'
On account of
You!

# Bad Morning

Here I sit
With my shoes mismated.
Lawdy-mercy!
I's frustrated!

## Could Be

Could be Hastings Street,
Or Lenox Avenue,
Could be 18th & Vine
And still be true.

Could be 5th & Mound,
Could be Rampart:
When you pawned my watch
You pawned my heart.

Could be you love me,
Could be that you don't.
Might be that you'll come back,
Like as not you won't.

Hastings Street is weary,
Also Lenox Avenue.
Any place is dreary
Without my watch and you.

## Midnight Raffle

I put my nickel
In the raffle of the night.
Somehow that raffle
Didn't turn out right.

I lost my nickel.
I lost my time.
I got back home
Without a dime.

When I dropped that nickel
In the subway slot,
I wouldn't have dropped it,
Knowing what I got.

I could just as well've
Stayed home inside:
My bread wasn't buttered
On neither side.

## Monroe's Blues

Monroe's fell on evil days—
His woman and his friend is dead.
Monroe's fell on evil days,
Can't hardly get his bread.

Monroe sings a little blues,
His little blues is sad.
Monroe sings a little blues—
*My woman and my friend is dead.*

## Raid

Late at night
When the wine's gone to your head
And the songs on the juke box
Get shorter and shorter,
*Baby, say when.*

But baby
Doesn't say when.

Suddenly
It's time to go.

*Where?*

The man is there!

## What?

Some pimps wear summer hats
Into late fall
Since the money that comes in
Won't cover it all—
Suit, overcoat, shoes—
And hat, too!

Got to neglect something,
So what would you do?

## Request for Requiems

Play the *St. Louis Blues*
For me when I die.
I want some fine music
Up there in the sky.

Sing the *St. James Infirmary*
When you let me down—
Cause there ain't a good man
Like me left around.

## Deceased

Harlem
Sent him home
In a long box—
Too dead
To know why:

The licker
Was lye.

## Final Curve

When you turn the corner
And you run into *yourself*
Then you know that you have turned
All the corners that are left.

## Boarding House

The graveyard is the
Cheapest boarding house:
Some of these days
We'll all board there.

Rich and poor
Alike will share.
The graveyard is the
Cheapest boarding house.
But me—if I can
Hang on here,
I ain't gonna
Go out there.
Let the graveyard be the
Cheapest boarding house!

## Funeral

Carried lonely up the aisle
In a box without a smile,
Resting near the altar where
Folks pass by and stare—

If I was alive
I'd say,
*I don't give a damn
Being this-a way!*

But I would give a damn.

## Migrant

(*Chicago*)

Daddy-o
Buddy-o
Works at the foundry.
Daddy-o
Buddy-o
Rides the State Street street car,
Transfers to the West Side,

Polish, Bohunk, Irish,
Grabs a load of sunrise
As he rides out on the prairie,
Never knew DuSable,
Has a lunch to carry.

Iron lifting iron
Makes iron of chocolate muscles.
Iron lifting iron
Makes hammer beat of drum beat
And the heat
Moulds and melts and moulds it
On red heart become an anvil
Until a glow is lighted
In the eyes once soft benighted
And the cotton field is frightened
A thousand miles away.

They draw up restrictive covenants
In Australia, too, they say.
Our President
Takes up important matters
Still left by V-J Day.
Congress cases Russia.
The *Tribune*'s hair
Turns gray.

Daddy-o
Buddy-o
Signs his name
In uphill letters
On the check that is his pay.
But if he wasn't in a hurry
He wouldn't write so
Bad that way,
Daddy-o.

## Third Degree

Hit me! Jab me!
Make me say I did it.
Blood on my sport shirt
And my tan suede shoes.

*Faces like jack-o'-lanterns*
*In gray slouch hats.*

Slug me! Beat me!
Scream jumps out
Like blowtorch.
Three kicks between the legs
That kill the kids
I'd make tomorrow.

*Bars and floor skyrocket*
*And burst like Roman candles.*

When you throw
Cold water on me,
I'll sign the
Paper . . .

## Jitney

Corners
Of South Parkway:
Eeeoooooo!
Cab!
31st,
35th,
39th,
43rd,
Girl, ain't you heard?
*No, Martha, I ain't heard.*
I got a Chinese boy-friend
Down on 43rd.
47th,
51st,
55th,
63rd,
Martha's got a Japanese!
Child, ain't you heard?
55th,
51st,
47th,
Here's your fare!
Lemme out!

I'm going to the Regal,
See what this week's jive is all about:
The Duke is mellow!
Hibbler's giving out!
43rd,
39th,
Night school!
Gotta get my teaching!
35th,
31st,
Bless God!
Tonight there's preaching!
31st! All out!
Hey, Mister, wait!
I want to get over to State.
*I don't turn, Madam!*
*Understand?*
*Take a street car*
*Over to the Grand.*

35th,
39th,
43rd,
I quit Alexander!
Honey, ain't you heard?
47th,
50th Place,
63rd,
Alexander's quit Lucy!
Baby, ain't you heard?
Eeeooooooooooo!
Cab!
If you want a good chicken
You have to get there early
And push and shove and grab!
I'm going shopping now, child.
Eeeeooooo!
Cab!
55th,
47th,
35th,
31st,
Hey!
Cab!

372

# Interne at Provident

White coats
White aprons
White dresses
White shoes
Pain and a learning
To take away to Alabama.
Practice on a State Street cancer,
Practice on a stockyards rupture,
Practice on the small appendix
Of 26-girl at the corner,
Learning skills of surgeons
Brown and wonderful with longing
To cure ills of Africa,
Democracy,
And mankind,
Also ills quite common
Among all who stand on two feet.

Brown hands
Black hands
Golden hands in white coat,
Nurses' hands on suture.
Miracle maternity:
Pain on hind legs rising,
Pain tamed and subsiding
Like a mule broke to the halter.

Charity's checked money
Aids triumphant entry squalling
After bitter thrust of bearing
Chocolate and blood:

Projection of a day!

Tears of joy
And Coca-Cola
Twinkle on the rubber gloves
He's wearing.
A crown of sweat
Gleams on his forehead.

In the white moon
Of the amphitheatre
Magi are staring.

The light on the Palmolive Building
Shines like a star in the East.

Nurses turn glass doorknobs
Opening into corridors.

A mist of iodine and ether
Follows the young doctor,
Cellophanes his long stride,
Cellophanes his future.

## To Be Somebody

Little girl
Dreaming of a baby grand piano
(Not knowing there's a Steinway bigger, bigger)
Dreaming of a baby grand to play
That stretches paddle-tailed across the floor,
Not standing upright
Like a bad boy in the corner,
But sending music
Up the stairs and down the stairs
And out the door
To confound even Hazel Scott
Who might be passing!

Oh!

Little boy
Dreaming of the boxing gloves
Joe Louis wore,
The gloves that sent
Two dozen men to the floor.
Knockout!
Bam! Bop! Mop!

There's always room,
*They say,*
At the top.

## Down Where I Am

Too many years
Beatin' at the door—
I done beat my
Both fists sore.

Too many years
Tryin' to get up there—
Done broke my ankles down,
Got nowhere.

Too many years
Climbin' that hill,
'Bout out of breath.
I got my fill.

I'm gonna plant my feet
On solid ground.
If you want to see me,
*Come down.*


## Catch

Big Boy came
Carrying a mermaid
On his shoulders
And the mermaid
Had her tail
Curved
Beneath his arm.

Being a fisher boy,
He'd found a fish
To carry—
Half fish,
Half girl
To marry.

## Island [1]

Wave of sorrow,
Do not drown me now:

I see the island
Still ahead somehow.

I see the island
And its sands are fair:

Wave of sorrow,
Take me there.


## Kid in the Park

Lonely little question mark
on a bench in the park:

See the people passing by?
See the airplanes in the sky?
See the birds
flying home
before
dark?

Home's just around
the corner
there—
*but not really*
*anywhere.*

# Poems 1951–1960

# Prelude to Our Age   A Negro History Poem

History's long page
Records the whole vast
Prelude to our age.

Across the chapters
Of recorded time
Shadows of so many hands
Have fallen,
Among them mine:
    *Negro.*

At first only
The spoken word of bard or chief,
And the beaten drum
That carried instant history
Across the night,
Or linked man with the mystery
Of powers beyond sight.
Pictures on stone, hieroglyphics,
Parchment, illuminated scrolls.

    Homer's
    "Blameless Ethiopians."

On all these rolls landmarking man,
The shadow of my hand:
    *Negro.*

Aesop, Antar, Terence,
Various Pharaohs,
Sheba, too.
Ethiopia, Ghana, Songhay.
Arab and African; the Moors
Gave Spain her castanets
And Senegal her prayers.

All this before the type that moved
in which Juan Latino spoke:
"Ad Catholicum-Pariter et Invictissimum"—
The shadow of my hand
Across the printed word:
    Granada, 1573.

    Yoruba, Benin, Guinea,
    Timbuctoo and Abderrahman Sadi's
    "Tarikh es Soudan."

Meanwhile Jamestown links its chains
Between the Gold Coast and our land.
    Jamestown, Virginia, 1619.

But lately dead Elizabeth the Queen.
But lately come to throne,
King James, whose Bible is our own.
As Sadi chronicles his great
    "Tarikh es Soudan,"
With Africa a link of chains connects our land.
Caught in those chains, my hand:
    *Negro.*

Yet Boston's Phillis Wheatley, slave, wrote her poems,
And Washington, the general, praised—
Washington who righted wrong—
But those of us who had no rights
    made an unwritten song:

    *Go down, Moses,*
    *Way down in Egypt land,*
    *And tell old Pharaoh*
    *To let my people go. . . .*

Black Crispus Attucks died
That our land might be free.
    His death
    Did not free me.
When Banneker made his almanac
    I was not free.
When Toussaint freed the blacks of Haiti,
    I was not free.

In other lands Dumas and Pushkin wrote—
    But we,
    Who could not write, made songs:

    *Swing low, sweet chariot,*
    *Coming for to carry me home . . .*
    *Oh, I looked over Jordan*
    *And what did I see—*

Phillis, Crispus, Toussaint,
Banneker, Dumas, Pushkin,

All of these were me—
    Not free:

    *As long as one*
    *Man is in chains,*
    *No man is free.*

Yet Ira Aldridge played Shakespeare in London.
Frederick Douglass ran away to freedom,
Wrote books, made speeches, edited "The North Star."
Sojourner Truth made speeches, too.
Harriet Tubman led her marches.
"Uncle Tom's Cabin" swept the nation—
While we, who were not free and could not write a word,
Gave freedom a song the whole earth heard:

    *Oh, Freedom!*
    *Freedom over me!*
    *Before I'd be a slave*
    *I'd be buried in my grave*
    *And go home to my Lord*
    *And be free.*

Nat Turner, Denmark Vesey
And thousands nameless went home.
Black men died at Harpers Ferry with John Brown.
Lovejoy, Garrison, Wendell Phillips spoke.
The North star guided men along the Quaker underground
To Canada—hills to cross, rivers to ford.
Sermons, revolt, prayers, Civil War—

    *Mine eyes have seen the glory*
    *Of the coming of the Lord!*

Lincoln:
1863.
Once slaves—
"Henceforth and forever free."

    *My Lord, what a morning,*
    *My Lord, what a morning,*

*My Lord, what a morning,*
*When the stars began to fall!*

Booker T.—
A school, Tuskegee.
Paul Laurence Dunbar—
A poem, a song, a "Lindy Lou."
Fisk University and its Jubilees.
Black Congressmen of Reconstruction days.
Black comics with their minstrel ways,
Then Williams & Walker, "In Dahomey," "Bandana Land"
Ragtime sets the pattern for a nation's songs
And Handy writes the blues
     For me—
     Now free.

Free to build my churches and my schools—
     Mary McLeod Bethune.
Free to explore clay and sweet potatoes—
     Dr. Carver.
Free to take our songs across the world—
     Anderson, Maynor, Robeson,
     Josephine Baker, Florence Mills,
Free to sit in councils of the nation—
     Johnson, Hastie, Dawson, Powell.
Free to make blood plasma—
     Charles R. Drew.
Free to move at will in great migrations
South to North across the nation—
Savannah to Sugar Hill,
Rampart Street to Paradise Valley,
Yamakraw to Yale.
Free to fight in wars as others do—
     Free—yet segregated.

     As man or soldier
     Underrated.

The 10th Cavalry at San Juan Hill:
     "As I heard one of the Rough Riders say,"
     Wrote Theodore Roosevelt,
     " 'They can drink out of our canteens.' "

The 369th Infantry at Champagne:
     To Henry Johnson

And to Needham Roberts,
The *Croix de Guerre*.

The 332nd Fighter Group over the Mediterranean:
        To more than eighty pilots,
        The Distinguished Flying Cross.

In the Pacific the Navy Cross to Dorie Miller.
        Me, hero and killer.
        (Yet segregated.)

        Me, peacemaker, too—
        Ralph Bunche
        Between the Arab
        And the Jew.

Du Bois, Woodson, Johnson, Frazier,
Robert S. Abbott, T. Thomas Fortune,
"The Afro-American," "The Black Dispatch."
All the time the written record grows—
"The Crisis," "Phylon," "Opportunity,"
Schomburg, McKay, Cullen, "Native Son,"
Papers, stories, poems the whole world knows—
The ever growing history of man
Shadowed by my hand:
        *Negro*.

Other hands whose fingers intertwine
With mine tell our story, too:
Park, Myrdal, Sinclair Lewis,
Smith, Van Vechten, Bucklin Moon.
Surveys, novels, movies, plays
That trace the maze of patterns
Woven by democracy and me,
        Now free.

And all the while
The rising power of my vote
Helping build democracy—
My vote, my labor, lodges, clubs,
My N.A.A.C.P.—
        The National Association
        For The Advancement
        Of Colored People—
All the way from a Jim Crow dining car

To the United States Supreme Court—
For the right to get a meal on a train.

All the way from a Jim Crow school
To the United States Supreme Court—
For the right to equal education.

All the way from ghetto covenants
To the United States Supreme Court—
For the right to housing free from segregation.

Thus I help to build democracy
For our nation.
Thus by decree across the history of our land—
The shadow of my hand:
    *Negro*

All this
A prelude to our age:
Today.

Tomorrow
Is another
Page.

## Where Service Is Needed

For the Negro Nurse there's been no easy way.
The bars have been high, the day a long day
When the hand that could tend the sick or the hurt
Must also combat Jim Crow's dirt.

No caution, no gloves, no antiseptic, no mask
Could protect her from prejudice as she stuck to her task.
Only devotion, and the will to be what she set out to be,
Kept the Negro nurse on her road to today's victory.

From America's garden now
The ugly weeds are being weeded:
Only five states bar their doors to dark hands
That would serve where service is needed.

In the Army, the Navy, colored nurses attend.
Her long gallant struggle portends a good end.
"Negro nurse" is a phrase men no longer need say.
"American nurse" means all nurses today.

The bars have been high. There is no magic wand;
Only unity and faith have brought this new dawn
Where the rights of democracy to all are ceded:
Her skilled hands may serve where service is needed.

## American Heartbreak

I am the American heartbreak—
Rock on which Freedom
Stumps its toe—
The great mistake
That Jamestown
Made long ago.

## Consider Me

Consider me,
A colored boy,
Once sixteen,
Once five, once three,
Once nobody,
Now me.
Before me
Papa, mama,
Grandpa, grandma,
So on back
To original
Pa.

(A capital letter there,
*He*
Being Mystery.)

Consider me,
Colored boy,

Downtown at eight,
Sometimes working late,
Overtime pay
To sport away,
Or save,
Or give my Sugar
For the things
She needs.

My Sugar,
Consider her
Who works, too—
Has to.
One don't make enough
For all the stuff
It takes to live.
Forgive me
What I lack,
Black,
Caught in a crack
That splits the world in two
From China
By way of Arkansas
To Lenox Avenue.

Consider me,
On Friday the eagle flies.
Saturday laughter, a bar, a bed.
Sunday prayers syncopate glory.
Monday comes,
To work at eight,
Late,
Maybe.

Consider me,
Descended also
From the
Mystery.

# MONTAGE
# OF A
# DREAM DEFERRED

In terms of current Afro-American popular music and the sources from which it has progressed—jazz, ragtime, swing, blues, boogie-woogie, and be-bop—this poem on contemporary Harlem, like be-bop, is marked by conflicting changes, sudden nuances, sharp and impudent interjections, broken rhythms, and passages sometimes in the manner of the jam session, sometimes the popular song, punctuated by the riffs, runs, breaks, and disctortions of the music of a community in transition.

[LH]

## Dream Boogie

Good morning, daddy!
Ain't you heard
The boogie-woogie rumble
Of a dream deferred?

Listen closely:
You'll hear their feet
Beating out and beating out a—

*You think
It's a happy beat?*

Listen to it closely:
Ain't you heard
something underneath
like a—

*What did I say?*

Sure,
I'm happy!
Take it away!

*Hey, pop!
Re-bop!
Mop!*

*Y-e-a-h!*


## Parade

Seven ladies
and seventeen gentlemen
at the Elks Club Lounge
planning planning a parade:
Grand Marshal in his white suit
will lead it.
Cadillacs with dignitaries
will precede it.

And behind will come
with band and drum
on foot . . . on foot . . .
on foot . . .

Motorcycle cops,
white,
will speed it
out of sight
if they can:
Solid black,
can't be right.

Marching . . . marching . . .
marching . . .
noon till night . . .

*I never knew*
*that many Negroes*
*were on earth,*
*did you?*

*I never knew!*

PARADE!

A chance to let

PARADE!

the whole world see

PARADE!

old black me!

# Children's Rhymes

When I was a chile we used to play,
"One—two—buckle my shoe!"
and things like that. But now, Lord,
listen at them little varmints!

> *By what sends*
> *the white kids*
> *I ain't sent:*
> *I know I can't*
> *be President.*

There is two thousand children
in this block, I do believe!

> *What don't bug*
> *them white kids*
> *sure bugs me:*
> *We knows everybody*
> *ain't free!*

Some of these young ones is cert'ly bad—
One batted a hard ball right through my window
and my gold fish et the glass.

> *What's written down*
> *for white folks*
> *ain't for us a-tall:*
> *"Liberty And Justice—*
> *Huh—For All."*

> *Oop-pop-a-da!*
> *Skee! Daddle-de-do!*
> *Be-bop!*

Salt' peanuts!

De-dop!

## Sister

That little Negro's married and got a kid.
Why does he keep on foolin' around Marie?
Marie's my sister—not married to me—
But why does he keep on foolin' around Marie?
Why don't she get a boy-friend
I can understand—some decent man?

> *Did it ever occur to you, son,*
> *the reason Marie runs around with trash*
> *is she wants some cash?*

Don't decent folks have dough?
*Unfortunately usually no!*

Well, anyway, it don't have to be a married man.

> *Did it ever occur to you, boy,*
> *that a woman does the best she can?*

> *Comment on Stoop*
> *So does a man.*


## Preference

I likes a woman
six or eight and ten years older'n myself.
I don't fool with these young girls.
Young girl'll say,
> *Daddy, I want so-and-so.*
> *I needs this, that, and the other.*
But a old woman'll say,
> *Honey, what does YOU need?*
> *I just drawed my money tonight*
> *and it's all your'n.*
That's why I likes a older woman
who can appreciate me:
When she conversations you
it ain't forever, *Gimme!*

391

## Necessity

Work?
I don't have to work.
I don't have to do nothing
but eat, drink, stay black, and die.
This little old furnished room's
so small I can't whip a cat
without getting fur in my mouth
and my landlady's so old
her features is all run together
and God knows she sure can overcharge—
Which is why I reckon I *does*
have to work after all.

## Question [2]

Said the lady, *Can you do*
*what my other man can't do—*
*That is*
*love me, daddy—*
*and feed me, too?*

*Figurine*

De-dop!

## Buddy

That kid's my buddy,
still and yet
I don't see him much.
He works downtown for Twelve a week.
Has to give his mother Ten—
she says he can have
the other Two
to pay his carfare, buy a suit,
coat, shoes,
anything he wants out of it.

# Juke Box Love Song

I could take the Harlem night
and wrap around you,
Take the neon lights and make a crown,
Take the Lenox Avenue busses,
Taxis, subways,
And for your love song tone their rumble down.
Take Harlem's heartbeat,
Make a drumbeat,
Put it on a record, let it whirl,
And while we listen to it play,
Dance with you till day—
Dance with you, my sweet brown Harlem girl.


# Ultimatum

Baby, how come you can't see me
when I'm paying your bills
each and every week?

If you got somebody else,
tell me—
else I'll cut you off
without your rent.
I mean
without a cent.


# Warning

Daddy,
don't let your dog
curb you!

## Croon

I don't give a damn
For Alabam'
Even if it is my home.

## New Yorkers

I was born here,
that's no lie, he said,
right here beneath God's sky.
*I wasn't born here, she said,*
*I come—and why?*
*Where I come from*
*folks work hard*
*all their lives*
*until they die*
*and never own no parts*
*of earth nor sky*
*So I come up here.*
*Now what've I got?*
            *You!*

She lifted up her lips
in the dark:
The same old spark!

## Wonder

Early blue evening.
Lights ain't come on yet.
        *Looky yonder!*
        *They come on now!*

## Easy Boogie

Down in the bass
That steady beat
Walking walking walking
Like marching feet.

Down in the bass
That easy roll,
Rolling like I like it
In my soul.

Riffs, smears, breaks.

Hey, Lawdy, Mama!
Do you hear what I said?
Easy like I rock it
In my bed!


## Movies

The Roosevelt, Renaissance, Gem, Alhambra:
Harlem laughing in all the wrong places
        at the crocodile tears
        of crocodile art
        that you know
        in your heart
        is crocodile:

            (Hollywood
            laughs at me,
            black—
            so I laugh
            back.)

## Tell Me

Why should it be *my* loneliness,
Why should it be *my* song,
Why should it be *my* dream
    deferred
    overlong?

## Not a Movie

Well, they rocked him with road-apples
because he tried to vote
and whipped his head with clubs
and he crawled on his knees to his house
and he got the midnight train
and he crossed that Dixie line
now he's livin'
on a 133rd.

He didn't stop in Washington
and he didn't stop in Baltimore
neither in Newark on the way.
Six knots was on his head
but, thank God, he wasn't dead!
And there ain't no Ku Klux
on a 133rd.

Neon Signs

WONDER BAR
•
•  •
•
WISHING WELL
•
•  •
•
MONTEREY
•
•  •
•
MINTON'S
(ancient altar of Thelonious)
•
•  •
•
MANDALAY
Spots where the booted
and unbooted play
•
•  •
•
SMALL'S
•
•  •
•
CASBAH
•
•  •
•
SHALIMAR
•
•  •
•
Mirror-go-round
where a broken glass
in the early bright
smears re-bop
sound
•
•  •
•

## Numbers

If I ever hit for a dollar
gonna salt every dime away
in the Post Office for a rainy day.

I ain't gonna
play back a cent.

(Of course, I might
combinate *a little*
with my rent.)

## What? So Soon!

I believe my old lady's
pregnant again!
Fate must have
some kind of trickeration
to populate the
cullud nation!

  *Comment against Lamp Post*
*You call it fate?*

  *Figurette*
*De-daddle-dy!*
*De-dop!*

## Motto

I play it cool
And dig all jive.
That's the reason
I stay alive.

My motto,
As I live and learn,
  is:
*Dig And Be Dug*
*In Return.*

## Dead in There

Sometimes
A night funeral
Going by
Carries home
A cool bop daddy.

Hearse and flowers
Guarantee
He'll never hype
Another paddy.

It's hard to believe,
But dead in there,
He'll never lay a
Hype nowhere!

He's my ace-boy,
Gone away.
*Wake up and live!*
He used to say.

Squares
Who couldn't dig him,
Plant him now—
Out where it makes
No diff' no how.

## Situation

When I rolled three 7's
in a row
I was scared to walk out
with the dough.

## Dancer

Two or three things in the past
failed him
that had not failed people
of lesser genius.

In the first place
he didn't have much sense.
He was no good at making love
and no good at making money.
So he tapped,
    trucked,
    boogied,
    sanded,
    jittered,
until he made folks say,
    *Looky yonder*
    *at that boy!*
    *Hey!*
But being no good at lovin'—
the girls left him.
(When you're no good for dough they go.)
With no sense, just wonderful feet,
What could possibly be all-reet?
Did he get anywhere? No!

Even a great dancer
can't C.P.T.
a show.

## Advice

Folks, I'm telling you,
birthing is hard
and dying is mean—
so get yourself
a little loving
in between.

## Green Memory

A wonderful time—the War:
when money rolled in
and blood rolled out.
        But blood
        was far away
        from here—
Money was near.


## Wine-O

Setting in the wine-house
Soaking up a wine-souse
Waiting for tomorrow to come—
Then
Setting in the wine-house
Soaking up a new souse.
Tomorrow . . .
Oh, hum!


## Relief

My heart is aching
for them Poles and Greeks
on relief way across the sea
because I was on relief
once in 1933.

I know what relief can be—
it took me two years to get on WPA.
If the war hadn't come along
I wouldn't be out the barrel yet.
Now, I'm almost back in the barrel again.

To tell the truth,
if these white folks want to go ahead

and fight another war,
or even two,
the one to stop 'em won't be me.

Would you?


## Ballad of the Landlord

Landlord, landlord,
My roof has sprung a leak.
Don't you 'member I told you about it
Way last week?

Landlord, landlord,
These steps is broken down.
When you come up yourself
It's a wonder you don't fall down.

Ten Bucks you say I owe you?
Ten Bucks you say is due?
Well, that's Ten Bucks more'n I'll pay you
Till you fix this house up new.

What? You gonna get eviction orders?
You gonna cut off my heat?
You gonna take my furniture and
Throw it in the street?

Um-huh! You talking high and mighty.
Talk on—till you get through.
You ain't gonna be able to say a word
If I land my fist on you.

*Police! Police!*
*Come and get this man!*
*He's trying to ruin the government*
*And overturn the land!*

Copper's whistle!
Patrol bell!
Arrest.

Precinct Station.
Iron cell.
Headlines in press:

MAN THREATENS LANDLORD
.
. .
TENANT HELD NO BAIL
.
. .
JUDGE GIVES NEGRO 90 DAYS IN COUNTY JAIL.


## Corner Meeting

> Ladder, flag, and amplifier:
> what the soap box
> used to be.
> The speaker catches fire
> looking at their faces.
> His words
> jump down to stand
> in listeners' places.


## Projection

> On the day when the Savoy
> leaps clean over to Seventh Avenue
> and starts jitterbugging
> with the Renaissance,
> on that day when Abyssinia Baptist Church
> throws her enormous arms around
> St. James Presbyterian
> and 409 Edgecombe

stoops to kiss 12 West 133rd,
on that day—
Do, Jesus!
Manhattan Island will whirl
like a Dizzy Gillespie transcription
played by Inez and Timme.
On that day, Lord,
Sammy Davis and Marian Anderson
will sing a duet,
Paul Robeson
will team up with Jackie Mabley,
and Father Divine will say in truth,

 *Peace!*
 *It's truly*
 *wonderful!*


## Flatted Fifths

Little cullud boys with beards
re-bop be-bop mop and stop.

Little cullud boys with fears,
frantic, kick their draftee years
into flatted fifths and flatter beers
that at a sudden change become
sparkling Oriental wines
rich and strange
silken bathrobes with gold twines
and Heilbroner, Crawford,
Nat-undreamed-of Lewis combines
in silver thread and diamond notes
on trade-marks inside
Howard coats.

Little cullud boys in berets
 *oop pop-a-da*
horse a fantasy of days
 *ool ya koo*
and dig all plays.

## Tomorrow

Tomorrow may be
a thousand years off:

TWO DIMES AND A NICKEL ONLY

says this particular
cigarette machine.

Others take a quarter straight.

*Some dawns*
*wait.*

## Mellow

Into the laps
of black celebrities
white girls fall
like pale plums from a tree
beyond a high tension wall
wired for killing
which makes it
more thrilling.

## Live and Let Live

Maybe it ain't right—
but the people of the night
will give even
a snake
a break.

## Gauge

> Hemp . . .
> A stick . . .
> A roach . . .
> Straw . . .

## Bar

> That whiskey will cook the egg.
> *Say not so!*
> *Maybe the egg*
> *will cook the whiskey.*
> You ought to know!

## Café: 3 a.m.

> Detectives from the vice squad
> with weary sadistic eyes
> spotting fairies.
> *Degenerates,*
> some folks say.
>
> But God, Nature,
> or somebody
> made them that way.
>
> Police lady or Lesbian
> over there?
> *Where?*

## Drunkard

> Voice grows thicker
> as song grows stronger
> as time grows longer until day
> trying to forget to remember
> the taste of day.

## Street Song

> Jack, if you got to be a rounder
> Be a rounder right—
> Just don't let mama catch you
> Makin' rounds at night.

## 125th Street

> Face like a chocolate bar
> full of nuts and sweet.
>
> Face like a jack-o'-lantern,
> candle inside.
>
> Face like a slice of melon,
> grin that wide.

## Dive

> Lenox Avenue
> by daylight
> runs to dive in the Park
> but faster . . .
> faster . . .
> after dark.

## Warning: Augmented

> Don't let your dog curb you!
> Curb your doggie
> Like you ought to do,
> But don't let that dog curb you!
> You may play folks cheap,

Act rough and tough,
But a dog can tell
When you're full of stuff.
Them little old mutts
Look all scraggly and bad,
But they got more sense
Than some people ever had.
Cur dog, fice dog, kerry blue—
Just don't let your dog curb you!


## Up-Beat

In the gutter
boys who try
might meet girls
on the fly
as out of the gutter
girls who will
may meet boys
copping a thrill
while from the gutter
both can rise:
But it requires
plenty eyes.


## Jam Session

Letting midnight
out on bail
*pop-a-da*
having been
detained in jail
*oop-pop-a-da*
for sprinkling salt
on a dreamer's tail
*pop-a-da*

## Be-Bop Boys

Imploring Mecca
to achieve
six discs
with Decca.

## Tag

Little cullud boys
with fears,
frantic,
nudge their draftee years.

*Pop-a-da!*

## Theme for English B

The instructor said,

*Go home and write*
*a page tonight.*
*And let that page come out of you —*
*Then, it will be true.*

I wonder if it's that simple?
I am twenty-two, colored, born in Winston-Salem.
I went to school there, then Durham, then here
to this college on the hill above Harlem.
I am the only colored student in my class.
The steps from the hill lead down into Harlem,
through a park, then I cross St. Nicholas,
Eighth Avenue, Seventh, and I come to the Y,
the Harlem Branch Y, where I take the elevator
up to my room, sit down, and write this page:

It's not easy to know what is true for you or me
at twenty-two, my age. But I guess I'm what
I feel and see and hear, Harlem, I hear you:

hear you, hear me—we two—you, me, talk on this page.
(I hear New York, too.) Me—who?
Well, I like to eat, sleep, drink, and be in love.
I like to work, read, learn, and understand life.
I like a pipe for a Christmas present,
or records—Bessie, bop, or Bach.
I guess being colored doesn't make me *not* like
the same things other folks like who are other races.
So will my page be colored that I write?
Being me, it will not be white.
But it will be
a part of you, instructor.
You are white—
yet a part of me, as I am a part of you.
That's American.
Sometimes perhaps you don't want to be a part of me.
Nor do I often want to be a part of you.
But we are, that's true!
As I learn from you,
I guess you learn from me—
although you're older—and white—
and somewhat more free.

This is my page for English B.


## College Formal: Renaissance Casino

Golden girl
in a golden gown
in a melody night
in Harlem town
lad tall and brown
tall and wise
college boy smart
eyes in eyes
the music wraps
them both around
in mellow magic
of dancing sound
till they're the heart
of the whole big town
gold and brown

## Low to High

How can you forget me?
But you do!
You said you was gonna take me
Up with you—
Now you've got your Cadillac,
you done forgot that you are black.
How can you forget me
When I'm you?

*But you do.*

How can you forget me,
fellow, say?
How can you low-rate me
this way?
You treat me like you damn well please,
Ignore me—though I pay your fees.
How can you forget me?

*But you do.*

## Boogie: 1 a.m.

Good evening, daddy!
I know you've heard
The boogie-woogie rumble
Of a dream deferred
Trilling the treble
And twining the bass
Into midnight ruffles
Of cat-gut lace.

## High to Low

God knows
We have our troubles, too—
One trouble is you:
you talk too loud,

cuss too loud,
look too black,
don't get anywhere,
and sometimes it seems
you don't even care.
The way you send your kids to school
stockings down,
(not Ethical Culture)
the way you shout out loud in church,
(not St. Phillip's)
and the way you lounge on doorsteps
just as if you were down South,
(not at 409)
the way you clown—
the way, in other words,
you let me down—
me, trying to uphold the race
and you—
well, you can see,
we have our problems,
too, with you.


## Lady's Boogie

See that lady
Dressed so fine?
She ain't got boogie-woogie
On her mind—

But if she was to listen
I bet she'd hear,
Way up in the treble
The tingle of a tear.

*Be-Bach!*

## So Long

*So long*
is in the song
and it's in the way you're gone
but it's like a foreign language
in my mind
and maybe was I blind
I could not see
and would not know
you're gone so long
so long.

## Deferred

*This year, maybe, do you think I can graduate?*
*I'm already two years late.*
*Dropped out six months when I was seven,*
*a year when I was eleven,*
*then got put back when we come North.*
*To get through high at twenty's kind of late—*
*But maybe this year I can graduate.*

Maybe now I can have that white enamel stove
I dreamed about when we first fell in love
eighteen years ago.
But you know,
rooming and everything
then kids,
cold-water flat and all that.
But now my daughter's married
And my boy's most grown—
quit school to work—
and where we're moving
there ain't no stove—
Maybe I can buy that white enamel stove!

*Me, I always did want to study French.*
*It don't make sense—*
*I'll never go to France,*
*but night schools teach French.*
*Now at last I've got a job*
*where I get off at five,*

*in time to wash and dress,*
*so, s'il vous plaît, I'll study French!*

Someday,
I'm gonna buy two new suits
at once!

*All I want is*
*one more bottle of gin.*

All I want is to see
my furniture paid for.

*All I want is a wife who will*
*work with me and not against me. Say,*
*baby, could you see your way clear?*

Heaven, heaven, is my home!
This world I'll leave behind
When I set my feet in glory
I'll have a throne for mine!

*I want to pass the civil service.*

I want a television set.

*You know, as old as I am,*
*I ain't never*
*owned a decent radio yet?*

I'd like to take up Bach.

> *Montage*
> *of a dream*
> *deferred.*

Buddy, have you heard?

## Request

> Gimme $25.00
> and the change.
> I'm going
> where the morning
> and the evening
> won't bother me.

## Shame on You

> If you're great enough
> and clever enough
> the government might honor you.
> But the people will forget—
> Except on holidays.
>
> A movie house in Harlem named after Lincoln,
> Nothing at all named after John Brown.
> Black people don't remember
> any better than white.
>
> If you're not alive and kicking,
> *shame on you!*

## World War II

> What a grand time was the war!
> Oh, my, my!
> What a grand time was the war!
> My, my, my!
> In wartime we had fun,
> Sorry that old war is done!
> What a grand time was the war,
> My, my!
>
> Echo:
> *Did*
> *Somebody*
> *Die?*

# Mystery

When a chile gets to be thirteen
and ain't seen Christ yet,
she needs to set on de moaner's bench
night and day.

*Jesus, lover of my soul!*

Hail, Mary, mother of God!

*Let me to thy bosom fly!*

Amen! Hallelujah!

*Swing low, sweet chariot,*
*Coming for to carry me home.*

Sunday morning where the rhythm flows,
how old nobody knows—
yet old as mystery,
older than creed,
basic and wondering
and lost as my need.

    *Eli, eli!*

    *Te deum!*

    *Mahomet!*

    *Christ!*

Father Bishop, Effendi, Mother Horne,
Father Divine, a Rabbi black
as black was born,
a jack-leg preacher, a Ph.D.

    *The mystery*
    *and the darkness*
    *and the song*
    *and me.*

## Sliver of Sermon

When pimps out of loneliness cry:
*Great God!*
Whores in final weariness say:
*Great God!*
*Oh, God!*
*My God!*

Great
God!

## Testimonial

If I just had a piano,
if I just had a organ,
if I just had a drum,
how I could praise my Lord!

But I don't need no piano,
neither organ
nor drum
for to praise my Lord!

## Passing

On sunny summer Sunday afternoons in Harlem
when the air is one interminable ball game
and grandma cannot get her gospel hymns
from the Saints of God in Christ
on account of the Dodgers on the radio,
on sunny Sunday afternoons
when the kids look all new
and far too clean to stay that way,
and Harlem has its
washed-and-ironed-and-cleaned-best out,
the ones who've crossed the line
to live downtown
miss you,
Harlem of the bitter dream,
since their dream has
come true.

## Nightmare Boogie

I had a dream
and I could see
a million faces
black as me!
A nightmare dream:
*Quicker than light*
*All them faces*
*Turned dead white!*
Boogie-woogie,
Rolling bass,
Whirling treble
of cat-gut lace.

## Sunday by the Combination

I feel like dancin', baby,
till the sun goes down.

But I wonder where
the sunrise
Monday morning's gonna be?

I feel like dancin'!
Baby, dance with me!

## Casualty

He was a soldier in the army,
But he doesn't walk like one.
He walks like his soldiering
Days are done.

Son! . . . Son!

# Night Funeral in Harlem

Night funeral
In Harlem:

*Where did they get*
*Them two fine cars?*

Insurance man, he did not pay—
His insurance lapsed the other day—
Yet they got a satin box
For his head to lay.

Night funeral
In Harlem:

*Who was it sent*
*That wreath of flowers?*

Them flowers came
from that poor boy's friends—
They'll want flowers, too,
When they meet their ends.

Night funeral
In Harlem:

*Who preached that*
*Black boy to his grave?*

Old preacher man
Preached that boy away—
Charged Five Dollars
His girl friend had to pay.

Night funeral
In Harlem:

When it was all over
And the lid shut on his head
and the organ had done played
and the last prayers been said
and six pallbearers
Carried him out for dead
And off down Lenox Avenue
That long black hearse done sped,

The street light
At his corner
Shined just like a tear—
That boy that they was mournin'
Was so dear, so dear
To them folks that brought the flowers,
To that girl who paid the preacher man—
It was all their tears that made
That poor boy's
Funeral grand.

Night funeral
In Harlem.

## Blues at Dawn

I don't dare start thinking in the morning.
I don't dare start thinking in the morning.
If I thought thoughts in bed,
Them thoughts would bust my head—
So I don't dare start thinking in the morning.

I don't dare remember in the morning
Don't dare remember in the morning.
If I recall the day before,
I wouldn't get up no more—
So I don't dare remember in the morning.

## Dime

Chile, these steps is hard to climb.

*Grandma, lend me a dime.*

Montage of a dream deferred:

*Grandma acts like*
*She ain't heard.*

Chile, Granny ain't got no dime.

*I might've knowed*
*It all the time.*

## Argument [2]

White is right,
Yellow mellow,
Black, get back!

*Do you believe that, Jack?*

Sure do!

*Then you're a dope*
*for which there ain't no hope.*
*Black is fine!*
*And, God knows,*
*It's mine!*

## Neighbor

Down home
he sets on a stoop
and watches the sun go by.
In Harlem
when his work is done
he sets in a bar with a beer.
He looks taller than he is
and younger than he ain't.
He looks darker than he is, too.
And he's smarter than he looks,

*He ain't smart.*
*That cat's a fool.*

Naw, he ain't neither.
He's a good man,

except that he talks too much.
In fact, he's a great cat.
But when he drinks,
he drinks fast.

    *Sometimes*
    *he don't drink.*

True,
he just
lets his glass
set there.


## Evening Song

A woman standing in the doorway
Trying to make her where-with-all:
*Come here, baby, darlin'!*
*Don't you hear me call?*

If I was anybody's sister,
I'd tell her, *Gimme a place to sleep.*
But I ain't nobody's sister.
I'm just a poor lost sheep.

Mary, Mary, Mary,
Had a little lamb.
Well, I hope that lamb of Mary's
Don't turn out like I am.


## Chord

Shadow faces
In the shadow night
Before the early dawn
Bops bright.

## Fact

There's been an eagle on a nickel,
An eagle on a quarter, too.
But there ain't no eagle
On a dime.

## Joe Louis [1]

They worshipped Joe.
A school teacher
whose hair was gray
said:
> *Joe has sense enough to know*
> *He is a god.*
> *So many gods don't know.*

"They say" . . . "They say" . . . "They say" . . .
But the gossips had no
"They say"
to latch onto
for Joe.

## Subway Rush Hour

Mingled
breath and smell
so close
mingled
black and white
so near
no room for fear.

## Brothers

We're related—you and I,
You from the West Indies,
I from Kentucky.

Kinsmen—you and I,
You from Africa,
I from the U.S.A.

Brothers—you and I.

## Likewise

The Jews:
    Groceries
    Suits
    Fruits
    Watches
    Diamond rings
    THE DAILY NEWS
Jews sell me things.
Yom Kippur, no!
Shops all over Harlem
close up tight that night.

Some folks blame high prices on the Jews.
(Some folks blame too much on Jews.)
But in Harlem they don't answer back,
Just maybe shrug their shoulders,
"What's the use?"
What's the use
in Harlem?
What's the use?
What's the Harlem
use in Harlem
what's the lick?

*Hey!*
*Baba-re-bop!*
*Mop!*
*On a be-bop kick!*

Sometimes I think
Jews must have heard
the music of a
dream deferred.

## Sliver

Cheap little rhymes
A cheap little tune
Are sometimes as dangerous
As a sliver of the moon.
A cheap little tune
To cheap little rhymes
Can cut a man's
Throat sometimes.

## Hope [2]

He rose up on his dying bed
and asked for fish.
His wife looked it up in her dream book
and played it.

## Dream Boogie: Variation

Tinkling treble,
Rolling bass,
High noon teeth
In a midnight face,
Great long fingers
On great big hands,
Screaming pedals
Where his twelve-shoe lands,

Looks like his eyes
Are teasing pain,
A few minutes late
For the Freedom Train.


## Harlem [2]


What happens to a dream deferred?

Does it dry up
like a raisin in the sun?
Or fester like a sore —
And then run?
Does it stink like rotten meat?
Or crust and sugar over —
like a syrupy sweet?

Maybe it just sags
like a heavy load.

*Or does it explode?*


## Good Morning


Good morning, daddy!
I was born here, he said,
watched Harlem grow
until colored folks spread
from river to river
across the middle of Manhattan
out of Penn Station
dark tenth of a nation,
planes from Puerto Rico,
and holds of boats, chico,
up from Cuba Haiti Jamaica,
in buses marked New York
from Georgia Florida Louisiana
to Harlem Brooklyn the Bronx

but most of all to Harlem
dusky sash across Manhattan
I've seen them come dark
  wondering
  wide-eyed
  dreaming
out of Penn Station—
but the trains are late.
The gates open—
   Yet there're bars
   at each gate.

    What happens
    to a dream deferred?

    Daddy, ain't you heard?


## Same in Blues

   I said to my baby,
   Baby, take it slow.
   I can't, she said, I can't!
   I got to go!

    *There's a certain*
    *amount of traveling*
    *in a dream deferred.*

   Lulu said to Leonard,
   I want a diamond ring.
   Leonard said to Lulu,
   You won't get a goddamn thing!

    *A certain*
    *amount of nothing*
    *in a dream deferred.*

   Daddy, daddy, daddy,
   All I want is you.

You can have me, baby—
but my lovin' days is through.

> *A certain*
> *amount of impotence*
> *in a dream deferred.*

Three parties
On my party line—
But that third party,
Lord, ain't mine!

> *There's liable*
> *to be confusion*
> *in a dream deferred.*

From river to river,
Uptown and down,
There's liable to be confusion
when a dream gets kicked around.


## Comment on Curb

> You talk like
> they don't kick
> dreams around
> downtown.

> > *I expect they do—*
> > *But I'm talking about*
> > *Harlem to you!*

# Letter

*Dear Mama,*
        *Time I pay rent and get my food*
*and laundry I don't have much left*
*but here is five dollars for you*
*to show you I still appreciates you.*
*My girl-friend send her love and say*
*she hopes to lay eyes on you sometime in life.*
*Mama, it has been raining cats and dogs up*
*here. Well, that is all so I will close.*
        *Your son baby*
            *Respectably as ever,*
                *Joe*


# Island [2]

Between two rivers,
North of the park,
Like darker rivers
The streets are dark.

Black and white,
Gold and brown—
Chocolate-custard
Pie of a town.

*Dream within a dream,*
*Our dream deferred.*

Good morning, daddy!

Ain't you heard?

# Tomorrow's Seed

Proud banner of death,
I see them waving
There against the sky,
Struck deep in Spanish earth
Where your dark bodies lie
Inert and helpless—
So they think
Who do not know
That from your death
New life will grow.
For there are those who cannot see
The mighty roots of liberty
Push upward in the dark
To burst in flame—
A million stars—
And one your name:
    Man
Who fell in Spanish earth:
Human seed
For freedom's birth.

# Hero—International Brigade

Blood,
Or a flag,
Or a flame
Or life itself
Are they the same:
Our dream?
    I came.
An ocean in-between
And half a continent.
Frontiers,
And mountains skyline tall,
And governments that told me NO,
YOU CANNOT GO!
    I came.
On tomorrow's bright frontiers
I placed the strength and wisdom
Of my years.
Not much,

For I am young.
(*Was* young,
Perhaps it's better said—
For now I'm dead.)

But had I lived four score and ten
Life could not've had
A better end.
I've given what I wished
And what I had to give
That others live.
And when the bullets
Cut my heart away,
And the blood
Gushed to my throat
I wondered if it were blood
Gushing there.
Or a red flame?
Or just my death
Turned into life?
They're all the same:
Our dream!
    My death!
    Your life!
    Our blood!
    One flame!
They're all the same!

## The Christmas Story

Tell me again the Christmas story:
Christ is born in all His glory!

Baby born in Manger dark
Lighting ages with the spark
Of innocence that is the Child
Trusting all within His smile.

Tell again the Christmas story
With the halo of His glory:
Halo born of humbleness

432

By the breath of cattle blest,
By the poverty of stall
Where a bed of straw is all,
By a door closed at the Inn,
Only men of means get in
By a door closed to the poor,
Christ is born on earthen floor
In a stable with no lock—
Yet kingdoms tremble at the shock
Of a King in swaddling clothes
At an address no one knows
Because there is no painted sign—
Nothing but a star divine,
Nothing but a halo bright
About His young head in the night,
Nothing but the wondrous light
Of innocence that is the Child
Trusting all within His smile.

Mary's Son of golden star:
Wise Men journey from afar.
Mary's Son in Manger born:
Music of the Angel's horn.
Mary's Son in straw and glory:

Wonder of the Christmas story!


## No Regrets

Out of love,
No regrets—
Though the goodness
Be wasted forever.

Out of love,
No regrets—
Though the return
Be never.

# Vari-Colored Song

If I had a heart of gold,
As have some folks I know,
I'd up and sell my heart of gold
And head North with the dough.

But I don't have a heart of gold.
My heart's not even lead.
It's made of plain old Georgia clay.
That's why my heart is red.

I wonder why red clay's so red
And Georgia skies so blue.
I wonder why it's *yes* to me,
But *yes, sir,* sir, to you.

I wonder why the sky's so blue
And why the clay's so red.
Why down South is always *down,*
And never *up* instead.

# A Ballad of Negro History   (So Much to Write About)

Written especially for The Authors Association at the request
of Dr. M. A. Majors, June, 1951.

There is so much to write about
In the Negro race.
On each page of history
Glows a dusky face.
Ancient Pharaohs come to mind
Away back in B.C.
Ethiopia's jewelled hand
Writes a scroll for me.
It was a black man bore the Cross
For Christ at Calvary.
There is so much to write about
In the Negro race.
Though now of Ghana's Empire
There remains no trace,
Once Africa's great cultures
Lighted Europe's dark
As Mandingo and Songhay
Cradled learning's ark

Before the Moors crossed into Spain
To leave their mark.
There is so much to write about
In the Negro race.
Ere the ships of slavery sailed
The seas of dark disgrace,
Once Antar added
Winged words to poetry's lore
And Juan Latino searched
The medieval heart's deep core—
All this before black men in chains
At Jamestown were put ashore.
There is so much to write about
In the Negro race,
So many thrilling stories
Time cannot erase:
Crispus Attuck's blow for freedom,
Denmark Vesey's, too.
Sojourner Truth, Fred Douglass,
And the heroes John Brown knew—
Before the Union Armies gave
Black men proud uniforms of blue.
1863—Emancipation!
The Negro race
Began its mighty struggle
For a rightful place
In the making of America
To whose young land it gave
Booker T. and Carver—
Each genius born a slave—
Yet foreordained to greatness
On the crest of freedom's wave.
Paul Laurence Dunbar
Penned his rhymes of lyric lace—
All the sadness and the humor
Of the Negro race.
To the words of colored Congressmen
The Halls of Congress rang.
Handy wrote the blues.
Williams and Walker sang.
Still on southern trees today
Dark bodies hang.
The story is one of struggle
For the Negro race—
But in spite of all the lynch ropes,

We've marched on to take our place:
Woodson, Negro History Week,
Du Bois, Johnson, Drew,
Cullen, Maynor, Bunche,
The cultural record grew.
Edith Sampson went around the world
To tell the nations what she knew—
And Josephine came home from France
To claim an equal chance
Through song and dance.
There is so much to write about
To sing about, to shout about
In the Negro race!
On each page of history
America sees my face—
On each page of history
We leave a shining trace—
On each page of history
    My race!
        My race!
            My race!

## Hope for Harlem

There's a new skyline in Harlem,
It's tall and proud and fine.
At night its walls are gleaming
Where a thousand windows shine.

There's a new skyline in Harlem
That belongs to you and me
As the dark old ugly houses
Tumble into memory—

Memory of those dingy stairs,
Memory of my helpless prayers,
Memory of the landlord's stares
When you asked him for a few repairs.

Now there's a new skyline in Harlem.
It's rising tall and free—

And if it keeps on rising
There'll be a brand new *me*.

Don't you know it makes a difference
When you got a clean new house?
I used to hear those old rats gnawing.
Now I don't even hear a mouse.

I used to climb those old steps,
Up dark old creaking stairs —
And sometimes I said a cuss word
Before I said my prayers.

But there's a new skyline in Harlem,
And I'm thankful when I pray
That the yard is bigger than a park,
And kids have a chance to play.

That the walls are painted pretty,
And the bathroom has a shower —
For folks who never thought they'd live
In a house that's got a tower.

> *A stone to throw*
> *Or a stone to build with?*
> *A brick for a brickbat*
> *Or a brick for a wall?*
> *Stones are better*
> *For building,*
> *Bricks are better*
> *For a wall.*

That's why I'm mighty happy
When I see those old walls fall,
When I see dead trees uprooted
For new trees to grow tall.

And I'm mighty glad I'm lucky
My name stayed on the list
To get a new apartment
Where I *live* — not just exist.

But I can't forget my brothers
Nor my sisters down the street

In those broken down old houses
Where both ends never meet.

Houses where the steps are creaking,
Where rats gnaw at the floors,
And a dozen names are sticking
In the doorbells at the doors.

Where clean clothes hang like banners
From dingy wall to wall—
Clothes that are *really* banners
Waving for us all—

Waving to the glory
Of those who climb the stairs
To wash the clothes of trying
In the soapsuds of their prayers.

But the old skyline is sagging.
It looks sadder than before.
So I hope the day is coming
When there won't be any more.

Houses where the steps are creaking
And rats gnaw at the floors
And a dozen names are sticking
In each doorbell at the doors.

For there's a new skyline in Harlem.
It's rising here and there.
We're waiting for that skyline
To start rising everywhere!

*A new skyline in Harlem—*
*The answer to a prayer!*

# Ultimatum: Kid to Kid

Go home, stupid,
And wash your dirty face.
Go home, stupid,
This is not your place.

Go home, stupid,
You don't belong here.
If you don't go,
I will pull your ear.

I ask you if you'd like to play.
"Huh?" is all you know to say,
Standing 'round here
In the way.

So go home, stupid!
I'll spit in your eye!
Stupid, go home —
Before I cry.

# Ballad of the Two Thieves

When Jesus died at Calvary
For what our world believes,
On either side upon a Cross
They hung two thieves —

Two members of a lowly mob
Who stole to get their bread
Were tied upon a Cross that day
To taste of death instead.

One thief looked at Christ and said,
*If you're so great*
*As your followers swear —*
*Save yourself! Save me!*
*And save my brother thief there —*
*If you're as great*
*As your followers swear!*

But he did not speak for his brother thief
Hanging on the gallows tree,

For the other thief cried only,
*Lord, remember me!*

Christ had the thorns upon His head
And in His mouth was gall.
From His palms the blood ran red
And on the ground did fall.

*For the sins of man I suffer.*
*For the sins of man I die—*
*My body and my blood*
*Are the answer to your cry.*

*In the garden one betrayed me,*
*And Peter denied me thrice*
*But you who cry, Remember me!*
*Go with me to Paradise.*


## Bible Belt

It would be too bad if Jesus
Were to come back black.
There are so many churches
Where he could not pray
In the U.S.A.,
Where entrance to Negroes,
No matter how sanctified,
Is denied,
Where race, not religion,
Is glorified.
But say it—
*You* may be
Crucified.

# Africa

Sleepy giant,
You've been resting awhile.
Now I see the thunder
And the lightning
In your smile.
Now I see
The storm clouds
In your waking eyes:
The thunder,
The wonder,
And the young
Surprise.
Your every step reveals
The new stride
In your thighs.

# Envoy to Africa

My name is Lord Piggly-Wiggly Wogglesfoot Brown.
I was born in a quaint old English manor town.
I now find myself engaged in a diplomatic chore
That looks as though it might turn into a bit of a bore.
I was sent to inform the natives of this dark place
That the Atlantic Charter will eventually apply to their race.
Of course, at the moment, we could hardly afford
To stretch the Atlantic Charter that broad.
But I will say this to each native race:
    *Some day you'll be equal—*
    *If you'll just stay in your place.*

# Ballad of Booker T.

Booker T.
Was a practical man.
He said, Till the soil
And learn from the land.
Let down your bucket
Where you are.

Your fate is here,
Not afar.
To help yourself
And your fellow man,
Train your head,
Your heart, and your hand.
For smartness alone
Is surely not meet—
If you haven't
At the same time
Got something to eat.
At Tuskegee
He built a school
With book-learning there
Plus the workman's tool.
He started out
In a simple way—
For yesterday
Was not today.
Sometimes he had
Compromise in his talk—
A man must crawl
Before he can walk:
In Alabama in '85
To be alive.
But Booker T.
Was nobody's fool:
A Negro was lucky
You may carve a dream
With a humble tool.
The tallest tower
Can tumble down
If it is not rooted
In solid ground.
So, being a far-seeing
Practical man,
He said, Train your head,
Your heart, and your hand.
Your fate is here,
Not afar,
Let down your bucket
Where you are.

## Addition [2]

Put 5 and 5 together
And see if it makes 10.

It does—
If 5 is exactly 5.

But don't let women
Come between—
Or men.

## Poet to Bigot

I have done so little
For you,
And you have done so little
For me,
That we have good reason
Never to agree.

I, however,
Have such meagre
Power,
Clutching at a
Moment,
While you control
An hour.

But your hour is
A stone.

My moment is
A flower.

## Room

Each little room
Should be
Protective and alone
When there are two—

But wide open
To the air
When only one
Is there.


## Do You Reckon?

Mr. White Man, White Man,
How can it be,
You sleep with my sister,
Yet you won't shake hands with me?

Miss White Lady, Lady,
Tell me, if you can,
Why you hard-work my mother,
Yet take my brother for your man?

White Man, White Lady,
What's your story, anyway?
You love me in the night time
And hate me in the day.

Dixie, Dixie, Dixie,
What make you do me like you do?
*But I guess if I was white*
*I would act the same way, too.*


## Lincoln University: 1954

This is the dream grown young
By but a hundred years,
The dream so bravely tended
Through a century of fears,
The dream so gently nourished
By a century of tears—
The dream grown ever younger,
Greener, fresher
Through the years of working,
Praying, striving, learning,
The dream become a beacon
Brightly burning.

# Draftees

Leave your Coras
And your Oras
In the candy stores
And the cocktail bars.

Leave your papas
And your mamas
And your sisters
And your brothers
And your cousins
By the dozens
Behind.

Take your little bag
With a toothbrush and a comb
And leave home.

*What's on your mind?*

Goodbye, Ora!
Goodbye, Cora!
Goodbye, Kiddie!

*Hello, Biddie,*
*Overseas.*

Basic training
(That is basic)
Is basic
In these.

# Azikiwe in Jail

The British said to Azikiwe,
*We're tired of you running around loose.*
*We're going to grab you—*
*And cook your goose.*

Azikiwe said to the British,
*That may be—*
*But you'll have a tough goose*
*If you cook me!*

## Old Walt

Old Walt Whitman
Went finding and seeking,
Finding less than sought
Seeking more than found,
Every detail minding
Of the seeking or the finding.

Pleasured equally
In seeking as in finding,
Each detail minding,
Old Walt went seeking
And finding.

## Without Benefit of Declaration

Listen here, Joe,
Don't you know
That tomorrow
You got to go
Out yonder where
The steel winds blow?

Listen here, kid,
It's been said
Tomorrow you'll be dead
Out there where
The rain is lead.

Don't ask me why.
Just go ahead and die.
Hidden from the sky
Out yonder you'll lie:
A medal to your family—
In exchange for
    A guy.

*Mama, don't cry.*

## Us: Colored

So strange,
We are completely out of range—
Becomes a cause
Beyond the laws—
So strange.

## Miss Blues'es Child

If the blues would let me,
Lord knows I would smile.
If the blues would let me,
I would smile, smile, smile.
Instead of that I'm cryin'—
I must be Miss Blues'es child.

You were my moon up in the sky,
At night my wishing star.
I love you, oh, I love you so—
But you have gone so far!

Now my days are lonely,
And night-time drives me wild.
In my heart I'm crying,
I'm just Miss Blues'es child!

## Delinquent

Little Julie
Has grown quite tall.
Folks say she don't like
To stay home at all.

Little Julie
Has grown quite stout.
Folks say it's not just
Stomach sticking out.

Little Julie
Has grown quite wise—

A tiger, a lion, and an owl
In her eyes.

Little Julie
Says she don't care!
What she means is:
*Nobody cares*
*Anywhere.*


## Georgia Dusk

Sometimes there's a wind in the Georgia dusk
That cries and cries and cries
Its lonely pity through the Georgia dusk
Veiling what the darkness hides.

Sometimes there's blood in the Georgia dusk,
Left by a streak of sun,
A crimson trickle in the Georgia dusk.
Whose blood? . . . Everyone's.

Sometimes a wind in the Georgia dusk
Scatters hate like seed
To sprout its bitter barriers
Where the sunsets bleed.


## Mean Old Yesterday

That mean old yesterday
Keeps on following me.
The things I've said and done
Haunt me like a misery.

What I did last year—
How come it matters still today?
The snow that fell last winter's
Melted away.

I thought you'd done forgotten
What happened way last week,
But when I saw you this morning,
You turned your head and would not speak.

Memory like an elephant,
Never forget a thing!
Well, if you feel like that, baby,
Gimme back my diamond ring.

## In Explanation of Our Times

The folks with no titles in front of their names
all over the world
are raring up and talking back
to the folks called Mister.

You say you thought everybody was called Mister?

No, son, not everybody.
In Dixie, often they won't call Negroes Mister.
In China before what happened
They had no intention of calling coolies Mister.
Dixie to Singapore, Cape Town to Hong Kong
the Misters won't call lots of other folks Mister.
They call them, Hey George!
 Here, Sallie!
 Listen, Coolie!
 Hurry up, Boy!
 And things like that.

George Sallie Coolie Boy gets tired sometimes.
So all over the world today
folks with not even Mister in front of their names
are raring up and talking back
to those called Mister.
From Harlem past Hong Kong talking back.

Shut up, says Gerald L. K. Smith.
Shut up, says the Governor of South Carolina.

Shut up, says the Governor of Singapore.
Shut up, says Strydom.

Hell no shut up! say the people
with no titles in front of their names.
Hell, no! It's time to talk back now!
History says it's time,
And the radio, too, foggy with propaganda
that says a mouthful
and don't mean half it says—
but is true anyhow:
    LIBERTY!
    FREEDOM!
    DEMOCRACY!
True anyhow no matter how many
Liars use those words.

The people with no titles in front of their names
hear those words and shout them back
at the Misters, Lords, Generals, Viceroys,
Governors of South Carolina, Gerald L. K. Strydoms.

    Shut up, people!
    Shut up! Shut up!
    Shut up, George!
    Shut up, Sallie!
    Shut up, Coolie!
    Shut up, Indian!
    Shut up, Boy!

George Sallie Coolie Indian Boy
black brown yellow bent down working
earning riches for the whole world
with no title in front of name
just man woman tired says:

    No shut up!
    Hell no shut up!
    So, naturally, there's trouble
    in these our times
    because of people with no titles
    in front of their names.

# Little Song on Housing

Here I come!
Been saving all my life
To get a nice home
For me and my wife.

*White folks flee—*
*As soon as you see*
*My problems*
*And me!*

Neighborhood's clean,
But the house is old,
Prices are doubled
When I get sold:
Still I buy.

*White folks fly—*
*Soon as you spy*
*My wife*
*And I!*

Next thing you know,
Our neighbors all colored are.
The candy store's
Turned into a bar:
White folks have left
The whole neighborhood
To my black self.

*White folks flee!*
*Still—there is me!*
*White folks, fly!*
*Here am I!*


# Plaint

Money and art
Are far apart

## The Thorn

Now there will be nobody, you say,
To start a *cause célèbre*,
To snatch a brand from the burning,
Or be a thorn in the side.

*You must be forgetting*
*The cause not yet célèbre,*
*The brand that's in the burning,*
*The thorn that awaits turning—*
*That turns with nobody there*
*To start the turning.*


## Mississippi

Oh, what sorrow!
Oh, what pity!
Oh, what pain
That tears and blood
Should mix like rain
And terror come again
To Mississippi.

Again?
Where has terror been?
On vacation? Up North?
In some other section
Of the Nation,
Lying low, unpublicized,
Masked—with only
Jaundiced eyes showing
Through the mask?

What sorrow, pity, pain,
That tears and blood
Still mix like rain
In Mississippi!

# Brotherly Love

A Little Letter to the White Citizens of the South

In line of what my folks say in Montgomery,
In line of what they're teaching about love,
When I reach out my hand, will *you* take it—
Or cut it off and leave a nub above?

If I found it in my heart to love you,
And if I thought I really could,
If I said, "Brother, I forgive you,"
I wonder, would it do *you* any good?

So long, so *long* a time you've been calling
Me *all* kinds of names, pushing me down—
I been swimming with my head deep under water,
And you wished I would stay under till I drown.

But I didn't! I'm still swimming! Now you're mad
Because I won't ride in the back end of your bus.
When I answer, "Anyhow, I'm gonna love you,"
Still and yet *you* want to make a fuss.

Now listen, white folks!
In line with Reverend King down in Montgomery—
Also because the Bible says I must—
I'm gonna love you—*yes, I will! Or BUST!*

# Two Somewhat Different Epigrams

I

Oh, God of dust and rainbows, help us see
That without dust the rainbow would not be.

II

I look with awe upon the human race
And God, who sometimes spits right in its face.

## Last Call

I look out into the Yonder
And I don't know where I go—
So I cry, *Lord! Lord!*

Yours is the only name I know.

Some folks might say Your ear is deaf
To one who never called before.
Some folks might say You'll scorn me
Since I never sought Your door.

Yet I cry, *Lord! Lord!*

Lord, that is Your name?

I never knew You,
Never called You.
Still I call You now.

I'm game.


## Late Corner

The street light
On its lonely arm
Becomes
An extension
Of the Cross—
The Cross itself
A lonely arm
Whose light is lost.

*Oh, lonely world!*
*Oh, lonely light!*
*Oh, lonely Cross!*

## Acceptance

God, in His infinite wisdom
Did not make me very wise—
So when my actions are stupid
They hardly take God by surprise.

## Testament

*What shall I leave my son*
*When I am dead and gone?*
    Room in hell to join me
    When he passes on.
*What shall I leave my daughter,*
*The apple of my eye?*
    A thousand pounds of salt
    For tears if she should cry.
*What shall I leave my wife*
*Who nagged me to my death?*
    I'll leave her more to nag about
    Than she's got breath.

## Gone Boy

Playboy of the dawn,
Solid gone!
Out all night
Until 12—1—2 a.m.

Next day
When he should be gone
To work—
*Dog-gone!*
He ain't gone.

## Where? When? Which?

When the cold comes
With a bitter fragrance
Like rusty iron and mint,
And the wind blows
Sharp as integration
With an edge like apartheid,
And it is winter,
And the cousins of the too-thin suits
Ride on bitless horses
Tethered by something worse than pride,
Which areaway, or bar,
Or station waiting room
Will not say,
*Horse and horseman, outside!*
With old and not too gentle
Apartheid?

## Memo to Non-White Peoples

They will let you have dope
Because they are quite willing
To drug you or kill you.

They will let you have babies
Because they are quite willing
To pauperize you—
Or use your kids as labor boys
For army, air force, or uranium mine.

They will let you have alcohol
To make you sodden and drunk
And foolish.

They will gleefully let you
Kill your damn self any way you choose
With liquor, drugs, or whatever.

It's the same from Cairo to Chicago,
Cape Town to the Caribbean,

Do you travel the Stork Club circuit
To dear old Shepherd's Hotel?
(Somebody burnt Shepherd's up.)
I'm sorry but it is
The same from Cairo to Chicago,
Cape Town to the Carib Hilton,
Exactly the same.

## Expendable

We will take you and kill you,
Expendable.

We will fill you full of lead,
Expendable.

And when you are dead
In the nice cold ground,
We'll put your name
above your head—

If your head
Can be found.

## Bouquet

Gather quickly
Out of darkness
All the songs you know
And throw them at the sun
Before they melt
Like snow.

## Impasse

I could tell you,
If I wanted to,
What makes me
What I am.

But I don't
Really want to—
And you don't
Give a damn.

## Departure

She lived out a decent span of years
And went to death as should a queen,
Regal in her bravery, hiding fears
More generous than mean—
    Yet even these,
    Lest loved ones weep,
    She carried hidden
    In her heart
    To sleep.

## Dixie South Africa

All the craziness
Of your craziness—
Is an Alka-Seltzer tablet
In the late-night glass of the world:
Watch it melt away
In the dew
Of day.

# Communiqué

I'm sorry for you
Sitting in the driver's seat
With bebop hands
And ragtime feet.
It would indeed
Be good news
Could you but learn
To sing a blues
Or play a boogie-
Woogie beat
So heart might leap
To head or feet.
It is too bad,
Indeed it's sad,
With all the culture
That you've had,
At this late date
Your rhythms don't
Coordinate.
I'm sorry, man!
With all the billing
That you've got,
You're still
Not so hot.

# Casual

Death don't ring no doorbells.
Death don't knock.
Death don't bother to open no doors,
Just comes on through the walls like TV,
Like King Cole on the radio, cool. . . .

Next thing you know, Death's there.
You don't know where Death came from:
Death just comes in
And don't ring no bell.

# Numbered

I think my days are numbered.
I think my days are few.
I think my days are numbered,
Baby, yes, I do!

Which is the reason
I spend my nights with you.


# The Last Man Living

When the last man living
Is left alive on earth,
And somebody knocks at the door—
If I am the last man living
I will be no more!

Who's that? No answer.
Who is that, I say?
If you don't intend to answer,
Then—just—go—away.

Might you be human—
Or might you be a ghost?
Or can you be myself
Imagining things, at most?

If you're somebody else,
And I'm the last man left alive,
Just get on away from here—
'Cause I don't want no jive!


# On a Pallet of Straw

They did not travel in an airplane.
They did not travel by car.
They did not travel on a streamline train.
They traveled on foot from afar.

They traveled on foot from afar.
They did not seek for a fine hotel,
They did not seek an inn,
They did not seek a bright motel,
They sought a cattle bin.
They sought a cattle bin.
Who were these travelers on the road?
And where were they going? And why?
They were Three Wise Men who came from the East,
And they followed a star in the sky,
A star in the sky.
What did they find when they got to the barn?
What did they find near the stall?
What did they find on a pallet of straw?
They found there the Lord of all!
They found the Lord of all!

## Carol of the Brown King

Of the three Wise Men
Who came to the King,
One was a brown man,
So they sing.
Of the three Wise Men
Who followed the Star,
One was a brown king
From afar.
They brought fine gifts
Of spices and gold
In jeweled boxes
Of beauty untold.
Unto His humble
Manger they came
And bowed their heads
In Jesus' name.
Three Wise Men,
One dark like me—
Part of His
Nativity.

# On a Christmas Night

In Bethlehem on a Christmas night
All around the Child shone a holy light.
All around His head was a halo bright
On a Christmas night.
"We have no room," the innkeeper called,
So the glory fell where the cows were stalled,
But among the guests were Three Kings who called
On a Christmas night.
How can it be such a light shines here
In this humble stable once cold and drear?
Oh, the Child has come to bring good cheer
On a Christmas night!
And what is the name of the little One?
His name is Jesus—He's God's own Son.
Be happy, happy, everyone
On a Christmas night!

# Ballad of Mary's Son

It was in the Spring.
The Passover had come.
There was fasting in the streets and joy.
But an awful thing
Happened in the Spring—
Men who knew not what they did
Killed Mary's Boy.

He was Mary's Son,
And the Son of God was He—
Sent to bring the whole world joy.
There were some who could not hear,
And some were filled with fear—
So they built a Cross
For Mary's Boy.

To His Twelve Disciples
He gave them of His bread.
He gave them to drink of His wine.
*This is my body*
*And this is my blood,* He said.
*My Cross for you*
*Will be a sign.*

He went into the garden
And He knelt there to pray.
He said, *Oh, Lord, Thy will be done!*
The soldiers came
And took my Lord away.
They made a Cross
For Mary's Son.

*This is my body*
*And this is my blood!*
His body and His blood divine!
He died on the Cross
That my soul should not be lost.

His body and His blood
Redeem mine.

## Pastoral

Between the little clouds of heaven
They thought they saw
The Saviour peeping through.
For little tears of heaven
They mistook the gentle dew,
And believed the tiny flowers
That grew upon the plain
To be souvenirs of Jesus,
The Child, come back again.

## Little Cats

What happens to little cats?
    Some get drowned in a well,
    Some run over by a car—
    But none goes to hell.

What happens to little cats,
  New born, not been here long?
    Some live out their
    Full nine lives—
As mean as they are strong.

## Not Else—But

Hip boots
Deep in the blues
(And I never had a hip boot on).
Hair
Blowing back in the wind
(And I never had that much hair).
Diamonds in pawn
(And I never had a diamond
In my natural life).
Me
In the White House
(And ain't never had a black house).
Do, Jesus!
Lord!
Amen!

## Angola Question Mark

Don't know why I,
Black,
Must still stand
With my back
To the last frontier
Of fear
In my own land.

Don't know why I
Must turn into
A Mau Mau
And lift my hand
Against my fellow man
To live on my own land.

But it is so—
And being so
I know
*For you and me*
*There's*
*Woe.*

# Tambourines

Tambourines!
Tambourines!
Tambourines
To the glory of God!
Tambourines
To glory!

A gospel shout
And a gospel song:
Life is short
*But God is long!*

Tambourines!
Tambourines!
Tambourines
To glory!

# As Befits a Man

I don't mind dying—
But I'd hate to die all alone!
I want a dozen pretty women
To holler, cry, and moan.

I don't mind dying
But I want my funeral to be fine:
A row of long tall mamas
Fainting, fanning, and crying.

I want a fish-tail hearse
And sixteen fish-tail cars,
A big brass band
And a whole truck load of flowers.

When they let me down,
Down into the clay,
I want the women to holler:
*Please don't take him away!*
　　*Ow-ooo-oo-o!*
*Don't take daddy away!*

## Maybe

I asked you, baby,
If you understood—
You told me that you didn't,
But you thought you would.

## Blue Monday

No use in my going
Downtown to work today,
    It's eight,
    I'm late—
And it's marked down that-a-way.

Saturday and Sunday's
Fun to sport around.
But no use denying—
Monday'll get you down.

That old blue Monday
Will surely get you down.

## To Artina

I will take your heart.
I will take your soul out of your body
As though I were God.
I will not be satisfied
With the little words you say to me.
I will not be satisfied
With the touch of your hand
Nor the sweet of your lips alone.
I will take your heart for mine.
I will take your soul.
I will be God when it comes to you.

## Uncle Tom [2]

Within—
The beaten pride.
Without—
The grinning face,
The low, obsequious,
Double bow,
The sly and servile grace
Of one the white folks
Long ago
Taught well
To know his
Place.


## Jim Crow Car

Get out the lunch-box of your dreams
And bite into the sandwich of your heart,
And ride the Jim Crow car until it screams
And, like an atom bomb, bursts apart.


## Abe Lincoln

Well, I know
You had a hard time in your life.
And I know
You knew what hard times meant.
And I guess you understood
That most folks ain't much good,
Also soon as good things come,
They went.
But I think you hoped
Some folks *sometimes* would act
Somewhat according to the fact
That black or white
Ain't just white
Or black.

# Imagine

Imagine!
They are afraid of you—
*Black dog*
That they have kicked
So long.

Imagine!
They are afraid of you—
*Monkey*
They've laughed at
So long.

Imagine!
They are afraid of you—
*Donkey*
Driven so long.

Imagine—
*Nigger*
They are afraid
Of you!

# "The Jesus"[1]

Until the crumpets and the christians,
Altars of grass bled paths
From Congo to Cape, shifting sacrificially
Through river beds, shifting
From saberthroat to sand
Voodoo rain drummed juju
Away and spring came,
Came with Galilee
Upon its back to chop
The naked bone of mumbo
Dangling like a dice
Swung from a mirror,

1. A ship lent to Sir John Hawkins by
Queen Elizabeth as support to his business
venture in the slave traffic off Cape Verde
in the latter half of the sixteenth century.

Captain of the stumps of Sir John
Lumped cargoes for Cuba
Among feathered kings rolling
Their skins in flax, moulded
To shaftsteel and psalm.
Through helms of smoke
Balloon dreams of grabber kings
Mooned at groaning girls
Bred on black sheets of seahull.
Was the deacon of pits blessing
The mumble of crumbs or
Trying to suck at his knuckles?
In this tambourine of limbs
Where crisscross droves of blackbirds croak
The Jesus weptwashed and slumped
Toward the mines of sugar cane.

# Poems **1961–1967**

# LANGSTON HUGHES

ALFRED · A · KNOPF

NEW YORK   1961

# ASK YOUR MAMA

# 12 MOODS FOR JAZZ

HESITATION BLUES
(Traditional)

The traditional folk melody of the "Hesitation Blues"
is the leitmotif for this poem. In and around it,
along with the other recognizable melodies employed,
there is room for spontaneous jazz improvisation,
particularly between verses,
where the voice pauses.
The musical figurine indicated after each "Ask your mama" line
may incorporate the impudent little melody of the old break,
"Shave and a haircut, fifteen cents."

SHAVE AND A HAIRCUT
(Figurine)

# CULTURAL EXCHANGE

IN THE
IN THE QUARTER
IN THE QUARTER OF THE NEGROES
WHERE THE DOORS ARE DOORS OF PAPER
DUST OF DINGY ATOMS
BLOWS A SCRATCHY SOUND.
AMORPHOUS JACK-O'-LANTERNS CAPER
AND THE WIND WON'T WAIT FOR MIDNIGHT
FOR FUN TO BLOW DOORS DOWN.

BY THE RIVER AND THE RAILROAD
WITH FLUID FAR-OFF GOING
BOUNDARIES BIND UNBINDING
A WHIRL OF WHISTLES BLOWING
NO TRAINS OR STEAMBOATS GOING —
YET LEONTYNE'S UNPACKING.

IN THE QUARTER OF THE NEGROES
WHERE THE DOORKNOB LETS IN LIEDER

*The*
*rhythmically*
*rough*
*scraping*
*of a guira*
*continues*
*monotonously*
*until a lonely*
*flute call,*
*high and*
*far away,*
*merges*
*into piano*
*variations*
*on German*
*lieder*
*gradually*
*changing*
*into*

MORE THAN GERMAN EVER BORE,                    *old-time*
HER YESTERDAY PAST GRANDPA—                     *traditional*
NOT OF HER OWN DOING—                            *12-bar*
IN A POT OF COLLARD GREENS                       *blues*
IS GENTLY STEWING.                               *up strong*
                                                 *between verses*

THERE, FORBID US TO REMEMBER,                    *until*
COMES AN AFRICAN IN MID-DECEMBER                 *African*
SENT BY THE STATE DEPARTMENT                     *drums*
AMONG THE SHACKS TO MEET THE BLACKS:             *throb*
LEONTYNE SAMMY HARRY POITIER                     *against*
LOVELY LENA MARIAN LOUIS PEARLIE MAE             *blues*

GEORGE S. SCHUYLER MOLTO BENE                    *fading*
COME WHAT MAY LANGSTON HUGHES                    *as the*
IN THE QUARTER OF THE NEGROES                    *music*
WHERE THE RAILROAD AND THE RIVER                 *ends.*
HAVE DOORS THAT FACE EACH WAY                    TACIT
AND THE ENTRANCE TO THE MOVIE'S
UP AN ALLEY UP THE SIDE.

                                                 *"Hesitation*
PUSHCARTS FOLD AND UNFOLD                        *Blues" with*
IN A SUPERMARKET SEA.                            *full band*
AND WE BETTER FIND OUT, MAMA,                    *up strong*
WHERE IS THE COLORED LAUNDROMAT,                 *for a chorus*
SINCE WE MOVED UP TO MOUNT VERNON.               *in the clear*
                                                 *between verses*
RALPH ELLISON AS VESPUCIUS                       *then down*
INA-YOURA AT THE MASTHEAD                        *under voice*
ARNA BONTEMPS CHIEF CONSULTANT                   *softly as*
MOLTO BENE MELLOW BABY PEARLIE MAE               *deep-toned*

SHALOM ALEICHEM JIMMY BALDWIN SAMMY     *distant*
COME WHAT MAY—THE SIGNS POINT:     *African*
    *GHANA*    *GUINEA*     *drums*
AND THE TOLL BRIDGE FROM WESTCHESTER     *join the*
IS A GANGPLANK ROCKING RISKY     *blues until*
BETWEEN THE DECK AND SHORE     *the music*
OF A BOAT THAT NEVER QUITE     *dies. . . .*
KNEW ITS DESTINATION.

IN THE QUARTER OF THE NEGROES     TACIT
ORNETTE AND CONSTERNATION
CLAIM ATTENTION FROM THE PAPERS
THAT HAVE NO NEWS THAT DAY OF MOSCOW.

IN THE POT BEHIND THE
PAPER DOORS WHAT'S COOKING?
WHAT'S SMELLING, LEONTYNE?     *Delicate*
LIEDER, LOVELY LIEDER     *lieder*
AND A LEAF OF COLLARD GREEN.     *on piano*
LOVELY LIEDER LEONTYNE.     *continues*
    *between verses*
IN THE SHADOW OF THE NEGROES     *to merge*
   NKRUMAH     *softly*
IN THE SHADOW OF THE NEGROES     *into the*
   NASSER NASSER     *melody of the*
IN THE SHADOW OF THE NEGROES     *"Hesitation*
   ZIK AZIKIWE     *Blues" asking*
CUBA CASTRO GUINEA TOURÉ     *its haunting*
FOR NEED OR PROPAGANDA     *question,*
   KENYATTA     *"How long*
AND THE TOM DOGS OF THE CABIN     *must I*

THE COCOA AND THE CANE BRAKE
THE CHAIN GANG AND THE SLAVE BLOCK
TARRED AND FEATHERED NATIONS
SEAGRAM'S AND FOUR ROSES
$5.00 BAGS A DECK OR DAGGA.
FILIBUSTER VERSUS VETO
LIKE A SNAPPING TURTLE—
WON'T LET GO UNTIL IT THUNDERS
WON'T LET GO UNTIL IT THUNDERS
TEARS THE BODY FROM THE SHADOW
WON'T LET GO UNTIL IT THUNDERS
IN THE QUARTER OF THE NEGROES

AND THEY ASKED ME RIGHT AT CHRISTMAS
IF MY BLACKNESS, WOULD I RUB OFF?
I SAID, ASK YOUR MAMA.

DREAMS AND NIGHTMARES . . .
NIGHTMARES . . . DREAMS! OH!
DREAMING THAT THE NEGROES
OF THE SOUTH HAVE TAKEN OVER—
VOTED ALL THE DIXIECRATS
RIGHT OUT OF POWER—
COMES THE *COLORED HOUR:*
MARTIN LUTHER KING IS GOVERNOR OF GEORGIA,
DR. RUFUS CLEMENT HIS CHIEF ADVISOR,
ZELMA WATSON GEORGE THE HIGH GRAND WORTHY.
IN WHITE PILLARED MANSIONS
SITTING ON THEIR WIDE VERANDAS,
WEALTHY NEGROES HAVE WHITE SERVANTS,

*wait?*
*Can I*
*get it*
*now—or*
*must I*
*hesitate?"*
*Suddenly*
*the drums*
*roll like*
*thunder*
*as the*
*music ends*
*sonorously.*
TACIT

*Figure impishly*
*into "Dixie"*
*ending in high*
*shrill flute call.*
TACIT

WHITE SHARECROPPERS WORK THE BLACK PLANTATIONS,
AND COLORED CHILDREN HAVE WHITE MAMMIES:

    MAMMY FAUBUS
    MAMMY EASTLAND
    MAMMY PATTERSON.
DEAR, *DEAR* DARLING OLD WHITE MAMMIES—
SOMETIMES EVEN BURIED WITH OUR FAMILY!
    *DEAR* OLD
    MAMMY FAUBUS!
*CULTURE*, THEY SAY,, *IS* A *TWO-WAY STREET:*
HAND ME MY MINT JULEP, MAMMY.
      MAKE HASTE!

*"When the Saints
Go Marching In"
joyously for two
full choruses
with maracas. . . .*

# RIDE, RED, RIDE

I WANT TO SEE MY MOTHER MOTHER
WHEN THE ROLL IS CALLED UP YONDER
IN THE QUARTER OF THE NEGROES:
    *TELL ME HOW LONG —*
    *MUST I WAIT?*
    *CAN I GET IT NOW?*
    *ÇA IRA! ÇA IRA!*
    *OR MUST I HESITATE?*
    *IRA! BOY, IRA!*

IN THE QUARTER OF THE NEGROES
TU ABUELA, ¿DÓNDE ESTÁ?
LOST IN CASTRO'S BEARD?
TU ABUELA, ¿DÓNDE ESTÁ?
BLOWN SKY HIGH BY MONT PELÉE?
¿DÓNDE ESTÁ? ¿DÓNDE ESTÁ?
WAS SHE FLEEING WITH LUMUMBA?
(GRANDPA'S GRANDMA'S GRANNY

*Maracas*
*continue*
*rhythms*
*of*
*"When*
*the*
*Saints*
*Go*
*Marching*
*In"*
*until*
*the*
*piano*
*gently*
*supplies*
*a softly*
*lyrical*
*calypso*
*joined now*

ALWAYS TOOK THE OTHER SIDE.)
A LITTLE RUM WITH SUGAR.
AY, MORENA, ¿DÓNDE ESTÁ?
GRENADINE GRANADA OR
DE SANGRE ES LA GOTA?

*by the*
*flute*
*that ends*
*in a high*
*discordant*
*cry.*
TACIT

SANTA CLAUS, FORGIVE ME,
BUT YOUR GIFT BOOKS ARE SUBVERSIVE,
YOUR DOLLS ARE INTERRACIAL.
YOU'LL BE CALLED BY EASTLAND.
WHEN THEY ASK YOU IF YOU KNEW ME,
DON'T TAKE THE FIFTH AMENDMENT.

IN THE QUARTER OF THE NEGROES
RIDING IN A JAGUAR, SANTA CLAUS,
SEEMS LIKE ONCE I MET YOU
WITH ADAM POWELL FOR CHAUFFEUR
AND YOUR HAIR WAS BLOWING BACK
IN THE WIND.

*Loud and*
*lively*
*up-tempo*
*Dixieland*
*jazz for*
*full chorus*
*to end.*

# SHADES OF PIGMEAT

IN THE QUARTER OF THE NEGROES                              TACIT
BELGIUM SHADOW LEOPOLD
PREMIER DOWNING AGING
GENERAL BOURSE BELEAGUERED
EASTLAND AND MALAN DECEASED
DEAD OR LIVE THEIR GHOSTS CAST SHADOWS
IN THE QUARTER OF THE NEGROES                              *Humming:*
WHERE NEGROES SING SO WELL                                *"All God's*
NEGROES SING SO WELL                                      *Chillun*
SING SO WELL                                              *Got*
SO WELL.                                                  *Shoes"*
WELL?
WHERE IS LOTTE LENYA                                      TACIT
AND WHO IS MACK THE KNIFE
AND WAS PORGY EVER MARRIED
BEFORE TAKING BESS TO WIFE
AND WHY WOULD MAI (NOT MAY)
BECOME JEWISH
THE HARD
WAY?                                                      *"Eli Eli"*

IN THE QUARTER OF THE NEGROES
ANSWER QUESTIONS ANSWER
AND ANSWERS WITH A QUESTION
AND THE TALMUD IS CORRECTED
BY A STUDENT IN A FEZ
WHO IS TO JESUIT
AS NORTH POLE IS TO SOUTH
OR ZIK TO ALABAMA
OR BIG MAYBELL TO
THE MET.

HIP BOOTS
DEEP IN THE BLUES
(AND I NEVER HAD A HIP BOOT ON)
    HAIR
BLOWING BACK IN THE WIND
(AND I NEVER HAD THAT MUCH HAIR)
DIAMONDS IN PAWN
(AND I NEVER HAD A DIAMOND
IN MY NATURAL LIFE)
    ME
IN THE WHITE HOUSE
(AND AIN'T NEVER HAD A BLACK HOUSE)
    DO, JESUS!
    LORD!
    AMEN!

*merging*
*into a*
*wailing*
*Afro-*
*Arabic*
*theme*
*with*
*flutes*
*and*
*steady*
*drum beat*
*changing*
*into*
*blues*
*with*
*each*
*instrument*
*gradually*
*dropping*
*out one*
*by one*
*leaving*
*only the*
*flute at*
*the end*
*playing a*
*whimsical*
*little*
*blues of*
*its own. . . .*

# ODE TO DINAH

IN THE QUARTER OF THE NEGROES                    TACIT
WHERE TO SNOW NOW ACCLIMATED
SHADOWS SHOW UP SHARPER,
THE ONE COIN IN THE METER
KEEPS THE GAS ON WHILE THE TV
FAILS TO GET PEARL BAILEY.
SINCE IT'S SNOWING ON THE TV
THIS LAST QUARTER OF CENTENNIAL
100-YEARS EMANCIPATION
MECHANICS NEED REPAIRING
FOR NIAGARA FALLS IS FROZEN
AS IS CUSTOM BELOW ZERO.
MAMA'S FRUITCAKE SENT FROM GEORGIA          *Traditional*
CRUMBLES AS IT'S NIBBLED                     *blues*
TO A DISC BY DINAH                           *in gospel*
IN THE RUM THAT WAFTS MARACAS                *tempo*
FROM ANOTHER DISTANT QUARTER                 *à la Ray*
TO THIS QUARTER OF THE NEGROES               *Charles*
WHERE THE SONG'S MAHALIA'S DAUGHTER          *to fade*
STEP-FATHERED BY BLIND LEMON                 *out*

STEP-FATHERED BY                                         *slowly.* . . .
BLIND LEMON. . . .

WHEN NIAGARA FALLS IS FROZEN                             TACIT
THERE'S A BAR WITH WINDOWS FROSTED
FROM THE COLD THAT MAKES NIAGARA
GHOSTLY MONUMENT OF WINTER
TO A BAND THAT ONCE PASSED OVER                          *Verse of*
WITH A WOMAN WITH TWO PISTOLS                            *"Battle*
ON A TRAIN THAT LOST NO PASSENGERS                       *Hymn*
ON THE LINE WHOSE ROUTE WAS FREEDOM                      *of the Republic"*
THROUGH THE JUNGLE OF WHITE DANGER                       *through*
TO THE HAVEN OF WHITE QUAKERS                            *refrain*
WHOSE HAYMOW WAS A MANGER MANGER                         *repeated*
WHERE THE CHRIST CHILD ONCE HAD LAIN.                    *ever*
SO THE WHITENESS AND THE WATER                           *softer*
MELT TO WATER ONCE AGAIN                                 *to*
AND THE ROAR OF NIAGARA                                  *fade*
DROWNS THE RUMBLE OF THAT TRAIN                          *out*
DISTANT ALMOST NOW AS DISTANT                            *slowly*
AS FORGOTTEN PAIN IN THE QUARTER                         *here*
QUARTER OF THE NEGROES                                   TACIT
WITH A BAR WITH FROSTED WINDOWS
NO CONDUCTOR AND NO TRAIN.                               *Drums*
    BONGO-BONGO! CONGO!                *up strong*
    BUFFALO AND BONGO!                 *for*
    NIAGARA OF THE INDIANS!            *interlude*
    NIAGARA OF THE CONGO!              *and out.*

BUFFALO TO HARLEM'S OVERNIGHT:                           TACIT
IN THE QUARTER OF THE NEGROES
WHERE WHITE SHADOWS PASS,

DARK SHADOWS BECOME DARKER BY A SHADE
SUCKED IN BY FAT JUKEBOXES
WHERE DINAH'S SONGS ARE MADE
FROM SLABS OF SILVER SHADOWS.
AS EACH QUARTER CLINKS
INTO A MILLION POOLS OF QUARTERS
TO BE CARTED OFF BY BRINK'S,
THE SHADES OF DINAH'S SINGING
MAKE A SPANGLE OUT OF QUARTERS RINGING
TO KEEP FAR-OFF CANARIES
IN SILVER CAGES SINGING.
    TELL ME, PRETTY PAPA,
    WHAT TIME IS IT NOW?
    PRETTY PAPA, PRETTY PAPA,
    WHAT TIME IS IT NOW?
    DON'T CARE WHAT TIME IT IS —
    GONNA LOVE YOU ANYHOW
WHILE NIAGARA FALLS IS FROZEN.

SANTA CLAUS, FORGIVE ME,
BUT BABIES BORN IN SHADOWS
IN THE SHADOW OF THE WELFARE
IF BORN PREMATURE
BRING WELFARE CHECKS MUCH SOONER
YET NO PRESENT DOWN THE CHIMNEY.

IN THE SHADOW OF THE WELFARE
CHOCOLATE BABIES BORN IN SHADOWS
ARE TRIBAL NOW NO LONGER
SAVE IN MEMORIES OF GANGRENOUS ICING
ON A TWENTY-STORY HOUSING PROJECT
THE CHOCOLATE GANGRENOUS ICING OF

*"Hesitation Blues" softly asking over and over its old question, "Tell me how long?" until music DIES. . . . TACIT*

491

JUST WAIT.
TRIBAL NOW NO LONGER PAPA MAMA
IN RELATION TO THE CHILD,
ONCE YOUR BROTHER'S KEEPER
NOW NOT EVEN KEEPER TO YOUR CHILD—
SHELTERED NOW NO LONGER.
BORN TO GROW UP WILD—
TRIBAL NOW NO LONGER ONE FOR ALL
AND ALL FOR ONE NO LONGER
EXCEPT IN MEMORIES OF HATE
UMBILICAL IN SULPHUROUS CHOCOLATE:
    GOT TO WAIT—
THIS LAST QUARTER OF CENTENNIAL:
    GOT TO WAIT.


I WANT TO GO TO THE SHOW, MAMA.
    NO SHOW FARE, BABY—
    NOT THESE DAYS.


ON THE BIG SCREEN OF THE WELFARE CHECK
A LYNCHED TOMORROW SWAYS. . . .
WITH ALL DELIBERATE SPEED A
LYNCHED TOMORROW SWAYS.


LIVING 20 YEARS IN 10
BETTER HURRY, BETTER HURRY
BEFORE THE PRESENT BECOMES WHEN
    AND YOU'RE 50
    WHEN YOU'RE 40
    40 WHEN YOU'RE 30
    30 WHEN YOU'RE 20
    20 WHEN YOU'RE 10

*Drums*
*alone*
*softly*
*merging*
*into*
*the*
*ever-*
*questioning*
*"Hesitation*
*Blues"*
*beginning*
*slowly*
*but*
*gradually*
*building to*
*up-tempo*
*as the*
*metronome*
*of*
*fate*
*begins*
*to*
*tick*
*faster*
*and*
*faster*

*as the*
*music*

IN THE QUARTER OF THE NEGROES                    *dies*
WHERE THE PENDULUM IS SWINGING
TO THE SHADOW OF THE BLUES,
EVEN WHEN YOU'RE WINNING
THERE'S NO WAY NOT TO LOSE.

WHERE THE SHADOWS MERGE WITH SHADOWS           TACIT
THE DOOR MARKED *LADIES* OPENS INWARD
AND CAN KNOCK THE HADES
OUT OF ONE IN EXIT
IF PUSHED BY HURRIED ENTRANCE.
IN THE SHADOW OF THE QUARTER
WHERE THE PEOPLE ALL ARE DARKER
NOBODY NEED A MARKER.
AMEN IS NOT AN ENDING
BUT JUST A PUNCTUATION.
WHITE FOLKS' RECESSION
IS COLORED FOLKS' DEPRESSION.

THEY ASKED ME RIGHT AT CHRISTMAS,
WOULD I MARRY POCAHONTAS?
MEANWHILE DINAH EATING CHICKEN
NEVER MISSED A BITE
WHEN THE MAN SHOT AT THE WOMAN            *Rim shot.*
AND BY MISTAKE SHOT OUT THE LIGHT.        *Dixieland*
                                          *up-tempo*
                                          *for full chorus*
                                          *to ending.*

# BLUES IN STEREO

YOUR NUMBER'S COMING OUT!                                    TACIT
BOUQUETS I'LL SEND YOU
AND DREAMS I'LL SEND YOU
AND HORSES SHOD WITH GOLD
ON WHICH TO RIDE IF MOTORCARS
WOULD BE TOO TAME—
TRIUMPHAL ENTRY SEND YOU—
SHOUTS FROM THE EARTH ITSELF
BARE FEET TO BEAT THE GREAT DRUMBEAT
OF GLORY TO YOUR NAME AND MINE
ONE AND THE SAME:
YOU BAREFOOT, TOO,
IN THE QUARTER OF THE NEGROES
WHERE AN ANCIENT RIVER FLOWS
PAST HUTS THAT HOUSE A MILLION BLACKS
AND THE WHITE GOD NEVER GOES
FOR THE MOON WOULD WHITE HIS WHITENESS
BEYOND ITS MASK OF WHITENESS

AND THE NIGHT MIGHT BE ASTONISHED
AND SO LOSE ITS REPOSE.

IN A TOWN NAMED AFTER STANLEY
NIGHT EACH NIGHT COMES NIGHTLY                          *African*
AND THE MUSIC OF OLD MUSIC'S                            *drum-*
BORROWED FOR THE HORNS                                 *beats*
THAT DON'T KNOW HOW TO PLAY                            *over*
ON LPs THAT WONDER                                     *blues*
HOW THEY EVER GOT THAT WAY.                            *that*
                                                       *gradually*
    *WHAT TIME IS IT, MAMA?*                 *mount*
    *WHAT TIME IS IT NOW?*                   *in*
    *MAKES NO DIFFERENCE TO ME—*             *intensity*
    *BUT I'M ASKING ANYHOW.*                 *to*
    *WHAT TIME IS IT, MAMA?*                 *end*
    *WHAT TIME NOW?*                         *in*
                                                       *climax.*
DOWN THE LONG HARD ROW THAT I BEEN HOEING              TACIT
I THOUGHT I HEARD THE HORN OF PLENTY BLOWING.
BUT I GOT TO GET A NEW ANTENNA, LORD—
MY TV KEEPS ON SNOWING.

# HORN OF PLENTY

SINGERS                                                           TACIT
SINGERS LIKE O-
SINGERS LIKE ODETTA — AND THAT STATUE
ON BEDLOE'S ISLAND MANAGED BY SOL HUROK
DANCERS BOJANGLES LATE LAMENTED     $ $ $ $
KATHERINE DUNHAM AL AND LEON       $ $ $ $ $
ARTHUR CARMEN ALVIN MARY       $ $ $ $ $ $ $ $
JAZZERS DUKE AND DIZZY ERIC DOLPHY      $ $ $
MILES AND ELLA AND MISS NINA      $ $ $ $ $ $ $
STRAYHORN HIS BACKSTAGE WITH LUTHER      $ $
*DO YOU READ MUSIC?* AND LOUIS SAYING        $ $
*NOT ENOUGH TO HURT MY PLAYING*    $ $ $ $ $
GOSPEL SINGERS WHO PANT TO PACK        $ $ $ $
GOLDEN CROSSES TO A CADILLAC      $ $ $ $ $ $
BONDS AND STILL AND MARGARET STILL        $ $
GLOBAL TROTTERS BASEBALL BATTERS        $ $
JACKIE WILLIE CAMPANELLA      $ $ $ $ $ $ $ $
FOOTBALL PLAYERS LEATHER PUNCHERS        $ $
UNFORGOTTEN JOES AND SUGAR RAYS       $ $ $

WHO BREAK AWAY LIKE COMETS   $ $ $ $ $ $
FROM LESSER STARS IN ORBIT   $ $ $ $ $ $ $
TO MOVE OUT TO ST. ALBANS   $ $ $ $ $ $ $ $
WHERE THE GRASS IS GREENER   $ $ $ $ $ $ $
SCHOOLS ARE BETTER FOR THEIR CHILDREN $
AND OTHER KIDS LESS MEANER THAN   ¢ ¢ ¢ ¢
IN THE QUARTER OF THE NEGROES   ¢ ¢ ¢ ¢ ¢
WHERE WINTER'S NAME IS HAWKINS   ¢ ¢ ¢
AND NIAGARA FALLS IS FROZEN   ¢ ¢ ¢ ¢ ¢ ¢
IF SHOW FARE'S MORE THAN 30¢ ¢ ¢ ¢ ¢ ¢ ¢ ¢

I MOVED OUT TO LONG ISLAND
EVEN FARTHER THAN ST. ALBANS
(WHICH LATELY IS STONE NOWHERE)
I MOVED OUT EVEN FARTHER FURTHER FARTHER
ON THE SOUND WAY OFF THE TURNPIKE—
AND I'M THE ONLY COLORED.

GOT THERE! YES, I MADE IT!
NAME IN THE PAPERS EVERY DAY!
FAMOUS—THE HARD WAY—
FROM NOBODY AND NOTHING TO WHERE I AM.
THEY KNOW ME, TOO, DOWNTOWN,
ALL ACROSS THE COUNTRY, EUROPE—
ME WHO USED TO BE NOBODY,
NOTHING BUT ANOTHER SHADOW
IN THE QUARTER OF THE NEGROES,
NOW A NAME! MY NAME—A NAME!

YET THEY ASKED ME OUT ON MY PATIO
WHERE DID I GET MY MONEY!

*"Hesitation
Blues"* 8 *bars.*
TACIT

499

I SAID, FROM YOUR MAMA!                                        *Figurine.*
THEY WONDERED WAS I SENSITIVE
AND HAD A CHIP ON MY SHOULDER?
DID I KNOW CHARLIE MINGUS?
AND WHY DID RICHARD WRIGHT
LIVE ALL THAT WHILE IN PARIS
INSTEAD OF COMING HOME TO DECENT DIE
IN HARLEM OR THE SOUTH SIDE OF CHICAGO
OR THE WOMB OF MISSISSIPPI?
AND ONE SHOULD LOVE ONE'S COUNTRY
FOR ONE'S COUNTRY IS YOUR MAMA.

LIVING IN ST. ALBANS
SHADOW OF THE NEGROES
WESTPORT AND NEW CANAAN
IN THE SHADOW OF THE NEGROES—
HIGHLY INTEGRATED
MEANS TOO MANY NEGROES
EVEN FOR THE NEGROES—
ESPECIALLY FOR THE FIRST ONES
WHO MOVE IN UNOBTRUSIVE                                        *Gently*
BOOK-OF-THE-MONTH IN CASES                                     *yearning*
SEEKING SUBURB WITH NO JUKEBOX                                 *lieder*
POOL HALL OR BAR ON CORNER                                     *on*
SEEKING LAWNS AND SHADE TREES                                  *piano*
SEEKING PEACE AND QUIET                                        *delicately*
AUTUMN LEAVES IN AUTUMN                                        *sedate,*
HOLLAND BULBS IN SPRING                                        *quietly*
DECENT GARBAGE SERVICE                                         *fading*
BIRDS THAT REALLY SING                                         *on the*
$40,000 HOUSES—                                                *word*

PAYMENTS NOT BELATED—
THE ONLY NEGROES IN THE BLOCK
INTEGRATED.

*belated. . . .*
TACIT

HORN OF PLENTY
IN ESCROW TO JOE GLASSER.
THE SERMON ON THE MOUNT
IN BILLINGTON'S CHURCH OF RUBBER.
LOVE THY NEIGHBOR AS THYSELF
IN GEORGE SOKOLSKY'S COLUMN.
BIRDS THAT REALLY SING.
EVERY DAY'S TOMORROW
AND ELECTION TIME
IS ALWAYS FOUR YEARS
FROM THE OTHER
AND MY LAWN MOWER
NEW AND SHINY
FROM THE BIG GLASS SHOPPING CENTER
CUTS MY HAIR ON CREDIT.

*Again
the old
"Hesitation
Blues"
against the
trills
of birds,
but the
melody
ends in
a thin
high
flute call.*

THEY RUNG MY BELL TO ASK ME
COULD I RECOMMEND A MAID.
I SAID, YES, YOUR MAMA.

TACIT

*Figurine.*

# GOSPEL CHA-CHA

IN THE QUARTER OF THE NEGROES
WHERE THE PALMS AND COCONUTS
CHA-CHA LIKE CASTANETS                          *Maracas . . .*
IN THE WIND'S FRENETIC FISTS                    *in*
WHERE THE SAND SEEDS AND THE                    *cha-cha*
SEA GOURDS MAKE MARACAS OUT OF ME,              *tempo,*
ERZULIE PLAYS A TUNE                            *then*
ON THE BONGO OF THE MOON.                       *bongo drums*
THE PAPA DRUM OF SUN                            *joined*
AND THE MOTHER DRUM OF EARTH                    *by*
KNOW TOURISTS ONLY FOR                          *the*
THE MONEY THAT THEY'RE WORTH                    *piano,*
IN THE QUARTER OF THE NEGROES                   *guitar*
MAMA MAMACITA PAPA PAPIAMENTO                   *and*
DAMBALLA WEDO OGOUN AND THE HORSE               *claves,*
THAT LUGGED THE FIRST WHITE                     *eerie*
FIRST WHITE TOURIST UP THE MOUNTAIN             *and*
TO THE CITADELLE OF SHADOWS SHADOWS             *strange*

WHERE THE SHADOWS OF THE NEGROES
ARE THE GHOSTS OF FORMER GLORY
TOUSSAINT WITH A THREAD
THREAD STILL PULLS HIS
PROW OF STONE STONE.
I BOIL A FISH AND SALT IT
(AND MY PLANTAINS)
WITH HIS GLORY.

    ¡AY, BAHIA!
    ¡AY, BAHIA!
SUNSETS STAINED WITH BLOOD
CLEAR GREEN CRYSTAL WATER
AND THE CRY THAT TURNED TO MUSIC
WHERE THE SEA SAND AND THE SEA GOURDS
MAKE CLAVES OF MY SORROWS
IN THE WIND'S FRENETIC FISTS.
MAMACITA! PAPA LEGBA! SHANGO!
BEDWARD! POCOMANIA! WEDO! OGOUN!
THE BOAT BEYOND THE FORTALEZA
TO THE VILLE OF NAÑIGO.
A LONG WAY TO BAHIA —
HOW I GOT THERE I DON'T KNOW.
WHAT'S HIS NAME, MY COUSIN,
WHO SEDUCED MARIE LAVEAU?
DAMBALLA WEDO! THE VIRGIN! BEDWARD!
JOHN JASPER! JESUS! DADDY GRACE!
    I TRIED
    LORD KNOWS I TRIED
    DAMBALLA
    I PRAYED

*like*
*bones*
*rattling*
*in a*
*sort*
*of off-*
*beat mambo*
*up strong*
*between verse*
*then*
*down*
*under*
*voice*
*to*
*gradually*
*die away*
*in the*
*lonely*
*swish-*
*swish of*
*the*
*maracas . . .*
TACIT

*Gospel*
*music*
*with a*
*very*
*heavy*

LORD KNOWS I PRAYED                               *beat*
DADDY                                             *as if*
I CLIMBED                                          *marching*
UP THAT STEEP HILL                                *forward*
THE VIRGIN                                         *against*
WITH A CROSS                                       *great*
LORD KNOWS I CLIMBED                              *odds,*
BUT WHEN I GOT                                     *climbing*
JOHN JASPER JESUS                                  *a*
WHEN I GOT TO CALVARY                             *high*
UP THERE ON THAT HILL                             *hill—*
ALREADY THERE WAS THREE —                         *to again*
AND ONE, YES, ONE                                 *fade into*
WAS BLACK AS ME.                                   *the dry*
                                                   *swish of*
CHA-CHA . . . CHA-CHA                             *maracas*
CHA. . . .                                         *in cha-cha*
                                                   *time.*

# IS IT TRUE?

FROM THE SHADOWS OF THE QUARTER                    TACIT
SHOUTS ARE WHISPERS CARRYING
TO THE FARTHEREST CORNERS SOMETIMES
OF THE NOW KNOWN WORLD
UNDECIPHERED AND UNLETTERED
UNCODIFIED UNPARSED
IN TONGUES UNANALYZED UNECHOED
UNTAKEN DOWN ON TAPE—
NOT EVEN FOLKWAYS CAPTURED
BY MOE ASCH OR ALAN LOMAX
NOT YET ON SAFARI.
WHERE GAME TO BAG'S ILLUSIVE
AS A SILVER UNICORN
AND THE GUN TO DO THE KILLING'S
STILL TO BE INVENTED,
TO FERTILIZE THE DESERT
THE FRENCH MAY HAVE THE SECRET.                    *Deep*
TURN, OH, TURN, DARK LOVERS                         *drum*
ON YOUR BED OF WHISPERED ECHOES:                    *vibrato*

*¡AY DIOS!*
　　*¡AY DIOS!*
　　　*¡AY DIOS!*

　　　　　　　　　　　　　　　　　　　　　　*into a*
　　　　　　　　　　　　　　　　　　　　　　*single high*
　　　　　　　　　　　　　　　　　　　　　　*flute*
　　　　　　　　　　　　　　　　　　　　　　*note. . . .*

TWENTY HOURS
FOR THE MILL WHEEL TO BE MILL WHEEL
WAITED TWENTY DAYS
FOR THE BISQUIT TO BE BREAD
WAITED TWENTY YEARS
FOR THE SADNESS TO BE SORROW.
WAITED TWENTY MORE
TO CATCH UP WITH TOMORROW
AND I CANNOT WRITE COMMERCIALS —
TO MY CHAGRIN — NOT EVEN SINGING —
AND THE WHISPERS ARE UNECHOED
ON THE TAPES — NOT EVEN FOLKWAYS.

TACIT

　　YES, SUBURBIA
　　WILL EVENTUALLY BE
　　ONLY IN THE SEA. . . .
　　MEANWHILE
　　OF COURSE
　　OF COURSE
　　OF COURSE
　　ON A MUDDY TRACK
IN THE QUARTER OF THE NEGROES
　　NEGROES
　　NEGROES
　　SOME HORSE MIGHT
　　SLIP AND BREAK
　　ITS BACK:

BUT SCRIPT-WRITERS WHO KNOW BETTER
WOULD HARDLY WRITE IT IN THE SCRIPT—
OR SPORTS-WRITERS IN THEIR STORY.
YET THE HORSE WHOSE BACK IS BROKEN
GETS SHOT RIGHT INTO GLORY.

THEY ASKED ME AT THE PTA
IS IT TRUE THAT NEGROES——?
I SAID, ASK YOUR MAMA.

*High
flute
call.*

# ASK YOUR MAMA

FROM THE SHADOWS OF THE QUARTER
SHOUTS ARE WHISPERS CARRYING
TO THE FARTHEREST CORNERS
OF THE NOW KNOWN WORLD:
5TH AND MOUND IN CINCI, 63RD IN CHI,
23RD AND CENTRAL, 18TH STREET AND VINE.
I'VE WRITTEN, CALLED REPEATEDLY,
EVEN RUNG THIS BELL ON SUNDAY, YET
YOUR THIRD-FLOOR TENANT'S NEVER HOME.
DID YOU TELL HER THAT OUR CREDIT OFFICE
HAS NO RECOURSE NOW BUT TO THE LAW?
*YES, SIR, I TOLD HER.*
WHAT DID SHE SAY?
*SAID, TELL YOUR MA.*                    *Figurine.*

17 SORROWS
AND THE NUMBER
6–0–2.

HIGH BALLS, LOW BALLS:
THE 8-BALL
IS YOU.
7–11!
COME 7
*PORGY AND BESS*
AT THE PICTURE SHOW.
I NEVER SEEN IT.
BUT I WILL.
YOU KNOW.
IF I HAVE
THE MONEY
TO GO.

FILLMORE OUT IN FRISCO, 7TH ACROSS THE BAY,                     *Delicate*
                                                                *post-bop*
18TH AND VINE IN K.C., 63RD IN CHI,                             *suggests*
ON THE CORNER PICKING SPLINTERS                                 *pleasant*
OUT OF THE MIDNIGHT SKY                                         *evenings and*
IN THE QUARTER OF THE NEGROES                                   *flirtatious*
AS LEOLA PASSES BY                                              *youth*
THE MEN CAN ONLY MURMUR                                         *as it*
MY! . . . MY! MY!                                               *gradually*
                                                                *weaves*
                                                                *into its*
LUMUMBA LOUIS ARMSTRONG                                         *pattern*
PATRICE AND PATTI PAGE                                          *a*
HAMBURGERS PEPSI-COLA                                           *musical*
KING COLE JUKEBOX PAYOLA                                        *echo of*
IN THE QUARTER OF THE NEGROES                                   *Paris*
GOD WILLING DROP A SHILLING                                     *which*
FORT DE FRANCE, PLACE PIGALLE                                   *continues*

VINGT FRANCS NICKEL DIME                                      *until*
BAHIA LAGOS DAKAR LENOX                                       *very*
KINGSTON TOO GOD WILLING                                      *softly*
A QUARTER OR A SHILLING. PARIS—                               *the*
AT THE DOME VINGT FRANCS WILL DO                              *silver*
ROTONDE SELECT DUPONT FLORE                                   *call*
TALL BLACK STUDENT                                            *of a*
IN HORN-RIM GLASSES,                                          *hunting*
WHO AT THE SORBONNE HAS SIX CLASSES,                          *horn*
IN THE SHADOW OF THE CLUNY                                    *is*
CONJURES UNICORN,                                             *heard*
SPEAKS ENGLISH FRENCH SWAHILI                                 *far away.*
HAS ALMOST FORGOTTEN MEALIE.                                  *African*
BUT WHY RIDE ON MULE OR DONKEY                                *drums*
WHEN THERE'S A UNICORN?                                       *begin*
                                                             *a softly*
NIGHT IN A SÉKOU TOURÉ CAP                                    *mounting*
DRESSED LIKE A TEDDY BOY                                      *rumble*
BLOTS COLORS OFF THE MAP.                                     *soon*
PERHAPS IF IT BE GOD'S WILL                                   *to fade*
AZIKIWE'S SON, AMEKA,                                         *into a*
SHAKES HANDS WITH EMMETT TILL.                                *steady*
BRICKBATS BURST LIKE BUBBLES                                  *beat*
STONES BURST LIKE BALLOONS                                    *like*
BUT HEARTS KEEP DOGGED BEATING                                *the*
    SELDOM BURSTING                       *heart*
    UNLIKE BUBBLES
    UNLIKE BRICKBATS                       TACIT
    FAR FROM STONE.
IN THE QUARTER OF THE NEGROES

WHERE NO SHADOW WALKS ALONE
LITTLE MULES AND DONKEYS SHARE
THEIR GRASS WITH UNICORNS.

*Repeat high*
*flute call*
*to segue into*
*up-tempo blues*
*that continue*
*behind the*
*next sequence. . . .*

# BIRD IN ORBIT

DE—                                          *Happy*
DELIGHT—                                      *blues*
DELIGHTED! INTRODUCE ME TO EARTHA             *in*
JOCKO BODDIDLY LIL GREENWOOD                  *up-beat*
BELAFONTE FRISCO JOSEPHINE                    *tempo*
BRICKTOP INEZ MABEL MERCER                    *trip*
AND I'D LIKE TO MEET THE                      *merrily*
ONE-TIME SIX-YEAR-OLDS                        *along*
FIRST GRADE IN NEW ORLEANS                    *until*
IN THE QUARTER OF THE NEGROES                 *the music*
WHERE SIT-INS ARE CONDUCTED                   *suddenly*
BY THOSE YET UNINDUCTED                       *stops in*
AND BALLOTS DROP IN BOXES                     *a loud*
WHERE BULLETS ARE THE TELLERS.                *rim shot.*

THEY ASKED ME AT THANKSGIVING                 TACIT
DID I VOTE FOR NIXON?
I SAID, VOTED FOR YOUR MAMA.                   *Figurine.*

METHUSELAH SIGNS PAPERS W. E. B.              *Cool*
ORIGINAL NIAGARA N.A.A.C.P.                   *bop*

ADELE RAMONA MICHAEL SERVE BAKOKO TEA          *very*
IRENE AND HELEN ARE AS THEY USED TO BE         *light*
AND SMITTY HAS NOT CHANGED AT ALL.             *and*
ALIOUNE AIMÉ SEDAR SIPS HIS NEGRITUDE.         *delicate*
THE REVEREND MARTIN LUTHER                     *rising*
KING MOUNTS HIS UNICORN                         *to an*
OBLIVIOUS TO BLOOD                             *ethereal*
AND MOONLIGHT ON ITS HORN                      *climax . . .*
WHILE MOLLIE MOON STREWS SEQUINS               *completely*
AS LEDA STREW HER CORN                         *far*
AND CHARLIE YARDBIRD PARKER                    *out. . . .*
IS IN ORBIT.

    *¡AY, MI NEGRA!*                    TACIT
    *¡AY, MORENA!*

GRANDPA, WHERE DID YOU MEET MY GRANDMA?
AT MOTHER BETHEL'S IN THE MORNING?
I'M ASKING, GRANDPA, ASKING.
WERE YOU MARRIED BY JOHN JASPER
OF THE DO-MOVE COSMIC CONSCIENCE?
GRANDPA, DID YOU HEAR THE
HEAR THE OLD FOLKS SAY HOW
HOW TALL HOW TALL THE CANE GREW
SAY HOW WHITE THE COTTON COTTON
SPEAK OF RICE DOWN IN THE MARSHLAND
SPEAK OF FREDERICK DOUGLASS'S BEARD
AND JOHN BROWN'S WHITE AND LONGER          *"The*
LINCOLN'S LIKE A CLOTHESBRUSH               *Battle*
AND OF HOW SOJOURNER HOW SOJOURNER          *Hymn*
TO PROVE SHE WAS A WOMAN WOMAN              *of*
BARED HER BOSOMS, BARED IN PUBLIC           *the*
TO PROVE SHE WAS A WOMAN?                    *Republic"*

WHAT SHE SAID ABOUT HER CHILDREN       *as a*
ALL SOLD DOWN THE RIVER.       *flute*
*I LOOK AT THE STARS,*       *solo*
*AND THEY LOOK AT THE STARS,*       *soft*
*AND THEY WONDER WHERE I BE*       *and*
*AND I WONDER WHERE THEY BE.*       *far*
STARS AT STARS STARS. . . .       *away*
    TOURÉ DOWN IN GUINEA       *fading*
    LUMUMBA IN THE CONGO       *in the*
    JOMO IN KENYATTA. . . . STARS. . . .       *distance. . . .*
GRANDPA, DID YOU FIND HER IN THE TV SILENCE       TACIT
OF A MILLION MARTHA ROUNDTREES?
IN THE QUARTER OF THE NEGROES
DID YOU EVER FIND HER?

THAT GENTLEMAN IN EXPENSIVE SHOES
MADE FROM THE HIDES OF BLACKS
WHO TIPS AMONG THE SHADOWS
SOAKING UP THE MUSIC
ASKED ME RIGHT AT CHRISTMAS
DID I WANT TO EAT WITH WHITE FOLKS?       *Flute cry. . . .*

THOSE SIT-IN KIDS, HE SAID,       TACIT
    MUST BE RED!
KENYATTA RED! CASTRO RED!
    NKRUMAH RED!
RALPH BUNCHE INVESTIGATED!
MARY McLEOD BETHUNE BARRED BY
THE LEGION FROM ENGLEWOOD
NEW JERSEY HIGH SCHOOL!
HOW ABOUT THAT N.A.A.C.P.
AND THE RADICALS IN THAT
THERE SOUTHERN CONFERENCE?

AIN'T YOU GOT NO INFORMATION
ON DR. ROBERT WEAVER?
INVESTIGATE THAT SANTA CLAUS
WHOSE DOLLS ARE INTERRACIAL!
INVESTIGATE THEM NEGRAS WHO
BOUGHT A DOBERMAN PINSCHER.

THAT GENTLEMAN IN EXPENSIVE SHOES
MADE FROM THE HIDES OF BLACKS
TIPS AMONG THE SHADOWS
SOAKING UP THE MUSIC. . . .
MUSIC. . . .

*Flute*
*call*
*into*
*very*
*far-out*
*boopish*
*blues.* . . .

# JAZZTET MUTED

IN THE NEGROES OF THE QUARTER

PRESSURE OF THE BLOOD IS SLIGHTLY HIGHER

IN THE QUARTER OF THE NEGROES

WHERE BLACK SHADOWS MOVE LIKE SHADOWS

CUT FROM SHADOWS CUT FROM SHADE

IN THE QUARTER OF THE NEGROES

SUDDENLY CATCHING FIRE

FROM THE WING TIP OF A MATCH TIP

ON THE BREATH OF ORNETTE COLEMAN.

IN NEON TOMBS THE MUSIC

FROM JUKEBOX JOINTS IS LAID

AND FREE-DELIVERY TV SETS

ON GRAVESTONE DATES ARE PLAYED.

EXTRA-LARGE THE *KINGS* AND *QUEENS*

AT EITHER SIDE ARRAYED

HAVE DOORS THAT OPEN OUTWARD

TO THE QUARTER OF THE NEGROES

*Bop*
*blues*
*into*
*very*
*modern*
*jazz*
*burning*
*the*
*air*
*eerie*
*like*
*a neon*
*swamp-*
*fire*
*cooled*
*by*
*dry*
*ice*

WHERE THE PRESSURE OF THE BLOOD
IS SLIGHTLY HIGHER—
DUE TO SMOLDERING SHADOWS
THAT SOMETIMES TURN TO FIRE.

    *HELP ME, YARDBIRD!*
    *HELP ME!*

*until*
*suddenly*
*there is*
*a single*
*ear-*
*piercing*
*flute*
*call. . . .*

# SHOW FARE, PLEASE

TELL ME, MAMA, CAN I GET MY SHOW
TELL ME FARE FROM YOU?
OR DO YOU THINK THAT PAPA'S
GOT CHANGE IN HIS LONG POCKET?
IN THE QUARTER OF THE NEGROES
WHERE THE MASK IS PLACED BY OTHERS
IBM ELECTRIC BONGO DRUMS ARE COSTLY.
TELL ME, MAMA, TELL ME,
STRIP TICKETS STILL ILLUSION?
GOT TO ASK YOU — GOT TO ASK!
TELL ME, TELL ME, MAMA,
ALL THAT MUSIC, ALL THAT DANCING
CONCENTRATED TO THE ESSENCE
OF THE SHADOW OF THE DOLLAR
PAID AT THE BOX OFFICE
WHERE THE LIGHTER IS THE DARKER
IN THE QUARTER OF THE NEGROES
AND THE TELL ME OF THE MAMA
IS THE ANSWER TO THE CHILD.

*TACIT*

*Rhythmic*
*bop,*
*ever*
*more*
*ironic,*
*laughs*
*itself*
*softly*
*into a*
*lonely*
*flute*
*call. . . .*

DID YOU EVER SEE TEN NEGROES
WEAVING METAL FROM TWO QUARTERS
INTO CLOTH OF DOLLARS
FOR A SUIT OF GOOD-TIME WEARING?
WEAVING OUT OF LONG-TERM CREDIT
INTEREST BEYOND CARING?

THE HEADS ON THESE TWO QUARTERS
ARE *THIS* OR *THAT*
OR *LESS* OR *MOST*—
SINCE BUT TWO EXIST
BEYOND THE HOLY GHOST.
OF THESE THREE.
IS ONE
ME?

THE TV'S STILL NOT WORKING.
SHOW FARE, MAMA, PLEASE.
SHOW FARE, MAMA. . . .
SHOW FARE!

*"The Hesitation
Blues" very loud,
lively and
raucously. Two
big swinging
choruses—
building full
blast to a
bursting climax.*

# LINER NOTES

*For the Poetically Unhep*

# CULTURAL EXCHANGE

In Negro sections of the South where doors have no resistance to violence, danger always whispers harshly. Klansmen cavort, and havoc may come at any time. Negroes often live either by the river or the railroad, and for most there is not much chance of going anywhere else. Yet *always* one of them has been away and has come home. The door has opened to admit something strange and foreign, yet tied by destiny to a regional past nourished by a way of life in common—in this case collard greens.

A State Department visitor from Africa comes, wishing to meet Negroes. He is baffled by the "two sides to every question" way of looking at things in the South. Although he finds that in the American social supermarket blacks for sale range from intellectuals to entertainers, to the African all cellophane signs point to ideas of change—in an IBM land that pays more attention to Moscow than to Mississippi.

What—wonders the African—is really happening in the shadow of world events, past and present—and of world problems, old and new—to an America that seems to understand so little about its black citizens? Even so little about itself. Even so little.

# RIDE, RED, RIDE

In the restless Caribbean there are the same shadows as in Mississippi, where, according to *Time*, Leontyne comes in the back door. Yet some persons in high places in Washington consider it subversive for ordinary people to be concerned with problems such as back doors anywhere—even suspecting those citizens of color who legitimately use the ballot in the North to elect representatives to front doors. But in spite of all, some Negroes occasionally do manage—for a moment—to get a brief ride in somebody's American chariot.

# SHADES OF PIGMEAT

Oppression by any other name is just about the same, casts a long shadow, adds a dash of bitters to each song, makes of almost every answer a question, and of men of every race or religion questioners.

# ODE TO DINAH

Hard times endure from slavery to freedom—to Harlem where most of the money spent goes downtown. Only a little comes back in the form of relief checks, which leaves next to nothing for show fare for children who must live in a hurry in order to live at all. Yet in a milieu where so many untoward things happen, one cannot afford to take to heart too deeply the hazards. Remember Harriet Tubman? One of the runaway slaves in her band was so frightened crossing from Buffalo into Canada that on the very last lap of his journey he hid under the seat of the train and refused to glance out the window. Harriet said: "You old fool! Even on your way to freedom, you might at least look at Niagara Falls."

# BLUES IN STEREO

Sometimes you are lucky, or at least you can dream lucky—even if you wake up cold in hand. But maybe with a new antenna you will get a clearer picture.

# HORN OF PLENTY

Certainly there are some who make money—and others who folks *think* make money. It takes money to buy gas to commute to the suburbs and keep one's lawns sheared like one's white neighbors who wonder how on earth a Negro got a lawn mower in the face of so many ways of keeping him from getting a lawn.

# GOSPEL CHA-CHA

Those who have no lawns to mow seek gods who come in various spiritual and physical guises and to whom one prays in various rhythms in various lands in various tongues.

# IS IT TRUE?

It seems as if everything is annotated one way or another, but the subtler nuances remain to be captured. However, the atom bomb may solve all this—since it would end the end results of love's own annotation. Meanwhile, although the going is rough, triumph over difficulties at least brings subjective glory. Everybody thinks that Negroes have the *most* fun, but, of course, secretly hopes they do not—although curious to find out if they do.

# ASK YOUR MAMA

In spite of a shortage of funds for the movies and the frequent rude intrusions of those concerned with hoarding hard metals, collective coins for music-making and grass for dreams to graze on still keep men, mules, donkeys, and black students alive.

# BIRD IN ORBIT

Those who contribute most to the joy of living and the stretching of the social elastic are not stymied by foolish questions, but keep right on drawing from the well of the past buckets of water in which to catch stars. In their pockets are layovers for meddlers—although somewhere grandma lost her apron.

# JAZZTET MUTED

Because grandma lost her apron with all the answers in her pocket (perhaps consumed by fire) certain grand- and great-grandsons play music burning like dry ice against the ear. Forcing cries of succor from its own unheard completion—not resolved by Charlie Parker—can we look to monk or Monk? Or let it rest with Eric Dolphy?


# SHOW FARE, PLEASE

If the answers were on tickets in long strips like those that come from slots inside the cashier's booth at the movies, and if I had the money for a ticket—like the man who owns *all* tickets, *all* booths, and *all* movies and who pays the ticket seller who in turn charges me—would I, with answer in my hand, become one of the three—the man, the ticket seller, me? Show fare, mama, please. . . .

## Lumumba's Grave

Lumumba was black
And he didn't trust
The whores all powdered
With uranium dust.

Lumumba was black
And he didn't believe
The lies thieves shook
Through their "freedom" sieve.

Lumumba was black.
His blood was red—
And for being a man
They killed him dead.

They buried Lumumba
In an unmarked grave.
But he needs no marker—
For air is his grave.

Sun is his grave,
Moon is, stars are,
Space is his grave.

My heart's his grave,
And it's marked there.
*Tomorrow will mark*
*It everywhere.*


## If You Would

You could stop the factory whistles blowing,
Stop the mine machines from going,
Stop the atom bombs exploding,
Stop the battleships from loading,
Stop the merchant ships from sailing,
Stop the jail house keys from turning,
Stop the trains from running,
Wheels from rolling where they roll,
    Mouths from eating
    Hearts from beating—

Starve and die to save your soul —
    If you would.
    You could
    If you
    Would.

## Encounter

I met You on Your way to death,
Though quite by accident
I chose the path I did,
Not knowing there You went.

When I heard the hooting mob
I started to turn back
But, curious, I stood my ground
Directly in its track
And sickened suddenly
At its sound,
Yet did not
Turn back.

So loud the mob cried,
Yet so weak,
Like a sick and muffled sea.
On Your head You had sharp thorns.
You did not look at me —
But on Your back You carried
My own Misery.

## Slave

To ride piggy-back
to the market of death
there to purchase a slave,
a slave who died young,
having given up breath—
unwittingly,
of course—
a slave who died young,
perhaps from a fix
with a rusty needle
infected,
to purchase a slave
to the market of death
I ride protected.

## Pair in One

The strangeness
And the stranger
Walk ambiently
Body-rounded:
The life bell
And the death knell
Both at once
Are sounded.

## Good Bluffers

Pity all the frightened ones
Who do not *look* afraid—
And so receive no pity from
The ones who make the grade.

## Number

When faith in black candles
and in the nothing at all
on clocks runs out
and the time that has gone
and the time to come
is done—
What is the number then
that hasn't yet
been won?
???
??
?

## The Dove

. . . and here is
old Picasso and the dove
and dreams as fragile
as pottery with dove
in white on clay
dark brown as
earth is brown
from our old
battle ground . . .

## Silent One

This little silent one—
He's all the atoms from the sun
And all the grass blades
From the earth
And all the songs
The heart gives birth
To when the throat
Stops singing—
He's my son—
This little
Silent
One.

# doorknobs

The simple silly terror
of a doorknob on a door
that turns to let in life
on two feet standing,
walking, talking,
wearing dress or trousers,
maybe drunk or maybe sober,
maybe smiling, laughing, happy,
maybe tangled in the terror
of a yesterday past grandpa
when the door from out there opened
into here where I, antenna,
recipient of your coming,
received the talking image
of the simple silly terror
of a door that opens
at the turning of a knob
to let in life
walking, talking, standing
wearing dress or trousers,
drunk or maybe sober,
smiling, laughing, happy,
or tangled in the terror
of a yesterday past grandpa
not of our own doing.

# Go Slow

Go *slow*, they say—
While the bite
Of the dog is fast.
Go *slow*, I hear—
While they tell me
*You can't eat here!*
*You can't live here!*
*You can't work here!*
*Don't demonstrate! Wait!*—
While they lock the gate.
Am I supposed to be God,
Or an angel with wings
And a halo on my head
While jobless I starve dead?
Am I supposed to forgive

And meekly live
Going slow, slow, slow,
Slow, slow, slow,
Slow, slow,
Slow,
Slow,
Slow?
????
???
??
?

## We, Too

Oh, Congo brother
With your tribal marks,
We, too, emerge
From ageless darks.
We, too, emit
A frightening cry
From body scarred,
Soul that won't die.
We encarnadine the sky.
We, who have no
Tribal marks to bear,
Bear in our souls
The great welts there
That years have cut
Through skin and lashed
Through bone
In silent cry,
In unheard moan—
We, too,
Congo brother,
Rise with you.

# Junior Addict

The little boy
who sticks a needle in his arm
and seeks an out in other worldly dreams,
who seeks an out in eyes that droop
and ears that close to Harlem screams,
cannot know, of course,
(and has no way to understand)
a sunrise that he cannot see
beginning in some other land—
but destined sure to flood—and soon—
the very room in which he leaves
his needle and his spoon,
the very room in which today the air
is heavy with the drug
of his despair.

      (Yet little can
      tomorrow's sunshine give
      to one who will not live.)

Quick, sunrise, come—
Before the mushroom bomb
Pollutes his stinking air
With better death
Than is his living here,
With viler drugs
Than bring today's release
In poison from the fallout
Of our peace.

      *"It's easier to get dope*
      *than it is to get a job."*

Yes, easier to get dope
than to get a job—
daytime or nighttime job,
teen-age, pre-draft,
pre-lifetime job.

Quick, sunrise, come!
Sunrise out of Africa,
Quick, come!
Sunrise, please come!
Come! Come!

## For Russell and Rowena Jelliffe

And so the seed
Becomes a flower
And in its hour
Reproduces dreams
And flowers.

And so the root
Becomes a trunk
And then a tree
And seeds of trees
And springtime sap
And summer shade
And autumn leaves
And shape of poems
And dreams—
And more than tree.

And so it is
With those who make
Of life a flower,
A tree, a dream
Reproducing (on into
Its own and mine
And your infinity)
Its beauty and its life
In you and me.

And so it was
And is with you:
The seed, the flower,
The root, the tree,
The dream, the you.

This poem I make

(From poems you made)

For you.

## Northern Liberal

And so
we lick our chops at Birmingham
and say, "See!
Southern dogs have vindicated me—
I knew that this would come."
But who are we to be
so proud that savages
have proven a point
taken late in time
to show how liberal I am?
Above the struggle
I can quite afford to be:
well-fed, degreed,
not beat—elite,
up North.
I send checks,
support your cause,
and lick my chops
at Jim Crow laws
and Birmingham—
where you,
*not I*
am.

## Slum Dreams

Little dreams
Of springtime
Bud in sunny air
With no roots
To nourish them,
Since no stems
Are there—
Detached,
Naïve,
So young,
On air alone
They're hung.

## Dream of Freedom

There is a dream in the land
With its back against the wall.
By muddled names and strange
Sometimes the dream is called.

There are those who claim
This dream for theirs alone—
A sin for which we know
They must atone.

Unless shared in common
Like sunlight and like air,
The dream will die for lack
Of substance anywhere.

The dream knows no frontier or tongue,
The dream no class or race.
The dream cannot be kept secure
In any one looked place.

This dream today embattled,
With its back against the wall—
To save the dream for one
It must be saved for ALL—
Our dream of freedom!

## Small Memory

I have this
Strange small memory
Of death
And seven trees
And winds that have
No ecstasies
To search
And find
And search
And find
The search
That is
Not mine.

# Ghosts of 1619

Ghosts of all too solid flesh,
Dark ghosts come back to haunt you now,
These dark ghosts to taunt you—
Yet ghosts so solid, ghosts so real
They may not only haunt you—
But rape, rob, steal,
Sit-in, stand-in, stall-in, vote-in
(Even vote for real in Alabam')
And in voting not give a damn
For the fact that white *was* right
Until last night.

Last night?
What happened then?
Flesh-and-blood ghosts
Became flesh-and-blood men?
Got tired of asking, *When?*
Although minority,
Suddenly became majority
(Metaphysically speaking)
In seeking authority?

How can one man be ten?
Or ten be a hundred and ten?
Or a thousand and ten?
Or a million and ten
Are but a thousand and ten
Or a hundred and ten
Or ten—or one—
Or none—
Being ghosts
Of then?

# Drums

I dream of the drums
And remember
Nights without stars in Africa.

Remember, remember, remember!

I dream of the drums
And remember

Slave ships, billowing sails,
The Western Ocean,
And the landing at Jamestown.

Remember, remember, remember!

I dream of drums
And recall, like a picture,
Congo Square in New Orleans—
Sunday—the slaves' one day of "freedom"—
The juba-dance in Congo Square.

I dream of the drums
And hear again
Jelly Roll's piano,
Buddy Bolden's trumpet,
Kid Ory's trombone,
St. Cyr's banjo,
They join the drums . . .
And I remember.

Jazz!

I dream of the drums
And remember.

Africa!
The ships!
New shore
And drums!

Remember!
I remember!
Remember!

# Final Call

SEND FOR THE PIED PIPER AND LET HIM PIPE THE RATS AWAY.
SEND FOR ROBIN HOOD TO CLINCH THE ANTI-POVERTY CAMPAIGN.
SEND FOR THE FAIRY QUEEN WITH A WAVE OF THE WAND
TO MAKE US ALL INTO PRINCES AND PRINCESSES.
SEND FOR KING ARTHUR TO BRING THE HOLY GRAIL.
SEND FOR OLD MAN MOSES TO LAY DOWN THE LAW.
SEND FOR JESUS TO PREACH THE SERMON ON THE MOUNT.
SEND FOR DREYFUS TO CRY, "J'ACCUSE!"
SEND FOR DEAD BLIND LEMON TO SING THE B FLAT BLUES.
SEND FOR ROBESPIERRE TO SCREAM, "ÇA IRA! ÇA IRA! ÇA IRA!"
SEND (GOD FORBID—HE'S NOT DEAD LONG ENOUGH!)
FOR LUMUMBA TO CRY, "FREEDOM NOW!"
SEND FOR LAFAYETTE AND TELL HIM, "HELP! HELP ME!"
SEND FOR DENMARK VESEY CRYING, "FREE!"
FOR CINQUE SAYING, "RUN A NEW FLAG UP THE MAST."
FOR OLD JOHN BROWN WHO KNEW SLAVERY COULDN'T LAST.
SEND FOR LENIN! (DON'T YOU DARE!—HE CAN'T COME HERE!)
SEND FOR TROTSKY! (WHAT? DON'T CONFUSE THE ISSUE, PLEASE!)
SEND FOR UNCLE TOM ON HIS MIGHTY KNEES.
SEND FOR LINCOLN, SEND FOR GRANT.
SEND FOR FREDERICK DOUGLASS, GARRISON, BEECHER, LOWELL.
SEND FOR HARRIET TUBMAN, OLD SOJOURNER TRUTH.
SEND FOR MARCUS GARVEY (WHAT?) SUFI (WHO?) FATHER DIVINE (WHERE?)
DUBOIS (WHEN?) MALCOLM (OH!) SEND FOR STOKELY. (NO?) THEN
SEND FOR ADAM POWELL ON A NON-SUBPOENA DAY.
SEND FOR THE PIED PIPER TO PIPE OUR RATS AWAY.

(And if nobody comes, send for me.)


# Old Age

Having known robins on the window sill
And loves over which to grieve,
What can you dream of now
In which you still believe?

Having known snow in winter
And the burst of blooms in spring,

What can you seek now
To make your heart still sing?

If there should be nothing new,
Might not the self-same wonders do?
And if there should be nothing old,
Might not new wonders still unfold?

Should nothing new or old appeal,
Still friends will ask,
"How do you feel?"

## To You

To sit and dream, to sit and read,
To sit and learn about the world
Outside our world of here and now—
        our problem world—
To dream of vast horizons of the soul
Through dreams made whole,
Unfettered free—help me!
All you who are dreamers, too,
Help me make our world anew.
I reach out my hands to you.

## Not What Was

By then the poetry is written
and the wild rose of the world
blooms to last so short a time
before its petals fall.
The air is music
and its melody a spiral
until it widens
beyond the tip of time
and so is lost
to poetry and the rose—
belongs instead to vastness beyond form,
to universe that nothing can contain,
to unexplored space

which sends no answers back
to fill the vase unfilled
or spread in lines
upon another page—
that anyhow was never written
because the thought could not escape
the place in which it bloomed
before the rose had gone.


## Long View: Negro

Emancipation: 1865
Sighted through the
Telescope of dreams
Looms larger,
So much larger,
So it seems,
Than truth can be.

But turn the telescope around,
Look through the larger end—
And wonder why
What was so large
Becomes so small
Again.


## Dinner Guest: Me

I know I am
The Negro Problem
Being wined and dined,
Answering the usual questions
That come to white mind
Which seeks demurely
To probe in polite way
The why and wherewithal
Of darkness U.S.A.—
Wondering how things got this way
In current democratic night,

Murmuring gently
Over *fraises du bois*,
"I'm so ashamed of being white."

The lobster is delicious,
The wine divine,
And center of attention
At the damask table, mine.
To be a Problem on
Park Avenue at eight
Is not so bad.
Solutions to the Problem,
Of course, wait.

## Christmas Eve: Nearing Midnight in New York

The Christmas trees are almost all sold
And the ones that are left go cheap.
The children almost all over town
Have almost gone to sleep.

The skyscraper lights on Christmas Eve
Have almost all gone out.
There's very little traffic,
Almost no one about.

Our town's almost as quiet
As Bethlehem must have been
Before a sudden angel chorus
Sang PEACE ON EARTH!
GOOD WILL TO MEN!

Our old Statue of Liberty
Looks down almost with a smile
As the Island of Manhattan
Awaits the morning of the Child.

# Frederick Douglass: 1817–1895

Douglass was someone who,
Had he walked with wary foot
And frightened tread,
From very indecision
Might be dead,
Might have lost his soul,
But instead decided to be bold
And capture every street
On which he set his feet,
To route each path
Toward freedom's goal,
To make each highway
Choose *his* compass' choice,
To all the world cried,
*Hear my voice!* . . .
*Oh, to be a beast, a bird,*
*Anything but a slave!* he said.

*Who would be free*
*Themselves must strike*
*The first blow,* he said.

He died in 1895.
*He is not dead.*

# Question and Answer

Durban, Birmingham,
Cape Town, Atlanta,
Johannesburg, Watts,
The earth around
Struggling, fighting,
Dying—for what?

*A world to gain.*

Groping, hoping,
Waiting—for what?

*A world to gain.*

Dreams kicked asunder,
Why not go under?

549

*There's a world to gain.*

But suppose I don't want it,
Why take it?

*To remake it.*


## Frosting

Freedom
Is just frosting
On somebody else's
Cake —
And so must be
Till we
Learn how to
Bake.


## Metropolitan Museum

I came in from the roar
Of city streets
To look upon a Grecian urn.

I thought of Keats —
To mind came verses
Filled with lovers' sweets.

Out of ages past there fell
Into my hands the petals
Of an asphodel.

## Emperor Haile Selassie    On Liberation Day, May 5, 1966

That he is human . . . and living . . .
And of our time . . .
Makes it seem a miracle
All the more sublime
That he becomes a symbol
Of our Negritude,
Our dignity . . . and food
On which men who are neither
Kings of Kings nor Lions of Judah
Yet may feed their pride . . .
And live to hope for that great day
When all mankind is one
And each is king in common
Of all his eyes survey.
And each man shares
The strength derived from head held high . . .
And holds his head, King of Kings . . .
Our symbol of a dream
That will not die.


## Crowns and Garlands

Make a garland of Leontynes and Lenas
And hang it about your neck
        Like a lei.
Make a crown of Sammys, Sidneys, Harrys,
Plus Cassius Mohammed Ali Clay.
Put their laurels on your brow
        Today—
Then before you can walk
To the neighborhood corner,
Watch them droop, wilt, fade
        Away.
Though worn in glory on my head,
They do not last a day—
        Not one—
Nor take the place of meat or bread
Or rent that I must pay.
Great names for crowns and garlands!
        Yeah!
I love Ralph Bunche—
But I can't eat him for lunch.

# The Backlash Blues

Mister Backlash, Mister Backlash,
Just who do you think I am?
Tell me, Mister Backlash,
Who do you think I am?
You raise my taxes, freeze my wages,
Send my son to Vietnam.

You give me second-class houses,
Give me second-class schools,
Second-class houses
And second-class schools.
You must think us colored folks
Are second-class fools.

When I try to find a job
To earn a little cash,
Try to find myself a job
To earn a little cash,
All you got to offer
Is a white backlash.

But the world is big,
The world is big and round,
Great big world, Mister Backlash,
Big and bright and round—
And it's full of folks like me who are
Black, Yellow, Beige, and Brown.

Mister Backlash, Mister Backlash,
What do you think I got to lose?
Tell me, Mister Backlash,
What you think I got to lose?
I'm gonna leave you, Mister Backlash,
Singing your mean old backlash blues.

*You're the one,*
*Yes, you're the one*
*Will have the blues.*

# Suburban Evening

A dog howled.
Weird became the night.
No good reason
For my fright—
But reason often
May play host
To quiet
Unreasonable
Ghosts.

# Demonstration

Did you ever walk into a firehose
With the water turned up full blast?
Did you ever walk toward police guns
When each step might be your last?
Did you ever stand up in the face of snarling dogs
And not move as the dogs came?
Did you ever feel the tear gas burn
Your day, your night, your dawn?
  *Your dawn*
When the water's a rainbow hue,
  *Your dawn*
When the guns are no longer aimed at you,
  *Your dawn*
When the cops forget their jails,
  *Your dawn*
When the police dogs wag their tails,
  *Your dawn*
When the tear-gas canisters are dry,
  *Your dawn*
When you own the star in the sky,
  *Your dawn*
When the atom bomb is yours—
  *Your dawn*
When you have the keys to all doors—
  *Your dawn*
Will you ever forget *your dawn?*

## Prime

Uptown on Lenox Avenue
Where a nickel costs a dime,
In these lush and thieving days
When million-dollar thieves
Glorify their million-dollar ways
In the press and on the radio and TV—
    But won't let me
    Skim even a dime—
I, black, come to my prime
In the section of the niggers
Where a nickel costs a dime.

## Lenox Avenue Bar

Weaving
between assorted terrors
is the Jew
who owns the place—
one Jew,
fifty Negroes:
embroideries
(heirloomed
from ancient evenings)
tattered
in this neon
place.

## Death in Yorkville

(James Powell, Summer, 1964)

How many bullets does it take
To kill a fifteen-year-old kid?
How many bullets does it take
To kill me?

How many centuries does it take
To bind my mind—chain my feet—
Rope my neck—lynch me—
Unfree?

From the slave chain to the lynch rope
To the bullets of Yorkville,
Jamestown, 1619 to 1963:
Emancipation Centennial—
100 years NOT free.

Civil War Centennial: 1965.
How many Centennials does it take
To kill me,
Still alive?

When the long hot summers come
Death ain't
No jive.

## Black Panther

Pushed into the corner
Of the hobnailed boot,
Pushed into the corner of the
"I-don't-want-to-die" cry,
Pushed into the corner of
"I don't want to study war no more,"
Changed into "Eye for eye,"
The Panther in his desperate boldness
Wears no disguise,
Motivated by the truest
Of the oldest
Lies.

## Office Building: Evening

When the white folks get through,
    Here come you:

    Got to clean awhile.

When daytime folks
Have made their dough,
    Away they go:

You clean awhile.

When white collars get done,
    You have your "fun"
    Cleaning awhile.

*"But just wait, chile . . ."*


## Special Bulletin


Lower the flags
For the dead become alive,
Play hillbilly dirges
That hooded serpents may dance,
Write obituaries
For white-robed warriors
Emerging to the fanfare
Of death rattles.
Muffled drums in Swanee River tempo.
Hand-high salutes—*heil!*
Present arms
With ax handles
Made in Atlanta,
    *Sieg*
    *Heil!*
Oh, run, all who have not
Changed your names.
As for you others—
The skin on your black face,
Peel off the skin,
    Peel peel
    Peel off
    The skin.

# Birmingham Sunday (September 15, 1963)

          Four little girls
Who went to Sunday School that day
And never came back home at all
But left instead
Their blood upon the wall
With spattered flesh
And bloodied Sunday dresses
Torn to shreds by dynamite
That China made aeons ago —
Did not know
That what China made
Before China was ever Red at all
Would redden with their blood
This Birmingham-on-Sunday wall.

          Four tiny girls
Who left their blood upon that wall,
In little graves today await
The dynamite that might ignite
The fuse of centuries of Dragon Kings
Whose tomorrow sings a hymn
The missionaries never taught Chinese
In Christian Sunday School
To implement the Golden Rule.

          Four little girls
Might be awakened someday soon
By songs upon the breeze
As yet unfelt among magnolia trees.

# Bombings in Dixie

          It's not enough to mourn
          And not enough to pray.
          Sackcloth and ashes, anyhow,
          Save for another day.

          The Lord God Himself
          Would hardly desire
          That men be burned to death —
          *And bless the fire.*

## Mother in Wartime

As if it were some noble thing,
She spoke of sons at war,
As if freedom's cause
Were pled anew at some heroic bar,
As if the weapons used today
Killed with great élan,
As if technicolor banners flew
To honor modern man —
Believing everything she read
In the daily news,
(No in-between to choose)
She thought that only
One side won,
Not that *both*
Might lose.

## Official Notice

Dear Death:
I got your message
That my son is dead.
The ink you used
To write it
Is the blood he bled.
You say he died with honor
On the battlefield,
And that I am honored, too,
By this bloody yield.
Your letter
Signed in blood,
With his blood
Is sealed.

## Last Prince of the East

Futile of me to offer you my hand,
Last little brown prince
Of Malaysia land.
Your wall is too high
And your moat is too wide —

For the white world's gunboats
Are all on your side.
So you lie in your cradle
And shake your rattle
To the jingo cry
Of blood and battle
While Revolt in the rice fields
Puts on a red gown.

Before you are king,
He'll come to town.

## War

The face of war is my face.
The face of war is your face.
 *What color*
 *Is the face*
 *Of war?*
Brown, black, white—
Your face and my face.

Death is the broom
I take in my hands
To sweep the world
 Clean.
I sweep and I sweep
Then mop and I mop.
I dip my broom in blood,
My mop in blood—
And blame you for this,
Because you are *there*,
 Enemy.
It's hard to blame me,
Because I am here—
So I kill you.
And you kill me.
 My name,
Like your name,
 Is war.

## Sweet Words on Race

Sweet words that take
Their own sweet time to flower
And then so quickly wilt
Within the inner ear,
Belie the budding promise
Of their pristine hour
To wither in the
Sultry air of fear.
Sweet words so brave
When danger is not near,
I've heard
So many times before,
I'd just as leave
Not hear them
Anymore.

## Un-American Investigators

The committee's fat,
Smug, almost secure
Co-religionists
Shiver with delight
In warm manure
As those investigated—
Too brave to name a name—
Have pseudonyms revealed
In Gentile game
    Of who,
    Born Jew,
    Is who?
*Is not your name Lipshitz?*
    Yes.
*Did you not change it*
*For subversive purposes?*
    No.
*For nefarious gain?*
    Not so.
*Are you sure?*
The committee shivers
With delight in
Its manure.

# Undertow

The solid citizens
Of the country club set,
Caught between
Selma and Peking,
Feel the rug of dividends,
Bathmats of pride,
Even soggy country club
Pink paper towels
Dropped on the MEN'S ROOM floor
Slipping out from under them
Like waves of sea
Between Selma, Peking,
Westchester
And me.

# Stokely Malcolm Me

i have been seeking
what i have never found
what i don't know what i want
but it must be around
i been upset
since the day before last
but that day was so long
i done forgot when it passed
yes almost forgot
what i have not found
but i know it must be
*somewhere* around.

you live in the Bronx
so folks say.

Stokely,
did i ever live
up your
way?
???
??
?

## Freedom [3]

Some folks think
By burning churches
They burn
Freedom.
Some folks think
By imprisoning me
They imprison
Freedom.
Some folks think
By killing a man
They kill
Freedom.
But Freedom
Stands up and laughs
In their faces
And says,
*No—*
*Not so!*
No!

## Flotsam

On the shoals of Nowhere,
Cast up—my boat,
Bow all broken,
No longer afloat.

On the shoals of Nowhere,
Wasted—my song—
Yet taken by the sea wind
And blown along.

# Appendix 1
## Poems Circulated by the Associated Negro Press

# Song of the Refugee Road

Refugee road, refugee road
Where do I go from here?
Weary my feet! Heavy the road!
My heart is filled with fear.
The ones I left far behind—
    Home nowhere!
Dark winds of trouble moan through my mind.
    None to care!
Bitter my past! Tomorrow—What's there?
Refugee road! Refugee road!
Where do I go from here?
Walking down the refugee road.
Must I beg? Must I steal?
Must I lie? Must I kneel?
Or driven like dumb war-weary sheep,
Must we wander the high road and weep?
Or will the world listen to my appeal?
From China where the war gods thunder and roar.
From all the dark lands where freedom is no more.
Vienna, city of light and gladness,
Once gay with waltzes, now bowed in sadness.
Dark Ethiopia, stripped of her mirth.
Spain, where the shells plant steel seeds in the earth.
Oh, Statue of Liberty, lighting tomorrow,
Look! And have pity on my sorrow:
    Home nowhere! None to care!
    Bitter my past! Tomorrow—what's there?
    Refugee road! Refugee road!
    Where do I go from here?
    Walking down the refugee road.

# America's Young Black Joe!

One tenth of the population
Of this mighty nation
Was sun-tanned by nature long ago,
But we're Americans by birth and training
So our country will be gaining
When every citizen learns to know
That I'm America's Young Black Joe!

Manly, good natured, smiling and gay,
My sky is sometimes cloudy
But it won't stay that way.
I'm comin', I'm comin'—
But my head AIN'T bending, low!
I'm walking proud! I'm speaking out loud!
I'm America's Young Black Joe!

This is my own my native land,
And I'm mighty glad that's true.
Land where my fathers worked
The same as yours worked, too.
So from every mountain side
Let freedom's bright torch glow—
Standing hand in hand with democracy,
I'm America's Young Black Joe!

Besides Joe Louis there's Henry Armstrong,
Three titles to his name,
Beat everybody that was his size
In the fighting game.
Then there was Kenny Washington
In a football suit,
Run, pass, kick, tackle, and block to boot.

And don't forget track men like Ellerbe
Who piles up points for Tuskegee,
Or Jessie Owens with his laurel wreath
That made old Hitler grit his teeth.
Look at those dark boys streaking by,
Feet just flying and head held high.
Looky yonder at Metcalf, Johnson,
Tolan! Down the field they go,
Swift and proud before the crowd—
They're America's Young Black Joe!

This is our own, our native land,
And I'm mighty glad that's true.
Land where my fathers worked
The same as yours worked, too.
So from every mountain side
Let freedom's bright torch glow—
Standing hand in hand with democracy
I'm  America's Young Black Joe!

# Ballad of the Fool

Poor, poor fool!
No sense at all.
Best he can do's
Walk around and not fall.

He don't have no place except
Up and down the block
In what's happening to the world
He takes no stock.

He just sits and grins
And laughs in the sun
And looks like
He's having fun.

He don't know there is a war.
He ain't on WPA.
Gee! Sometimes I wish I
Was a fool that way.


# Ballad of Walter White

Now Walter White
Is mighty light.
Being a colored man
Who looks like white,
He can go down South
Where a lynching takes place
And the white folks never
Guess his race —
So he investigates
To his heart's desire
Whereas if he was brownskin
They'd set him on fire!
By being himself
Walter finds out
What them lynchers
Was all about.
But back to New York
Before going to press —

Cause if the crackers ever got him
There'd be one Negro less!
Yes, it's our good fortune
He was born so light
Cause it's swell to have a leader
That can pass for white.

## The Mitchell Case

I see by the papers
Where Mitchell's won his case.
Down South the railroads now
Must give us equal space.
Even if we're rich enough
    To want a Pullman car,
The Supreme Court says we get it—
And a diner and a bar!
Now since the Court in Washington
Can make a rule like that,
If we went to court enough we might
Get Jim Crow on the mat
And pin his shoulders to the ground
And drive him from the land—
Since the Constitution ain't enough—
To protect a colored man—
And we have to go to court to make
The crackers understand.
But for poor people
It's kinder hard to sue.
Mr. Mitchell, you did right well—
But the rest of us ain't you.
Seems to me it would be simpler
If the Government would declare
They're tired of all this Jim Crow stuff
And just give it the air.
Seems to me it's time to realize
That in the U.S.A.
To have Jim Crow's too Hitler-like
In this modern age and day—
Cause fine speeches sure sound hollow
About Democracy
When all over America,
They still Jim Crowing me.

To earn a dollar sometimes
Is hard enough to do—
Let alone having to take that dollar
To go and sue!

## Explain It, Please

I see by the papers
What seems mighty funny to me.
The British are fighting for freedom
But India ain't free.
The colored weeklies tell me
In the British colonies
The white man stands on his two feet
But the black man's on his knees.
And they tell me that in Africa
The color line's drawn tight,
So when the English holler freedom
Can it be that they are right?
Course there's a mighty lot of fog and smoke,
But I'm trying hard to see
How folks can have a mouth full of freedom—
And a handful of dung for me.

## Ballad of the Black Sheep

My brother,
He never left the old fireside.
I was the one
Who liked to ride.

I always felt I
Had to wander and roam.
Never met nobody's got
What it takes to keep me home.

Every job I have
I throw away my pay
And raise sand each and
Every day.

My brother gathers
What the folks call
Moss.
But me—
I am a
Total loss.

Help me, Jesus!

## Epitaph [2]

Uncle Tom,
When he was alive,
Filled the white folks
Full of jive.
But the trouble was
His jive was bad.
Now, thank God,
Uncle Tom
Is dead.

## So Tired Blues

I'm gonna wake up some mornin'
With the sun in my hand.
Gonna throw the sun
Way across the land—
    Cause I'm tired,
    Tired as I can be.

Gonna throw the sun
In somebody's face
  Recreate
The human race—
    Cause I'm tired,
    Tired as I can be.

When the sunstroke strikes,
Gonna rise and shine,

Take this world and
Make it mine—
        Cause I'm tired,
        Tired as I can be.

Don't try to figger
Out these words I sing.
They'll keep you figgerin'
To way next spring—
        Cause I'm tired,
        Tired as I can be.

## Return to Sea

Today I go back to the sea
And the wind-beaten rise of the foam.
Today I go back to the sea
And it's just as though I was home.

It's just as though I was home again
On this ship of iron and steam.
It's just as though I'd found again
The broken edge of a dream.

## Jazz Girl

Jazz?
Remember that song
About the wind in the trees
Singing me pretty melodies?
Was nice, wasn't it?
Hear that violin?
Say, Buddy, you know
It's spring in the country
Where flowers grow.
Play, jazz band! Play!
I'm tired! Oh, gee!
Sure, go ahead,
Buy a drink for me.

## Pathological Puzzle

There are so many diseases
From rabies to the wheezes
That people can contract
Till it's hard to understand
    How any man
      remains intact.

## Dixie Man to Uncle Sam

How can you
Shake a fist at tyranny
Everywhere else
But here?

Do you not see?
I, too, in Dixie
Stand in need
Of being free:

Jim Crow's
Too Hitler-like
For you—
Or me.

## Governor Fires Dean

I see by the papers
Where Governor Talmadge get real mad
Cause one of Georgia's teachers
Thinks Democracy ain't bad.
The Governor has done had him
Kicked plumb out of school
Just because that teacher
Believes the Golden Rule.
Governor Talmadge says that white folks
And black folks cannot mix
Unless they want to put

The sovereign State of Georgia
In an awful kind of fix.
The Governor says equality
(Even just in education)
Is likely to lead us all
Right straight to ruination—
So I reckon Governor Talmadge
Must be a Hitler man
Cause that's just what Hitler'd say
If he ruled the land.
Ain't it funny how some white folks
Have the strangest way
Of acting just like Hitler
In the U.S.A.?

## Get Up Off That Old Jive

White folks,
You better get some new jive.
That old jive is wearing thin.
I been listening to that old jive
Since I don't know when.

Fact of the matter,
To tell you the truth
Instead of just words
I want action to boot.

You been making fine speeches
For a long long while
Now give some democracy
To each brown-skin child.

A war's taking place.
We ain't fighting for fun.
We're fighting to win—
This fight's got to be won.

We want just what
The president said:
    Freedom from fear,
    And from want—

To be men,
And have bread.

So get up off that old jive.
Let's start clearing the way:
Put an end to Jim Crow
*Right now, today.*

A man can fight
Better that way.


## Fourth of July Thought

Remember on our far-flung fronts
This Fourth of July,
Soldiers of Democracy
Guard our earth and sky.

Those of us who stay at home
Have grave duties, too:
    The WAR FRONT
    Depends on
    THE HOME FRONT—
The HOME FRONT is YOU!


## Battle Ground

The soldier said to the general,
General, what shall I shoot?
The general said, Man, shoot your gun—
And you better shoot straight to boot.
The soldier said to the general,
What shall my target be?
The general said, Man, I don't care,
Just so your target ain't me!
The soldier said to the general,
I can't see nothing but space,

Yet every time I lift my head
The bullets pass my face.
The general said to the soldier,
You do not need to see
Who you're fighting nor what for.
Just take your orders from me.
The soldier said to the general,
They shootin' in front and behind.
The general said to the soldier,
Don't pay them bullets no mind.
The soldier said, Then, general,
Why don't YOU come out here with me?
The general said, That isn't right—
Cause I'm the general! See?

# Joe Louis [2]

Joe Louis is a man
For men to imitate—
When this country needed him,
He did not stall or fail.

Joe took up the challenge
And joined up for war.
Nobody had to ask him,
"What are you waiting for?"

As a private in the army
Of his talents he gave free
Two mighty boxing matches
To raise funds for liberty.

That's more than lots of others
Who still try to jim-crow Joe
Have either heart or mind to do—
So this is to let them know

That Joe Louis is a man for any
    man to imitate.
If everybody was like Joe Louis
    there'd be no
"Too little" or "too late."

## Crow Goes, Too

Uncle Sam—
And old Jim Crow—
Right along with you
Wherever you go.

Done gone to England
Took Jim Crow there—
But England don't like
The feathers you wear.

Driberg in Commons
The other day
Said, kindly take that
Bird away.

Uncle Sam,
Why don't you get hep?
Stop marching with
A Jim Crow step.

This is a war
To free all men.
Throw Jim Crow out—
And let decency in.
That's the way
To win!

## Lonely Nocturne

When dawn lights the sky
And day and night meet,
I climb my stairs high
Above the grey street.
I lift my window
To look at the sky
Where moon kisses star
Goodbye.

When dawn lights the sky
I seek my lonely room.
The halls as I go by
Echo like a tomb.
And I wonder why
As I take out my key,

There is nobody there
But me—
When dawn lights the sky.

## Troubled Water

Between us, always, loved one,
There lies this troubled water.
You are my sky, my shining sun
Over troubled water.

I journey far to touch your hand.
The trip is troubled water.
We see yet cannot understand
This fateful troubled water.

Deep hearts, dear, dream of happiness
Balked by troubled water.
Between us always—love, and this—
This sea of troubled water.

## Total War

The reason Dixie
Is so mean today
Is because it wasn't licked
In the proper way.
And I reckon old Hitler
A cracker must be—
Because he, too,
Wants to Jim Crow me.

So I'm in favor of beating
Hitler to his knees—
Then beating him some more
Until he hollers, Please!

Cause if we let our enemies
Breathe again—
They're liable to live
To be another pain.

# Ghandhi Is Fasting

Mighty Britain, tremble!
Let your empire's standard sway
Lest it break entirely—
Mr. Ghandhi fasts today.

You may think it foolish—
That there's no truth in what I say—
That all of Asia's watching
As Ghandhi fasts today.

All of Asia's watching,
And I am watching, too,
For I am also jim crowed—
As India is jim crowed by you.

You know quite well, Great Britain,
That it is not right
To starve and beat and oppress
Those who are not white.

Of course, we do it too,
Here in the U.S.A.
May Ghandhi's prayers help us, as well,
As he fasts today.


# Judge William Hastie

Now you take
This Bill Hastie guy—
He resigned
And told the world why;
He can't see why
Colored boys can't fly!
And neither do I.

## What I Think

The guys who own
The biggest guns
Are the lucky ones
These days.
Being hip
To your marksmanship
Is what pays.
On the other hand
There's some demand
For a world plan.
Some folks wish
The human race might
Try to do right—
Instead of just fight.
But others still feel
That any old heel
Has a right
To laissez faire
Anywhere,
And that Empire's right.
As for me,
I can't agree,
To my nose colonies stink.
People ought to be FREE
And have liberty—
That's what I think.


## Just an Ordinary Guy

He's just an ordinary guy.
He doesn't occupy
A seat of government
Or anything like that.

He works hard every day,
Saturday brings home his pay—
He may take a glass of beer
Sometimes at that.

He never had his name in lights,
He's never front page news.

He stands up for his rights,
Yet doesn't beef or sing the blues.

But when his country gets in trouble
And it's time to fight and die,
He doesn't ask for a deferment—
He's just an ordinary guy.

Listen, Hitler!
About this ordinary guy,
You may wonder why
He's taken such an awful
Hate to you.

But you'll never understand
His kind of man.
You won't need to—
You'll be dead when he gets through.

He doesn't bully or act rough.
You never hear him bluff.
But there's one thing certain, Nazi,
He won't stand for your type of stuff.

He just doesn't like the idea
Of men being in a cage,
And the way you try to boss folks
Puts him in a rage.

You've got the whole round world in trouble
With your boastings and your lies.
But you'll never beat us, Hitler—
Not us ordinary guys!

## Speaking of Food

I hear folks talking
About coffee's hard to get,
And they don't know how
They're going to live without it.

I hear some others saying
They can't buy no meat to fry,

And the way they say it
You'd think they're gonna die.

If I was to sit down
And write to Uncle Sam,
I'll tell him that I reckon
I can make it without ham.

I'd say, "Feed those fighting forces
For they're the ones today
That need to have their victuals
To wipe our foes away!"

Looks to me
That's what we ought to say.

## Puzzlement

I don't know why
They're so hard on me and you?
We don't do nothing in the jook joints
Rich folks don't do.

But the rich folks have clubs
And licenses and such,
Only trouble is, we
Can't afford that much.

## The Bells Toll Kindly

Many clocks in many towers
Have struck for me delightful hours.
Many cities, many towns
Have gathered laughter,
Scattered frowns.
Many clocks in many towers
Have laughed their hours.

Some day in some higher tower
A clock will strike its final hour.

When it tolls I shall go
Not wishing that the hour be slow.

I shall then remember still
How it struck one gay December
Near the Kremlin white with snow
And the midnight a warm ember
Of love's glow.

I shall then still sweet recall
How one evening in Les Halles
We walked together arm in arm
Hearing Notre Dame's grave charm.

Then I shall still realize
How, round the world, the bells are wise,
So when I hear that last bell toll,
Willingly, I'll bare my soul.

For many clocks in many towers,
Have struck for me delightful hours,
So there shall be no need to fear
The final hour drawing near.


## Madam and the Crime Wave

I said, I believe
This world's gone mad,
Never heard of folks
Acting so bad.

Last night a man
Knocked a woman down,
Robbed her and raped her
On the ground.

Such a fate, folks say,
Is worse than death!

When I read it
I held my breath.

With your money gone
Where is death's sting?
(Course you always got
That other thing.)

## Madam's Christmas (or Merry Christmas Everybody)

I forgot
to send a card to Jennie
But the truth about cousins is
There's too many.

I also forgot
A card for Joe
But I believe I'll let
The old rascal go.

I disremembered
My old friend Jack
But he's been evil
Long as he's been black.

I done bought
Four boxes now,
And I can't afford
No more nohow.

So MERRY CHRISTMAS
Everybody!
Cards or no cards
Here's HOWDY!

## Song After Lynching

I guess DEMOCRACY'S meant to be
Just a high-flown sound
Flying around . . .
Cause the crackers get mad
If I try to pin it down.

I guess LIBERTY'S supposed
To be just a hope.
When Negroes try to make it real
They look for a rope.

White folks oughtn't to use
Those fine words that way
When they don't mean a thing
Those words say . . .

Getting on the radio
About DEMOCRACY'S star . . .
And herded up
In a Jim Crow car!

Speeches like theirs
Puzzle me.
JUSTICE don't jibe
With a lynching tree.

## Bonds for All

Buy a Bond for Grandma—
Grandma's growing old.
Buy a Bond for Baby—
Bless his little soul.

Buy a Bond for Papa,
Though it's Father's Day.
Buy a Bond for Mama
To salt away.

Buy a Bond for Uncle.
Get one for Auntie, too.

Then buy one for your Buddy
Who's fighting for you.

BACK THE ATTACK
Is the slogan this fall.
Back it, Mr. Citizen,
With War Bonds for all.

## Poor Girl's Ruination

I went to Chicago
At the age of three.
Chicago nearly
Ruined me.

I went to Detroit
At twenty-one.
What Chicago started
Detroit's done.

If I'd a-growed up
With a little money
I might not a-been
Ruined, honey.

Before you give
A girl damnation,
Take what is in
Consideration.

## Poem to Uncle Sam

Uncle Sam
With old Jim Crow—
Like a shadow
Right behind you—
Everywhere
You go.

Uncle Sam,
Why don't you
Turn around,
And before you
Tackle Hitler—
Shoot Jim down?


## Song of Adoration

I would like to be a white man, wouldn't you?
There's so many lovely things that I could do.
      I could lynch a Negro—
      And never go to jail, you know,
I would love to be a white man, wouldn't you?

I would love to be a white man, wouldn't you?
So many tasty things that I could do.
      I could tell the starving Indian nation
      To go straight to damnation,
Oh, I would love to be a white man, wouldn't you?

I would love to be a white man, wouldn't you?
There's such intriguing things that one could do.
      I could say to Stalin, listen kid,
      You're just an Asiatic mongrel Red.
Ah, I would love to be a white man, wouldn't you?

I would love to be a white woman also, too.
There's so many cultural things that I could do.
      I could belong to the D.A.R.
      Tell Marian Anderson, stay . . . out the D.A.R.!
I could ADORE being a white woman, wouldn't you?

I'd love to be a white congressman, too.
There's so many helpful things I could do.
      Just to get the Negro's goat
      I wouldn't let NO soldiers vote.
I would love to be a white congressman, wouldn't you?

Oh, I'd love to be a white Christian, ain't it true.
I'd act just like my fellow Christians do.
            For Jesus I would search
            With no black folks in my church.
Amen, I'd love to be a white man, wouldn't you?
        Halleloo! . . . O Halleloo . . .
            Hallelloo-o-o

## Bonds: In Memoriam

Written Especially for the Writers' War Board, War Loan Drive, by Langston Hughes
(For ANP)


Eddie and Charlie and Jack and Ted
And Harry and Arthur and Ken
        Have all gone down
        Where heroes are found
In the land of the lost fighting men.

Eddie and Charlie and Ted and Ken
And Harry and Arthur and Jack
        All fought well
        Through a living hell
To a land where there's no coming back.

But Eddie and Charlie and Ted and Ken
And all the men who are gone
        Still look to you
        To see it through—
The least you can do is buy a Bond.

The least you can do is do your job well—
They fought that your future'd be sunny.
        These men who gave all
        That our cause might not fall
Only ask that you lend your money.

# Worriation

There's something disturbing
To a cat, no doubt,
Seeing birds with wings
Flying about.
Is there something disturbing
To Aryans in the way
That Negroes, being black,
Keep looking that way?

# Ballad of Harry Moore

(Killed at Mims, Florida, on Christmas night, 1951)

Florida means land of flowers.
It was on Christmas night
In the state named for the flowers
Men came bearing dynamite.

Men came stealing through the orange groves
Bearing hate instead of love,
While the Star of Bethlehem
Was in the sky above.

Oh, memories of a Christmas evening
When Wise Men travelled from afar
Seeking out a lowly manger
Guided by a Holy Star!

Oh, memories of a Christmas evening
When to Bethlehem there came
"Peace on earth, good will to men"—
Jesus was His name.

But they must've forgotten Jesus
Down in Florida that night
Stealing through the orange groves
Bearing hate and dynamite.

It was a little cottage,
A family, name of Moore.
In the windows wreaths of holly,
And a pine wreath on the door.

Christmas, 1951,
The family prayers were said
When father, mother, daughter,
And grandmother went to bed.

The father's name was Harry Moore.
The N.A.A.C.P.
Told him to carry out its work
That Negroes might be free.

So it was that Harry Moore
(So deeply did he care)
Sought the right for men to live
With their heads up everywhere.

Because of that, white killers,
Who like Negroes "in their place,"
Came stealing through the orange groves
On that night of dark disgrace.

It could not be in Jesus' name,
Beneath the bedroom floor,
On Christmas night the killers
Hid the bomb for Harry Moore.

It could not be in Jesus' name
The killers took his life,
Blew his home to pieces
And killed his faithful wife.

It could not be for the sake of love
They did this awful thing—
For when the bomb exploded
No hearts were heard to sing.

And certainly no angels cried,
"Peace on earth, good will to men"—
But around the world an echo hurled
A question: When? . . . When? . . . When?

When will men for sake of peace
And for democracy
Learn no bombs a man can make
Keep men from being free?

It seems that I hear Harry Moore.
From the earth his voice cries,

No bomb can kill the dreams I hold—
For freedom never dies!

I will not stop! I will not stop—
For freedom never dies!
I will not stop! I will not stop!
Freedom never dies!

So should you see our Harry Moore
Walking on a Christmas night,
Don't run and hide, you killers,
He has no dynamite.

In his heart is only love
For all the human race,
And all he wants is for every man
To have his rightful place.

And this he says, our Harry Moore,
As from the grave he cries:
No bomb can kill the dreams I hold
For freedom never dies!

Freedom never dies, I say!
Freedom never dies!


## Message to the President

Mr. President, kindly please,
May I have a word with you?
There's one thing, for a long time,
I've been wishing you would do.
In your fireside chats on the radio
I hear you telling the world
What you want them to know,
And your speeches in general
Sound mighty fine,
But there's one thing, Mr. President,
That worries my mind.
I hear you talking about freedom
        For the Finn,
        The Jew,
        And the Czechoslovak—

But you never seem to mention
Us folks who're black!
We're all Americans, Mr. President,
And I've had enough
Of putting up with this
Jim Crow stuff.
I want the self-same rights
Other Americans have today.
I want to fly a plane
Like any other man may.
I don't like this Jim Crow army
Or this Jim Crow navy,
Or the lily-white marines
Licking up the gravy.
We're one-tenth of the nation,
Mr. President, fourteen million strong.
If you help to keep us down,
You're wrong.
We work and pay our taxes.
Our patriotism's good.
We try to live like
Decent Americans should.
That's why as citizens, Mr. President,
We have the right to demand
The next time you make a speech,
Take an all-out stand
And make your meaning
Just as clear to me
As you do when talking to
Those Englishmen across the sea.
Since, for our land's defense
If we have to fight—
We ought to be together,
Black and white.
So what I'm asking, Mr. President,
Is to hear you say
No more segregation in the U.S.A.
And when you mention the Finns,
    And the Jew,
    And the Czechoslovak,
Don't forget the fourteen million
Here who're black.
Such a speech, Mr. President, for me
Would put a whole lot more meaning
In Democracy.
So the next time you sit down

To that radio,
Just like you lambast Hitler,
Give Jim Crow a blow—
For all I'm asking, Mr. President,
Is to hear you say,
No more segregation in the U.S.A.
My friends, NO more
Segregation in the U.S.A.


## Promised Land

The Promised Land
Is always just ahead.
You will not reach it
Ere you're dead.

But your children's children
By their children will be led
To a spot from which the Land—
Still lies ahead.


## Chicago Blues    (moral: go slow)

Chicago is a town
That sure do run on wheels.
Runs so fast you don't know
How good the ground feels.

I got in town on Monday
Tuesday rolling drunk
Wednesday morning
I pawned my trunk.

Thursday morning
Cutting aces high

My stock went up
Head in the sky.

Friday riding
In a Cadillac,
She said, Daddy, you can ride
Long as you stay black.

Saturday I said, Baby,
You been good to me—
But I'm no one-woman man,
I need two or three.

Sunday I was living
In a ten room flat
Monday I was back
Where I started at.

Chicago is a town
That sure do run on wheels.
Runs so fast you don't know
How good the ground feels.

# Appendix 2
## Poetry for Children

# Fairies

Out of the dust of dreams
Fairies weave their garments.
Out of the purple and rose of old memories
They make rainbow wings.
No wonder we find them such marvellous things!

# Winter Sweetness

This little house is sugar.
    Its roof with snow is piled,
And from its tiny window
    Peeps a maple-sugar child.

# April Rain Song

Let the rain kiss you.
Let the rain beat upon your head with silver liquid drops.
Let the rain sing you a lullaby.

The rain makes still pools on the sidewalk.
The rain makes running pools in the gutter.
The rain plays a little sleep-song on our roof at night—

And I love the rain.

# Signs of Spring

Bright, jolly sunshine and clear blue skies,
Green trees and gardens and gay butterflies,
Soft little winds that balmy blow,
A golden moon with love light glow,
And the music of bird songs, blithe and clear,
Are the things which tell us that Spring is here.

## The Lament of a Vanquished Beau

Willy is a silly boy,
    Willy is a cad.
Willy is a foolish kid,
    Sense he never had.
Yet all the girls like Willy—
    Why I cannot see,—
    He even took my best girl
Right away from me.

I asked him did he want to fight,
    But all he did was grin
And answer, "Don't be guilty
    Of such a brutal sin."

Oh, Willy's sure a silly boy,
    He really is a cad,
Because he took the only girl
    That I 'most ever had.

Her hair's so long and pretty
    And her eyes are very gay;
I guess that she likes Willy
    'Cause he's handsome, too, they say.
But for me, he's not good looking;
    And he sure has made me mad,
'Cause he went and took the only girl
    That I 'most ever had.


## Mister Sandman

The Sandman walks abroad tonight,
    With his canvas sack o' dreams filled tight.

Over the roofs of the little town,
    The golden face of the moon looks down.

Each Mary and Willy and Cora and Ned
    Is sound asleep in some cozy bed,

When the Sandman opens his magic sack
    To select the dreams from his wonder pack.

"Ah," says the Sandman, "To this little girl
    I'll send a dream like a precious pearl."

So to Mary Jane, who's been good all day,
    A fairy comes in her sleep to play;

But for Corinne Ann, who teased the cat,
    There's a horrid dream of a horrid rat,

And the greedy boy, with his stomach too full,
    Has a bad, bad dream of a raging bull;

While for tiny babes, a few days old,
    Come misty dreams, all rose and gold.

And for every girl and every boy
    The Sandman has dreams that can please or annoy.

When at pink-white dawn, with his night's work done,
    He takes the road toward the rising sun,

He goes straight on without a pause
    To his house in the land of Santa Claus.

But at purple night-fall he's back again
    To distribute his dreams, be it moon light or rain;

And good little children get lovely sleep toys,
    But woe to the bad little girls and boys!

For those who'd have dreams that are charming and sweet,
    Must be good in the day and not stuff when they eat,

'Cause old Mister Sandman, abroad each night,
    Has a dream in his sack to fit each child just right.

## Thanksgiving Time

When the night winds whistle through the trees and blow the crisp brown leaves
  a-crackling down,
When the autumn moon is big and yellow-orange and round,
When old Jack Frost is sparkling on the ground,
 It's Thanksgiving time!

 When the pantry jars are full of mince-meat and the shelves are laden with sweet
  spices for a cake,
When the butcher man sends up a turkey nice and fat to bake,
When the stores are crammed with everything ingenious cooks can make,
 It's Thanksgiving time!

When the gales of coming winter outside your window howl,
When the air is sharp and cheery so it drives away your scowl,
When one's appetite craves turkey and will have no other fowl,
 It's Thanksgiving time!


## Autumn Thought

   Flowers are happy in summer.
   In autumn they die and are blown away.
    Dry and withered,
   Their petals dance on the wind
   Like little brown butterflies.


## Trip: San Francisco

   I went to San Francisco.
   I saw the bridges high
   Spun across the water
   Like cobwebs in the sky.

## Garment

The clouds weave a shawl
Of downy plaid
For the sky to put on
When the weather's bad.


## The Kids in School with Me

When I studied my A-B-C's
And learned arithmetic,
I also learned in public school
What makes America tick:

The kid in front
And the kid behind
And the kid across the aisle,
The Italian kid
And the Polish kid
And the girl with the Irish smile,
The colored kid
And the Spanish kid
And the Russian kid my size,
The Jewish kid
And the Grecian kid
And the girl with the Chinese eyes—
We were a regular Noah's ark,
Every race beneath the sun,
But our motto for graduation was:
One for All and All for One!
The kid in front
And the kid behind
And the kid across from me—
Just American kids together—
The kids in school with me.

## We're All in the Telephone Book

We're all in the telephone book,
Folks from everywhere on earth—
Anderson to Zabowski,
It's a record of America's worth.

We're all in the telephone book.
There's no priority—
A millionaire like Rockefeller
Is likely to be behind me.

For generations men have dreamed
Of nations united as one.
Just look in your telephone book
To see where that dream's begun.

When Washington crossed the Delaware
And the pillars of tyranny shook,
He started the list of democracy
That's America's telephone book.


## City

In the morning the city
Spreads its wings
Making a song
In stone that sings.

In the evening the city
Goes to bed
Hanging lights
About its head.


## To Make Words Sing

To make words sing
Is a wonderful thing—
Because in a song
Words last so long.

# Gypsies

Gypsies are picture-book people
Hanging picture-book clothes on a line.
The gypsies fill the vacant lots
With colors gay as wine.

The gypsies' skins are olive-dark,
The gypsies' eyes are black fire.
The gypsies wear bright headcloths dyed
By some elfin dyer.

The gypsies wear gay glassy beads
Strung on silver threads
And walk as though forever
They've had suns about their heads.


# There's Always Weather

There's always weather, weather,
Whether we like it or not.
Some days are nice and sunny,
Sunny and bright and hot.

There's always weather, weather,
Whether we like it or don't.
Sometimes so cold and cloudy!
Will it soon snow, or won't?

If days were always just the same,
Out-of-doors would be so tame—
Never a wild and windy day,
Never a stormy sky of gray.

I'm glad there's weather, weather,
Dark days, then days full of sun.
Summer and fall and winter—
Weather is so much fun!

## New Flowers

So many little flowers
Drop their tiny heads—
But newer buds come to bloom
In their place instead.

I miss the little flowers
That have gone away,
But the newly budding blossoms
Are equally gay.

## Year Round

Summertime
Is warm and bright,
With light-bugs
At night.

Autumn time
Is not so sunny,
But Halloween
Is funny.

Winter
Changes most of all,
Bright, then gray,
Then snowflakes fall.

But Spring
I like the very best
When birds come back
To nest.

Also in the
Springtime rain
Flowers start
To bloom again.

## Country

My mother said,
A house we'll buy
In the country where the sky
Is not hidden by tall buildings.

I said,
We'll have a hill
For coasting in the wintertime
Or climbing in the summertime —
    I love to coast!
    I love to climb!

## Grandpa's Stories

The pictures on the television
Do not make me dream as well
As the stories without pictures
Grandpa knows how to tell.

Even if he does not know
What makes a Spaceman go,
Grandpa says back in his time
Hamburgers only cost a dime,
Ice cream cones a nickel,
And a penny for a pickle.

## Piggy-Back

My daddy rides me piggy-back.
My mama rides me, too.
But grandma says her poor old back
Has had enough to do.

## Shearing Time

It must be nice to be a sheep
With nothing to do but graze and sleep.
But when it's time the wool to shear,
That poor old sheep bleats, "Oh, dear!"

## Brand New Clothes

My mama told me,
Kindly, please,
Do not get down
On your knees
With your brand new
Clothes on.

I said, Mom,
I'm already down.
Can't I stay
On the ground
With my brand new
Clothes on?

My mother said,
No, I say!
So my mother had her way—
That's why I'm so clean today
With my brand new
Clothes on.

## Problems

2 and 2 are 4.
4 and 4 are 8.

But what would happen
If the last 4 was late?

And how would it be
If one 2 was me?

Or if the first 4 was you
Divided by 2?

## Not Often

I seldom see
A kangaroo
Except in a zoo.

At a whale
I've never had a look
Except in a book.

Another thing
I never saw
Is my great-
Great-great-grandpa—
Who must've been
A family fixture,
But there's no
Picture.

## Grocery Store

Jimmy, go
To the store, please,
And bring me back
A can of peas.

Also, get
A sack of flour,
And kindly do not
Stay an hour.

## Poor Rover

Rover was in clover
With a bone
On the front lawn—
But Rover's fun was over
When his bone
Was gone.
Poor Rover!

## The Blues

When the shoe strings break
On *both* your shoes
And you're in a hurry—
That's the blues.

When you go to buy a candy bar
And you've lost the dime you had—
Slipped through a hole in your pocket somewhere—
That's the blues, too, *and bad!*

## Silly Animals

The dog ran down the street
The cat ran up the drain
The mouse looked out and said,
        *There they go again!*

## Old Dog Queenie

Old Dog Queenie
Was such a meanie,
She spent her life
Barking at the scenery.

# Little Song

Carmencita loves Patrick.
Patrick loves Si Lan Chen.
Xenophon loves Mary Jane.
Hildegarde loves Ben.

Lucienne loves Eric.
Giovanni loves Emma Lee.
Natasha loves Miguelito—
And Miguelito loves me.

Ring around the Maypole!
Ring around we go—
Weaving our bright ribbons
Into a rainbow!


# Friendly in a Friendly Way

I nodded at the sun
And the sun said, *Howdy do!*
I nodded at the tree
And the tree said, *Howdy, too!*

I shook hands with the bush.
The bush shook hands with me.
I said to the flower,
*Flower, how do you be?*

I spoke to the man.
The strange man touched his hat.
I smiled at the woman—
The world is smiling yet.

Oh, it's a holiday
When everybody feels that way!
What way?—*Friendly
In a friendly way.*

# Shepherd's Song at Christmas

Look there at the star!
I, among the least,
Will arise and take
A journey to the East.
*But what shall I bring*
*As a present for the King?*
*What shall I bring to the Manger?*

I will bring a song,
A song that I will sing,
A song for the King
In the Manger.

Watch out for my flocks,
Do not let them stray.
I am going on a journey
Far, far away.
*But what shall I bring*
*As a present for the Child?*
*What shall I bring to the Manger?*

I will bring a lamb,
Gentle, meek, and mild,
A lamb for the Child
In the Manger.

I'm just a shepherd boy,
Very poor I am—
But I know there is
A King in Bethlehem.
*What shall I bring*
*As a present just for Him?*
*What shall I bring to the Manger?*

I will bring my heart
And give my heart to Him.
I will bring my heart
To the Manger.

# Appendix 3
## Additional Poems

The following poems did not appear in the first edition (Knopf, 1994) of *The Collected Poems of Langston Hughes*. We would like to thank Thomas H. Wirth of The Fire!! Press for his help in confirming that they were indeed published during Hughes's lifetime or (in one instance) submitted for publication by Hughes before his death. We also gratefully acknowledge the help of Diane Roberts of the University of Georgia library.

## Bulwark

You were the last bulwark of my dreams,
And now you, too, have tumbled down into the dust.
You, too, are no more than a broken lie.
    Something
    came between us
    green and slimy
    like sickly laughter
    and a bowl was broken
    from which
    we could not drink thereafter
    and we turned around
    and threw
    the scattered bits
    upon the ground
    and went our separate ways
    into the town
    and a clock
    somewhere in a tower
    boomed out slowly
    hour after hour
    a great cracked
    broken sound.
You were the last bulwark of my dreams,
And now you, too, have tumbled down.


## Old Youth

I heard a child's voice,
Strong, clear, and full of youth,
But I looked into his face
And the face was old,—
Not old with age,
But old with city knowledge,
Old with work
And the dust and grime
Of the factories.
O little child's voice,
O face like a flowerless spring!

## Moscow

Here are the red flags
That wave
In the bright silver glory
Of the dawn—
The red flags
That ask no pardon
Of the past—
Dead and gone.

## Madrid

*Damaged by shells, many of the clocks*
*on the public buildings in Madrid have*
*stopped. At night, the streets are pitch*
*dark.*

*—News Item*

Put out the lights and stop the clocks.
Let time stand still.
Again man mocks himself
And all his human will to build and grow.
Madrid!
The fact and symbol of man's woe.
Madrid!
Time's end and throw-back,
Birth of darkness,
Years of light reduced:
The ever minus of the brute,
The nothingness of barren land
And stone and metal,
Emptyness of gold,
The dullness of a bill of sale:
BOUGHT AND PAID FOR! SOLD!
Stupidity of hours that do not move
Because all clocks are stopped.
Blackness of nights that do not see
Because all lights are out.
Madrid
Beneath the bullets!
Madrid
Beneath the bombing planes!

Madrid
In the fearful dark!

Oh, mind of man!
So long to make a light
Of fire,
        of oil,
                of gas,
And now electric rays.
So long to make a clock
Of sun-dial,
        sand-dial,
                figures,
And now two hands that mark the hours.
Oh, mind of man!
So long to struggle upward out of darkness
To a measurement of time—
And now:
These guns,
These brainless killers in the hills
Trained on Madrid
To stop the clocks in the towers
And shatter all their faces
Into a million bits of nothingness
In the city
That will not bow its head
To darkness and to greed again:
That dares to dream a cleaner dream!
Oh, mind of man
Moulded into a metal shell—
Left-overs of the past
That rain dull hell and misery
On the world again—
Have your way
And stop the clocks!
Bomb out the lights!
And mock yourself!
Mock all the rights of those
Who live like decent folk.
Let guns alone salute
The wisdom of our age
With dusty powder marks
On yet another page of history.
Let there be no sense of time,
Nor measurement of light and dark.

In fact, no light at all!
Let mankind fall
Into the deepest pit that ignorance can dig
For us all!
Descent is quick.
To rise again is slow.
*In the darkness of her broken clocks,*
*Madrid cries NO!*
*In the timeless midnight of the Fascist guns,*
*Madrid cries No!*
*To all the killers of man's dreams,*
*Madrid cries NO!*


To break that NO apart
Will be to break the human heart.


## Chicago


It is not Lake Michigan's lapping waves,
Dun-colored without glow,
Nor the scorching summers and freezing winters
Where the lake winds blow,
Nor the elevated trains that coil,
Nor the uncoiled lines of cars
That stretch to the very prairie's edge
When "time to quit" drops go-home bars,
It's not the stockyards' hearty stench
Delicate on the breeze,
Nor the gamblers' dice
Nor the sinners' vice
Nor the righteous on their knees,
And it's not the Civic Opera
Nor the Wrigley Building's light
Nor Marshall Field's
Or the Merchandise Mart
Or the bars that blaze at night,
And it's not the memory of Al Capone
Or Sandburg or McCormick
Or Harriet Monroe
Or Mrs. Potter Palmer.
Armour, Swift,
Insul or DuSable—Negro—

Or any names we know—
But it's *all* the names
In the phone book,
Their relatives and friends
And Pa's and Ma's and Grandpa's
Back generations to other nations
That sent the names
With un-anglo spellings.
The faces with un-anglo shapes,
The skins not always white
And the tongues not always English
And the polyglot hands
And the polyglot ways
To make headline nights and headline days
That flash beyond the Wrigley light
And forge of Chicago a sun not a moon—
But a *sun* that blazes and turns and glows
And lightens and brightens
All orbits beyond it's looped center
And lake bordered edge
And prairie backdrop
And motorized cop
And multi-ranged sky
And the image of God
     *Chicago!*
That's found in its eye:

## Bitter Brew

Whittle me down
To a strong thin reed
With a piercing tip
To match my need.

Spin me out
To a tensile wire
To derrick the stones
Of my problems higher.

Then simmer me slow
In the freedom cup
Till only an essence
Is left to sup.

May that essence be
The black poison of me
To give the white bellies
The third degree:

Concocted by history
Brewed by fate—
A bitter concentrate
    Of hate.

# Notes to the Poems

The two volumes of Hughes's autobiography are always referred to by their full titles:

The following anthologies are always referred to by their full titles:

Where the title of a poem is used more than once, the title is followed by a number in brackets, as in "Question [1]."

23    "The Negro Speaks of Rivers": First published in *Crisis* (June 1921), p. 71. Included in *TWB*, *LHR*, and *SP*.

In *The Big Sea*, p. 55, Hughes describes the composition of this poem. "Now it was just sunset, and we crossed the Mississippi, slowly, over a long bridge. I looked out the window of the Pullman at the great muddy river flowing down toward the heart of the South, and I began to think what that river, the old Mississippi, had meant to Negroes in the past—how to be sold down the river was the worst fate that could overtake a slave in times of bondage. . . . Then I began to think about other rivers in our past—the Congo, and the Niger, and the Nile in Africa—and the thought came to me: 'I've known rivers,' and I put it down on the back of an envelope I had in my pocket, and within the space of ten or fifteen minutes, as the train gathered speed in the dusk, I had written this poem, which I called 'The Negro Speaks of Rivers.' "

In *TWB*, the poem includes the following dedication: "(To W. E. B. Du Bois)." The dedication does not appear in earlier or later printings of the poem. Hughes dedicated the poem to Du Bois at the urging of Jessie Fauset, the literary editor of *The Crisis*. See Rampersad, vol. I, p. 116.

*The Crisis*, the official publication of the NAACP, was founded in 1910 by W. E. B. Du Bois, who served as its first editor. It is now the oldest African American periodical in existence. The magazine featured news, essays, fiction, and poetry by and about African Americans. It is fitting that Hughes's first and last published poems appeared in *The Crisis*, since more of his poems appeared in this magazine than in any other journal.

"Aunt Sue's Stories": First published in *Crisis* (July 1921), p. 121. Included in *TWB* and *SP*.

In *The Big Sea*, p. 17, Hughes recalled his maternal grandmother's stories: "Through my grandmother's stories life always moved, moved heroically toward an end. Nobody ever cried in my grandmother's stories. They worked, schemed, or fought. But no crying."

24    "Negro": First published as "The Negro" in *Crisis* (Jan. 1922), p. 113, and *Current Opinion* (March 1922), p. 397. It appeared as "Proem" in *TWB*, but the title "The Negro" was used again in *TDK* and *SP*.

Line 15, "The Belgians cut off my hands in the Congo": During the rule of King Leopold of the Belgians as sovereign of the Congo Free State (1885–1908), a labor tax of 10 percent was instituted. According to F. Scott Babb (*Historical Dictionary of Zaire* [London and Metuchen, N.J.: Scarecrow Press, 1988], p. 55), "Failure to pay the tax was punished by flogging, execution, and occasionally destruction of entire villages. Soldiers were required to produce the right hand of villagers who had been executed for not paying the tax and the procurement of hands became an end in itself, reportedly leaving thousands of maimed victims."

Line 16, "They lynch me still in Mississippi": "They lynch me now in Texas" (all printings before *SP*). In the summer of 1919, the Ku Klux Klan was responsible for several lynchings and other acts of violence against African Americans in Longview, Texas. James Weldon Johnson called the period the "Red Summer." In 1955, a number of lynchings were recorded in Mississippi, the most notorious of which was the killing of fourteen-year-old Emmett Till.

24 "Question" [1]: Published in *Crisis* (March 1922), p. 210. Included in *Seven Poets in Search of an Answer*, p. 49.

25 "Mexican Market Woman": First published in *Crisis* (March 1922), p. 210. Included in *TWB*, *TDK*, and *SP*. Although Hughes spent at least a year with his father in Mexico between 1919 and 1921, this is his only published poem with a Mexican theme.

"New Moon": First published in *Crisis* (March 1922), p. 210. Included in *FOW*.

"My Loves": Published in *Crisis* (May 1922), p. 32.

26 "To a Dead Friend": Published in *Crisis* (May 1922), p. 21.

"The South": First published in *Crisis* (June 1922), p. 72. Included in *TWB* and *SP*.

27 "Laughers": Published as "My People" in *Crisis* (June 1922), p. 72. The title was changed when the poem was included in *FCTTJ*. In the first version, lines 15 and 16 read: "Porters,/Hairdressers." Lines 20 and 22 were added when the poem was reprinted in 1927.

28 "Danse Africaine": In the first version of the poem, published in *Crisis* (Aug. 1922), p. 167, and *Southern Workman* (April 1924), p. 180, lines 4 and 5 read:

> *Slow . . . slow*
> *Low . . . slow—*

Hughes also made changes in the line lengths for *TWB*. The *TWB* text was reprinted in *SP*.

"After Many Springs": First published in *Crisis* (Aug. 1922), p. 167. Included in *TWB* and *TDK*.

29 "Beggar Boy": First published in *Crisis* (Sept. 1922), p. 219, and *Southern Workman* (April 1924), p. 179. Included in *TWB* and *TDK*.

"Song for a Banjo Dance": First published in *Crisis* (Oct. 1922), p. 267, and *Southern Workman* (April 1924), p. 180. Included in *TWB* and *TDK*.
   In *The Crisis* and *Southern Workman*, line 7 read: "Get on over, darling"; in *TWB* it read: "Walk on over, darling."

30 "Mother to Son": First published in *Crisis* (Dec. 1922), p. 87. Included in *Four Negro Poets*, p. 26, *TDK*, and *SP*.

"When Sue Wears Red": The first version of the poem, in *Crisis* (Feb. 1923), p. 174, reads:

> *When Susanna Jones wears red*
> *Her face is like an ancient cameo*
> *Turned brown by the ages.*

> *When Susanna Jones wears red*
> *A queen from some time-dead Egyptian night*
> *Walks once again.*

> *And the beauty of Susanna Jones in red*
> *Wakes in my heart a love-fire sharp like pain.*

The varied refrain which follows these lines was added in *TWB*. Hughes also changed the word "Wakes" to "Burns" in line 11 of the *TWB* text. The *TWB* text was reprinted in *TDK* and *SP*.

Hughes claimed that he wrote the poem for a girl he had met in high school. "I met her at a dance at the Longwood Gym [in Cleveland]. She had big eyes and skin like rich chocolate. Sometimes she wore a red dress that was very becoming to her." (*The Big Sea*, p. 52.) Hughes then quotes the final version of the poem.

31    "A Black Pierrot": First published in *Amsterdam News* [New York] (April 4, 1923), p. 12, and, also in English, in *Les Continents* [Paris] (July 15, 1924), p. 2. Included in *TWB*, *TDK*, and *SP*.

Pierrot is a traditional figure in French pantomime, often depicted as an adult with the mind of a child. He was usually thin, with a face covered with flour or "whiteface" to distinguish him from the "blackface" of the conniving character Harlequin. The French symbolist poet Jules Laforgue wrote a number of poems in the "voice" of Pierrot in the late nineteenth century. Because of the influence of Laforgue, Pierrot often appeared in early-twentieth-century American poetry, such as the work of Edna St. Vincent Millay. What differentiates Hughes's Pierrot from those of Laforgue and the other writers mentioned is the racial significance attached to the mask of Pierrot, which thematically links it to other Hughes poems, such as "The Jester."

"Justice": First published in *Amsterdam News* (April 25, 1923), p. 12. Included in *SL*.

"Monotony": Published in *Crisis* (May 1923), p. 35.

32    "Dreams": First published in *World Tomorrow* (May 1923), p. 147. Included in *TDK*. In the first version, lines 1 and 5 read, respectively:

> *Hold fast to dreams,* my son,
> *Hold fast to dreams,* O boy,

The unitalicized phrases were omitted in subsequent printings.

"Poem" [1]: First published in *World Tomorrow* (May 1923), p. 147. Paul Gauguin (1848–1903) was one of the major French post-impressionist painters. He moved to Tahiti in 1891, where the local people and their customs provided a new inspiration for his art. Included in *TWB*.

"Our Land": The first published version of the poem, in *World Tomorrow* (May 1923), p. 147; *Opportunity* (May 1924), p. 142; and *Survey Graphic* (March 1, 1925), p. 678, ended with line 15: "And not this land where joy is wrong." The last two lines were added in *TWB* and *Four Negro Poets*, p. 29.

The magazine *Opportunity* was begun by Charles S. Johnson in 1923 as the official publication of the National Urban League. It served as a major outlet for Hughes's verse until it folded in 1949.

33   "The Last Feast of Belshazzar": Published in *Crisis* (Aug. 1923), p. 162. In the Book of Daniel, Belshazzar was the last Chaldean king of Babylon before its conquest by the Medians. He saw a mysterious hand write the words *Mene Mene Tekel Upharsin* on the wall of his banquet hall—an event which signaled the end of his reign.

"Young Prostitute": First published in *Crisis* (Aug. 1923), p. 162. Included in *TWB*.

34   "Jazzonia": First published in *Crisis* (Aug. 1923), p. 162. Included in *TWB*.

"Shadows": Published in *Crisis* (Aug. 1923), p. 162.

35   "Cabaret": First published in *Crisis* (Aug. 1923), p. 162, and *Vanity Fair* (Sept. 1925), p. 62. Included in *TWB*.

"Winter Moon": First published in *Crisis* (Aug. 1923), p. 162. Included in *TWB*, *TDK*, and *SP*.

"Young Singer": First published in *Crisis* (Aug. 1923), p. 162. Included in *TWB*.
   Line 1: "Chansons vulgaires" are popular songs, but "vulgaire" can also have the connotation of "crude" and "low."

"Prayer Meeting": First published in *Crisis* (Aug. 1923), p. 162. Reprinted in *FCTTJ* and *SP* with different line lengths.

36   "My People": First published as "Poem" in *Crisis* (Aug. 1923), p. 162, and *TWB*. The title "My People" was used in *TDK* and *SP*.

"Migration": First published as "The Little Frightened Child" in *Crisis* (Oct. 1923), p. 280. The title was changed in *FOW*.

"My Beloved": Published in *Crisis* (March 1924), p. 202.

37   "The White Ones": First published in *Opportunity* (March 1924), p. 68. Included in *TWB*.

"Gods": Published in *Messenger* (March 1924), p. 94. *The Messenger* (1917–28) was edited by the labor leaders A. Philip Randolph and Chandler Owen. Hughes often contributed to the magazine, especially when his friend Wallace Thurman worked on the staff in 1927.

"Grant Park": Published in *Messenger* (March 1924), p. 75. Hughes appears to be referring to Bryant Park, which is at 42nd St. and the Avenue of the Americas (Sixth Avenue), behind the New York Public Library.

38   "Fire-Caught": Published in *Crisis* (April 1924), p. 254.

38 "Exits": First published as "Song for a Suicide," with different line lengths, in *Crisis* (May 1924), p. 23. When Hughes became aware that some African Americans were reading this poem as a comment on race, he responded that "people are taking it all wrong. It's purely personal, not racial. If I choose to kill myself, I'm not asking anybody else to die, or to mourn either. Least of all the Negro race." (Quoted in Rampersad, vol. I, p. 89.) The title was changed for *FOW*.

"Prayer for a Winter Night": Published in *Messenger* (May 1924), p. 153.

39 "Lament for Dark Peoples": First published in *Crisis* (June 1924), p. 60. Included in *TWB*.

"Fascination": Published in *Crisis* (June 1924), p. 86. Circulated as "Love Song" by ANP (see Appendix 1).

"Youth": This poem was entitled "Poem" in *TWB*; *Crisis* (August 1924), p. 163; and *Survey Graphic* (March 1, 1915), p. 664. The title was changed to "Youth" when the poem appeared in *TDK*. *The Crisis* contained the final line "We march!" which was omitted from the version published in *TWB*. The line was restored in *TDK*. In *LHR*, pp. 147–48, Hughes says: To help us all remember what America is, and how its future belongs to all of us, recently I added two new lines to an old poem of mine—the last two lines to help us remember to work together. . . .

> *We march!*
> *Americans together,*
> *We march!*

40 "Mammy": First published as "Poem (I am waiting for my mother)" in *Crisis* (Aug. 1924), p. 173. The title was changed in *FCTTJ* with "mother" changed to "mammy."

"Dream Variations": The title was "Dream Variation" in *Crisis* (July 1924), p. 128; *Current Opinion* (Sept. 1924), p. 361; *The New Negro*, p. 143; *Opportunity* (April 1927), p. 111; *TWB*; and *TDK*. The change was made in *SP*. In *The New Negro*, the poem was not divided into stanzas, although the stanza structure is used in the earliest versions of the poem. Hughes returned to the two-stanza format in *TWB* and kept it for subsequent appearances in *TDK* and *SP*. Hughes also made several changes in punctuation when the poem was included in his first book of verse.

"Subway Face": Published in *Crisis* (Dec. 1924), p. 71.

41 "Afraid": First published in *Crisis* (Nov. 1924), p. 21. Included in *TWB* with slight changes in punctuation.

"A Song to a Negro Wash-woman": Published in *Crisis* (Jan. 1925), p. 115.

42 "Poppy Flower": First published in *Crisis* (Feb. 1925), p. 167, in two three-line stanzas. The revised version appears in *FOW*.

"Troubled Woman": First published in *Opportunity* (Feb. 1925), p. 56. Included in *TWB* and *SP* with slight changes in punctuation.

43 "Johannesburg Mines": First published in *Messenger* (Feb. 1925), p. 93, and *Crisis* (Feb. 1928), p. 52, in which the poem spanned only four long lines. The nine-line version appeared in *Africa South* (April–June 1957), p. 20.

"To Certain Intellectuals": Published in *Messenger* (Feb. 1925), p. 103.

"Steel Mills": Published in *Messenger* (Feb. 1925), p. 103. Hughes says that he wrote this poem in high school (*The Big Sea*, p. 29). During this time, his stepfather worked in a steel mill in Cleveland.

44 "Negro Dancers": First published in *Crisis* (March 1925), p. 221. Included in *TWB* and *TDK*. In a letter to Countee Cullen, Hughes wrote of this poem: "Do you like it? Do you get it? We'll dance! Let the white world tear itself to pieces. Let the white folks worry. We know two more joyous steps—two more ways to do de buck! C'est vrai?" (Quoted in Rampersad, vol. I, p. 89.)
   Lines 3, 6, and 15: "Two mo' ways to do de Charleston" appeared as "Two mo' ways to do de buck" in the first version, in *The Crisis* and *TWB*. The lines were changed to the present text for *TDK*.

"Liars": Published in *Opportunity* (March 1925), p. 90.

"Sea Charm": First published in *Survey Graphic* (March 1, 1925), p. 664. Included in *TWB* and *TDK*. This special Negro issue of *Survey Graphic*, edited by Howard University professor Alain Locke, is considered by many as the official beginning of the Harlem Renaissance. Locke selected ten poems by Hughes for the issue.

45 "The Dream Keeper": First published in *Survey Graphic* (March 1, 1925), p. 664. Included in *TWB* and *TDK*.

"Song": First published in *Survey Graphic* (March 1, 1925), p. 664. Included in *The New Negro* and *TDK*.

"Walkers with the Dawn": First published in *Survey Graphic* (March 1, 1925), p. 664. Reprinted in *The New Negro*, p. 142, as "Poem" and in *Lincoln University Poets*, p. 3, as "Being Walkers with the Dawn." Included in *TDK* with the present title.

46 "Earth Song": First published in *Survey Graphic* (March 1, 1925), p. 664. Reprinted in *The New Negro*, p. 142. Included in *FOW*.

"I, Too": First published in *Survey Graphic* (March 1, 1925), p. 683. It appeared in *The New Negro*, p. 145, and, under the title "Epilogue," in *TWB*.
   In the early version of the poem, in *The New Negro*, *TWB*, and *TDK*, line 9 read: "I'll sit at the table." Hughes changed this line to "I'll be at the table" in *SP*.
   The first line probably alludes to the poetry of Walt Whitman.

47 "Drama for Winter Night (Fifth Avenue)": Published in *Workers Monthly* (March 1925), p. 225. This magazine was published by the Workers Party of the United States of America, a communist organization. The publication has had various titles: *Labor Herald* (1922–24); *Workers Monthly* (1924–27); *The Communist* (1927–44); and finally *Political Affairs*. Hughes's appearance in *Workers Monthly* as early as 1925 reveals that his attraction to the left began well before the 1930s.

48   "God to Hungry Child": Published in *Workers Monthly* (March 1925), p. 234.

"Rising Waters": Published in *Workers Monthly* (April 1925), p. 267.

"Poem to a Dead Soldier": Published in *Workers Monthly* (April 1925), p. 261.

49   "Park Benching": Published in *Workers Monthly* (April 1925), p. 261.

50   "The Weary Blues": First published in *Opportunity* (May 1925), p. 143. Included in *TWB*, *TDK*, *LHR*, and *SP*.

    This poem won a first prize in the literary contest sponsored by *Opportunity* in 1925. In *The Big Sea*, p. 215, Hughes says: "It was a poem about a working man who sang the blues all night and then went to bed and slept like a rock. That was all. And it included the first blues verse I'd ever heard way back in Lawrence Kansas, when I was a kid.

> *I got de weary blues*
> *And I can't be satisfied.*
> *I got de weary blues*
> *And can't be satisfied.*
> *I ain't happy no mo'*
> *And I wish that I had died.*

That was my lucky poem—because it won first prize."

    Line 4, "Down on Lenox Avenue the other night": Lenox Avenue, now Malcolm X Boulevard, runs from West 110th Street for two miles to the Esplanade Garden Apartments. Lenox Avenue came to epitomize the spirit of Harlem.

51   "Empty House": Published in *Buccaneer* (May 1925), p. 20.

"Prayer" [1]: First published in *Buccaneer* (May 1925), p. 20. Included in *FCTTJ*, *TDK*, and *SP*.

"Ways": Published in *Buccaneer* (May 1925), p. 20.

52   "Poem" [2]: First published in *Crisis* (May 1925), p. 11. Included in *TWB* with changes in the line lengths. "F.S." has not been plausibly identified.

"America": Published in *Opportunity* (June 1925), p. 175, where it won third prize in a literary contest.

    Line 35, "I am Crispus Attucks at the Boston Tea Party": Crispus Attucks (1723–70), born a slave, ran away from his master's residence in Framingham, Massachusetts, in 1750. He was killed in the Boston Massacre on March 5, 1770, while urging a crowd to protest the beating of a barber's apprentice by British soldiers.

    Lines 36–37 refer to the service of African Americans in the U.S. Armed Forces during World War I. Hughes speaks about their bravery at the front and the treatment of their families at home in his poem "The Colored Soldier" in *The Negro Mother*.

    Line 38, "I am Sojourner Truth preaching and praying": Sojourner Truth (1797–1883) was a former slave who became a prominent speaker for abolition. She recounts her own story in her autobiography, *The Narrative of Sojourner Truth*.

53  "Better": Hughes left a published tear sheet stating that this poem, along with the next two, appeared in *Reflexus* in 1925. This journal has not been located.

54  "Change": Ascribed to *Reflexus* (1925). (See note for "Better" above.)

"Poem" [3]: Ascribed to *Reflexus* (1925). (See note for "Better" above.)

"Love Song for Antonia": Hughes left a published tear sheet stating that this poem, with the next poem, appeared in *American Life* in July 1925. This journal has not been located.

55  "A Wooing": Ascribed to *American Life* (July 1925). (See note for "Love Song for Antonia" above.)

"To Certain 'Brothers' ": Published in *Workers Monthly* (July 1925), p. 406.

"Suicide's Note": First published in *Vanity Fair* (Sept. 1925), p. 62. Included in *TWB* and *SP*.

56  "Fantasy in Purple": First published in *Vanity Fair* (Sept. 1925), p. 62, with no stanza breaks and with the ending not divided into three separate lines. These changes were made for *TWB* and reprinted in *SP*.

"Young Bride": First published in *Crisis* (Oct. 1925), p. 278. Included in *TWB*.

"The Jester": In *Opportunity* (Dec. 1925), p. 357, the end of the poem reads:

> *Shall I*
> *Be wise*
> *Again?*

The three lines form one line in *TWB* and *Four Negro Poets*, p. 25.

57  "Soledad": First published in *Opportunity* (Dec. 1925), p. 378. Included in *TWB* with changes in the line lengths. *Soledad* is the Spanish word for "solitude" or "loneliness."

"To Midnight Nan at Leroy's": First published in *Vanity Fair* (Sept. 1925), p. 62, with only the first four stanzas. The last stanza was added when the poem appeared in *TWB* and *Opportunity* (Jan. 1926), p. 23.

58  "Poem" [4]: First published in *Crisis* (Dec. 1925), p. 67. Included in *TWB*.

"Cross": First published in *Crisis* (Dec. 1925), p. 66. Included in *TWB* and *SP*. In *The Big Sea*, Hughes said that from his childhood he "had been intrigued with the problem of those so-called 'Negroes' of immediate white-and-black blood, whether they were light enough to pass for white or not" (*The Big Sea*, pp. 262–63). He then quotes the poem "Cross" and connects it thematically to his play *Mulatto* and his short story "Father and Son."

59  "Summer Night": First published in *Crisis* (Dec. 1925), p. 66. Included in *TWB*.

60    "Disillusion": First published in *Crisis* (Dec. 1925), p. 67. Included in *TWB*.

"Jazz Band in a Parisian Cabaret": The original title in *Crisis* (Dec. 1925), p. 67, was "To a Negro Jazz Band in a Parisian Cabaret."
    Lines 7 and 8 in *FCTTJ* formed one line in the *Crisis* version ("And the school teachers out for a spree"). The second stanza of the early version was significantly different from the text in *FCTTJ*.

> *May I?*
> *Mais oui,*
> *Mein Gott!*
> *Parece una rumba!*

> *Play it, jazz band!*
> *You've got seven languages to speak in*
> *And then some.*

> *Can I?*
> *Sure.*

    This poem and several others set in Paris probably draw on Hughes's experience as a dishwasher in the Paris nightclub Le Grand Duc in the spring of 1924 (see *The Big Sea*, pp. 158–63, 171–83).

61    "Minstrel Man": First published in *Crisis* (Dec. 1925), pp. 66–67, and *The New Negro*, p. 144. In *The New Negro*, the last lines of both stanzas ended with periods ("So long." and "I die."). Line 12 ended with a comma ("My inner cry,"). The question marks were added for *TDK*.

"Nude Young Dancer": First published in *The New Negro*, p. 227. Included in *TWB*.

"Songs to the Dark Virgin": First published in *Palms* (Jan. 1926), p. 115, in three stanzas but without the Roman-numeral headings. These were added when the poem appeared in *TWB*.

62    "Young Sailor": First published in *Palms* (Jan. 1926), p. 114. *TWB* has the following two lines after line 15:

> *And tomorrow?*
> *For joy.*

These lines are omitted from the version of the poem published in *Palms* and the version included in *SP*. Also in *TWB*, the last line ("And nothing hereafter") is not set apart from the rest of the poem, as it is in the other printings.

63    "Joy": First published in *Crisis* (Feb. 1926), p. 173. Included in *TWB*, *TDK*, and *SP*.

"Fog": First published as "African Fog" in New York *Herald Tribune* (Feb. 14, 1926), sect. VI, p. 4. The title was changed when the poem appeared in *Palms* (Oct. 1926), p. 24.

Line 3, "In the thick white fog at Sekondi": Sekondi is a port town in the West African nation of Ghana. Hughes describes landing at Sekondi in 1923, when the area was still a British colony (*The Big Sea*, p. 106).

63 "Strange Hurt": First published as "Strange Hurt She Knew" in the New York *Herald Tribune* (Feb. 14, 1926), sect. VI, p. 4. Included with the new title in *FOW* and *SP*.

64 "Star Seeker": Published in New York *Herald Tribune* (Feb. 14, 1926), sect. VI, p. 4.

"Lullaby": First published in *Crisis* (March 1926), p. 224, in three stanzas. The seven-stanza format was made for *TDK*.

65 "The Ring": Published in *Crisis* (April 1926), p. 284.

"Midwinter Blues": First published in *New Republic* (April 14, 1926), p. 223. When the poem appeared in *FCTTJ* and *Four Negro Poets*, p. 23, Hughes used dialect forms such as "de" for "the," "ma" for "my," and "an' " for "and." In *SP*, however, Hughes changed all of the dialect forms back to standard spelling. Thus the final version of the poem mirrors the first printed version. Lines 23 and 24 in *FCTTJ* read:

*So when I'm dead, they*
*Won't need no flowers from the store.*

66 "Gypsy Man": First published in *New Republic* (April 14, 1926), p. 223, and *Anthology of Magazine Verse: 1926*, ed. W. S. Braithwaite (New York: G. Sully, 1927), pp. 109–10. Included in *FCTTJ*.

"Ma Man": First published in *New Republic* (April 14, 1926), p. 223 under the title "My Man." In *FCTTJ*, Hughes changed all instances of "my" to "ma" (lines 1, 2, 3, and 4) and inserted the other dialect forms.
Lines 13 and 14, "Eagle-rockin' / Daddy, eagle-rock with me": The Eagle Rock was a popular dance step in the 1920s.

67 "Teacher": Published in *Opportunity* (May 1926), p. 167.

"Love Song for Lucinda": Published in *Opportunity* (May 1926), p. 164.

68 "Minnie Sings Her Blues": First published in *Messenger* (May 1926), p. 132.
The present stanza 3 was originally two stanzas. Hughes changed all the instances of "and" to "an' " for *FCTTJ* (lines 2, 6, 8, and 17) and replaced all other dialect forms with standard spelling. He also made the following changes: line 13, "If ma daddy" was "If daddy"; line 15, "If he" was "If my man"; line 19, "Blue, blue, blues" was "Blue blue-blues."

69 "Listen Here Blues": First published in *Modern Quarterly* (May–July 1926), p. 203. Included in *FCTTJ*.

"Lament over Love": First published in *Vanity Fair* (May 1926), p. 70. The early version contained a number of differences from *FCTTJ*: lines 1 and 3, "I hope my child'll" was "I hope my chile'll"; line 5, "Love can hurt you" was "Cause love can hurt you"; lines 7 and 9, "the river" was "de river"; line 12, "And I'm goin' there to think about him" was "I'm goin' there to think about him"; line 15, "Love is like whiskey" was "O, love is like whiskey"; line 19, "I'm goin' up in a tower" was "Goin' up in a tower."

Hughes made only one change to the *FCTTJ* version when he republished the poem in *SP*. Lines 23 and 24—"Gonna think about my man an' / Let my fool-self fall."—became "Gonna think about my man— / And let my fool-self fall."

70     "Fortune Teller Blues": Published in *Vanity Fair* (May 1926), p. 70.

"Judgment Day": In *Measure* (June 1926), p. 17; *FCTTJ*; and *TDK*, the first refrain, *Lord Jesus!*, occurs after line 2. This refrain was omitted in *SP*. The last word in line 6 of *SP* was changed from "heaben" to "heaven."

71     "Wide River": First published in *Measure* (June 1926), p. 15. Included in *TDK*.

72     "Homesick Blues": First published in *Measure* (June 1926), p. 16, and *Literary Digest* (July 3, 1926), p. 30. Included in *FCTTJ* and *TDK*.

"Pale Lady": Hughes left a published tear sheet saying that this poem appeared in *American Life* (June 1926), p. 17. See note for "Love Song for Antonia," page 619.

73     "Ruby Brown": First published in *Crisis* (Aug. 1926), p. 181. Included in *FCTTJ* and *SP*.

"New Year": Published in *Messenger* (Sept. 1926), p. 277.

74     "Epitaph" [1]: Published in *Messenger* (Sept. 1926), p. 284, under the pseudonym J. Crutchfield Thompson.

"Autumn Note": Published in *Messenger* (Sept. 1926), p. 276, under the pseudonym J. Crutchfield Thompson.

"Formula": Published in *Messenger* (Sept. 1926), p. 276.

75     "For Dead Mimes": First published in *Messenger* (Sept. 1926), p. 276, under the pseudonym Earl Dane. Included in *FOW*.

"To Beauty": Published in *Crisis* (Oct. 1926), p. 317.

76     "Bound No'th Blues": In the early versions in *Opportunity* (Oct. 1926), p. 315; *FCTTJ*; and *TDK*, "de" and other dialect forms are used; these are replaced by standard spelling in *SP*.

"Lonesome Place": Published in *Opportunity* (Oct. 1926), p. 314.

77     "Misery": Previous versions of the poem—in *Opportunity* (Oct. 1926), p. 315, and *FCTTJ*—used "de" for "the" in lines 1 and 2. Hughes eliminated much of the dialect from the poems of *FCTTJ* he included in *SP*.

78 "Bad Luck Card": The poem first appeared in *Opportunity* (Oct. 1926), p. 315, as "Hard Luck." It was reprinted as "Bad Luck Card" in *FCTTJ* and *SP*.

"Feet o' Jesus": First published in *Opportunity* (Oct. 1926), on the cover, with "de" for "the" in lines 1 and 5. This version was retained in *FCTTJ* and *TDK*, but the dialect was changed for *SP*.

"Down and Out": The poem originally had three stanzas in *Opportunity* (Oct. 1926), p. 314, and *SIH*, but the last was deleted for *SP*. The deleted stanza read:

> *Oh, talk about yo' friendly friends*
> *Bein' kind to you —*
> *Yes, talk about yo' friendly friends*
> *Bein' kind to you —*
> *Just let yo'self git down and out*
> *And then see what they'll do.*

79 "Pictures to the Wall": Published in *Palms* (Oct. 1926), p. 24.

"Walls": First published in *Palms* (Nov. 1926), p. 37, where lines 2 and 6 read "Oh, so much pain" and "Oh, so much sorrow," respectively. The lines were changed when the poem was included in *FOW*.

80 "Beale Street Love": First published in *Palms* (Nov. 1926), p. 36. Included in *FCTTJ*. Beale Street was the center of black life in Memphis, Tennessee, and well known for bars and halls where jazz and blues were played. Richard Wright gives a description of life on Beale Street in chapter 11 of his autobiography, *Black Boy* (1945).

"Dressed Up": First published in *Palms* (Nov. 1926), p. 37. Included in *FCTTJ* and *TDK*.

"A House in Taos": First published in *Palms* (Nov. 1926), pp. 35–36. Included in *FOW* and *SP*.

Hughes wrote in *The Big Sea*: "It was a strange poem for me to be writing in a period when I was writing mostly blues and spirituals. I do not know why it came to me in just that way, but I made hardly a change in it after I put it down." Although Hughes had never visited Taos, New Mexico, he later received a letter from Mabel Dodge Luhan, who claimed that her house was the one described in the poem. She sent snapshots to support her assertion. Hughes comments: "At that time I had never heard Mrs. Luhan's name, nor did I know she had married an Indian, or that Jean Toomer had been a guest in their house. The red, yellow, and white of my poem came from the Indian corn colors of the desert. Three was the mystic number. The rain, sun, and moon, and other nature words I used in contrast to the art-houses being built by exotics from the Village." (*The Big Sea* pp. 260–61.) Despite Hughes's statement, he may have known of Toomer's relations with Luhan, and the poem perhaps reflects that knowledge (see Rampersad, vol. I, pp. 120–22).

82    "Suicide": First published in *Poetry* (Nov. 1926), p. 91, where lines 2 and 4 contain the dialect form "an'." This was changed to "and" in *FCTTJ*, but the "de" in lines 13, 15, and 17 was kept.

"Hard Luck": First published in *Poetry* (Nov. 1926), p. 88. Included in *FCTTJ*.

83    "Po' Boy Blues": First published in *Poetry* (Nov. 1926), p. 89. Included in *FCTTJ* and *TDK*.

"Red Roses": Published in *Poetry* (Nov. 1926), p. 90.

84    "Railroad Avenue": First published in *FIRE!!* (Nov. 1926), p. 21. Included in *FCTTJ* and *SP*.

85    "Elevator Boy": First published in *FIRE!!* (Nov. 1926), p. 21. Included in *FCTTJ* and *SP*.

"Stars": First published in *Lincoln University News* (Nov. 1926), p. 4. Included in *FOW* and *SP* with altered line lengths.

86    "Brass Spittoons": First published in *New Masses* (Dec. 1926), p. 10. Included in *FCTTJ*.

87    "The New Cabaret Girl": First published as "New Girl" in *New Masses* (Dec. 1926), p. 10. The title was changed for *FCTTJ*.

"Argument" [1]: Published in *New Masses* (Dec. 1926), p. 10.

88    "Saturday Night": First published in *New Masses* (Dec. 1926), p. 10. Included in *FCTTJ*.

89    "The Cat and the Saxophone (2 a.m.)": Published in *TWB*. Hughes interspersed lines from the 1924 song "Everybody Loves My Baby, but My Baby Don't Love Nobody but Me," by Jack Palmer and Spencer Williams.

"To a Little Lover-Lass, Dead": Published in *TWB*.

90    "Harlem Night Club": Published in *TWB*.

91    "Midnight Dancer": First published as "To a Black Dancer in 'The Little Savoy' " in *TWB*. The title was changed when the poem was included in *SP*.

"Blues Fantasy": Published in *TWB*.

92    "Lenox Avenue: Midnight": Published in *TWB*. For Lenox Avenue, see the notes to "The Weary Blues," page 618.

"Poème d'Automne": Published in *TWB*.

93    "March Moon": Published in *TWB* and *SP*.

93     "As I Grew Older": Published in *TWB*, *TDK*, and *SP*.

94     "Harlem Night Song": In *TWB*, two additional lines appeared at the end of the second stanza:

> *In the cabaret*
> *The jazz-band's playing.*

These lines were omitted when the poem was included in *SP*.

95     "Ardella": Published in *TWB* and *SP*. Appeared as "Quiet Girl" in *TDK*.

"Pierrot": Published in *TWB*. (See note for "A Black Pierrot," page 614.)

96     "Water-Front Streets": Published in *TWB*, *TDK*, and *SP*.

"A Farewell": Published in *TWB*.

97     "Long Trip": Published in *TWB*, *TDK*, and *SP*.

"Port Town": Published in *TWB* and *SP*.

"Sea Calm": Published in *TWB*, *TDK*, and *SP*.

98     "Caribbean Sunset": Published in *TWB*.

"Seascape": Published in *TWB*, *TDK*, and *SP*.

"Natcha": Published in *TWB* and *SP*.

99     "Death of an Old Seaman": Published in *TWB* and *TDK*.

"Sick Room": Published in *TWB*.

"To the Dark Mercedes of 'El Palacio de Amor' ": Published in *TWB*. During his voyage to Africa in 1923, Hughes's ship stopped at Las Palmas, in the Azores. Hughes and several shipmates spent the night at a brothel called El Palacio de Amor, Spanish for "The Palace of Love" (see Rampersad, vol. I, pp. 76–77).

100     "Mulatto": Line 11 of the text in *SP* ("What's a body but a toy?") does not appear in the earlier version in *Saturday Review of Literature* (Jan. 29, 1927), p. 547, and *FCTTJ*.

101     "A Letter to Anne": *Lincoln University News* (Feb. 1927), p. 4. The poem is probably addressed to Anne Marie Coussey, a young West African woman with whom Hughes was romantically involved in Paris in 1924. Although in *The Big Sea*, p. 168, Hughes says that the young lovers were separated by Anne's family, he may have decided to end the relationship (see Rampersad, vol. I, pp. 86–90).

"In the Mist of the Moon": *Lincoln University News* (Feb. 1927), p. 4. Line 2: "Nanette" probably refers to Anne Marie Coussey (see note for "A Letter to Anne" above).

102 "Spirituals": First published as "Song" in *Bookman* (Feb. 1927), p. 729, and *Home Quarterly* [Nashville] (July–Sept. 1944), p. 5. Hughes also altered the line lengths when he included the poem in *FOW*, but changed only one word: on line 7, "when you hurt her" became "when life hurt her."

"For an Indian Screen": Published in *Opportunity* (March 1927), p. 85.

103 "Day": Published in *Opportunity* (March 1927), p. 85.

"Passing Love": First published in *Opportunity* (March 1927), p. 85. Included in *TDK*.

"Lincoln Monument: Washington": Published in *Opportunity* (March 1927), p. 85, without stanza breaks. Lines 6 and 7 form a single line in this version. The changes were made when the poem appeared in *TDK*. In *Lincoln University News* (Nov. 1926), p. 4, the poem ends after line 5.

104 "Song for a Dark Girl": First published in *Saturday Review of Literature* (April 19, 1927), p. 712, and *Crisis* (May 1927), p. 94. Included in *FCTTJ*.

"Gal's Cry for a Dying Lover": First published in *Saturday Review of Literature* (April 19, 1927), p. 712. Included in *FCTTJ*.

105 "Desire": First published in *Messenger* (May 1927), p. 151. Included in *FOW*.

"Poem for Youth": Published in *Messenger* (June 1927), p. 186.

106 "The Naughty Child": Published in *Messenger* (June 1927), p. 186.

"Girl": First published as "Mona" in *Opportunity* (June 1927), p. 161. The title was changed for *FOW*.

107 "Wise Men": Published in *Messenger* (June 1927), p. 180.

"Ma Lord": First published in *Crisis* (June 1927), p. 123. Included in *TDK*.

"Tapestry": Published in *Crisis* (July 1927), p. 158.

108 "Success": Published in *Messenger* (July 1927), p. 236.

"Nocturne for the Drums": Published in *Messenger* (July 1927), p. 225.

109 "For Salome": Published in *Messenger* (July 1927), p. 236. This poem appeared as "Salome" in *Lincoln University News* (March 1926), p. 7. After Salome had pleased her father, Herod, with her dancing, she was urged to choose any gift she liked. She asked for the head of John the Baptist on a platter (see Mark 6:17–28 and Matthew 14:3–11; the only source which provides the name of Herod's daughter is the historian Flavius Josephus in *Jewish Antiquities* 18:36). Hughes is alluding to Oscar Wilde's famous play entitled *Salome*.

"Being Old": Published in *Crisis* (Oct. 1927), p. 265.

110    "Freedom Seeker": Published in *Crisis* (Oct. 1927), p. 265.

"Parisian Beggar Woman": Published as "Montmartre Beggar Woman" in *Crisis* (Nov. 1927), p. 303, and *Lincoln University News* (Feb. 1927), p. 4. The title changed when the poem appeared in *TDK*.

"I Thought It Was Tangiers I Wanted": Published in *Opportunity* (Dec. 1927), p. 368. Tangier (or Tangiers) is a city in northwestern Morocco.

111    "Dreamer": Published in *Ebony and Topaz*, ed. C. S. Johnson (New York: National Urban League, 1927), p. 36.

112    "Hey!": Published in *FCTTJ*. See note for "Hey! Hey!" below.

"Hey! Hey!": Published in *FCTTJ*. This, the last poem of the book, was written as a companion to the previous poem, which opened the book. The two poems were published as one work with two stanzas under the title "Night and Morn" in *TDK*.

"Bad Man": Published in *FCTTJ*.

113    "Closing Time": Published in *FCTTJ*.

"Prize Fighter": Published in *FCTTJ*.

114    "Crap Game": Published in *FCTTJ*.

"Ballad of Gin Mary": First published in *FCTTJ*.

115    "Death of Do Dirty: A Rounder's Song": Published in *FCTTJ*.

116    "Porter": Published in *FCTTJ* and *SP*.

"Sport": Published in *FCTTJ*.

117    "Shout": Published in *FCTTJ* and *SP*.

"Fire": Published in *FCTTJ* and *SP*.

118    "Moan": In the first version, which Hughes attributed to *American Life* (July 1926), the final three stanzas are:

> *Moanin', moanin',*
> *Nobody cares just why.*
>
> *Moanin', moanin',*
> *Feels lak I could die.*
>
> *O, Little Lord,*
> *Dere's peace up in de sky.*

These were changed to three-line stanzas in *FCTTJ*. (For *American Life*, see note to "Love Song for Antonia," page 619.)

118     "Angels Wings": In *FCTTJ*, "de" was used for "the" throughout the poem. The dialect was changed to standard spelling when the poem was included in *SP*.

119     "Sinner": Published in *FCTTJ*, *TDK*, and *SP*.

    "Cora": Published in *FCTTJ* and *SP*.

    "Workin' Man": Published in *FCTTJ*.

120     "Baby": Published in *FCTTJ*, *TDK*, and *SP*.

    "Evil Woman": Published in *FCTTJ*.

    "A Ruined Gal": Published in *FCTTJ*.

121     "Black Gal": Published in *FCTTJ*. Line 15: "rinney" stands for "marinney"—a light-skinned black person.

122     "Sun Song": Published in *FCTTJ*, *TDK*, and *SP*.

    "Magnolia Flowers": In *FCTTJ*, lines 8–9 and 12–13 are not italicized. The change was made for *SP*.

    "Red Silk Stockings": Published in *FCTTJ*. Of the critics of *FCTTJ*, Hughes complained: "An ironic poem like 'Red Silk Stockings' they took for literal truth" (*The Big Sea*, p. 266).

123     "Young Gal's Blues": In *Four Negro Poets*, p. 24, and *FCTTJ*, "de" is used for "the" throughout. The dialect was altered when the poem was published in *Negro Caravan*, ed. Sterling Brown (New York: Dryden, 1941), p. 369.

124     "Hard Daddy": Once again, "de" is used throughout the poem in *FCTTJ* and is replaced by "the" in *SP*.

    "Sunset—Coney Island": Published in *New Masses* (Feb. 1928), p. 13.

125     "Lover's Return": In a special commencement issue of *Lincoln University News* (Oct. 1928); *Poetry* (Oct. 1931), p. 16; and *SIH*, the final two lines are not italicized. The italics were added in *SP*.

    "Nonette": Published anonymously in *Crisis* (June 1928), p. 196. In 1927, driven by a concern for his artistic reputation, Hughes wrote *The Crisis* asking that the magazine not print any poems by him contained in their files. He no longer believed that some of these poems, which he had submitted before 1926, were worthy to appear in print. *The Crisis* did not honor his request, but in this one instance refrained from attaching his name to the poem (see Rampersad, vol. I, p. 161). Circulated by ANP as "Beloved," under Hughes's name.

126 "Alabama Earth": First published in Tuskegee *Messenger* (June 1928), on the cover, and later in *Epworth Era* (Oct. 1930), p. 93. Reprinted in *Golden Slippers*.

Booker T. Washington, the founder of Tuskegee Institute and the foremost leader of black America around 1900, advocated a policy of economic opportunity for African Americans without social integration with whites, for which he was challenged by W. E. B. Du Bois and others. Washington gives an account of his life and opinions in his autobiography, *Up from Slavery* (1901). In the summer of 1927, Hughes visited Tuskegee with Zora Neale Hurston and was asked to write an anthem for the school. He sent "Alabama Earth."

"Mazie Dies Alone in the City Hospital": Published in the magazine *Harlem* (Nov. 1928), p. 38, and *Lincoln University News* (Oct. 1928), p. 7.

"Hurt": Published in *Harlem* (Nov. 1928), p. 38.

127 "Lady in Cabaret": Published in *Harlem* (Nov. 1928), p. 38.

"Dear Lovely Death": First published in *Opportunity* (June 1930), p. 182. Included in *DLD* and *LHR*.

"Flight": Lines 5 and 6 ("No I didn't touch her / White flesh ain't for me") are in quotation marks in *DLD*, not italics as in *OWT*. They are in neither quotation marks nor italics in *Opportunity* (June 1930), p. 182.

128 "Aesthete in Harlem": First published in *Opportunity* (June 1930), p. 182. Included in *DLD*. Later reprinted under the title "Life Face to Face" in the *American Review* (Spring 1961), p. 10.

"Anne Spencer's Table": Published in *Crisis* (July 1930), p. 235. The poet Anne Spencer (1882–1976) lived in Lynchburg, Virginia. Hughes stayed with the Spencers when he gave a lecture in the city in 1927 (see Rampersad, vol. I, p. 158). Spencer's poetry has been collected in J. Lee Greene's *Time's Unfading Garden: Anne Spencer's Life and Poetry* (Baton Rouge: Louisiana State University Press, 1977).

"Spring for Lovers": Published in *Crisis* (July 1930), p. 235.

"Tower": First published in *Crisis* (July 1930), p. 235. Included in *DLD*.

129 "The English": Published in *Crisis* (July 1930), p. 235.

"Afro-American Fragment": Hughes changed the length of many of the lines of the version in *Crisis* (July 1930), p. 235, and *DLD* when the poem appeared in *SP*:

Lines 6 and 7 in *SP* were originally one line ("Save those that songs beat back into the blood—").

Lines 13–15 were originally two lines ("Subdued and time-lost are the drums— / And yet, through some vast mist of race").

Lines 19 and 20 were originally one line ("Of bitter yearnings lost, without a place—").

130  "Rent-Party Shout: For a Lady Dancer": Published in *Amsterdam News* (August 20, 1930), p. 9. Parties with an admission charge to raise money for home rentals were a feature of Harlem life in the 1920s (see *The Big Sea*, pp. 228–33).

"Black Seed": Published in *Opportunity* (Dec. 1930), p. 371.

131  "Militant": The poem originally appeared under the title "Pride" in *Opportunity* (Dec. 1930), p. 371, and ANS. The title and the end of the poem were changed for *TPATL*. The final five lines of the first version read:

> Your spit is in my face.
> And so my fist is clenched—
> Too weak I know
>
> But longing to be strong
> To strike your face.

"Negro Servant": In *Opportunity* (Dec. 1930), p. 371, lines 12–14 read as follows:

> The el, the sub.
> Pay-nights,
> A taxi through the park.

The text was changed in *OWT*.

132  "Merry Christmas": Published in *New Masses* (Dec. 1930), p. 4.


POEMS 1931–1940

135  "Tired": Published in *New Masses* (Feb. 1931), p. 4.

"Call to Creation": Published in *New Masses* (Feb. 1931), p. 4.

136  "To Certain Negro Leaders": The poem appears with a stanza break after line 3 in *Negro: An Anthology*, ed. Nancy Cunard (1934; rpt. 1970), p. 263. In *New Masses* (Feb. 1931), p. 4, the seven lines appear as one unit.

The poem may have been a response to W. E. B. Du Bois, Marcus Garvey, A. Philip Randolph, and other prominent African Americans who did not endorse the communist belief that uniting black and white workers was essential to black progress (see Rampersad, vol. I, p. 217).

"A Christian Country": Published in *New Masses* (Feb. 1931), p. 4.

"To the Little Fort of San Lazaro on the Ocean Front, Havana": Published in *New Masses* (May 1931), p. 11.

Line 4, "DRAKE": Sir Francis Drake (1540–96), the English pirate and admiral, commanded the English ships against the attack of the Spanish Armada (1588). He later led an English expedition against the Spanish possessions in the West Indies, to which Hughes refers in this poem. During this campaign, Drake died off the coast of Panama.

Line 5, "DE PLAN": Unidentified. Perhaps a pirate or corsair in the Caribbean during the sixteenth or seventeenth century.

Line 6, "EL GRILLO": Domingo Grillo was a Genovese slave trader who obtained a contract from the Spanish crown to import 24,500 African slaves to Spanish colonies in the New World at the price of 2.1 million pesos.

137    "Drum": In *Poetry Quarterly* (Spring 1931), p. 12, and *DLD* the last three lines read:

*Calling all life*
*To Come! Come!*
*Come!*

The line lengths were altered in *SP*.

"Snake": First published in *Poetry Quarterly* (Spring 1931), p. 12. Included in *SIH*.

"Negro Ghetto": First published in *New Masses* (March 1931), p. 19. Included in *ANS*.

138    "House in the World": Published as "White Shadows" in the magazine *Contempo* (Sept. 15, 1931), p. 1. The title was changed when the poem appeared in *Negro: An Anthology*, p. 263.

"Union": The first version of the poem, in *New Masses* (Sept. 1931), p. 12, and *Negro Worker* (July 1934), p. 32, ends with line 10, "Too well defended." The final two lines were added in *ANS*.

"Prayer" [2]: First published in *Contemporáneos* (Sept.–Oct. 1931), p. 158, and then as "Big City Prayer" in *Opportunity* (Oct. 1940), p. 308. The title and line lengths were changed for *FOW*.

139    "Dying Beast": Published in *Poetry* (Oct. 1931), pp. 18–19.

"Sailor": First published in *Poetry* (Oct. 1931), p. 18; *Literary Digest* (Nov. 21, 1931), p. 26; and *DLD*. Included in *TDK*.

140    "God": Published in *Poetry* (Oct. 1931), p. 19.

"Sylvester's Dying Bed": In *Poetry* (Oct. 1931), pp. 17–18, and *Literary Digest* (Nov. 21, 1931), p. 26, "everything" in line 27 was written "ever'thing." The standard spelling is used in *SIH* and *SP*.

141    "October 16: The Raid": Published as "October The Sixteenth" in *Opportunity* (Oct. 1931), p. 299, where the final four lines appeared as follows:

*Come again to town—*
*Perhaps,*

*You will recall*
*John Brown.*

In *Volunteer for Liberty* (Oct. 14, 1937), p. 16, as "October 16," the first two lines read:

> *Perhaps today*
> *You will recall John Brown.*

The version printed in this volume appeared in *JCLS, OWT, SP,* and *TPATL.* The subtitle was added in *TPATL.*

142   "Scottsboro": First published in *Opportunity* (Dec. 1931), p. 379. Included in *SL.* See note for "The Town of Scottsboro," page 634.

143   "Christ in Alabama": First published in *Contempo* (Dec. 1931), p. 1, after the magazine asked Hughes for a comment on the Scottsboro case. Reprinted in *SL* and *TPATL.*

     "Advertisement for the Waldorf-Astoria": Published in *New Masses* (Dec. 1931), pp. 16–17. In *The Big Sea,* pp. 320–21, Hughes says that the poem was "modeled after an ad in *Vanity Fair* announcing the opening of New York's greatest hotel. (Where no Negroes worked and none were admitted as guests.)"

146   "Helen Keller": Published in *Double Blossoms: A Helen Keller Anthology,* ed. E. Porter (New York: Copeland, 1931), p. 19. Helen Keller (1880–1968), the internationally known American educator and writer, was blind, deaf, and mute. In 1931, Hughes was asked to contribute a poem to this book of verse in her honor.

147   "The Colored Soldier": This poem, along with the next five poems in the order in which they appear here, formed the contents of the volume *The Negro Mother.* Published later as "The Negro Soldier" but without the prefatory and marginal texts in *A Negro Looks at War,* ed. John Henry Williams (New York: Workers Library Publishers, 1940), pp. 2–3.

148   "Broke": Line 47, Sugar Hill was once the most prosperous section of Harlem.

150   "The Black Clown": Reprinted in *Crisis* (Feb. 1932), p. 32.

153   "The Big-Timer": Reprinted in *Trend* (March–May 1932), p. 20.

155   "The Negro Mother": Reprinted in *SP.*

156   "Dark Youth of the U.S.A.": Reprinted in *Common Sense Historical Review* (August 1953), p. 12.

157   "The Consumptive": In the poem's first appearance, in *DLD* (1931), the last two stanzas were:

> *All night in bed*
> *Waiting for sleep*
> *He lay*
> *Feeling death creep—*

*Steady—like fire*
*From a slow spark*
*Choking his breath*
*And burning the dark.*

The revised version appeared in *Crisis* (Feb. 1933), p. 31.

158    "Two Things": Published in *DLD*.

"Demand": First published as "Request to Genius," *Poetry Quarterly* [New York] (Spring 1931), p.12. The title was changed for *DLD* and *SP*.

"Florida Road Workers": The first two lines of the poem in *OWT* ("Hey Buddy! / Look at me!") were not in the early versions published in the New York *Herald Tribune* (Nov. 23, 1930); *DLD*; and *Negro: An Anthology*, p. 263.
    Line 4 was originally two lines ("For the cars / to fly by on").
    Line 8 was not followed by a stanza break.
    Lines 10 and 11, "For the rich to sweep over / In their big cars" was "For the rich old white men / To sweep over in their big cars."
    Lines 19 and 20 were originally three lines instead of two:

*Hey Buddy!*
*Look at me!*
*I'm makin' a road!*

Reprinted in *OWT* and *TPATL*.

159    "Garden": The work originally appeared under the title "Poem" in *DLD*. The change was made for *SP*.

"Pennsylvania Station": Originally published under the title "Terminal" in *Opportunity* (Feb. 1932), p. 52. The title was changed when the poem was reprinted in *Approach* (Spring 1962), p. 4. "Penn" Station and Grand Central are the two major railway terminals of New York City.

160    "Open Letter to the South": Published as "Red Flag over Tuskegee" in Baltimore *Afro-American* (June 25, 1932), p. 17, and *Negro Worker* (July 1932), pp. 31–32. In these printings, as well as that in the *New Masses* (June 1932), p. 10, with the title "Open Letter to the South," line 21 read "He knew he lied" (a reference to Booker T. Washington's reputation in some quarters for duplicity). The line was deleted in ANS.
    Line 16, "At Harlan, Richmond, Gastonia, Atlanta, New Orleans": Harlan County, Kentucky, was called "Bloody Harlan" after three persons died and twenty were injured during strikes by miners in the thirties. Gastonia, North Carolina, was the site of a major strike by textile workers in 1929.

161    "Ph.D.": Published in *Opportunity* (Aug. 1932), p. 249.

162    "Good Morning Revolution": Published in *New Masses* (Sept. 1932), p. 5. The poem may be a parody of Carl Sandburg's "Good Morning America."

164 "Chant for Tom Mooney": This poem appeared as "For Tom Mooney" in *New Masses* (Sept. 1932), p. 16. The title was changed for *ANS*. Tom Mooney (1882–1942) was a labor leader in the San Francisco area. Arrested in 1916 in connection with a bomb thrown during a Preparedness Parade, which was sponsored by a group favoring American involvement in World War I, he was sentenced to die on the basis of perjured testimony. His sentence was commuted to life in prison in 1918, and he was finally released in 1939. Mooney's fate was a rallying cry for leftists during the 1920s and 1930s. Hughes visited Mooney in prison in 1932 (see Rampersad, vol. I, p. 238).

165 "Always the Same": First appeared in *Negro Worker* (Sept.–Oct. 1932), pp. 31–32, under the title "The Same." Subsequent printings as "Always the Same" in *Liberator* (Nov. 4, 1932), p. 4, and *Negro: An Anthology*. p. 263.

  Line 4, "In the diamond mines of Kimberley": Kimberley is the center of the diamond industry in the north of Cape Province, South Africa.

166 "Goodbye Christ": Published in *Negro Worker* (Nov.–Dec. 1932), p. 32, and *Negro: An Anthology*, p. 264. Reprinted without permission in *Saturday Evening Post* (Dec. 21, 1940), p. 34.

  Line 26, "Saint Ghandi" [*sic*]: Mohandas K. Gandhi (1869–1948) was the leader of the Indian independence movement and the advocate of nonviolent resistance to the British.

  Line 27, "And Saint Pope Pius": Pius XI was pope from 1922 to 1939. The Catholic Church strongly opposed not only communism, but the labor movement in general. For such conservative stances, Catholicism was often linked with fascism by the American left.

  Line 28, "Saint Aimee McPherson": Aimee Semple McPherson was a well-known evangelist and the founder of the Church of the Four Square Gospel, based in Echo Park, California. McPherson was involved in several financial and sexual scandals in the 1920s, one of which caused her mother to sue her for control of the church. Hughes's allusion to McPherson later came back to haunt him. Her followers picketed an appearance by him in the Los Angeles area in 1940 and handed out copies of "Goodbye Christ." The notoriety led *The Saturday Evening Post*, mentioned in line 13 of the poem, to reprint the poem without permission. The subsequent uproar moved Hughes to repudiate the poem (see Rampersad, vol. I, pp. 390–95).

  Line 29: George Wilson Becton (d. 1933) was the leader of a Harlem-based sect called The World's Gospel Feast, which included programs funded through donated "consecrated" dimes. Becton was murdered in Philadelphia while riding in his car. Hughes writes about Becton in *The Big Sea*, pp. 275–78.

167 "Irish Wake": First published as "Night Tears" in *Abbott's Monthly* (May 1932), p. 14. Included in *TDK*.

  "Reasons Why": Previously published in *Columbia University Spectator* (May 10, 1922), p. 2. Included in *TDK*.

168 "The Town of Scottsboro": Published in *SL*.

  The Scottsboro case began on March 25, 1931, when nine African American youths were accused of raping two white women on a freight train near Painted Rock, Alabama. They were taken to a jail in nearby Scottsboro. Eight of the defendants were quickly sentenced to die and one, thirteen-year-old Roy Wright, to life imprisonment. The communist-affiliated group International Labor Defense brought about a series of appeals and retrials, which after almost twenty years ended in the release of all the defendants. Hughes was particularly moved by the case, and his participation in fund-raising for the Scottsboro defense was a significant force in his move to the left in the early 1930s (see Rampersad, vol. I, pp. 216–18). Hughes visited the eight youths held in Kilby Prison during a tour of the South in 1931 and gives a description of the event in *I Wonder As I Wander*, pp. 61–62.

Hughes's book *Scottsboro Limited* contained four poems and a play. Three of the poems had been previously published. One, "Justice," was not written in response to the Scottsboro trial, but first appeared in *Amsterdam News* (April 25, 1923), p. 12.

168    "Columbia": Published in *International Literature*, no. 2 (1933), p. 54.

169    "Letter to the Academy": Published in *International Literature*, no. 5 (1933), p. 112.

170    "Song of the Revolution": Published in *Negro Worker* (March 1933), p. 32.

"A New Song": The end of the poem was substantially changed when it was included in ANS. The first version, in *Opportunity* (Jan. 1933), p. 23, and *Crisis* (March 1933), p. 59, reads after line 39:

> *New words are formed,*
> *Bitter*
> *With the past*
> *And sweet*
> *with the dream.*
> *Tense, silent,*
> *Without a sound,*
> *They fall unuttered—*
> *Yet heard everywhere:*

*Take care!*

> *Black world*
> *Against the wall,*
> *Open your eyes—*

*The long white snake of greed has struck to kill!*

> *Be wary and*
> *Be wise!*

> *Before*
> *The darker world*
> *The future lies.*

172    "Black Workers": Published in *Crisis* (April 1933), p. 80.

172     "Black Dancers": Published in *Crisis* (May 1933), p. 110.

173     "Havana Dreams": First published in *Opportunity* (June 1933), p. 181. Included in *FOW* and *SP*.

         Line 3: Batabano is a town in northwestern Cuba not far from Havana.

"Dream": First published in *Opportunity* (Sept. 1933), p. 282, with different line lengths and with lines 5 and 14 not italicized. The changes were made when the poem was included in *FOW*.

"Personal": First published in *Crisis* (Oct. 1933), p. 238. Included in *FOW* and *SP*.

174     "Wait": Published in *Partizan* [Los Angeles] (Dec. 1933), p. 4.

175     "Revolution": Published in *New Masses* (Feb. 20, 1934), p. 28, and *Harper's* (July 1935), p. 135.

"Cubes": Published in *New Masses* (March 13, 1934), p. 22. Pablo Picasso (1881–1973), the leading figure in the evolution of Modernist painting, was especially involved in the movement called Cubism.

         Line 30, "the *Marseillaise*": This refers to the national anthem of France, written at the time of the French Revolution.

176     "One More 'S' in the U.S.A.": Published in *Daily Worker* (April 2, 1934), p. 7. On April 1, 1947, Senator Albert Hawkes of New Jersey attacked Hughes as a radical subversive. As evidence, the senator read the text of this poem and "Good Morning Revolution" into the Senate record. (This was not the only time portions of "One More 'S' in the U.S.A." were read on Capitol Hill; see Rampersad, vol. II, pp. 90–91.)

178     "Moonlight Night: Carmel": First published in Carmel *Pine Cone* (June 15, 1934), p. 8, and *Opportunity* (July 1934), p. 217. Included in *FOW* and *SP*. Hughes lived in the home of millionaire Noël Sullivan in Carmel, California, for two extended periods, in 1933–34 and 1939–41 (for the first, see *I Wonder As I Wander*, pp. 281–85). In the spring of 1941, the Carmel *Pine Cone* published verse by Hughes on a regular basis.

"Ballad of Roosevelt": Published in *New Republic* (Nov. 14, 1934), p. 9. Reprinted in the same magazine on Nov. 22, 1954, p. 64. The title refers to Franklin Delano Roosevelt, who was still in his first term as president when the poem appeared.

179     "History": First published in *Opportunity* (Nov. 1934), p. 339, and *ANS* with different line lengths. The poem was revised when it was included in *TPATL*.

"Death in Harlem": First published in *Anthology of Magazine Verse: 1935*, ed. Alan Pater (New York: Poetry Digest Association, 1936), pp. 75–79, and *Literary America* (June 1935), pp. 437–40. Included in *SIH*.

183     "Park Bench": First published in *Anvil* (May 1933), p. 17, where the last two lines were "Move this park bench over/To Park Avenue." The version published in our text appeared in *Proletarian Literature* (1935), p. 168, *New Masses* (March 6, 1934), p. 6 and *ANS*.

183 "Ballads of Lenin": First published as "Ballad of Lenin" in *Anvil* (May 1933), p. 17, where the last line read "In death—behold our room." Included in *Proletarian Literature* (1935), pp. 166–67 and *ANS*. In the latter there is an obvious error in the second line of the last stanza, where the word "tomb" was omitted. In *Proletarian Literature*, the stanza read:

> Comrade Lenin of Russia
> Rises in the marble tomb:
> On guard with the fighters forever—
> The world is our room!

184 "Call of Ethiopia": Published in *Opportunity* (Sept. 1935), p. 276. The poem was written at the beginning of the Italian campaign to make Ethiopia a colony (1935). At this time, Ethiopia was one of only two independent countries in Africa, the other being Liberia.

185 "Share-Croppers": First published in *Proletarian Literature* (1935), p. 167. Included in *SIH* and *SP*.

"Air Raid over Harlem": Published in *New Theatre* (Feb. 1936), p. 19.
Line 37, "GUGSA A TRAITOR TOO": Gugsa Wele (1877–1930) was an Ethiopian nobleman who married Zewditu, the daughter of Emperor Menelik II. They separated in 1916 so that she could inherit the throne. Gugsa was appointed governor of a province, but fell under suspicion for secret dealings with local rebels and the Italians. He was killed in a clash with the Ethiopian army.

188 "Ballad of Ozie Powell": The version in *American Spectator* (April 1936), p. 36, includes a stanza omitted from *ANS*. It came between the third and fourth stanzas of the *New Song* version:

> One of the nine in law's lean claws,
>> Penniless Ozie Powell,
> Not one of the nine who pass the laws,
>> Ozie, Ozie Powell.

Ozie Powell was one of the Scottsboro boys. He was scheduled to die in 1932, until the Supreme Court of the United States granted his appeal on the grounds that he had not had adequate legal counsel. His case, *Powell* v. *Alabama*, remains important in legal history as the first time the court recognized the right of defendants to competent legal representation.

189 "Let America Be America Again": First published in *Esquire* (July 1936), p. 92. Included in *ANS*.

192 "Broadcast on Ethiopia": Published in *American Spectator* (July–August 1936), pp. 16–17.
Line 3, "Addis Ababa": the capital of Ethiopia.
Line 7 "Haile" Selassie: the emperor of Ethiopia from 1930 to 1974.
Line 13, "Il Duce" ("The Leader"): the title of Benito Mussolini, dictator of Italy from 1922 to 1943, who ordered the invasion of Ethiopia.

193    "Dusk": First published as "Poem" in *New Challenge* (June 1936), p. 34. The last line there read "Keep on!" The title was changed for *FOW*.

       "Elderly Leaders": Originally titled "Elderly Race Leaders" in *Race* (Summer 1936), p. 87, the poem appeared as "Public Dignitaries" in *Unquote* (1940), p. 4; "Elderly Politicians" in *LHR*; and then "Elderly Leaders" in *TPATL*.

194    "White Man": Published in *New Masses* (Dec. 1936), p. 34.

195    "Song of Spain": First published in *International Literature*, no. 6 (1937), pp. 67–68. Included in *ANS*. In 1937, Hughes went to Spain to cover the Spanish Civil War as the foreign correspondent of the Baltimore *Afro-American* and the Cleveland *Call and Post*. He describes his experience in *I Wonder As I Wander*, pp. 321–400.
       Line 20, "Goya, Velasquez, Murillo": Goya (1746–1828), Velásquez (1559–1660), and Murillo (1617–1682) are renowned Spanish painters.
       Line 23, "La Maja Desnuda's": *La Maja Desnuda (The Naked Maja)* is a celebrated oil painting by Goya in the Prado Museum, Madrid.
       Line 26, "*Don Quixote! España!*": *Don Quixote* is the title and also the name of the principal character of Miguel de Cervantes's monumental sixteenth-century novel.
       Lines 27–28 translate as "That corner of La Mancha that I don't want to remember."
       Line 66, "Lest some Franco steal into our backyard": Francisco Franco (1892–1975), the leader of the army rebellion against the Spanish government in 1936, ruled Spain from 1938 until his death.

197    "Sister Johnson Marches": First published in *Fight Against War and Fascism* (May 1937), p. 11. Included in *ANS*.

198    "Genius Child": In *Opportunity* (Aug. 1937), p. 239, the poem reads as follows after line 5:

> *Can you love an eagle tame or wild?*
> *Can you love an eagle, wild though tame?*
> *Can you love a monster of a frightening name?*
>     *Nobody can love a genius child.*
> *Kill him — and let his soul run wild.*

Lines 5, 11, and 12 were not italicized. The changes were made for *FOW* and *SP*.

       "Roar China!": Published in *Volunteer for Liberty* (Sept. 6, 1937), p. 3, and *New Masses* (Feb. 22, 1938), p. 20.
       Lines 16–18, "So they came with gunboats, / Set up Concessions, / Zones of influence": In a series of conflicts with Western governments during the last half of the nineteenth century, culminating in the Boxer Rebellion in 1900, the Chinese were required to offer freedom of trade and residence to Europeans in fifty cities in China. Hughes describes the situation in Shanghai in *I Wonder As I Wander*, pp. 246–48.

200    "Note in Music": Published in *Opportunity* (April 1937), p. 104.

       "Search": Published in *Opportunity* (July 1937), p. 207.

201   "Today": First published in *Opportunity* (Oct. 1937), p. 310. Included in *FOW*.

"Letter from Spain": Published in *Volunteer for Liberty* (Nov. 15, 1937), p. 3. Hughes tells of a visit to a hospital in Spain where he met dark-skinned Moroccans (Moors) who had fought in Franco's army. He ends his account: "The International Brigades were, of course, aware of the irony of the colonial Moors—victims themselves of oppression in North Africa—fighting against a Republic that had been seeking to work out a liberal policy toward Morocco. To try to express the feelings of some of the Negro fighting men in this regard, I wrote these verses in the form of a letter from an American Negro in the Brigades to a relative in Dixie." (*I Wonder As I Wander*, p. 353.)

202   "Postcard from Spain": Published in *Volunteer for Liberty* (April 9, 1938), p. 4.

203   "Convent": First published in *Opportunity* (March 1938), p. 82, with different line lengths. The text was altered when the poem was included in *FOW*.

"In Time of Silver Rain": First published in *Opportunity* (June 1938), p. 176. Included in *Golden Slippers*, *FOW*, and *SP*. Hughes altered the line lengths substantially for each new printing, but no words were changed.

204   "August 19th . . . ": *Daily Worker* (June 28, 1938), p. 7. Clarence Norris was one of the Scottsboro defendants. He was sentenced to death in 1933, but was granted a retrial by the Supreme Court of the United States on April 1, 1935, on the grounds that qualified blacks had been systematically excluded from jury duty in the first Alabama trial. In July of 1937, he was found guilty and once again sentenced to die, but the sentence was commuted to life in prison in June 1938.
    The following note appeared with the poem: "Read this poem aloud, and think of young Clarence Norris pacing his lonely cell in the death house of Alabama, doomed to die on August 18. When used for public performances, on the last two verses punctuate the poem with a single drumbeat after each line. AUGUST 18TH IS THE DATE. During the final stanza, let the beat go faster, and faster following the line, until at the end the drum goes on alone, unceasing, like the beating of a heart."

207   "Beauty": Published in *Opportunity* (July 1938), p. 203.

"Song for Ourselves": Published in New York *Post* (Sept. 19, 1938), p. 17.

"Air Raid: Barcelona": Published in *Esquire* (Oct. 1938), p. 40. Hughes describes the experience of his first air raid when he was in Barcelona in 1937 in *I Wonder As I Wander*, pp. 321–26.

209   "Chant for May Day": Published in *ANS*.

210   "Kids Who Die": Published in *ANS*.
    Line 36, "To believe an Angelo Herndon": At nineteen years of age already a communist activist, Angelo Herndon organized an interracial demonstration in Atlanta in January 1932. He was arrested for attempting to incite an insurrection and sentenced to eighteen to twenty years in jail. In 1937, in *Herndon v. Lowry*, the Supreme Court of the United States struck down Georgia's insurrection law as unconstitutional, and Herndon was released. Hughes used the facts of the case in his one-act play *Angelo Herndon Jones* (1936).

Line 42, "Or the rivers where you're drowned like Liebknecht": Karl Liebknecht was a prominent German labor leader and associate of Rosa Luxemburg, with whom he founded the German Communist Party. On June 15, 1919, Liebknecht and Luxemburg were arrested by the German police; they were executed without a trial on the same day.

211    "Six-Bits Blues": A third stanza of six lines, later dropped from the poem in *SIH*, appeared in the first version published in *Opportunity* (Feb. 1939), p. 54. It reads:

> *O, there ain't no place in*
> *This world to rest a-tall.*
> *Ain't no place for*
> *A man to rest a-tall—*
> *That's why I got to be a-sayin'*
> *Goodbye to you all.*

212    "Poet to Patron": Published in *American Mercury* (June 1939), p. 147.

"Red Clay Blues": Published in *New Masses* (Aug. 1, 1939), p. 14. This poem was the only literary collaboration of Hughes and Wright.

213    "Hey-Hey Blues": First published in *New Yorker* (Nov. 25, 1939), p. 70. Included in *SIH*.

214    "Lynching Song": Published in ANS and OWT. This poem, along with "Silhouette" and "Flight," appeared as "Three Songs About Lynching" in *Opportunity* (June 1936), p. 170. Because of Hughes's marginal notations in this version, the full text is given below.

### THREE SONGS ABOUT LYNCHING

| | |
|---|---|
| *The* | *SILHOUETTE* |
| *first with* | *(With Violins)* |
| *satirically* | |
| *sentimental* | *Southern gentle lady,* |
| *music.* | *Do not swoon.* |
| | *They've just hung a nigger* |

> *In the dark of the moon.*
> *They've hung a black nigger*
> *To a roadside tree*
> *In the dark of the moon*
> *For the world to see*
> *How Dixie protects*
> *Its white womanhood.*

> *Southern gentle lady,*
> *Be good! Be good!*

|                  | FLIGHT                                  |
|------------------|-----------------------------------------|
| The              | *FLIGHT*                                |
| second           | *(With Oboe and Drums)*                  |
| to a             |                                         |
| sylvan           | *Plant your toes in the cool swamp mud.* |
| air              | *Step and leave no track.*               |
| with an          | *Hurry, sweating runner!*                |
| under-           | *The hounds are at your back.*           |
| current of       |                                         |
| fear and         | *No, I didn't touch her.*                |
| death.           | *White flesh ain't for me.*              |

*The*
*second*
*to a*
*sylvan*
*air*
*with an*
*under-*
*current of*
*fear and*
*death.*

FLIGHT
*(With Oboe and Drums)*

*Plant your toes in the cool swamp mud.*
*Step and leave no track.*
*Hurry, sweating runner!*
*The hounds are at your back.*

*No, I didn't touch her.*
*White flesh ain't for me.*

*Hurry, black boy, hurry!*
*Or they'll swing you to a tree.*

*The*
*third to*
*a blast*
*of childish*
*trumpets*
*full of*
*empty*
*wonder—*
*and life*
*not dead*
*at all.*

LYNCHING SONG
*(With Trumpets)*

*Pull at the rope! O!*
*Pull it high!*
*Let the white folks live*
*And the nigger die.*

*Pull it, boys,*
*With a bloody cry*
*As the nigger spins*
*And the white folks die.*

*The white folks die?*
*What do you mean—*
*The white folks die?*

*The nigger's*
*Still body*
*Says*

NOT I.

---

214    "How Thin a Blanket": Published in *Opportunity* (Dec. 1939), p. 361, and *Span* (Oct.–Dec. 1946), p. 3.

215    "Visitors to the Black Belt": In *Opportunity* (Jan. 1940), p. 13, there are no stanza breaks. The last two lines read:

*Who're you, rich folks?*
*Ask me who am I.*

Hughes changed "rich folks" to "outsider" for *JCLS* and *SP*.

215   "Note on Commercial Theatre": First published in *Crisis* (March 1940), p. 79, and reprinted in *JCLS*, *OWT*, and *SP*.

     Line 2, "You sing 'em on Broadway" was "You sing 'em in Paris" in *The Crisis*. The last line was added in *JCLS* and read simply, "It'll be me." "Yes" was added at the beginning of the line for *SP*.

216   "Love Again Blues": In *Poetry* (April 1940), p. 21, lines 15–16 repeated lines 13–14 ("Tell me, tell me, / What makes love such an ache and pain?"). The lines were slightly changed for *SIH*.

217   "Out of Work": First published in *Poetry* (April 1940), p. 21. Included in *SIH*.

     Line 8, "WPA": the Works Project Administration, a Depression-era jobs program.

"Seven Moments of Love": When the poem first appeared in *Esquire* (May 1940), pp. 60–61, the dialect form "ole" was used for "old" in lines 9, 11, and 14 of "Twilight Reverie," line 8 of "Daybreak," and line 19 of "Letter." The words italicized in the text of *SIH* were capitalized in *Esquire*.

220   "Daybreak in Alabama": First published in *Unquote* [Yellow Springs, Ohio] (June 1940), p. 3. Included in *JCLS*, *OWT*, *SP*, and *TPATL*.

221   "Comment on War": Published in *Crisis* (June 1940), p. 190.

"Ballad of the Miser": Published in *Opportunity* (Dec. 1940), p. 363.

222   "Ballad of Little Sallie": Published in *Opportunity* (Dec. 1940), p. 364.

POEMS 1941–1950

225   "Evenin' Air Blues": First published in *Common Ground* (Spring 1941), p. 57. Included in *SIH*.

"Aspiration": First published in Carmel *Pine Cone* (March 7, 1941), p. 7. Included in *SIH*.

226   "Little Lyric (*Of Great Importance*)": First published in Carmel *Pine Cone* (March 21, 1941), p. 7. Included in *SIH* and *SP*.

"Curious": First published in Carmel *Pine Cone* (April 4, 1941), p. 7. Included in *OWT*.

"If-ing": First published in Carmel *Pine Cone* (April 4, 1941), p. 13. Included in *SIH*.

227   "Evil": First published in Carmel *Pine Cone* (April 25, 1941), p. 7. Included in *SIH* and *SP*.

227   "Southern Mammy Sings": First published in *Poetry* (May 1941), pp. 72–73. Included in *SIH* and *SP*. It also appeared under the title "Southern Mammy Song" in *Million*, no. 1 (1944), p. 14.

"Black Maria": In the early version of the poem in *Poetry* (May 1941), pp. 74–75, and *SIH*, the dialect form "de" was used for "the" throughout. The dialect was removed for *SP*. The poem originally had only three stanzas. The break after line 10 was made in *SP*. A "Black Maria" is a police van for carrying prisoners.

228   "Dustbowl": In *Poetry* (May 1941), p. 72, the poem appeared with different line lengths from the version included in *FOW*.

229   "Addition" [1]: Published in Carmel *Pine Cone* (May 2, 1941), p. 7.

"Kid Sleepy": First published in Carmel *Pine Cone* (May 2, 1941), p. 10. Included in *SIH* and *SP*.

230   "Stony Lonesome": First published in Carmel *Pine Cone* (May 2, 1941), p. 7. The poem was originally titled "Death Chant" in the *Pine Cone* and *SIH*. The change was made for *SP*. In the first publication, a stanza break occurred after line 11. Lines 14–16 are also arranged differently in *SP*. *SIH* reads:

> Yes, po' Buddy
> Jones has done been left.
> Now she's out in stony lonesome,
> Lordy! Sleepin' by herself.

"NAACP": Published in *Crisis* (June 1941), p. 201.

231   "Early Evening Quarrel": First published in *Living Age* (June 1941), p. 382. Included in *SIH* and *SP*.

232   "Watch Out, Papa": Published in Carmel *Pine Cone* (June 13, 1941), p. 7.

"Snob": First published in Carmel *Pine Cone* (June 27, 1941), p. 2. Included in *SIH*.

"Heaven": First published in Carmel *Pine Cone* (July 4, 1941), p. 7, and *Golden Slippers*, p. 144. Included in *FOW* and *SP*.

233   "Enemy": Published in Carmel *Pine Cone* (July 11, 1941), p. 7.

"Snail": In Carmel *Pine Cone* (July 18, 1941), p. 6, and *Golden Slippers*, p. 149, the last stanza consists of only four lines, without word changes. The present text is in *FOW* and *SP*.

234   "One": First published in Carmel *Pine Cone* (July 18, 1941), p. 6. Included in *FOW* and *SP*.

"Young Negro Girl": First published in Carmel *Pine Cone* (July 18, 1941), p. 6. Included in *SIH*.

234  "Silence": First published in Carmel *Pine Cone* (July 18, 1941), p. 6. Included in *FOW*.

235  "Big Sur": First published in Carmel *Pine Cone* (July 18, 1941), p. 6. Included in *FOW*. Big Sur, an area on the California coast south of Carmel, is renowned for its natural beauty.

"Gypsy Melodies": First published in Carmel *Pine Cone* (July 18, 1941), p. 6. Included in *FOW* and *SP*.

"Refugee": Published in Carmel *Pine Cone* (July 18, 1941), p. 6.

"It Gives Me Pause": Published in Carmel *Pine Cone* (July 25, 1941), p. 7.

236  "Some Day": Published in *Span* (June–July, 1941), p. 10.

"Death in Africa": Published in *Opportunity* (Aug. 1941), p. 237. Damballa Wedo is the venerable father of the sky, the most powerful god in the Afro-Caribbean religion of Haiti.

237  "Sunset in Dixie": Published in *Crisis* (Sept. 1941), p. 277.

"Gangsters": Published in *Crisis* (Sept. 1941), p. 295.

238  "Southern Negro Speaks": Published in *Opportunity* (Oct. 1941), p. 308.

"This Puzzles Me": Published in *Southern Frontier* (Nov. 1941), p. 1.
    Herbert Talmadge, governor of Georgia (1933–35 and 1941–43), opposed all forms of integration and the introduction of New Deal programs into his state.
    Martin Dies was a conservative congressman from Texas, 1931–45 and 1953–59, who chaired the special House Committee on Un-American Activities, which often viewed persons in favor of racial integration as subversives.

239  "Vagabonds": In *Opportunity* (Dec. 1941), p. 367, the last line of the text is "Who want to weep." Changed for *FOW* and *SP*.

"Me and the Mule": In *Negro Quarterly* (Spring 1942), p. 37, and *SIH*, the final stanza of the poem reads:

> *I'm like that old mule—*
> *Black*
> *And don't give a damn!*
> *So you got to take me*
> *Like I am.*

The structure of these lines was altered for *SP*, and the word "So" deleted.

240  "Big Buddy": First published in *Negro Quarterly* (Spring 1942), p. 38. Included in *JCLS*.

240 "Merry-Go-Round": First published in *Common Ground* (Spring 1942), p. 27. Included in *SIH*, *SP*, and *TPATL*.

241 "403 Blues": Published in *Fountain* (May 1942), p. 4. The number was that of a dismissal form from the WPA.

"Sunday Morning Prophecy": First published in *New Yorker* (June 20, 1942), p. 18. Included in *OWT* and *SP*.

242 "The Bitter River": First published in *Negro Quarterly* (Fall 1942), pp. 249–51. Included in *JCLS*.

245 "Hope" [1]: Published in *SIH* and *SP*.

"Harlem Sweeties": Published in *SIH*.

246 "Declaration": Published in *SIH*.

247 "Statement": Published in *SIH*.

"Present": Published in *SIH*.

"Free Man": Published in *SIH*.

"Brief Encounter": Published in *SIH*.

248 "Morning After": Published in *SIH* and *SP*.

249 "Mississippi Levee": Published in *SIH*.

"In a Troubled Key": Published in *SIH*.

250 "Only Woman Blues": Published in *SIH*.

"Wake": Published in *SIH*; *New Yorker* (June 10, 1944), p. 65; and *SP*.

251 "Cabaret Girl Dies on Welfare Island": Published in *SIH*.

"Crossing": Published in *SIH* and *SP*. Line 18, "Looked like me" in *SP*, was "That looked like me" in *SIH*. Line 20, "I walked" in *SP*, was "When I walked" in *SIH*. The poem is virtually the same as "Crossing Jordan," *Poetry* (May 1941), pp. 73–74, except for the last two lines: "Crossing Jordan! Crossing Jordan! / Alone and by myself."

252 "West Texas": The poem had five stanzas in *SIH*; the fourth was dropped for *SP*. Hughes also made minor changes in the third and fifth stanzas, which became the third and fourth in the text for *SP*, and he changed the dialect "de" to "the." The last three stanzas in *SIH* read:

*So we cranked up our old Ford*
*And we started down the road*
*And where*
*We was goin'*
*We didn't know—*

*Cause it's hard for a jigaboo*
*With a wife and children, too,*
*To make a livin'*
*Anywhere*
*Today.*

*But in West Texas where de sun*
*Shines like the evil one*
*There ain't no reason*
*For a man*
*To stay.*

252   "Ku Klux": Published in *SIH*, *SP*, and *TPATL*.

253   "Ballad of the Sinner": Published in *SIH*.

254   "Ballad of the Killer Boy": Published in *SIH*.

255   "Ballad of the Fortune Teller": Published in *SIH* and *SP*.

256   "Ballad of the Girl Whose Name Is Mud": In *SIH*, line 14 appeared as "(Just as though it was no sin)." The parentheses were removed in *SP*.

"Ballad of the Gypsy": Published in *SIH* and *SP*.

257   "Ballad of the Pawnbroker": Published in *SIH*.

258   "Ballad of the Man Who's Gone": Published in *SIH* and *SP*.

"Midnight Chippie's Lament": Published in *SIH*. "Chippie" is a term for a prostitute.

259   "Widow Woman": Published in *SIH* and *SP*.

260   "Shakespeare in Harlem": Published in *SIH*.

"Fired": Published in *SIH* and *SP*.

261   "Announcement": Published in *SIH*. Circulated by the Associated Negro Press as "Ballad of Some Changes Made."

"50–50": Published in *SIH* and *SP*.

262   "Evil Morning": Published in *SIH*.

"Reverie on the Harlem River": Published in *SIH* and *SP*.

263   "Love": First published in *Compass* (April 1941), p. 28. Included in *SIH* and *SP*.

"Freedom's Plow": First published in *Opportunity* (April 1943), pp. 66–69. Printed as a pamphlet in 1943 by Musette Publishers. Reprinted in *LHR* and *SP*. Hughes made extensive changes in the stanza and line lengths of the poem from its first appearance to the final version in *SP*, often simply cutting in half earlier verses. Hughes deleted one line from the first version. This deleted line ("The mind seeks a way to overcome these obstacles") appeared after line 16. He also reversed the order of lines 184–89, which originally read:

> To all the enemies of the great words:
> FREEDOM, BROTHERHOOD, DEMOCRACY
> We say, NO!

Changes were also made in lines 198–99, where a clause was dropped:

> That tree is not for Negroes alone,
> But for everybody, for all America, for all the world.

268   "Wisdom": In *Saturday Evening Post* (Jan. 30, 1943), p. 74, the poem comprises four lines instead of eight. When Hughes revised the poem for *FOW*, he cut each of the lines in the earlier version in two.

269   "Words Like Freedom": Titled "Refugee in America" in *Saturday Evening Post* (Feb. 6, 1943), p. 64, and *FOW*. The name was altered for *TPATL*. Hughes made the following changes at that time: line 5, "*Liberty*" replaced "democracy"; line 7, "know" replaced "knew"; line 8, "you would" replaced "you'd" (only *Saturday Evening Post*).

"Madam and the Number Writer": First published in *Contemporary Poetry* (Autumn 1943), pp. 5–6, in which the title was "Madam and the Number Runner," and *Negro Story* (March–April 1945), p. 47. Included in *OWT* and *SP*.

270   "Dimout in Harlem": In *Panorama* [Wayne State University] (March 1943), p. 7; *Span* (Dec. 1944–Jan. 1945), p. 14; and *FOW*, the second stanza consisted of five lines, the last two of which read:

> Veiling shadows cut by laughter
> Then a silence over laughter

In *Seven Poets in Search of an Answer*, p. 50, Hughes split these two lines and made a five-stanza poem out of what had been four stanzas.

271   "Little Old Letter": The poem was first published in *Old Line* (April 1943), p. 20, as "Little Old Letter Blues." It originally featured a six-line blues structure, which Hughes changed to the present four-line stanzas for *OWT*. The first version of the poem reads:

*It was yesterday morning*
*That I looked in my box for mail.*
*Yesterday morning*
*I looked in my box for mail.*
*The letter that I found there*
*Made me turn snow pale.*

*Just a little old letter*
*That wasn't but one page long.*
*A little old letter—*
*One little old page long,*
*But it made me wish I*
*Was in hell and gone.*

*I turned that letter over,*
*Nary a word writ on the back.*
*Turned it over,*
*Nothing on the back.*
*I never felt so lonesome*
*Since I was born black.*

*Just a pencil and a paper,*
*You don't need no gun or knife.*
*A pencil and a paper,*
*Don't need no gun or knife—*
*Cause a little old letter*
*Can take a person's life.*

271 "Dear Mr. President": Published in *People's Voice* [New York] (July 3, 1943), p. 23, and *Seven Poets in Search of an Answer*, pp. 46–47.

273 "Broadcast to the West Indies": Published in *People's Voice* (Aug. 14, 1943), p. 23.

275 "Madam and the Rent Man": In *Poetry* (Sept. 1943), pp. 312–13, and *Negro Story* (Dec. 1944–Jan. 1945), p. 50, "You" in line 24 is italicized. Included in *OWT* and *SP*.

276 "Madam and the Charity Child": First published in *Poetry* (Sept. 1943), pp. 311–12, and *Negro Story* (March–April 1945), p. 47. Included in *OWT* and *SP*.

277 "Blind": Published in *Span* (Oct.–Nov. 1943), p. 6.

278 "Shall the Good Go Down?": Published in *Span* (Oct.–Nov. 1943), p. 7.
   Line 3: Lidice was a town in Czechoslovakia not far from Prague. In June 1942, it was razed, the men were killed, and the women and children deported, because some of the inhabitants had aided the assassins of Reinhard Heydrich, the Nazi Reich Protector in Prague. Later that year, Hughes joined the Save Lidice Committee, which raised money to help the survivors.

"Crowing Hen Blues": Published in *Poetry* (Sept. 1943), pp. 313–14.

279   "The Underground": Published in *New Masses* (Sept. 28, 1943), p. 14, and *Seven Poets in Search of an Answer*, pp. 51–52.

Line 23: A Quisling is one who collaborates with the enemy, particularly an occupying enemy. The word came from Vidkun Quisling, the Norwegian who helped the Nazis take and hold Norway during World War II.

A different version of this poem appeared as "Our Spring," *International Literature*, no. 2 (1933), p. 4.

## OUR SPRING

*Bring us with our hands bound,*
*Our teeth knocked out,*
*Our heads broken,*
*Bring us shouting curses, or crying,*
*Or silent as tomorrow.*
*Bring us to the electric chair,*
*Or the shooting wall,*
*Or the guillotine.*
*But you can't kill all of us.*
*You can't silence all of us.*
*You can't stop all of us—*
*Kill Vanzetti in Boston and Huang Ping rises*
*In China.*
*We're like those rivers*
*That fill with the melted snow in spring*
*And flood the land in all directions.*

    *Our spring has come.*

*The pent-up snows of all the brutal years*
*Are melting beneath the rising sun of revolution.*
*The rivers of the world will be flooded with strength*
*And you will be washed away—*
*You murderers of the people—*
*Killers and cops and soldiers,*
*Priests and kings and billionaires,*
*Diplomats and liars,*
*Makers of gas and guns and guillotines.*
*You will be washed away,*
*And the land will be fresh and clean again,*
*Denuded of the past—*
*For time has given us*
*Our spring*
*At last.*

280 "Too Blue": First published in *Contemporary Poetry* (Autumn 1943), p. 5. Included in *OWT*.

281 "Beaumont to Detroit: 1943": Published in *Common Ground* (Autumn 1943), p. 104. From May 12 to August 8, 1943, the nation was rocked by a number of racial riots. Two of the most serious occurred in Beaumont, Texas, and Detroit, Michigan. Hughes wrote about yet another (New York City) in "The Ballad of Margie Polite" (below).

282 "The Ballad of Margie Polite": First published in *Amsterdam News* (Oct. 2, 1943), p. 10A. Included in *OWT*. On August 1, 1943, in Harlem, Margie Polite became involved in an altercation with a white policeman. After a black soldier intervened in Margie Polite's behalf, the policeman shot him. Polite went into the street screaming that her protector had been killed, which was not true. Civil unrest broke out in Harlem, leaving four dead, four hundred injured, and millions of dollars in damages. For Hughes's response to the riot, see Rampersad, vol. II, pp. 75–76.

283 "Madam and the Army": The text here is from *Negro Story* (Oct.–Nov. 1944), p. 55. In *Common Ground* (Summer 1943), p. 89, the poem appeared without stanza breaks.

284 "Madam and the Movies": Published in *Common Ground* (Summer 1943), p. 90, and *Negro Story* (Oct.–Nov. 1944), p. 55.

285 "Madam and Her Madam": Published in *Common Ground* (Summer 1943), pp. 89–90, and in *Negro Story* (Oct.–Nov. 1944), p. 55 (without stanza breaks). It also appeared in *Southern Frontier* (Dec. 1943), p. 2, under the title "Madam to You." Included in *OWT* and *SP*.

"Stalingrad: 1942": Published in *War Poems of the United Nations*, ed. J. Davidman (New York: Dial Press, 1943), pp. 321–24. Stalingrad, now Volgograd, is a city on the Volga River that was the site of a decisive battle in World War II. The Germans attacked the city in August 1942. By February 1943, Soviet troops had recovered it, killing or capturing 330,000 Nazi soldiers in the process. The battle marked the turning point in the war on the Eastern front.

288 "The Black Man Speaks": Published in *JCLS*.

289 "Freedom" [1]: The poem appeared in *JCLS*, *OWT*, and *SP* as "Democracy." The name was changed for *TPATL*. Line 1, "Freedom will not come" was "Democracy will not come" in *JCLS*, *OWT*, and *SP*.

290 "Color": The poem had only five lines in *JCLS*, where lines 1 and 4 read "I would wear it." The six-line version appeared in *TPATL*. The title was "My Color" when the poem was circulated by the Associated Negro Press.

"Freedom" [2]: Published in *JCLS*.

"Red Cross": Published in *JCLS*. This poem was written in response to the Red Cross policy of racially segregating blood donations.

291 "Note to All Nazis Fascists and Klansmen": Published in *JCLS*.

"How About It, Dixie": First published in *New Masses* (Oct. 20, 1942), p. 14. Included in *JCLS*.
Line 1: In 1941, in a major address, Roosevelt spoke to the American people about the need for Four Freedoms—of speech, of worship, from want, and from fear.
Line 14, "Club Roland Hayes": Roland Hayes (1887–1967) was a noted singer of classical songs and Negro spirituals. In 1942, he was assaulted by a white clerk in a segregated shoe store in Rome, Georgia, when he took his wife's part in an argument.

292 "Blue Bayou": In *Black Opals* 1.1 (Spring 1927), p. 6 and *JCLS*, the dialect form "de" was used for "the" throughout. Hughes eliminated the dialect in *SP*.

"Motherland": Published in *JCLS* and *FOW*.

293 "To Captain Mulzac": Published in *JCLS*. In 1920, Hugh Nathaniel Mulzac was the first African American to qualify as a captain in the U.S. Merchant Marine. Refusing to accept command of a vessel unless all the positions on the ship could be filled according to ability, not race, he waited over twenty years until he took charge of the integrated crew of the *Booker T. Washington*.

295 "Still Here": In *JCLS*, the first part of line 3 appears as "Snow has frize me," not "Snow has friz me." The last line is italicized in *SP*, but not in *OWT* or *TPATL*. In earlier versions, the first line reads, "I've been scarred and battered."

"Ballad of Sam Solomon": Published in *JCLS*. In May 1939, Samuel B. Solomon of the NAACP, in defiance of an open Ku Klux Klan threat, led more than one thousand blacks to the polls in the Miami city primaries.

296 "Me and My Song": Published in *JCLS*.

297 "Good Morning, Stalingrad": Published in *JCLS* and *Seven Poets in Search of an Answer*, pp. 44–46. See note to "Stalingrad: 1942," page 650.

299 "Jim Crow's Last Stand": Published in *JCLS*.
Line 15, "Nehru said": Jawaharlal Nehru, an activist for Indian independence and later the first prime minister of India, was jailed on August 9, 1942. He served 1,041 days.
Line 17, "Marian Anderson said to the DAR": Marian Anderson was the prominent concert singer who was the first African American to sing with the Metropolitan Opera Company in New York. Hughes refers to an incident in 1939, when the Daughters of the American Revolution (DAR) refused her request to perform in their Constitution Hall in Washington, D.C., presumably because of her race. Eleanor Roosevelt responded by resigning from the DAR and sponsoring a concert by Anderson at the Lincoln Memorial on Easter Sunday, 1939. An integrated audience of over seventy-five thousand attended, including the president, Cabinet members, members of Congress, and Supreme Court justices.
Line 19, "Paul Robeson said, out in Kansas City": Paul Robeson made it a rule never to perform before racially segregated audiences. During a tour in 1942, after he discovered that the audience at a Kansas City performance was segregated, he would not return for the second half of the concert until he had announced his protest to the crowd.

Line 21, "Mrs. Bethune told Martin Dies": Mary McLeod Bethune (1875–1955) was the founder of Bethune-Cookman College in 1904, when it was called the Daytona Normal and Industrial School for Negro Girls. In 1931, Hughes called her "America's leading Negro woman" (*The Big Sea*, p. 40). Martin Dies was the chairman of the House Committee on Un-American Affairs in the 1940s and 1950s, the counterpart to the committee in the Senate later chaired by Joe McCarthy. Like Hughes himself, Bethune was attacked for having left-wing sympathies.

Line 25, "Joe Louis said": The former heavyweight boxing champion.

Line 28, "When Dorie Miller": Dorie Miller gained fame when, although only a Navy mess attendant on the USS *Arizona*, he seized a machine gun and shot down four Japanese planes during the 1941 attack on Pearl Harbor. For his bravery, he was awarded the Navy Cross. He later died in action in the South Pacific.

299   "Salute to Soviet Armies": Published in *New Masses* (Feb. 15, 1944), p. 10, and, as "To the Red Army," in *Soviet Russia Today* (July 1944), p. 20.

300   "Poem for an Intellectual on the Way Up to Submit to His Lady": Published in *Contemporary Poetry* (Autumn 1944), p. 11.

301   "Madam's Past History": In the first publication, in *Negro Story* (Oct.–Nov. 1944), p. 54, there were no stanza breaks. These appear in *Common Ground* (Summer 1943), p. 88, and OWT and SP.

"Madam's Calling Cards": In *Negro Story* (Dec. 1944–Jan. 1945), p. 50, and *Poetry* (Sept. 1943), p. 310, the last line of the poem reads: "*Madam* that's me." Hughes changed "Madam" to "American" for OWT and SP.

302   "Uncle Tom" [1]: Published in *Span* (Dec. 1944–Jan. 1945), p. 14, and *Crisis* (July 1948), p. 209. A different poem with the same title appeared in SP.

303   "Will V-Day Be Me-Day Too?": Chicago *Defender* (Dec. 30, 1944), p. 9.

305   "Ennui": First published in *Maryland Quarterly* (1944), p. 74. Included in SP.

"Breath of a Rose": Published in *Thirteen Against the Odds*, p. 118. This poem was first published in *The Big Sea*, pp. 170–71. Hughes says there that he wrote it after the end of a romance with a woman named Mary. Her real name was Anne Marie Coussey (see Rampersad, vol. I, pp. 86–90). See also "A Letter to Anne," page 625.

"Silhouette": In *Seven Poets in Search of an Answer*, pp. 49–50, the last line of the poem was "Be good! Be good!" The phrases were made into two lines for OWT. Included in SP. The poem also appeared as part of "Three Songs About Lynching"; see also note to "Lynching Song," page 640.

306   "Moonlight in Valencia: Civil War": Published in *Seven Poets in Search of an Answer*, p. 51.

Valencia, on the Mediterranean coast, was the capital of Republican Spain during the Spanish Civil War. Hughes stayed in the city on his way to and from Madrid in 1937; see *I Wonder As I Wander*, pp. 326–31, 395–96.

Line 21 translates as "I feel it in my bones!"

307   "Madam and the Minister": First published in *Cross Section*, pp. 433–34. Included in *OWT* and *SP*.

308   "Madam and the Wrong Visitor": First published in *Cross Section*, pp. 435–36. Included in *OWT* and *SP*.

     "Madam and the Newsboy": Published in *Negro Story* (Dec. 1944–Jan. 1945), p. 50. Line 18: Marva Trotman and Joe Louis were married in 1935.

309   "Madam and Her Might-Have-Been": In *Cross Section*, pp. 434–35, and *OWT*, the fifth and eighth stanzas were divided in half to form two-line units each. They became four-line stanzas in *SP*.

310   "Madam and the Insurance Man": Published in *Negro Story* (March–April 1945), p. 47.

311   "I Dream a World": Published in *Teamwork* (Feb. 1945), p. 1. Previously it had been circulated by the Associated Negro Press (see *Amsterdam News* [July 19, 1941], p. 14). In *American Negro Poetry*, ed. Arna Bontemps (New York: Hill and Wang, 1963), pp. 71–72, the poem appears without stanza breaks, and the last line reads: "Of such I dream, our world!"
     This piece comes from the libretto of *Troubled Island*, an opera by Hughes and William Grant Still.

     "The Heart of Harlem": Published in *Hawk's Cry* [Tuskegee Army Air Field] (Aug. 18, 1945), p. 6.
     Line 14: Joe Louis, the heavyweight boxing champion, and W. E. B. Du Bois.
     Line 16: Father Divine, the evangelist whose real name was George Baker, and Earl "Fatha" Hines, the jazz pianist and band leader.
     Line 18: Dorothy Maynor, a noted classical singer, founded the Harlem School for the Arts in 1964.
     Line 19: The Schomburg Center of the New York Public Library, which was created when Arthur Schomburg sold his extensive collection of African American manuscripts and publications to the New York Public Library in 1926. The Apollo, at 125th Street near 8th Avenue, is the most famous theater in Harlem. It began in 1913 as a burlesque house, but after 1934 was used for vaudeville and musical acts.
     Line 20: Father Shelton Hale Bishop was the rector of St. Phillip's Episcopal Church in Harlem for twenty-four years before his retirement in 1954. Rosa Artemius Horn, or Horne, called Mother Horne or the "pray for me priestess," was a Harlem evangelist who claimed to have raised thousands from the dead.
     Line 21: "Rennie" is the Renaissance Casino, another Harlem dance hall.
     Line 22: Canada Lee (1907–51) was a champion boxer until he suffered an injury that ended his career. He then began a distinguished acting career on stage and in films. In 1941, he appeared as Bigger Thomas in the Orson Welles production of Richard Wright's *Native Son*.

313   "Little Green Tree": Published in *Tomorrow* (June 1945), p. 30, as "Little Green Tree Blues." Like "Little Old Letter," the poem originally had a six-line blues structure, which was altered to four-line stanzas in *OWT* and *SP*. The first version of the poem reads:

*Looks like to me*
*My good-time days done past.*
*Yes, it looks like*
*My good-time days done past.*
*Ain't nothing in the world*
*I reckon's due to last.*

*I used to play*
*And I played so hard.*
*Used to play,*
*I played so doggone hard.*
*But old age is got me,*
*Dealt me my bad-luck card.*

*I looked down the road*
*And I see a little tree.*
*Little piece down the road*
*I see a little tree.*
*Them sweet green leaves is*
*Waitin' to shelter me.*
*Aw, little tree!*

Hughes changed the last line to "O, little tree!" in *OWT*, but the line was not italicized until *SP*.

313 "Give Us Our Peace": Published in Chicago *Defender* (Aug. 25, 1945), p. 11.

314 "Lonesome Corner": First published in *Tomorrow* (July 1945), p. 60. Included in *OWT*.

"Harlem Night": First published as "Troubled Night" in *Crisis* (Oct. 1945), p. 302. The last three lines "Darkness, / Stars / Nowhere." Changed for *Public Opinion* [Kingston, Jamaica] (Oct. 9, 1948), p. 9.

315 "Graduation": First published in *Common Ground* (Autumn 1945), pp. 86–87. Included in *OWT* and *SP*.

316 "Peace Conference in an American Town": Published in *Common Ground* (Winter 1946), p. 25.

317 "Labor Storm": Published in *New Masses* (July 30, 1946), p. 19.

318 "Lenin": Published in *New Masses* (Jan. 22, 1946), p. 5.

"First of May": Published in *People's Voice* (May 4, 1946), p. s-9. In the late nineteenth century, May 1 was designated a labor holiday by the Second Socialist International. It is still observed as International Workers' Day in many countries.

319 "Conservatory Student Struggles with Higher Instrumentation": First published as "A Juilliard Student Struggles with Higher Instrumentation" in *Lionel Hampton's Swing Book* (Chicago: Negro Story Press, 1946), p. 142. The title was changed for *LHR*.

"Comment": Published in *Span*, vol. 5, no. 2 (Winter 1946), p. 6.

320 "Summer Evening (Calumet Avenue)": When the poem first appeared, in *Poetry Quarterly* [London] (Winter 1947), p. 232, the full title was "Summer Evening: Calumet Avenue, Chicago." "Chicago" was deleted when the poem was included in *OWT*.

321 "Yesterday and Today": First published in *Poetry* (Feb. 1947), p. 250. Included in *OWT*.

"Blues on a Box": First published in *Poetry* (Feb. 1947), pp. 248–49. Included in *OWT*.

322 "Who but the Lord?": Published in *Poetry* (Feb. 1947), p. 249; *OWT*; and *SP* without the last line. It was added for *TPATL*.

"Seashore Through Dark Glasses (Atlantic City)": First published in *Poetry* (Feb. 1947), p. 248. Included in *OWT* and *SP*.

323 "Birth": First published in *Christian Register, Unitarian* [Boston] (May 1947), p. 190. Included in *FOW*.

"Freedom Train": First published in the *New Republic* (Sept. 1947), p. 27; *Our World* (Oct. 1947), pp. 26–27; and *Welcome News* (Dec. 1947–Feb. 1948), pp. 8–9. Included in *SP*.
   The poem was written in response to a plan by the American Heritage Foundation to send the original text of the Declaration of Independence around the country on a special train. The tour never took place.
   Line 43, "Anzio": On January 22, 1944, American and British troops made an amphibious landing at the coastal town of Anzio, about forty miles southeast of Rome. They were pinned down near the sea for months by German guns on the surrounding high ground.

325 "Border Line": Published in *FOW* and *SP*.

326 "Night: Four Songs": Published in *FOW* and *SP*.

"Burden": First published in Carmel *Pine Cone* (Nov. 14, 1941), p. 6. Included in *FOW*.

"Beale Street": Published in *FOW* and *SP*. See note for "Beale Street Love," page 623.

327 "Circles": Published in *FOW*.

"Grave Yard": Published in *FOW*.

"Montmartre": Published in *FOW*.
   Line 1: In *The Big Sea*, p. 162, Hughes notes that the rue Pigalle was the center of jazz and blues in Paris in 1924, when he lived there.

328    "Fragments": Published in *FOW*.

"Desert": Published in *FOW*; *Negro Digest* (Dec. 1950), p. 68; and *SP*.

"End": In *FOW*, the last line of the poem is not italicized. Italics were added for *SP*.

329    "Heart": First published in *Abbott's Monthly* (May 1932), p. 14, with minor variations. Included in *FOW*.

"Remembrance": First published under the title "Pattern" in *Negro Voices: An Anthology of Contemporary Verse*, edited by Beatrice Murphy (New York: Henry Harrison, 1938), p. 79. Included in *FOW*.

330    "Fulfillment": Published in *FOW* and *SP*.

"Night Song": Published in *FOW*.

331    "Carolina Cabin": Published in *FOW*.

332    "Songs": Published in *FOW*.

"Sleep": Published in *FOW*.

"Juliet": Titled "On the Road to Mantova" in *Library* [Roswell, New Mexico] (March 15, 1927); *Lincoln University News* (March 1926), p. 7; and *FOW*. The first line of the early version read, "There are wonder." Line lengths differ from *SP*, but there are no other word changes.
    Juliet is, of course, the heroine of Shakespeare's *Romeo and Juliet*, which is set in the Italian city of Verona.

333    "Man": Published in *FOW*.

"Luck": The second stanza was added when the poem was reprinted in *SP*. The original version in *FOW* had only the first four lines. The second stanza also appeared as "Gifts" in *SIH*.

334    "Chippy": First published in *Poetry Magazine* [Australia] (Dec. 20, 1946), p. 9. Included in *FOW*. See note to "Midnight Chippie's Lament," page 646.

"Dancers": Published in *FOW*.

"Grief": Published in *FOW*.

335    "Old Sailor": Published in *FOW*.

"Faithful One": Published in *FOW*.

336    "Dream Dust": Published in *FOW*, *SP*, and *TPATL*.

"Little Song": Published in *FOW* and *Opportunity* (July 1948), p. 104.

"Jaime": Published in *FOW*.

337  "Sailing Date": Published in *FOW*.

"There": Published in *FOW*.

338  "Trumpet Player": The poem appeared in *Mainstream* (Winter 1949), pp. 44–45 and *FOW* with the title "Trumpet Player: 52nd Street." The title was shortened for *SP*.

339  "Harlem Dance Hall": Published in *FOW*.

"Communion": Published in *FOW*.

340  "When the Armies Passed": Published in *FOW*.

"Oppression": Published in *FOW* and *Lincoln University Poets*, pp. 28–29. Included in *TPATL*.

341  "Peace": First published in *Opportunity* (Summer 1948), p. 99. Included in *TPATL*.

"To Dorothy Maynor": Published in *Crisis* (July 1948), p. 209. See note to "The Heart of Harlem," line 18, page 653.

"Barefoot Blues": First published as "Don't You See My Shoes" in *Public Opinion* [Kingston, Jamaica] (Oct. 9, 1948), p. 9, where the last line read "Papa, don't you see my shoes?" This line and the title were changed when the poem appeared in *Masses and Mainstream* (Feb. 1949), p. 53.

342  "Wealth": Published in *Public Opinion* (Oct. 9, 1948), p. 9.

"Wisdom and War": Published in *Ebony Rhythm*, ed. B. Murphy (New York: Exposition Press, 1948), p. 88, and *Span* (Oct.–Dec. 1946), p. 3.

343  "From Selma": Published in *Ebony Rhythm*, p. 88.

"Ballad of the Seven Songs": Published in *Common Ground* (Winter 1949), pp. 21–27.
    Line 11: Cudjoe was a Jamaican slave who led the revolt in the Maroon War (1734–38), in which the Maroons won independence from the British in their section of the island.
    Line 17: Jackie Robinson, who played for the Brooklyn Dodgers, was the first African American major-league baseball player.
    Line 224: "*Depuis le jour*" is an aria from *Louise*, an opera by Gustave Charpentier.

350  "Dare": Published in *Voices* (Winter 1949), p. 31.

351  "Slave Song": Published in *Voices* (Winter 1949), p. 31.

"Second Generation: New York": Published in *Common Ground* (Spring 1949), p. 47.

352 "Homecoming": The poem was originally three stanzas, in *Experiment* (Summer 1949), p. 276. Hughes deleted this last stanza when the poem was republished in *SP*:

> *Little old empty bed, Lord!*
> *Little old empty room!*
> *Little old empty heart, Lord!*
> *Might as well be my tomb!*

"From Spain to Alabama": Published in *Experiment* (Summer 1949), p. 276.

353 "Madam and the Phone Bill": Published in *OWT* and *SP*.

354 "Madam and the Fortune Teller": First published in *Rocky Mountain Review* (Summer 1944), p. 122. Included in *OWT* and *SP*.

355 "Madam and the Census Man": Published in *OWT* and *SP*.

356 "Mama and Daughter": In *OWT*, line 17 reads: "*Mama, he couldn't still be young.*" "*He*" was changed to "*dad*" in *SP*.

357 "S-sss-ss-sh!": The final two lines do not appear in *OWT*. They were added to the text for *SP*.

358 "Life Is Fine": Published in *OWT* and *SP*.

359 "Honey Babe": Published in *OWT*. This poem was originally distributed by the Associated Negro Press.

"Stranger in Town": Published in *OWT*.

360 "Lincoln Theatre": Published in *OWT*.

"Song for Billie Holiday": Published in *OWT* and *SP*. Billie Holiday (1915–59) was one of the most influential jazz singers. The story of her professional success and personal tragedy is recounted in her autobiography, *Lady Sings the Blues* (1956). Hughes's poem was written after her first incarceration for possession of illicit drugs.

361 "One-Way Ticket": Published in *OWT* and *SP*.

"Restrictive Covenants": Published in *OWT*.

362 "Juice Joint: Northern City": Published in *OWT*. Earlier, a different version was published under the title "Barrel House: Chicago" in *Lincoln University News* (1928), p. 7.

> *There is a barrel house on the avenue,*
> *Where singing black boys dance and play each night*
> *Until the stars pale and the sky turns blue*
> *And dawn comes down the street all wanly white.*

They sell hard cider there in mug-like cups,
And gin is sold in glasses finger-tall,
And women of the streets stop in for sups
Of whiskey as they go by to the ball.
And all the time a singing black boy plays
A song that once was sung beneath the sun,
In lazy far-off sunny Southern days
Before that strange hegira had begun,
That brought black faces and gay dancing feet
Into this barrel house on the city street.

Play your banjos, grinning night-dark boys,
And let your songs drift through the swinging doors.
Let your songs hold all the sunny joys
That goad black feet to dancing on bare floors.
Then let the woman with her red lips
Turn from the bar and join you in your song,
And later lift her skirts and raise her head
To sing about the men who've done her wrong—
While blues as mellow as the Southern air
And weary as a drowsy Southern rain
Echo the age-less, age-long old despair
That fills all woman's age-less, age-long pain—
As every swaying banjo-playing boy
Forgets he ever sang a song of joy.

O, in this barrel house on the city street
Where black men come to drink and play and sing,
And women, too, whom anyone may meet
And handle easy like a purchased thing,
Where two old brown men stand behind the bar—
And sell those drinks white man's law forbids—
Dark dancers dance and dreamers dream a star
And some forget to laugh who still are kids.
Here on a keg a banjo-playing lad
Whose languid lean brings back the sunny South
Strikes up a tune all gay and bright and glad
To keep the gall from biting in his mouth,
Then drowsy as the rain soft sad black feet
Dance in this barrel house on the city street.

This version was reprinted with slight alterations as "Barrel House: Northern City"
in *Abbott's Monthly* (Oct. 1931), p. 1, and "Barrel House: Industrial City" in *Seven*

*Poets in Search of an Answer*, pp. 148–49. The only significant change occurred in the sixth line of the last stanza, the revision for *OWT* prompted by the end of Prohibition in 1933: in *Lincoln News*, "And sell those drinks the white man's law forbids"; in *Abbott's*, "And sell those drinks the nation's law forbids"; in *OWT* and *Seven*, "Still after hours pouring drinks the law forbids."

363 "Harlem" [1]: Titled "Puzzled" in *OWT* and *SP*. The title was changed for *TPATL*.

364 "Man into Men": Published in *OWT*.

365 "Warning": Published under the title "Roland Hayes Beaten [Georgia: 1942]" in *OWT*. On the incident, see the note for "How About It, Dixie," page 651. The change was made for *TPATL* along with, in line 5, "mind" for "minds."

"Late Last Night": Published in *OWT* and *SP*.

"Bad Morning": Published in *OWT* and *SP*.

366 "Could Be": Published in *OWT* and *SP*.

"Midnight Raffle": Published in *OWT* and *SP*.

367 "Monroe's Blues": Published in *OWT* and *SP*.

"Raid": Published in *OWT*.

"What?": The title of the poem in *OWT* was "White Felts in Fall." The change was made for *SP*.

368 "Request for Requiems": Published in *OWT*.

"Deceased": Published in *OWT*. This poem was originally distributed by the Associated Negro Press.

"Final Curve": Published in *OWT* and *SP*.

"Boarding House": Published in *OWT*.

369 "Funeral": Published in *OWT*.

"Migrant": First published in *Poetry Magazine* [Australia] (Sept. 30, 1946), pp. 9–10. Included in *OWT* and *SP*.
    Line 12, "Never knew DuSable": Jean Baptist Point du Sable was Chicago's first settler, in 1782 or 1783. His father was French and his mother was of African descent. His statue now stands outside the Museum of African-American History at 3806 South Michigan Avenue, Chicago.
    Line 29, "V-J Day": Victory over Japan Day (August 10, 1945) marked the end of World War II.

370 "Third Degree": First published in *Poetry Magazine* [Australia] (Sept. 30, 1946), p. 11. Included in *OWT*, *SP*, and *TPATL*.

371 "Jitney": Published in OWT and on the inside of the front cover of *Circuit* (Jan. 1947).
  Line 27: Albert "Al" Hibbler was born blind in 1915. He was a vocalist with Duke Ellington's band from 1943 to 1951.

373 "Interne at Provident": First published in *Poetry Magazine* [Australia] (Sept. 30, 1946), pp. 12–13 with minor variations. Included in OWT, SP, and TPATL.

374 "To Be Somebody": First published in *Phylon* (4th Quarter 1950) in two stanzas. The text was changed for SP.
  Line 11: Hazel Scott (1920–81), a popular singer and pianist once married to Adam Clayton Powell, Jr.

375 "Down Where I Am": First published in *Voices* (Winter 1950), p. 33. Included in TPATL.

  "Catch": First published in *Minnesota Quarterly* (Spring 1950), p. 22. Included in SP.

376 "Island" [1]: The poem was titled "Wave of Sorrow" in *Minnesota Quarterly* (Spring 1950), p. 22. The last line in the first version was "Let me stagger there," which was changed to "Take me there" in SP.

  "Kid in the Park": The title was "Waif" in *Minnesota Quarterly* (Spring 1950), p. 22. The title was changed for SP.


POEMS 1951–1960

379 "Prelude to Our Age": *Crisis* (Feb. 1951), pp. 87–90. A note reads: "Read by the author on October 15, 1950 at 25th Schomburg Collection dedication exercises, New York City."
  Lines 19–20, "Homer's 'Blameless Ethiopians' ": The Greeks believed that the Ethiopians had special reverence for the gods, which caused the divinities to attend in person the feasts of the East Africans. The reputation of the Ethiopians for piety was established by the time of composition of the Homeric epic poems (around 800 B.C.E.). Hughes probably found this information, as well as other material in the poem, in Arna Bontemps's *The Story of the Negro* (1948), a volume dedicated to Langston Hughes.
  Line 24: Aesop (c. 550 B.C.E.), a Thracian by birth, wrote fables in Ancient Greek. Antar-bin Shedad (c. 500 C.E.), was a medieval poet in Egypt who wrote works in the manner of the *Arabian Nights*; Terence, or Publius Terentius Afer (c. 195–159 B.C.E.), wrote Roman stage comedies; he was born in North Africa, and his surname "Afer" means "dark" or "black."
  Line 27: The West African kingdoms Ghana and Songhay were, with the Ethiopians, three of the most important civilizations in sub-Saharan Africa before the European colonization.
  Line 32: Juan Latino (1516–97), a black man from the Spanish city of Granada, was a poet and a professor at the University of Granada. He wrote verses honoring the return of Philip V of Spain from the victory against the Turks at Lepanto in 1571.

Line 33 translates as "To the Equally Catholic and Most Invincible."

Line 38: Abderrahman Sadi, or Abd al-Rahman ben Abd Allah al-Sadi, was a writer in Timbuctoo in the middle of the seventeenth century and the author of the *Ta'rikh al Sudan* or, as Hughes calls it, the "Tarikh es Soudan," one of the two major African historical works of the 1600s.

Line 51: The poet Phillis Wheatley (1753–84) was the first African American to publish a book. In 1775, Wheatley sent George Washington a poem that she had written about him. Washington responded by inviting her to visit his headquarters outside of Boston. She met with the general for about half an hour.

Line 60: Crispus Attucks, a runaway slave, was killed in the Boston Massacre in 1776. See the note to "America," page 618.

Line 64: Benjamin Banneker (1731–1806) wrote a Farmer's Almanac for the years 1792–1802, the first scientific work published by an African American.

Line 66: Toussaint L'Ouverture led the Haitian slave revolt of 1791.

Line 68: The authors Alexandre Dumas (1802–70) of France and Alexander Pushkin (1799–1857) of Russia were of partial African descent.

Line 82: Ira Aldridge (1805–67), an outstanding Shakespearean actor of African American descent, achieved international fame in England and in Continental Europe.

Lines 84, 100: *The North Star* was the name of the newspaper edited by Frederick Douglass.

Line 96: Nat Turner led the bloodiest slave revolt in American history, in Virginia in 1832; Denmark Vesey was accused of planning a slave revolt in South Carolina in 1822.

Line 99: Elijah Lovejoy, William Lloyd Garrison, and Wendell Phillips were prominent white leaders of the Abolition movement in the North.

Line 115: Paul Laurence Dunbar (1872–1906), the beloved poet and novelist, published verse in both dialect and standard English.

Line 116: "By the Watermelon Vine, Lindy Lou" was composed in 1914 by Thomas S. Allen.

Line 117: A reference to the Jubilee singers of Fisk University, who traveled the world raising money for the college between 1871 and 1878.

Line 120: Bert Williams and George Nash Walker formed a vaudeville team in 1895. They had a string of popular reviews in New York and London, including *In Dahomey* and *Bandana Land*.

Line 122: W. C. Handy (1873–1958), the musician and composer, is known as "The Father of the Blues" for being an early champion of the blues as an art form. His most famous composition was "St. Louis Blues."

Line 126: Mary McLeod Bethune founded Bethune-Cookman College in 1906. See note to "Jim Crow's Last Stand," page 651.

Line 130: Marian Anderson, Dorothy Maynor, and Paul Robeson.

Line 131: Josephine Baker (1906–75) was at one time the queen of cabaret in the city of Paris, and Florence Mills (1896–1927), despite the brevity of her life, had similar fame in England and among black Americans.

Line 133: Charles Spurgeon Johnson (1893–1956), sociologist, editor, and president of Fisk University, served on the Tennessee Valley Authority in the 1930s and on other government commissions after World War II. William H. Hastie (1904–76) became the first African American on the federal bench when Franklin D. Roosevelt appointed him to the U.S. District Court of the Virgin Islands in

1937. Truman raised him to the Third Circuit Court of Appeals in 1949. William L. Dawson (1886–1970) served in the U.S. House of Representatives for fourteen terms as a representative from Chicago. Adam Clayton Powell, Jr., of Harlem, served as the representative for Harlem in the U.S. House of Representatives from 1944 to 1970, with a brief interruption in 1967, when he was expelled for alleged financial improprieties.

Line 135: Charles Richard Drew (1904–50). His experiments with the preservation of blood plasma led to the creation of safe blood banks.

Line 140: Yamacraw is a historically black district in Savannah, Georgia.

Line 160: Ralph Bunche was awarded the Nobel Peace Prize in 1950 for his work in ending hostilities between Jews and Arabs after the British left Palestine in 1948.

Line 163: W. E. B. Du Bois, Carter G. Woodson (see note to "A Ballad of Negro History," line 65 [page 668]), James Weldon Johnson, and E. Franklin Frazier (1894–1962). Frazier, a sociologist and professor, was the author of *The Negro Family in the United States* (1939) and *The Black Bourgeoisie* (1957).

Line 164: Robert S. Abbott founded the Chicago *Defender* in 1905. T. Thomas Fortune (1856–1936), another well-known journalist, was a co-founder of the National Afro-American Press Association in 1898.

Line 165: The Baltimore *Afro-American* and Cincinnati's *Black Dispatch* were two influential black newspapers of the twentieth century.

Line 167: *The Crisis, Phylon,* and *Opportunity* were, along with *The Messenger,* the leading African American magazines during Hughes's career as a writer. Phylon means "race" in Greek.

Line 168: Arthur A. Schomburg, an enterprising book collector, founded the Negro Society for Historical Research in 1911. Claude McKay and Countee Cullen were, like Hughes, writers of the Harlem Renaissance. *Native Son,* the novel by Richard Wright, was published in 1940.

Lines 175–76: The sociologist Robert Ezra Park co-wrote *The Man Further Down* (1912) with Booker T. Washington and later collected his own essays on race in America in *Race and Culture* (1950). Gunnar Myrdal, a Swedish sociologist, published a landmark study on race in America entitled *An American Dilemma* (1944). Sinclair Lewis's *Kingsblood Royal* (1947) is a novel about racial "passing." Lillian Smith's best-selling anti-racist novel *Strange Fruit* appeared in 1944. Carl Van Vechten's *Nigger Heaven* (1926) depicts Harlem life in the 1920s. Bucklin Moon wrote several novels about African Americans, among them *The Darker Brother* (1943) and *White Magnolias* (1949).

384 "Where Service Is Needed": Published in a number of African American newspapers, including *Daily Express* [Ohio] (Feb. 17, 1951), p. 2, and *Herald News* [New Jersey] (Feb. 3, 1951). In the latter, the poem contains the following introduction: "Brilliant Langston Hughes, sepia poet laureate of America, wrote a poem especially for the Testimonial Dinner of *The National Association of Colored Graduate Nurses* at its dissolution and as a salute to the integration and crashing of 'Jim Crow' barriers."

385 "American Heartbreak": First published in *Phylon* (3rd Quarter 1951), p. 248. Included in SP and TPATL.

Line 5, "Jamestown": The earliest settlement in Virginia, where the first blacks brought from Africa landed in 1619.

385 "Consider Me": In the first appearance of the poem, in *American Scholar* (Winter 1951–52), pp. 100–101, the first stanza had an extra line and ended: "Pa— / Spelled G-o-d." The second stanza, however, did not include the present line 14 ("*He*"), which was added in *SP*. The fifth stanza had different line lengths:

> Consider me:
> On Friday
> The eagle flies.
> Saturday
> Laughter, a bar, a bed.
> Sunday
> Prayers syncopate glory.
> Monday, come eight
> To work, late—
> Maybe.

### Montage of a Dream Deferred   (1951)

Since Hughes clearly refers to the whole book as a "poem" and stresses that the parts should be read in sequence, we have preserved the order of *Montage of a Dream Deferred* intact, even though many sections of the work appeared independently in periodicals. The only major difference between the three printings of the work occurs after "Lady's Boogie." In *Montage*, it is followed by "Freedom Train." "Freedom Train" was removed from the text of *LHR*. In *SP*, "So Long" replaces "Freedom Train" in this position in the text.

Hughes made a number of minor changes in the text of *Montage of a Dream Deferred* when it was reprinted in its entirety in *SP*. Most of these changes involved italicizing words which had not been italicized when the sequence was published on its own and in *LHR*, or pairing lines that had been separated by spaces. For the sake of brevity, the addition of italics and the joining of lines which do not alter the stanzaic patterns will not be documented here. However, readers interested in the link between Hughes's verse and music should take note of such changes, since they affect the "be-bop" rhythms of the sequence to which Hughes refers in his prefatory note to *Montage*.

All poems appear in *Montage* and *LHR* unless noted. The text here is from *SP*. Three poems were later reprinted in *TPATL*: "Corner Meeting," "Motto," and "Children's Rhymes."

390 "Children's Rhymes": Part of the poem was included in *TPATL*.

392 "Question" [2]: In *Montage* and *LHR*, "de-dop!" was a poem entitled "Figurine."

393 "Juke Box Love Song": First published in *Voices* (Winter 1950), pp. 32–33.

394 "New Yorkers": Published as "New York" in *Phylon* (1st Quarter 1950), p. 14.

395 "Easy Boogie": Not in *SP*.

397 "Neon Signs": Line 5, "(ancient altar of Thelonius)," read simply "(altar of Thelo-nius)" in *Montage* and *LHR*. The line refers to Thelonius Monk, the jazz pianist. In earlier versions, the capitalized "signs" of the poem were separated by lines of three horizontal dots ( ... ) instead of the diamond-shaped patterns of four dots in *SP*.

398 "What? So Soon!": In *Montage* and *LHR*, "Comment against Lamp Post" and "Figurette" appear as separate poems within the verse sequence. In *SP*, Hughes made them subsections of the preceding poem, "What? So Soon!"

"Motto": In *TPATL*, the last line is not italicized.

399 "Dead in There": In line 4, Hughes made one of several word changes to the *Montage* sequence when it was reprinted in *SP*. The line "A re-bop daddy" in the earlier versions in *Montage* and *LHR* became "A cool bop daddy" in *SP*.

400 "Dancer": In *Montage* and *LHR*, line 13 was "kittered," not "jittered." A misprint? Line 25: "C.P.T." stands for "Colored People's Time."

"Advice": First published in *Senior Scholastic* (April 15, 1946), p. 19.

401 "Green Memory": First published in *Harlem Quarterly* (Winter 1949–50), p. 9. Not in *SP*.

"Relief": In *Harlem Quarterly* (Winter 1949–50), p. 10, line 2 read "for them Turks and Greeks." About this time, the Marshall Plan was sending millions of dollars in aid to Turkey and Greece to deter the spread of Communism. Hughes later changed the line to "for them Poles and Greeks," perhaps in response to the failed Polish attempts to liberate themselves during the 1950s.

402 "Ballad of the Landlord": This poem first appeared in *Opportunity* (Dec. 1940), p. 364, and was included in the volume *JCLS*. In the first version of the poem, which appeared in *Opportunity* (Dec. 1940), p. 364, there was no stanza break between lines 24 and 25, but line 30 ("Headlines in press:") was set apart by itself. Also in the *Opportunity* version the headlines occupied the final four lines of the poem, not three, and were not in capital letters. The lines become capitalized in *JCLS*, in which the last two lines are "JUDGE GIVES NEGRO 90 DAYS / IN COUNTY JAIL . . ." The two lines became one line in the final version of the poem, in *SP*.

403 "Corner Meeting": The following text appears in *TPATL*:

> *Ladder, flag, and amplifier*
> *now are what the soapbox*
> *used to be.*
>
> *The speaker catches fire,*
> *looking at listeners' faces.*
>
> *His words jump down*
> *to stand*
> *in their*
> *places.*

403    "Projection": First published as "Projection of a Day" in *New Masses* (Jan. 1, 1946), p. 11. Hughes made a number of changes for *Montage*: Line 2, "leaps clean" became "leaped clean"; line 3, "starts" became "started"; line 6, "throws" became "threw"; line 9, "stoops" became "stooped"; line 13, "like a Dizzy Gillespie transcription" became "like a Lionel Hampton transcription"; line 16, "Sammy Davis" became "Willie Bryant"; line 17, "will sing" became "sang"; line 19, "will team up" became "teamed up"; line 20, "Father Divine will say" became "Father Divine said." Lines 21–23 formed one line in *New Masses*. The most significant change was the omission of the last stanza of the first version of the poem. In *New Masses*, the poem ends:

> *On that day*
> *My Simple Minded Friend*
> *Was simple no more*
> *Because the time had come to be wise—*
> *On that day when Freedom*
> *Opened up our*
> *Skies!*

This was the only place in his verse that Hughes mentioned his Simple Minded Friend, also known as Simple or Jesse B. Semple, the hero of his weekly column in the Chicago *Defender*.

Line 13: Dizzy Gillespie (1917–93) was a renowned jazz trumpeter and band leader. The *Montage* version refers to the jazz vibraphonist Lionel Hampton. He played with Benny Goodman from 1936 to 1940, when he left to form his own band.

Line 14: Inez Cavanaugh began her career as the publicity agent for Duke Ellington. In the 1930s, she opened a night club in Paris. Timme may be Baron Timme Rosenkrantz, an afficionado of jazz from Denmark. Rosenkrantz published two books on jazz in Copenhagen before moving to the United States in the late 1940s, where he wrote for the jazz magazine *Down Beat*.

Line 16: Sammy Davis, Jr. The early version refers to William S. Bryant (1908–64), a big-band leader and vocalist in the 1930s and 1940s and star of a television show on CBS in 1949.

Line 19: Jackie "Moms" Mabley (1894–1975) was a popular comedian and vaudeville performer.

Line 20: Father Divine (1887–1965), born George Baker, was one of the best-known religious leaders in America through his Father Divine Peace Mission. Father Divine claimed that he was God on earth, and all people should try to please God—i.e., Father Divine. His Peace Mission fed and housed many poor people during the Depression.

404    "Flatted Fifths": In *Montage* and *LHR*, line 4 read "frantic, kick their C.C. years," which was changed to "frantic, kick their draftee years" in *SP*. "C.C." refers to the Conservation Corps, a Depression relief measure.

406    "Gauge": Slang for marijuana, as are hemp, stick, roach, and straw.

407    "125th Street": A section of this poem was published in *Voices* (Winter 1950), p. 32, under the title "Passersby." That version employed three-line stanzas. The first line of each stanza was simply the word "Face."

408 "Jam Session": In *Montage*, the poems "Jam Session," "Be-Bop Boys," and "Tag" appear as separate units, as they do in the text of *SP* printed here. In *LHR*, Hughes combined the three poems into a single poem with the title "Jam Session." In order to bring the three poems together, he put the title of "Be-Bop Boys" into the first line of the poem of that name and changed the form of the verb: "While Be-Bop boys implore Mecca." He also removed the title "Tag" from the text.

409 "Theme for English B": First published in *Common Ground* (Spring 1949), pp. 89–90.
    Line 9: The college, according to this description, is the City College of the City University of New York (CCNY).

410 "College Formal: Renaissance Casino": First published in *Holiday* (April 1949), p. 164. The Renaissance Casino was a club at 138th Street and Seventh Avenue in Harlem.

411 "Low to High": First published in *Midwest Journal* (Summer 1949), p. 25.

    "High to Low": In the first appearance of the poem, in *Midwest Journal* (Summer 1949), p. 26, line 6 read "look too black." This was changed to "look too bad" in *LHR*, but "look too black" was restored in *SP*.
    Line 12: "Ethical Culture" is the name of a historically integrated preparatory school in mid-Manhattan.
    Line 14: A leading Episcopal church in Harlem.
    Line 17: 409 Edgecombe Avenue, an apartment building that housed many prominent persons in Harlem.

413 "So Long": Not included in *Montage* and *LHR*.

415 "Shame on You": First published in *Phylon* (1st Quarter 1950), p. 15.

    "World War II": The title was simply "World War" in *Harlem Quarterly* (Winter 1949–50), p. 9.

416 "Mystery": Lines 21–22: Father Sheldon Hale Bishop was the rector of St. Phillip's Episcopal Church in Harlem. Effendi perhaps refers to Duse Mohammed Effendi, a leader of the Pan-African Movement in England at the turn of the century and editor of *The African Times and Orient Review*, a leading Pan-African periodical in London. Mother Horne, or Rosa Artemius Horne, and Father Divine were leaders of evangelical movements in Harlem (see the notes to "The Heart of Harlem" and "Projection," pages 661 and 674). "A Rabbi black" perhaps refers to A. Wentworth Matthews, the spiritual leader of the Black Jews of Harlem.

417 "Passing": First published in *Phylon* (1st Quarter 1950), p. 15.

418 "Casualty": The last line ("Son! . . . Son!") does not appear in the first version of the poem, in *Voices* (Winter 1950), p. 33.

419 "Night Funeral in Harlem": First published in *Tomorrow* (Dec. 1949), p. 46.

423 "Joe Louis" [1]: The poem appeared with the title "The Champ" in *Voices* (Winter 1950), p. 32.

424 "Brothers": First published in *Crisis* (Feb. 1924), p. 160, and *JCLS*. Hughes made slight modifications when the poem was reprinted in *Montage*. The first two words of the original final line ("We are brothers—you and I") were dropped. Hughes made one other change, in line 6, in which "I from these States" became "I from the U.S.A."

425 "Hope" [2]: Line 3: "Dream Book" refers to a text, consulted by gamblers, in which elements in dreams are assigned numbers.

426 "Harlem" [2]: Reprinted in *SP* under the title "Dream Deferred."

428 "Comment on Curb": The two stanzas of this poem originally formed the final two stanzas of the preceding poem, "Same in Blues," in *Montage* and *LHR*. They were separated to form another poem in *SP*.

429 "Letter": Line 11 is "Respectable as ever" in *LHR*, but "Respectably as ever" in *Montage* and *SP*.

431 "Tomorrow's Seed": Published in *The Heart of Spain*, p. 325. This poem and the one that follows were written for a volume memorializing the Spanish Civil War, which Hughes had reported on in the 1930s.

"Hero—International Brigade": Published in *The Heart of Spain*, p. 326.

432 "The Christmas Story": Published in *Catholic Interracialist* [Chicago] (Jan. 1952), p. 4. This poem was later incorporated into the musical play *Black Nativity*.

433 "No Regrets": First published in *Saturday Review of Literature* (Jan. 26, 1952), p. 22. Included in *SP*.

434 "Vari-Colored Song": First published in *Phylon* (1st Quarter 1952), p. 42. Included in *TPATL*.

"A Ballad of Negro History": Published in *Negro History Bulletin* (Feb. 1952), p. 92.
    Line 17: Mandingo and Songhay were the most important West African kingdoms in the centuries before the arrival of the Europeans.
    Line 25: On Antar bin-Shedad, see notes for "Prelude to Our Age," page 669.
    Line 27: On Juan Latino, see notes for "Prelude to Our Age," page 669.
    Line 57: On W. C. Handy, see notes for "Prelude to Our Age," page 670.
    Line 58: Bert Williams and George Nash Walker were a famous vaudeville act (see notes for "Prelude to Our Age," page 670).
    Line 65: The historian Carter G. Woodson, founder of the Association for the Study of Negro Life and History, began the observance of Negro History Week in 1926, which has now become Black History Month. In 1925, Hughes briefly worked as an assistant to Woodson on a large project titled *Free Negro Heads of Families in 1830* (see *The Big Sea*, pp. 210–12).
    Line 66: On W. E. B. Du Bois, James Weldon Johnson, and the scientist Charles Richard Drew, see notes to "Prelude to Our Age," page 671.
    Line 69: Edith Sampson was an actress.

436 "Hope for Harlem": Published in *Our World* (Aug. 1952), pp. 34–36.

439 "Ultimatum: Kid to Kid": Published in *Shenandoah* (Winter 1953), p. 25.

"Ballad of the Two Thieves": Published in *Shenandoah* (Winter 1953), pp. 26–27.

440 "Bible Belt": First published with the title "Not for Publication" in *Crisis* (March 1953), p. 167, and *Black Orpheus* (May 1959), p. 28. The following changes were made for *TPATL*: line 1, "Jesus" replaced "Christ"; lines 8 and 9 are one line in *Crisis* and *Black Orpheus*; line 11, "But say it" replaced "But, talk about it"; line 12, "*You*" replaced "You."

441 "Africa": First published in three stanzas in *Long Island University Review* (June 1952), p. 12, and *Crisis* (March 1953), p. 167. The poem appears without stanza breaks in *Africa South* (April–June 1957), p. 28.

"Envoy to Africa": Published in *Crisis* (April 1953), p. 252.

"Ballad of Booker T.": Published in *Common Sense Historical Review* (May 1953), p. 17. An early version appeared in *Southern Frontier* (July 1941), p. 1, with the following variations: line 8, "Not afar" was "And not afar"; line 12, "and your hand" was "*and your hand*"; line 14, "surely not meet" was "surely not mete"; lines 15 and 16 are one line in *Southern Frontier*; line 18, "At Tuskegee" was "So at Tuskegee"; line 25, "Was not today" was "Was *not* today"; line 34, "A Negro was lucky" was "A Joker was lucky"; line 44, "and your hand" was "*and your hand*"; line 47, "Let down" was "So let down."

443 "Addition" [2]: Published in *Voices* (May–Aug. 1953), p. 16.

"Poet to Bigot": First published in *Phylon* (2nd Quarter 1953), p. 206, and *Lincoln University Poets*, pp. 29–30. Included in *LHR*.

"Room": Published in *Voices* (May–Aug. 1953), p. 17.

444 "Do You Reckon?": Published in *Deer and the Dachshund* no. 6 (n.d., n.p.).

"Lincoln University: 1954": Published in *Lincoln University Poets*, p. 24. Lincoln University, in Pennsylvania, was founded in 1854 to educate "colored youth of the male sex." In the late 1950s, the student body became coeducational. Hughes attended Lincoln from 1926 to 1929, when he received a Bachelor of Arts degree. He received an honorary doctorate from the university in 1943.

445 "Draftees": Published in *Lincoln University Poets*, pp. 25–26.

"Azikiwe in Jail": Published in *Lincoln University Poets*, p. 29. An earlier version, identical except for the name, was circulated by the ANP in 1942 as "Ghandi in Jail." Benjamin Nnamdi Azikiwe became the first president of an independent Nigeria in 1960. He was often jailed for his actions against the continuation of British rule in Nigeria during the 1950s. Hughes later traveled to Nigeria at the invitation of Azikiwe (see Rampersad, vol. II, pp. 324–25). Azikiwe, who attended Lincoln University, contributed to the volume *Lincoln University Poets*.

446 "Old Walt": First published in *Beloit Poetry Journal Chapbook*, no. 3 (1954), p. 10, a volume dedicated to tributes to the poet Walt Whitman. Included in *SP*.

"Without Benefit of Declaration": First published in *Free Lance*, no. 1 (1955), p. 3, and *New Orlando Anthology* (1963), p. 61. Included in *TPATL*.

447 "Us: Colored": Published in *Free Lance*, no. 1 (1955), p. 4.

"Miss Blues'es Child": In *Olivant Quarterly* (2nd Quarter 1955), p. 135, the dialect form "chile" is used for "child" in the text of the poem, but not in the title. Hughes removed the dialect in *SP*. Line 9 of the *SP* text appeared as two indented lines in *Olivant* without the word "so" at the end: "I love you! / Oh, I love you!"

"Delinquent": First published as "Little Julie" in *Olivant Quarterly* (2nd Quarter 1955), p. 134, and without the last stanza, which was added for *SP*. Line 8, "stomach" was "her stomach" in *Olivant*.

448 "Georgia Dusk": First published in *Olivant Quarterly* (2nd Quarter 1955), p. 135. Included in *SP* and *TPATL*.

"Mean Old Yesterday": Published in *Olivant Quarterly* (2nd Quarter 1955), p. 134.

449 "In Explanation of Our Times": The poem has slightly different stanza breaks and line lengths in *SP*, *Africa South* (April–June 1957), pp. 100–101, and *Olivant Quarterly* (2nd Quarter 1955), pp. 136–37. The only lines in which the words are altered are lines 56–57, which read as follows in *Africa South*:
> Hell no shut up
> No! . . . No! . . . No!

In this version, the name Strydom is spelled Strijdom, a variation of the name of the South African leader Johannes Gerhardus Strydom (1893–1958). Prime minister of South Africa from 1954 until his death, he was a leader in the creation of apartheid.
Line 23: Gerald L. K. Smith was the leader of the right-wing America First Party, which organized boycotts of Hughes's poetry readings in the 1940s.

451 "Little Song on Housing": First published in *Phylon* (2nd Quarter 1955), p. 148. Included in *TPATL*.

"Plaint": Published in *Voices* (Sept.–Dec. 1955), p. 17.

452 "The Thorn": Published in *Voices* (Sept.–Dec. 1955), p. 17.

"Mississippi": First published as "Mississippi—1955" in *Amsterdam News* (Oct. 1, 1955), p. 4. On August 24, 1955, Emmett Till, a fourteen-year-old black youth from Chicago, allegedly whistled at and made suggestive remarks to Carolyn Bryant in a store in Money, Mississippi. One week later, Till was killed by Bryant's husband

and brother-in-law. They were acquitted of all charges by an all-white jury on September 23. Till's death and the jury verdict caused an outcry outside of the South.

453    "Brotherly Love": Published in *Nation* (Aug. 18, 1956), p. 142. Reprinted in *New Republic* (Aug. 21, 1961), p. 23, and *Negro Digest* (Sept. 1965), p. 57. Included in *TPATL*. Previously, the last three lines were:

> *And terror, fetid hot,*
> *Yet clammy cold,*
> *Remain.*

Line 18 refers to the Montgomery Bus Boycott of 1956, led by Martin Luther King, Jr., and Ralph Abernathy.

"Two Somewhat Different Epigrams": Published in *New Poems by American Poets, #2*, p. 81. The first section first appeared under the title "Prayer" in *Voices* (Sept.–Dec. 1955), p. 18. The second section appeared as "Awe" in *Black Orpheus* (May 1959), p. 29.

454    "Last Call": Published in *New Poems by American Poets, #2*, p. 82.

"Late Corner": Published in *New Poems by American Poets, #2*, p. 81.

455    "Acceptance": First published in *Beloit Poetry Journal Chapbook* (1957), p. 24, a special issue of poems for Robert Frost, and *New Poems by American Poets, #2*, p. 80. Included in *LHR*.

"Testament": First published in *New Poems by American Poets, #2*, p. 80. Included in *LHR*.

"Gone Boy": First published in *Voices* (Jan.–April 1957), p. 9, and *New Poems by American Poets, #2*, p. 82. Included in *SP*.

456    "Where? When? Which?": Several words were deleted from the text as it appeared in *Colorado Review* (Winter 1956–57), p. 34, and *New Poems by American Poets, #2*, p. 81, when this poem was reprinted in *TPATL*. Line 5 was originally "Fresh and sharp as integration"; line 6 was "With an edge like gentle apartheid"; line 16 was "Colorless apartheid?" In addition, lines 12 and 13 in *TPATL* were one line in the first version.

"Memo to Non-White Peoples": Published in *Africa South* (April–June 1957), p. 99.
Line 18: Shepherd's Hotel in Cairo, founded in 1845, is one of the most famous hotels in the world. On January 16, 1952, the original building was burned to the ground during a demonstration against the British presence in Egypt.

457    "Expendable": Published in *Voices* (Jan.–April 1957), p. 10.

"Bouquet": Published in *Colorado Review* (Spring–Summer 1957), p. 76.

458 "Impasse": Previously published as "So?" in *Colorado Review* (Spring–Summer 1957), p. 76, and *Black Orpheus* (May 1959), p. 29. Included in *TPATL*.

"Departure": Published in *Free Lance*, no. 1 (1958), p. 2.

"Dixie South Africa": Published in *Free Lance*, no. 1 (1958), p. 3.

459 "Communiqué": Published in *Free Lance*, no. 1 (1958), p. 3.

"Casual": Published in *Hearse*, no. 1 (n.d., n.p.).

460 "Numbered": Published in *Hearse*, no. 2 (n.d., n.p.).

"The Last Man Living": Published in *Hearse*, no. 7 (n.d., n.p.).

"On a Pallet of Straw": Published in *Crisis* (Dec. 1958), p. 614. This poem and the next three poems are all included in the musical play *Black Nativity*.

461 "Carol of the Brown King": Published in *Crisis* (Dec. 1958), p. 615. See note to "On a Pallet of Straw" above.

462 "On a Christmas Night": Published in *Crisis* (Dec. 1958), p. 616. See note to "On a Pallet of Straw" above.

"Ballad of Mary's Son": Published in *LHR*. See note to "On a Pallet of Straw" above.

463 "Pastoral": Published in *LHR*.

"Little Cats": Published in *Voices* (Jan.–April 1959), p. 16.

464 "Not Else—But": Published in *Voices* (Jan.–April 1959), p. 15. It appeared later as the third stanza of "Shades of Pigmeat" in *AYM*.

"Angola Question Mark": The poem was titled "African Question Mark" in *Black Orpheus* (May 1959), p. 29, and *Phylon* (3rd Quarter 1957), p. 212. Lines 3 to 4 and 18 to 19 of the text in *TPATL* formed single lines in the earlier printing. In addition, the first line of the second stanza (line 8) was "Don't know why I now" and line 16 was "All I know." The words "now" and "all" were deleted in *TPATL*.

465 "Tambourines": Published in *SP*. On a draft of this poem in the James Weldon Johnson Collection of the Beinecke Library, Yale University, Hughes noted: "Drafts of a poem written especially to fill an empty page in the final proofs of my *Selected Poems*."

"As Befits a Man": Published in *SP*.

466 "Maybe": Published in *SP*.

"Blue Monday": Published in *SP*.

466 "To Artina": Published in *SP*.

467 "Uncle Tom" [2]: Published in *SP*.

"Jim Crow Car": The title was originally "Lunch in a Jim Crow Car" in *SP*. The title was changed for *TPATL*.

"Abe Lincoln": Published in *Voices* (May–Aug. 1960), p. 17.

468 "Imagine": Published in *Chelsea Eight* (Oct. 1960), p. 42.

" 'The Jesus' ": Published in *Chelsea Eight* (Oct. 1960), pp. 41–42, under the pseudonym Durwood Collins.


POEMS 1961–1967

*Ask Your Mama: 12 Moods for Jazz*    (1961)

476 "Cultural Exchange": A portion of this poem was reprinted under the same title in *TPATL*.
Line 15: Leontyne Price (b. 1927), the opera soprano, made her debut with the New York Metropolitan Opera on January 27, 1961.
Line 27: Leontyne Price; Sammy Davis, Jr.; Harry Belafonte; Sidney Poitier.
Line 28: Lena Horne; Marian Anderson; Louis Armstrong; Pearl Bailey (see note to "Ode to Dinah," page 683).
Line 29: George S. Schuyler (b. 1895), author of the novel *Black No More*, worked as a journalist with the *Messenger* (1923–25) and the Pittsburgh *Courier*.
Line 41: Ralph Ellison (1914–94), the author of *Invisible Man* (1952). Vespucius, or Amerigo Vespucci (1454–1512), was an Italian explorer of the coastline of South America who demonstrated that America was not the Indies but a separate continent.
Line 42: Ina and Ura Quarrels were twin sisters and friends of Hughes. Ina was a teacher at Texas College (Tyler), and her sister was at Fisk University (see *Arna Bontemps–Langston Hughes Letters: 1925–1967*, ed. C. Nichols [New York: Dodd, Mead, 1980], p. 75).
Line 43: Arna Bontemps (1902–73) wrote *God Sends Sunday* (1931) and *Black Thunder* (1936). He was a close friend of Hughes, and together they collaborated on a number of literary projects, including *Popo and Fifina* (1932) and *The Poetry of the Negro* (1949).
Line 45: Shalom Aleichem ("Peace be with You") was the pen name of Solomon Rabinowitz (1859–1916), the Ukrainian-born Yiddish writer. James Baldwin (1924–89) was the author of acclaimed novels and the book of essays *The Fire Next Time*.
Line 54: Ornette Coleman (b. 1930) was a jazz saxophonist.
Line 62: "Lieder" means "songs" in German.
Line 64: Kwame Nkrumah (1909–72) was the leader of the independence movement in Ghana, and became that country's president in 1960. He attended Hughes's alma mater, Lincoln University.

Line 66: Gamal Abdel Nasser (1918–70) led the army revolt which deposed the monarchy in Egypt in 1952. He governed Egypt until his death.

Line 68: Benjamin Azikiwe became the first president of an independent Nigeria in 1960. He also attended Lincoln University. See the note for "Azikiwe in Jail," page 669.

Line 69: Fidel Castro had been in power for two years when *Ask Your Mama* was published. Ahmed Sékou Touré, a union official in the early 1950s, served as president of Guinea from 1958 to 1984.

Line 71: Jomo Kenyatta (1894–1978), leader of the independence movement in Kenya, served as the head of his country's government from 1964 until his death.

Line 92: In 1948, many Southern Democrats, upset over Truman's liberal racial policies, withdrew from the party and formed a separate political organization called the Dixiecrats, with Strom Thurmond as their presidential candidate.

Line 96: Dr. Rufus Clement (1900–1967) was president of Atlanta University from 1937 to 1967. In 1957, he became the first African American since Reconstruction to serve on a school board in a Southern state.

Line 97: Zelma George Watson (1903–94) was a musician and an educator. In 1960, she served as an alternate in the U.S. delegation to the UN General Assembly. She once stood and applauded a motion for ending colonial rule in Africa even though the U.S. abstained from a vote on the measure.

Line 103: Orval Faubus (1910–79), the Democratic governor of Arkansas from 1955 to 1967. In 1955, he summoned the Arkansas National Guard to stop the integration of Central High School in Little Rock, a move which prompted Eisenhower to send in the U.S. Army.

Line 104: James O. Eastland (1904–86) was a Democratic senator from Mississippi and an ardent segregationist.

Line 105: John M. Patterson was Democratic governor of Alabama from 1959 to 1963.

482 "Ride, Red, Ride":
Line 7: "Ça Ira," "It Will Succeed," was a popular song during the French Revolution. It originally celebrated national unity and France's resistance to her enemies, but a refrain added later spoke of hanging aristocrats from lamp posts.
Line 11 translates as "Your grandmother, where is she?"
Line 14: Mont Pelée is a volcano on the Caribbean island of Martinique. It erupted in 1902, killing 37,500 people.
Line 16: On Patrice Lumumba, see note for "Lumumba's Grave," page 686.
Line 22 translates as "Are you a drop from the blood?"
Line 32: Adam Clayton Powell, Jr., served as Harlem's representative in Congress from 1944 to 1970. See the note for "Final Call," page 689.

485 "Shades of Pigmeat": First published in *Village Voice* (July 6, 1961), p. 4. The third stanza appeared earlier as the poem "Not Elsewhere, But" in *Voices* (Jan.–Apr. 1959), p. 15.
Line 2: King Leopold of the Belgians was ruler of the Belgian Congo from 1885 to 1908.
Line 3: Hughes is not referring to a real person, but playing on the fact that 10 Downing Street is the official residence of the British prime minister.
Line 4: The Bourse is the stock exchange in Paris.

Line 5: James O. Eastland, Democratic senator from Mississippi, and Daniel François Malan (1874–1959), South African prime minister (1948–54) and one of the creators of apartheid.

Line 13: Lotte Lenya (1898–1981) was a successful musical and cabaret singer and the wife of the composer Kurt Weill, with whom Hughes worked on *Street Scene*.

Line 14: Mack the Knife is the main character in *The Threepenny Opera* (1928), a musical by Berthold Brecht and Kurt Weill.

Line 15: *Porgy and Bess*, the opera with music by George Gershwin, was based on *Porgy*, a novel about a beggar in South Carolina by Du Bose Heyward.

Line 17: Mai Britte or May Britt, a Swedish actress, was the second wife of Sammy Davis, Jr.

Line 24: The Talmud contains a codification of post-biblical oral Jewish law along with commentary on those texts.

Line 29: Mabel Louis Smith, known as "Big Maybelle" (1924–72), was a blues singer.

488   "Ode to Dinah":

Line 6: Pearl Bailey (1918–90), a singer and an actress, sang with Cab Calloway's band in the 1940s and performed in numerous movies and musical plays, including *Carmen Jones*.

Line 15: The singer Dinah Washington, born Ruth Jones (1924–63), was called the "Queen of the Blues."

Line 19: Mahalia Jackson (1911–72) was a renowned gospel singer.

Line 20: Blind Lemon Jefferson (1897–1919), blind from birth, was among the most popular of the early blues singers.

494   "Blues in Stereo":

Line 21: Stanleyville, now Kisangani in Zaire, was established at the furthest navigable point up the lower Zaire River. The town was named for the explorer Henry Stanley, who was hired in 1878 to help open up Belgian trade in the Congo.

497   "Horn of Plenty":

Line 3: Odetta Gordon (b. 1930) was a popular folk singer in the 1950s and 1960s.

Line 4: Sol Hurok was a prominent concert impresario whose clients included Marian Anderson and the pianist Errol Garner.

Line 6: Dancer and choreographer Katherine Dunham (b. 1910). Al Mims and Leon James began their careers as Lindy Hoppers at the Savoy Hotel in New York. In the 1950s, they teamed up to perform a program of early-twentieth-century dances of African American origin or influence.

Line 7: This line refers to the African American ballet dancers Arthur Mitchell, Carmen De Lavallade, Alvin Ailey, and Mary Hinkson.

Line 8: Duke Ellington; Dizzy Gillespie; and Eric Dolphy (1928–64), a jazz clarinetist.

Line 9: Miles Davis, Ella Fitzgerald, and Nina Simone.

Line 10: William "Billy" Strayhorn was the most important musical arranger for Duke Ellington. Luther Allison (b. 1939) was a blues musician and arranger.

Line 11: Louis Armstrong.

Line 15: The composers Margaret Bonds, whose work includes "Ballad of the Brown King" and "Three Dream Portraits," with lyrics by Hughes; and William Grant Still, who worked with Hughes on the opera *Troubled Island*.

Line 16: The Harlem Globe Trotters, a professional basketball team.

Line 17: Jackie Robinson, Willie Mays, and Roy Campanella.

Line 19: The boxers Joe Louis and Sugar Ray Robinson.

Line 22: St. Albans—a town in Long Island, at the edge of the borough of Queens, where it meets Nassau County—attracted an influx of black middle-class settlers in the 1950s.

Line 51: Charles Mingus (1922–79) was a jazz bass player, band leader, and composer.

Line 52: Richard Wright (1908–1960), author of *Native Son* and *Black Boy*, moved to France in 1947.

Line 61: Westport and New Canaan, towns in southwestern Connecticut, are wealthy suburbs of New York City.

Line 82: Hughes is possibly referring to Joseph Glaser, business agent for a number of famous black performers, including Duke Ellington, Louis Armstrong, and Billie Holiday.

Line 84: The line probably refers to Dallas Franklin Billington, a white evangelist and leader of the Akron Baptist Temple in Akron, Ohio, called the "rubber city" because of the presence of the Firestone Tire Company. Billington appeared on both radio and television and was the first evangelist to have a TV studio in his church.

Line 86: George Sokolsky (1893–1962) became a columnist for the New York *Herald Tribune* in 1935. He moved to the *Sun* newspapers in 1940 and the New York *Journal-American* in 1950. He often wrote about the communist menace and was a prominent supporter of Joe McCarthy. In the autumn of 1944, Sokolsky began attacking Hughes in his column (see Rampersad, vol. II, p. 91).

502    "Gospel Cha-Cha": A portion of this poem appeared under the title "Haiti" in *New Republic* (Sept. 1961), p. 22.

Line 7: Erzulie or Ezilie is a female spirit in Afro-Haitian religion identified with the Mater Dolorosa. She is sometimes thought of as a water spirit.

Line 14: Papiamento is a Spanish-based Creole dialect spoken in Surinam. It is also called Curcaleno or Curasesse.

Line 15: Damballah Wedo is the venerable sky father associated in Yoruba religion with weather and fertility. Ogoun is a Yoruban deity of war.

Line 18: The Citadel La Ferrière is the fortress at Cap Haïtien on Haiti. In *I Wonder As I Wander*, p. 16, Hughes says that earlier travelers had been "filled with wonder regarding this relic of Negro pride. I had read of Toussaint L'Ouverture, Dessalines, King Christophe, proud black names, symbols of a dream—freedom—building a citadel to guard that freedom." He describes his own visit to the citadel in the same volume, pp. 26–27.

Line 21: Toussaint L'Ouverture, leader of the Haitian slave revolt in 1791.

Line 27: "Ay Bahia" may refer to the Bahiano, an Afro-Brazilian improvised dance which originated in the province of Bahia, Brazil.

Line 35: Shango, the Yoruba god of thunder and lightning, is associated with St. John in Afro-Caribbean religion. Legba is the Afro-Haitian god of the crossroads and one of the most important voodoo gods. He is summoned at the start of every religious ceremony.

Line 36: Alexander Bedward (1859-?), a preacher in Kingston, Jamaica, founded Bedwardism, a sect centered on a vow ceremony and rigorous fasting. Pocomania is an Afro-Jamaican cult influenced by Christianity. Revival meetings often end with the faithful being taken by a frenzy. Wedo is Damballah Wedo, the sky father.

Line 37: The Fortaleza, or the fort of San Lazaro, overlooks the harbor of Havana. See Hughes's poem "To the Little Fort of San Lazaro on the Ocean Front, Havana," page 136.

Line 38: Nañigo is a secret sect for black men in Cuba.

Line 42: Marie Leveau (d. 1881) was a noted voodoo priestess in New Orleans in the nineteenth century. Her spirit was still considered dominant among devotees of the religion when Zora Neale Hurston arrived in the city to study voodoo practices in 1928. See Robert Hemenway, *Zora Neale Hurston* (Urbana: University of Illinois, 1977), pp. 117–23.

Line 44: John Jasper (1812–1901) was a preacher of the African Baptist Church in Richmond, Virginia, who became popular with both black and white audiences. He spoke in dialect, and his most famous sermon, "The Sun Do Move," asserted that the earth was the center of the universe. Hughes wrote a musical play with the same title.

506 "Is It True?":
Line 10: Moses "Moe" Asch was the founder of Folkways Records; Alan Lomax was another important collector of African American folklore.

510 "Ask Your Mama":
Line 45: Fort de France is the main city in Martinique. Place Pigalle in Paris is in the night-club district, where Hughes worked in 1924.

Line 47: Lagos, Nigeria; Dakar, Senegal; Lenox Avenue in Harlem.

Line 48: Kingston, Jamaica.

Lines 50–51 contain the names of famous cafés in Paris.

Line 52: The tall black student is probably Diallo Alpha, a young man from Guinea whom Hughes met in Paris in 1960 (see Rampersad, vol. II, p. 326).

Line 58: "Mealie" probably refers to "mel," the word for an indigenous group of related African languages in the area of Guinea and Sierra Leone.

Line 61: Sékou Touré, the first president of Guinea.

Line 65: Benjamin Azikiwe, first president of Nigeria.

Line 66: Emmett Till, a fourteen-year-old visiting Mississippi from Chicago, was abducted and murdered in Mississippi in 1955. See note for "Mississippi," page 678.

515 "Bird in Orbit": Charlie Parker, called "Bird" or "Yardbird" (1920–55), was one of the most influential jazz saxophonists.

Line 3: Eartha Kitt.

Line 4: Jocko, a famous disc jockey in Chicago; Bo Didley, the professional name of McDaniel Ellis, a rock 'n' roll guitarist who incorporated elements from the blues; Lillie "Lil" Greenwood, a concert singer who began as a vocalist for Duke Ellington.

Line 5: Harry Belafonte; perhaps Jocelyn "Frisco" Bingham, a Paris nightclub owner; Josephine Baker.

Line 6: Ada "Bricktop" Smith; Inez Cavanaugh (see note for "Projection," page 674); the singer Mabel Mercer.

Line 19: The Niagara Movement, the predecessor to the NAACP, began in 1905.

Line 20: Adele Glasgow and Ramona Lowe owned the Market Place Gallery in

Harlem. Hughes gave the first reading of *Ask Your Mama* at the Gallery on February 6, 1961 (see Rampersad, vol. II, p. 327).

Line 23: Alioune Diop was a founding editor of the journal *Présence Africaine*, published in Paris. Diop solicited advice from Hughes about the magazine (Rampersad, vol. II, p. 237). Aimé Césaire (b. 1913) represented Martinique in the National Assembly of France from 1945 and has advocated the independence of the island. He has had a distinguished career as a writer of poetry, essays, and plays. Among his best-known works are the dramas *Une Tempête, Une Saison au Congo*, and *La Tragédie du roi Christophe*. Léopold Sédar Senghor (b. 1906) represented Senegal in the French National Assembly from 1945 to 1958, then served as the president of the Republic of Senegal from 1960 to 1981. He was a noted writer; his *Collected Poems* appeared in 1977. In 1983, he was elected to the French Academy.

Line 28: Mollie Moon (1912–90) helped to found the National Urban League Guild of New York in 1942 and acted as president of the local civil-rights organization until her death. She was also active in the Urban League at the national level.

Line 29: In classical Greek mythology, Leda was raped by the god Zeus, who had taken the form of a swan.

Line 37: On John Jasper, see note for line 44 of "Gospel Cha-Cha," page 685.

Lines 47–50: In 1858, while speaking to an audience in Indiana, Sojourner Truth was challenged by a hostile minister who claimed she was a man. Truth bared her breast to the crowd.

Line 76: In 1942, the Board of Education in Englewood, New Jersey, refused to allow Mary McLeod Bethune to speak at a school because of her alleged communist affiliations. Support for Bethune forced the board to reverse its decision.

Line 83: Robert Clifton Weaver (b. 1907) received his doctorate in economics from Harvard in 1934. Appointed secretary of Housing and Urban Development by President Lyndon Johnson, he was the first African American to hold a U.S. Cabinet position.

520    "Jazztet Muted":
Line 9: Ornette Coleman (b. 1930), the jazz saxophonist.

523    "Show Fare, Please": First published in *Free Lance*, no. 2 (1961), p. 5.

533    "Lumumba's Grave": First published as "El Sepulcro de Lumumba" in *Magisterio* [Mexico City] (Nov. 1961), p. 280, in a Spanish translation by Manuel Gonzales Flores. Included in *TPATL*. Patrice Lumumba (1925–61) was the first prime minister of the newly independent Congo (now Zaire) in 1960. After the army rebelled, Lumumba requested UN assistance to end the uprising. He was removed from power in September 1960 by General Mobutu, who has since ruled the country. On February 13, 1961, Lumumba was killed, reportedly while trying to escape from custody.

"If You Would": Published in *Rong, Wrong*, no. 2 (n.d.), p. 2.

534    "Encounter": Published in *Voices* (Jan.–April 1962), p. 24.

535    "Slave": The end of the poem was substantially altered when the poem was republished in *TPATL*. The first version, in *Renaissance* [New York] (Winter–Spring 1962), p. 10, reads as follows after line 11:

to purchase a slave
whom life set free
to be a fantasy
slave to me,
utterly un-
protected.

535 "Pair in One": Published in *Approach* (Spring 1962), p. 5, and *New Orlando Anthology* (1963), p. 60.

"Good Bluffers": Published in *Approach* (Spring 1962), p. 5.

536 "Number": Published in *South and West Review* (Summer 1962), p. 9.

"The Dove": First published in *Outcry* (Summer 1962), p. 56. Included in *TPATL*.

"Silent One": Published in *New York Times* (Nov. 9, 1962), p. 34.

537 "doorknobs": Published in *Outsider* (Fall 1961), p. 30, and *New Orlando Anthology* (1963), p. 59.

"Go Slow": First published in *ETC* (July 1963), p. 186. Included in *TPATL*.

538 "We, Too": Published in *New Orlando Anthology* (1963), p. 60.

539 "Junior Addict": First published in *Liberator* (April 1963), p. 3, with the following explanation: "This poem is inspired by the Mario Jorrin photo in the article on NARCOTICS in the February 1963 LIBERATOR." In the magazine, line 34 reads "pre-life job." The phrase was changed for *TPATL*.

540 "For Russell and Rowena Jelliffe": Published in Cleveland *Call and Post* (April 6, 1963), p. 1B. The Jelliffes founded a neighborhood social-service organization in Cleveland, which later was named Karamu House. It is still a focal point for black culture in the city. Hughes first met the Jelliffes when he was a student at Central High in Cleveland. The poem was written for a dinner in their honor.

541 "Northern Liberal": First published under the title "Northern Liberal: 1963" in *Liberator* (July 1963), p. 4. The title was altered for *TPATL*.

"Slum Dreams": First published as "Little Dreams" in *New York Times* (May 8, 1964), p. 32. Hughes changed the title and the line lengths when the poem was included in *TPATL*.

542 "Dream of Freedom": Published in *Wayne State University Graduation Comment* (July 1964), p. 108, and NAACP *Freedom Journal* (April 1964), p. 11. This issue commemorates the tenth anniversary of the Supreme Court ruling in *Brown* v. *Board of Education*.

"Small Memory": Published in *Renaissance*, no. 3 (Aug. 1964), p. 7.

542     "Ghosts of 1619": First published in *Liberator* (July 1964), p. 21, under the title "Ghosts." The title was changed for *TPATL*. The poem refers to the arrival of the first African captives in Jamestown, Virginia, in 1619.

543     "Drums": Published in *Liberator* (Aug. 1964), p. 4, and *Negro Digest* (Oct. 1964), p. 53.

545     "Final Call": First published in *American Dialog* (Oct.–Nov. 1964), p. 37, as "Harlem Call: After the 1964 Riots." The title was changed for *TPATL*.

Line 8, "SEND FOR DREYFUS TO CRY, 'J'ACCUSE!' ": Alfred Dreyfus (1859–1935) was a French officer of Jewish descent who was accused, tried, and convicted of passing secrets to the Germans. Even though the documents used to convict Dreyfus were forgeries, the army refused to overturn its verdict. In 1898, Emile Zola published his famous essay entitled *"J'accuse"* (I accuse), which brought the case to the attention of the public. Paroled in 1899, Dreyfus returned to the army in 1906. His case aided the cause of Republicanism in France by damaging the reputation of the army, monarchy, and Catholic clergy.

Line 9: Blind Lemon Jefferson (1880–1929) was a celebrated blues musician born blind in Texas.

Line 10, "SEND FOR ROBESPIERRE": Maximilian Robespierre (1758–94) was a leader of the French Revolution and an instigator of the Reign of Terror, in which thousands of French were killed. He himself fell victim to the carnage he had unleashed when he was guillotined.

Line 12, "FOR LUMUMBA": See note for "Lumumba's Grave," page 686.

Line 14, "SEND FOR DENMARK VESEY": Denmark Vesey was a freedman in Charleston, South Carolina, who was accused in 1822 of planning a slave revolt. He was executed along with thirty-four others.

Line 15, "FOR CINQUE": Joseph Cinque (1811–78) led a successful mutiny on a Spanish slave ship and brought the vessel to Long Island, New York, where the ship and the mutineers were taken into American custody. A long legal battle then ensued. Were Cinque and the other forty-nine men intended for slavery to be sent as slaves to Cuba or freed? In 1841, John Quincy Adams, the former president, convinced the U.S. Supreme Court to uphold a lower-court decision freeing the mutineers. Cinque returned to Africa, where, ironically, he became involved in the slave trade.

Line 18, "SEND FOR TROTSKY!": Leon Trotsky (1879–1940), the most important Russian revolutionary after Lenin, was exiled in 1928 after a power struggle with Josef Stalin, and was assassinated by Stalin's agents in Mexico City.

Line 21, "SEND FOR FREDERICK DOUGLASS, GARRISON, BEECHER, LOWELL": William Lloyd Garrison, Henry Ward Beecher, and James Russell Lowell were all prominent white Northern Abolitionists.

Line 23, "SEND FOR MARCUS GARVEY (WHAT?) SUFI (WHO?)": The Jamaican-born Marcus Garvey (1887–1940) believed that black people could prosper only if independent of whites socially, economically, and politically. To this end, he founded the United Negro Improvement Association, which attracted many thousands of blacks. Garvey encouraged the formation of black-owned businesses which catered to blacks, such as the Black Star Steam Ship Line. In politics, he advocated the "Back to Africa" movement, which urged people of African descent to return to the continent of their ancestors. In 1925, he was convicted of using the U.S. mail to defraud investors in his shipping business. After two years in prison, he was deported to Jamaica. Garvey later died in London in relative obscurity.

"SUFI" is probably Sufi Abdul Hamid, a cult leader from Chicago who used boycotts to force stores in Harlem to hire blacks. He organized the Harlem Boycott of 1934 and the Jobs for Negroes Campaign. At one time, Hamid attempted an alliance with Father Divine and other Harlem evangelicals, but his racist and anti-Semitic rhetoric and inflammatory actions caused a break with the rest of the Harlem community. He died in a plane crash after he had lost most of his following.

Line 24, "DuBOIS (WHEN?) MALCOLM (OH!) SEND FOR STOKELY": W. E. B. Du Bois, Malcolm X, and Stokely Carmichael.

Line 25, "SEND FOR ADAM POWELL ON A NON-SUBPOENA DAY": Adam Clayton Powell, Jr. (1908–72), was a minister, civil-rights leader, and New York City politician who represented Harlem in the U.S. House of Representatives for eleven terms. Unseated by his colleagues in the House for ethical violations, he was re-elected to his seat and became the chairman of the Committee on Education and Labor in 1960. Powell lost the post a few years later, when he was again accused of misusing public funds.

545    "Old Age": Published in *Borderline* [Fort Smith, Arkansas] (Jan. 1965).

546    "To You": *Amsterdam News* (Jan. 30., 1965), p. 22. The poem appeared with the following explanatory comment: "Langston Hughes, the Negro Poet Laureate of America, wrote the following poem expressly for a new greeting card to be issued by CORE [the Congress of Racial Equality]."

"Not What Was": Published in *Massachusetts Review* (Winter–Spring 1965), p. 305.

547    "Long View: Negro": First published in *Harper's Magazine* (April 1965), p. 186. Included in *TPATL*.

"Dinner Guest: Me": First published in *Negro Digest* (Sept. 1965), p. 57. Included in *TPATL*.

548    "Christmas Eve: Nearing Midnight in New York": Published in *American Christmas*, ed. W. Schoo and R. Myers (Kansas City: Hallmark, 1965), p. 49.

549    "Frederick Douglass: 1817–1895": First published in *Liberator* (Dec. 1966), p. 21. Included in *TPATL*.

"Question and Answer": First published in *Crisis* (Oct. 1966), p. 525. Included in *TPATL*.

550    "Frosting": First published under the title "Black Economics" in *Crisis* (Dec. 1966), p. 525. The title was changed for *TPATL*.

"Metropolitan Museum": Published in *Crisis* (Dec. 1966), p. 525.

551 "Emperor Haile Selassie": Published in *Negro Digest* (Nov. 1966), p. 48. Haile Selassie I was the emperor of Ethiopia from 1930 until he was overthrown and placed under house arrest in 1974. In 1936, he was forced into exile following the Italian invasion of Ethiopia. On May 5, 1941, Selassie and triumphant Ethiopian and British forces entered Addis Ababa. He died in 1975. Hughes personally presented the poem to Selassie in Addis Ababa in 1966.

"Crowns and Garlands": Published in *Nation* (Jan. 16, 1967), p. 92, and *TPATL*.
    Line 1: Leontyne Price and Lena Horne.
    Line 4: Sammy Davis, Jr., Sidney Poitier, and Harry Belafonte.
    Line 19: Ralph Bunche (1904–71) was a teacher and diplomat who helped to write the UN Charter in 1946. He subsequently held a number of UN posts, including undersecretary general in 1968. He was awarded the Nobel Peace Prize in 1950.

552 "The Backlash Blues": Published in *Crisis* (June 1967), p. 251, and *TPATL*.

553 "Suburban Evening": Published in *Crisis* (April 1967), p. 131.

"Demonstration": Published in *Negro Digest* (Sept. 1966), p. 64.

554 "Prime": Published in *TPATL*.

"Lenox Avenue Bar": Published in *TPATL*.

"Death in Yorkville": Published in *TPATL*. On July 16, 1964, James Powell, a fifteen-year-old black youth, was shot in the predominantly white Upper East Side of Manhattan by a white off-duty police officer who claimed that Powell was armed with a knife. The shooting caused the worst civil disturbance in Harlem since 1943. Hughes joined thousands of other mourners at the viewing for Powell, which was held in Harlem in a funeral parlor a few blocks from Hughes's home.

555 "Black Panther": Published in *TPATL*.

"Office Building: Evening": Published in *TPATL*.

556 "Special Bulletin": Published in *TPATL*.

557 "Birmingham Sunday": Published in *TPATL*. On Sunday, Sept. 15, 1964, a bomb exploded in the black Sixteenth Street Baptist Church in Birmingham, Alabama, killing four girls attending Sunday School.

"Bombings in Dixie": Published in *TPATL*. See note for "Birmingham Sunday" above.

558 "Mother in Wartime": Published in *TPATL*.

"Official Notice": Published in *TPATL*.

"Last Prince of the East": Published in *TPATL*.

559  "War": Published in *TPATL*.

560  "Sweet Words on Race": Published in *TPATL*.

"Un-American Investigators": Published in *TPATL*. In 1953, Hughes was subpoenaed to testify before Joseph McCarthy and his Senate Permanent Sub-Committee because of his radical writings and activities, mainly in the 1930s (see Rampersad, vol. II, pp. 211–22). The poem may refer to this experience, or to other activities of McCarthy's subcommittee.

561  "Undertow": Published in *TPATL*.

"Stokely Malcolm Me": Published in *TPATL*. The title refers to Stokely Carmichael and Malcolm X.

562  "Freedom" [3]: Published posthumously in *Crisis* (Feb. 1968), p. 50. This is a revision of an earlier poem with the same name ("Freedom" [2]), but is so different that it deserves to be included as a separate text.

"Flotsam": Published posthumously in *Crisis* (June–July 1968), p. 194, to mark the first anniversary of Hughes's death. A note there says that this is the last of seven poems which Hughes submitted to the magazine before he died.


NOTES TO APPENDIX 1

The following poems were sent by Hughes to the Associated Negro Press in Chicago, which distributed them to African American newspapers throughout the country. Space does not allow all of the citations to be listed. Where possible, a reference to a newspaper readily available on microfilm is provided. In other cases, the Langston Hughes Papers provide information as to the month or year in which a poem was sent to the ANP. The poems in these two categories have been arranged in chronological order. Poems which are contained in the file of clippings in the Langston Hughes Papers, but for which no date can be given, are placed at the end. Readers and scholars interested in investigating Hughes's newspaper verse are directed to the box of clippings in the Langston Hughes Papers in the James Weldon Johnson Collection at the Beinecke Library, Yale University.

565  "Song of the Refugee Road": Feb. 1940.

"America's Young Black Joe!": Dec. 1940.
   Line 23: The boxers Joe Louis, a heavyweight champion, and Henry Armstrong, a welterweight and middleweight champion.
   Line 27: Kenny Washington was an All-American football player for UCLA in the late 1930s and one of the first blacks to play in the National Football League.
   Line 30: Mozelle Ellerbe, a track star at Tuskegee Institute, was the 1938 and 1939 National Champion in both the hundred- and two-hundred-yard dashes.
   Line 32: Jessie Owens won four gold medals in the 1936 Olympics in Berlin.
   Line 36: Ralph Metcalfe set the world record in the 220-yard dash on June 11,

1932, and tied the record in the hundred-yard dash on the same day. He competed for the U.S.A. in the 1932 and 1936 Olympics, but came in second behind Eddie Tolan (one and two hundred meters) in Los Angeles and Jessie Owens (two hundred meters) in Berlin. Cornelius Johnson won the high jump at the 1936 Olympics in Berlin. Until Johnson's victory, Hitler had invited all the winners to his box at the stadium to congratulate them. But Hitler left the stadium before he had to meet Johnson, and subsequently suspended such invitations to his box. Jessie Owens is often said to be the spurned athlete in this episode, but in fact it occurred the day before he won his first medal.

Line 37: Thomas "Eddie" Tolan won the hundred- and two-hundred-meter sprints at the 1932 Olympics in Los Angeles.

567   "Ballad of the Fool": Baltimore *Afro-American* (May 17, 1941), p. 7.

"Ballad of Walter White": Baltimore *Afro-American* (June 28, 1941), p. 7.

568   "The Mitchell Case": Baltimore *Afro-American* (June 7, 1941), p. 7. In 1934, Arthur Weigs Mitchell was the first black Democrat elected to Congress, from Chicago's 74th District. He served until 1943. In 1937, Mitchell took the Chicago Rock Island and Pacific Railway from Chicago to Hot Springs, Arkansas. When the train reached the Arkansas border, he was forced to leave the first-class Pullman car, for which he had purchased a ticket, for the Jim Crow Car. He sued the railroad on the grounds that interstate travel should be exempt from Arkansas's restrictions. He lost in the lower courts, but in April 1941 the Supreme Court ruled that the same accommodations offered to whites must be made available to blacks. This did not end segregation: it simply meant that the railroads had to provide separate first-class cars for African Americans. Despite Mitchell's victory, the service was rarely provided.

569   "Explain It, Please": *Amsterdam News* (June 14, 1941), p. 11.

"Ballad of the Black Sheep": Baltimore *Afro-American* (Aug. 16, 1941), p. 7.

570   "Epitaph" [2]: *Amsterdam News* (Oct. 18, 1941), p. 8.

"So Tired Blues": *Amsterdam News* (Nov. 1941), p. 12.

571   "Return to Sea": Baltimore *Afro-American* (May 9, 1941), p. 6. First published in *Black Opals* 1.1 (Spring 1927), p. 6, with no stanza break.

"Jazz Girl": Baltimore *Afro-American* (May 16, 1941), p. 7. First published in *Black Opals* 1.1 (Spring 1927), p. 7, with minor variations.

572   "Pathological Puzzle": April 1942.

"Dixie Man to Uncle Sam": Baltimore *Afro-American* (April 25, 1942), p. 6.

"Governor Fires Dean": July 1942. In May of 1942, Governor Eugene Talmadge of Georgia declared at a meeting of the Board of Regents of the University of Georgia that he would terminate "any person in the university system advocating communism or racial equality" (from William Anderson, *The Wild Man from Sugar Creek: The Political Career of Eugene Talmadge* [Baton Rouge: Louisiana State University

Press, 1975], p. 197). He then pushed through the dismissal of Walter Cocking, a respected educator, because of a study by Cocking's group that suggested integrated training sites for black and white rural teachers. The president of the university resigned over Cocking's dismissal, which led the Board of Regents to reverse itself. Talmadge then packed the board with his own supporters and fired Cocking a second time. The governor's action led to the loss of regional accreditation for the university and several high schools in Georgia. The crisis in Georgia education was a major factor in Talmadge's electoral defeat in the fall of 1942.

573 "Get Up Off That Old Jive": *Amsterdam News* (June 13, 1942), p. 6.

574 "Fourth of July Thought": *Amsterdam News* (July 4, 1942), p. 6.

"Battle Ground": *Amsterdam News* (Aug. 9, 1942), p. 14.

575 "Joe Louis" [2]: Baltimore *Afro-American* (Oct. 3, 1942), p. 7.

576 "Crow Goes, Too": *Amsterdam News* (Oct. 17, 1942), p. 6. On Sept. 29, 1942, Member of Parliament Tom Driberg rose in the House of Commons and said that "an unfortunate result of the presence here of American forces has been the introduction in some parts of Britain of discrimination against Negro troops." He asked "whether he [Prime Minister Churchill] will make friendly representations to the American authorities asking them to instruct their men that the colour bar is not a custom of this country and its non-observance by British troops and civilians should be regarded with equanimity." (Quoted in Francis Wheen, *Tom Driberg: His Life and Indiscretions* [London: Chatto and Windus, 1990], p. 182.)

"Lonely Nocturne": *Amsterdam News* (Oct. 24, 1942), p. 6.

577 "Troubled Water": *Amsterdam News* (Oct. 24, 1942), p. 6.

"Total War": Baltimore *Afro-American* (Feb. 6, 1943), p. 9.

578 "Ghandhi Is Fasting": Baltimore *Afro-American* (Feb. 20, 1943), p. 4.

"Judge William Hastie": *Amsterdam News* (March 6, 1943), p. 10.

579 "What I Think": *Amsterdam News* (March 27, 1943), p. 10.

"Just an Ordinary Guy": July 1943.

580 "Speaking of Food": Baltimore *Afro-American* (April 3, 1943), p. 7.

581 "Puzzlement": July 1943.

"The Bells Toll Kindly": July 1943.

582 "Madam and the Crime Wave": July 1943.

583 "Madam's Christmas (or Merry Christmas Everybody)": Aug. 1943.

584    "Song After Lynching": July 1943.

"Bonds for All": Aug. 1943.

585    "Poor Girl's Ruination": Sept. 1943.

"Poem to Uncle Sam": Nov. 1943.

586    "Song of Adoration": Winter 1943–44. In one clipping, the title is "Song of Odoration."

587    "Bonds: In Memoriam": Baltimore *Afro-American* (June 24, 1944), p. 2.

588    "Worriation": June 1948.

"Ballad of Harry Moore": Feb. 1952. Harry Moore, an NAACP leader in Florida, was killed when his house was bombed on December 25, 1951, after he had protested about the treatment of the African American defendants in the Groveland case, known as "Little Scottsboro."

The following poems could not be dated:

590    "Message to the President": The piece was obviously written during World War II.

592    "Promised Land"

"Chicago Blues"

NOTES TO APPENDIX 2

597    "Fairies": First published in *Brownie's Book* (Jan. 1921), p. 32. Included in *TDK*.

"Winter Sweetness": First published in *Brownie's Book* (Jan. 1921), p. 27. Included in *TDK* and *Golden Slippers*.

"April Rain Song": First published in *Brownie's Book* (April 1921), p. 111. Included in *TDK*.

"Signs of Spring": *Brownie's Book* (Aug. 1921), p. 229.

598    "The Lament of a Vanquished Beau": *Brownie's Book* (Aug. 1921), p. 229.

"Mister Sandman": *Brownie's Book* (Aug. 1921), p. 244.

600    "Thanksgiving Time": *Brownie's Book* (Nov. 1921), p. 328.

"Autumn Thought": First published in *Brownie's Book* (Nov. 1921), p. 307. Included in *TDK*.

600 "Trip: San Francisco": *Golden Slippers*, p. 132. Included in the essay "Poetry and Children" in *LHR*.

601 "Garment": *Golden Slippers*, p. 175. Included in the essay "Poetry and Children" in *LHR*.

"The Kids in School with Me": *Common Ground* (Autumn 1947), p. 31.

602 "We're All in the Telephone Book": *Common Ground* (Autumn 1947), p. 32.

"City": Included in the essay "Poetry and Children" in *LHR*. Reprinted in *Favorite Poems, Old and New*, ed. Helen Ferris (Garden City, N.Y.: Doubleday, 1957), p. 244.

"To Make Words Sing": Included in the essay "Poetry and Children" in *LHR*.

603 "Gypsies": Included in the essay "Poetry and Children" in *LHR*, p. 147. It was circulated by ANP and can be found in Baltimore *Afro-American* (Sept. 27, 1941), p. 7.

The remaining eighteen poems appeared under the heading "18 Poems for Children" in *LHR*. "New Flowers" was published previously as "Cycle," *Golden Slippers*, p. 180. The first two lines of "Shearing Time" appeared as "Days of Our Years," Carmel *Pine Cone* (July 25, 1941), p. 7.


NOTES TO APPENDIX 3

613 "Bulwark": Published in *Carolina Magazine* (May 1927), p. 32.

613 "Old Youth": Published in *A Little Book of Central Verse* (Central High School, Cleveland, 1928), p. 7.

614 "Moscow": Published in *Negro Voices: An Anthology of Contemporary Verse*, edited by Beatrice Murphy (New York: Henry Harrison, 1938), p. 79.

614 "Madrid": Published in *Fight for Peace and Democracy* (July 1938), p. 14.

616 "Chicago": Published in *Negro Digest* (September 1964), p. 55.

617 "Bitter Brew": Published in *Umbra Anthology* (1967–68), p. 16.

# Index of First Lines

# Index of Titles

# A Note About the Editors

ARNOLD RAMPERSAD, the author of the acclaimed two-volume *The Life of Langston Hughes*, is Woodrow Wilson Professor of Literature in the Department of English at Princeton University, where he is also director of the Program in American Studies and the program in Afro-American Studies. Among his other books are *The Art and Imagination of W. E. B. Du Bois* and, with the late Arthur Ashe, *Days of Grace: A Memoir*. In 1991, he was appointed a MacArthur Foundation Fellow.

DAVID ROESSEL is the author of many published essays on modern American poetry. Trained as a Classicist and in British and American literature at Rutgers, the State University of New York at Albany, and Princeton University, he has taught Greek and Latin at Howard University and at the Catholic University in Washington, D.C. He has been a Fulbright Fellow twice, in Italy and in Cyprus.